ENDORSEMENTS

"Scholars over the last few decades have challenged the construction of the religious/secular duality from a theoretical point of view. That was the easy part. In this fascinating volume, Andrew Jones does the hard work of historical analysis to deconstruct the religious/secular divide. In a richly detailed study of Louis IX's reign, Jones shows how anachronistic our categories of religious/secular, religion/politics, and Church/State are when we talk about the medieval period. Even more importantly, Jones suggests how those same categories operate ideologically when we talk about our own period, because they help to reinforce the notion that the way we divide up the world is natural, inevitable, and the summit of a process of evolution begun with our benighted medieval forebears. Jones' work is history at its best, helping us to understand not only the past, but ourselves, better."

—William T. Cavanaugh, DePaul University

"Even many of the best scholars still construe the Middle Ages in terms of tensions between Church and State that prefigure those of modernity and modern tensions between the religious and the secular. But in this exciting and scholarly new book Andrew Jones amply shows that in the thirteenth century the 'secular' time of this world and its concerns was still governed by processes of sacramental mediation. The West was originally more integrated than we like to think, in a way that may allow us to see that, if our legacy is significantly different from that of Islam, it may not be different in quite the way that we think. For this reason, amongst others, this book could not be more timely."

—John Milbank, University of Nottingham

"For the past half-century, social historians have been recovering a lost world of pre-modern, organic social relations. This scholarship has challenged modern readers to re-think basic modern assumptions about a range of social phenomena, most especially organization of work and family life. With *Before Church and State*, Andrew Willard Jones accomplishes a similar feat with respect to pre-modern politics. Here he challenges perhaps the most sacred cow of modernity: the privatization of religion. Building on the theoretical insights of historians and theologians who have identified 'religion' as itself a modern construct, Jones draws on extensive research to provide a masterful reconstruction of the political/religious imaginary of medieval Christendom at its peak in thirteenth-century France. He reveals a world in which there is no 'problem of Church and State' because there is no clear distinction between Church and State. Even more importantly, he shows that this organic integration of the Church into every aspect of political life was no 'theocracy'—a rule of the State by the Church—but rather a reflection of incarnational and Trinitarian theology. Medievals understood the temporal and the spiritual as distinct-yet-united by analogy to the human and divine natures of Christ, while they understood society as a communion of persons by analogy to the Trinity. By these standards, modernity has separated not only 'Church' and 'State,' but every person from every other person, leaving us with a peace that is merely a cessation of hostilities rather than true concord."

—CHRISTOPHER SHANNON, CHRISTENDOM COLLEGE

"It is often said, and rightly, that the past is a foreign country. Implicit in this statement is the conviction that when a genuine encounter takes place between the past and the present, the 'time-traveler' returns home enriched, with a capacity to see both the past and the present anew. While there are many books on medieval history that accomplish this task to a limited degree, I would place Andrew Jones' study of the sacramental kingdom of King Louis IX among an elite category of books that open up genuinely new ways of seeing both past and present.

"To effect such an encounter is not easy; for all too often, the 'traveler's' own habits of thought and action render the foreignness of the past invisible. With a keen and sympathetic eye for both medieval and modern ways of seeing, Jones carefully measures the distance between the two. Then, drawing on an impressive range of sources, he lets the past speak with its own voice, without being pre-empted or colonized by modern habits of perception. The reader wins a double prize—the political and religious world of thirteenth-century France, in all its exotic otherness; and a new standpoint from which to see, perhaps for the first time, the exotic otherness of today's political and religious landscape."

—David Foote, University of St. Thomas

"Dr. Jones has done the world of scholarship an immense service with the publication of *Before Church and State*. Thomas Kuhn famously spoke of paradigm shifts within science. Dr. Jones' volume has the potential to do just that: shift an entire paradigm within the history of the medieval period, which would have a ripple effect in a host of other fields: history of law, politics, theology, and philosophy. What Jones has done is shown the complexity of medieval Christendom which problematizes the universally assumed dichotomy between the sacred and the secular. With his thorough treatment of the historical context to St. Louis IX and Pope Clement IV, including copious primary sources, Jones has demonstrated that far from a raging battle between throne and altar, the evidence indicates a unified Christian society. Modern scholars have anachronistically read back into the historical record post-Enlightenment divisions between secular and sacred, where no such divisions actually existed. Instead, conflicts were aimed at the shared twin goal of both laity and clergy, namely the common temporal good and the eternal good of souls. Jones' immensely important volume represents a masterful treatment of the historical data which promises to have a profound impact on a number of disciplines, especially history, politics, and theology. Extremely well-written, erudite, and perspicacious, *Before Church and State* is a gripping historical narrative and should be read widely by any intellectual concerned with our common past, present, and future."

—Jeffrey L. Morrow, Seton Hall University

BEFORE
CHURCH
AND STATE

BEFORE CHURCH AND STATE

A Study of Social Order in the
Sacramental Kingdom of St. Louis IX

ANDREW WILLARD JONES

EMMAUS
ACADEMIC

Steubenville, Ohio
www.EmmausAcademic.com

EMMAUS
ACADEMIC

Steubenville, Ohio
www.emmausacademic.com
A Division of The St. Paul Center for Biblical Theology
Editor-in-Chief: Scott Hahn
1468 Parkview Circle
Steubenville, Ohio 43952

Library of Congress Cataloging-in-Publication Data
Names: Jones, Andrew Willard, 1980- author.
Title: Before church and state : a study of social order in St. Louis IX's
  sacramental kingdom / Andrew Willard Jones.
Description: Steubenville : Emmaus Academic, 2017. | Includes
  bibliographical references and index. | Description based on print version
  record and CIP data provided by publisher; resource not viewed.
Identifiers: LCCN 2017008738 (print) | LCCN 2017010988 (ebook) | ISBN
  9781945125409 (ebook) | ISBN 9781945125140 (hardcover)
Subjects: LCSH: Church and state--France--History--To 1500. | Church and
  state--History of doctrines--Middle Ages, 600-1500. | Louis IX, King of
  France, 1214-1270.
Classification: LCC BV630.3 (ebook) | LCC BV630.3 .J665 2017 (print) | DDC
  261.70944/09022--dc23
LC record available at https://lccn.loc.gov/2017008738

Front Cover image: St. Louis IX leaving Paris, 13th-Century manuscript.
© World History Archive / fotoLIBRA

Cover design and layout by Margaret Ryland

For Jerilou, my mother

CONTENTS

PREFACE

THIS BOOK has been with me for a long time. It began taking
shape ten years ago when I started writing graduate seminar
papers that focused on the French popes of the 1260s, Urban
IV and Clement IV. I was interested in these figures originally
simply because it seemed that no one else was—a wonderful
reason to settle on a dissertation topic, as I thought at the time.
As I read the documents that surrounded their activities, I increasingly came to know them, to understand their vision of
Christendom. This research also thrust me into the world of
St. Louis's France, both because these popes were subjects of
the great king and because his kingdom was at the very center
of mid-thirteenth-century affairs. And so, I started reading
the documents that surrounded St. Louis's reign. It was in this
manner that I came, slowly, to form an understanding of the
relationship between clergy and king, Church and State. And
this understanding was at odds with many of the narratives
that I had been taught since childhood. I found myself having
to jettison my established and everyday categories. Notions of
Church and State, of religious and secular, of worship and politics, of private and public, simply couldn't be made to express
what I saw in the sources.

By the time I defended the dissertation, I felt I had worked
through many of these problems and had come to a stable
understanding of the unity of the spiritual and the temporal powers within a coherent medieval Christian worldview.
However, due to the unfortunate isolation of the academic
disciplines, I, as a historian, was at that time largely unaware
of the work of the theologians, philosophers, sociologists, and
others who were proposing similar, but far more advanced,
arguments in their own disciplines. I recall clearly my first
encounter with John Milbank's *Theology and Social Theory*: I
was sleep deprived and on a flight to somewhere. It was ex-
hilarating. Milbank fully articulated so many of the ideas and

intuitions that I had been trying to make sense of. He clarified so much in my clouded thinking. What's more, Milbank gave me the courage to press ahead.

In the years that followed, I read more of the often spectacular work that was being done across many disciplines, especially in theology. When I took this new knowledge back to the body of historical research that I had assembled, I found that my original interpretation largely remained my interpretation, only now I had better tools to understand and explain it, to myself and hopefully to others. And so, over the course of the past five years the work has profoundly evolved. I dramatically reworked nearly all of it and it has about doubled in size. The chapters on Parlement were added first, and these then became the backbone of the whole second part of the book. In the records of Parlement I saw something that I had largely missed in the dissertation: I saw an ordered, juridical society that lacked sovereignty. This added a whole new layer to the book, from beginning to end.

My reading in theology continued, especially after I came to the St. Paul Center at Franciscan University. My understanding of how the Scripture was approached in the High Middle Ages was greatly deepened during this period, which helped me to see the implications of many of my "institutional" observations. It was also at the Center that I really engaged, finally, with St. Thomas. I had known, of course, that St. Thomas was the book's "elephant in the room." "Yes, but Aquinas says..." was the way over the years that so many protests against my thesis had begun. It is almost certainly imprudent and certainly naive for a historian such as myself to wade into the arguments of theologians. But, I just didn't see how the book could avoid engaging the great doctor. I decided that maybe I could get away with it by treating his writings as yet another body of documents from the period. Was I qualified to offer a reading of them as a historian? I don't know the answer, but the fourth part of the book, the *Conclusions*, is the result of my attempt. Working on Thomas added another thick layer to the work, and another revision was made.

It was in this way that the book took its current form, and its current form is odd, even somewhat accidental. It is most certainly a work of history, a history that focuses narrowly on a particular time and place, but it is also a history that is aware of its broader theoretical and even theological implications and which attempts to articulate them. The method I adopted was one of simply following the sources and recording what I thought about them. It vacillates between minute detail and grandiose conclusions. In the end, the book has come to propose a narrative structure that emerges from the Christian tradition and that is, I think, capable of making sense of the data of the sources while telling a story rather different than that which is normally told. This has resulted in a work that trespasses in the territory of multiple specialties, in none of which can I call myself a master, as the actual masters will quickly perceive. This leaves immense purchase for criticism. I likely don't have good responses for many of the criticisms that the specialists will levy. I simply beg the reader's pardon and I hope the book might be of some value, even if just as an occasion for discussion. I hope that I have captured something of the medieval social vision, and I hope that I have in some measure shown how that vision can help us understand our own.

As I mentioned, the book came to be over the course of about ten years. Over this time, I have been helped by so many wonderful family members, friends, and colleagues that it would be impossible to list them all here. I owe a profound debt to my dissertation advisor Damian J. Smith and to my graduate student friends, Adam Hoose, Scott McDermott, and Luke Ritter. It was in conversations with them that the seeds of most of the ideas in this work were planted. My colleagues at the St. Paul Center, Rob Corzine and Scott Hahn, are largely responsible for getting me to finally publish the book. Without Scott's support and insistence that the work was of value, I doubt I would ever have "finished" it. Jacob Wood and Jeff Morrow read the work and offered invaluable comments, sparing me much embarrassment, and adding depth to my reasoning. Likewise, David Foote and Gregory Lippiatt read the manuscript and offered extremely helpful comments and corrections. Portions of the work have benefited from being discussed in the Wednesday evening graduate seminar at the St. Paul Center and I thank all the participants for their efforts. Brett Kendall, Melissa Girard, Katie Takats, Kathryn Hogan, and especially Chris Erickson did amazing editorial work. No one has spent more time with the work, however, than has my mother, Jerilou. She has read it all the way through in every one of its iterations and has offered constant editorial guidance and direction. More than this, though, she is responsible for planting in me the seed of intellectual curiosity and of always tending it, sometimes pruning it, as it grew. Thanks, Mom. Finally, I thank my wife, Sara. She sacrificed hundreds of Saturdays and has provided the love and support without which, as far as I can tell, such projects simply cannot be done, at least not happily.

ABBREVIATIONS

Actes	*Actes du Parlement de Paris*
AE	*Annales Ecclesiastici*
Annales Minorum	*Annales Minorum seu trium ordinum a S. Francisco institutorum*
CAAP	*Correspondance administrative d'Alfonse de Poitiers*
CGN	*Concilia Galliae Narbonensis*
Clément IV, Reg.	*Les Registres de Clément IV (1265–1268)*
JC-1582	*Corpus Juris Canonici, emendatum et notis illustratum.* Rome, 1582.
EAAP	*Enquêtes Administratives d'Alfonse de Poitiers*
Établissements	*Les Établissements de Saint Louis*
Eudes, Reg.	Sydney M. Brown, *The Register of Eudes of Rouen*
Foedera	*Foedera, Conventiones, Literae, et Cujuscunque Generis Acta Publica*
Gal. Christ.	*Gallia Christiana*
HGL	*Histoire générale de Languedoc*
Hist. Frid.	*Historia Diplomatica Friderici Secundi*
HUP	*Historia universitatis parisiensis*
LTC	*Layettes du Trésor des chartes*
Mansi	*Sacrorum conciliorum nova et amplissima collectio*, ed. Joannes D. Mansi.
MGH *Leges Capit.* I	*Monumenta Germaniae Historica, Capitularia regum Francorum*
MGH *Leges Capit.* II	*Monumenta Germaniae Historica, Capitularia regum Francorum*, Series II
MGH *Leges Const.*	*Monumenta Germaniae Historica, Constitutiones et Acta Publica Imperatorum et Regum*
MGH SS	*Monumenta Germaniae Historica, Scriptores*
Olim	*Les Olim ou registres des arrêts rendus par la cour du roi*

Ordonnances	*Ordonnances des Roys de la France de la Troisième Race*
PL	Migne, *Patrologia latina*
RGALF	*Recueil Général Anciennes Lois Francaises*
RHGF	*Recueil des historiens des Gaules et de la France*
SCG	Aquinas, *Summa contra gentilles*
ST	Aquinas, *Summa theologiae*
Super eth.	Aquinas, *Sententia libri Ethicorum*
Super Ioan	Aquinas, *Super Evangelium S. Ioannis lectura*
Super Jer	Aquinas, *Super Jeremiam*
Super Ps	Aquinas, *Super Psalmos*
Super sent.	Aquinas, *Scriptum super Sententiis*
Tanner	*Decrees of the Ecumenical Councils.* Edited and Translated by Norman P. Tanner, S.J.
TNA	*Thesaurus novus anecdotorum*
Urban IV, Reg.	*Les Registres d'Urbain IV (1261–1264)*
X	*Liber extravagantium decretalium*

CHURCH AND STATE?

And therefore, where there is not this righteousness whereby the one supreme God rules the obedient city according to His grace, so that it sacrifices to none but Him, and whereby, in all the citizens of this obedient city, the soul consequently rules the body and reason the vices in the rightful order, so that, as the individual just man, so also the community and the people of the just, live by faith, which works by love, that love whereby man loves God as He ought to be loved, and his neighbor as himself—there, I say, there is not an assemblage associated by a common acknowledgement of right, and by a community of interests. But if there is not this, there is not a people, if our definition be true, and therefore there is no republic; for where there is no people there can be no republic.

—St. Augustine (ca. 413)

Let both swords of the faithful fall upon the necks of the foe, in order to destroy every high thing exalting itself against the knowledge of God, which is the Christian faith, lest the Gentiles should then say, "Where is their God?"

—St. Bernard of Clairvaux (ca. 1130)

These three types, namely, the laity, the secular clergy, and the religious, are a trinity: but in the holy union of the Church and in the Catholic faith they are a unity. Likewise, the Persons of the Father and the Son and the Spirit are a Trinity, but in essence and divinity a unity.

—Hostiensis (Cardinal Henry of Susa) (1254)

In the Church there are two powers, the spiritual and the temporal.

—Vincent of Beauvais (1260)

THIS BOOK IS A STUDY of France during the life of St. Louis IX (1214–1270). In it, I hope to overcome the limitations of modern political and religious categories and, in doing so, to reframe our discussion of government in the Middle Ages, especially with regard to the spiritual and temporal powers. I argue that thirteenth-century France was not a world of the secular and the religious vying for position and power, but a world in which the material and the spiritual were totally dependent on each other and penetrated one another at every level. This was a world not of the religious and the secular, but of the New Testament and the Old, of virtue and vice, of grace and law, of peace and violence. This world offered a coherent vision of the whole in which mankind moved through grace from the lesser to the greater, from the fallen to the redeemed.

It was an integral vision which included all of social reality and it was far removed from our own.

Our own vision is secular. Even when we acknowledge the importance of religion, we do so from within the assumption of the secular: that reality itself is ultimately free of the religious. Religions come and go; they are relative. The secular is permanent; it is absolute and universal. To us, the secular is the field on which the game of history—including religious history—is played. Within this secular vision, religion as a sociological category is often considered inessential to the concept of society itself. In this view, religious societies are, in a sense, accidentally religious: their religion can fade away. Secular societies, for their part, do not seem to have a religion proper to themselves at all, even if some individuals within them are religious.

To us moderns, the secular is fundamental. Even when religion is considered a universal sociological category, we almost always first translate it into something secular, such as its function: it synthesizes diverse perspectives and experiences, it knits people together, it makes the world coherent, it assuages the fear of death, it provides legitimacy for power, it constructs social roles, and so on. In this way, we are perhaps willing to accept that every society has a religion, but only if we first reduce religion to yet another aspect of the fundamental secular, to yet another ideology or worldview. In such an approach, "religion" is a category that functions *within* the secular.

Through this framework, we recognize that the societies of the Middle Ages were religious. But we do so because we recognize in the Middle Ages characteristics that we, from the vantage point of the fundamental secular, now call religious. When we say that the Middle Ages were religious, we mean something similar, I think, to when we say that a particular person is religious. He goes to church, he prays, he talks about God, and so on. Religion is important in his life. It might even be the most important thing in his life, having influence in everything that he does. But it could go away; he could abandon his religion and become secular and he would still be him.

And this is so because the secular is always actually there: it is the "there" where religion functions. In this way, even the most religious person does a great deal that we coherently call secular. He goes to work; he votes; he mows his lawn. We view the Middle Ages in a similar manner, and activities of our secular world that we recognize in the behavior of the religious people of the Middle Ages we deem to have always really been secular, even if they mentioned God when they did them. The people of the Middle Ages could have cultivated the land, they could have elected kings, they could have administered justice, and they could have fought wars without God because farming, elections, courts, and wars are constants and so ultimately secular. On the other hand, things that we recognize in the past and now think of as being religious and so optional to our secular society we deem to have always belonged to the "religious" sphere—the Scripture, liturgy, prayer, sacraments, the clergy.

The current book is a challenge to this conception of the Middle Ages and to the categories that underpin it. In it, I hope to add my voice to the growing chorus of scholars from diverse disciplines who are challenging notions of the "religious" and the "secular" wherever they appear. I contend that the Middle Ages were neither religious nor secular because the religious and the secular are two features of a single construction: the modern, Western social architecture of "Church" and "State," "private" and "public," "individual" and "market," and so on. The societies of the Middle Ages had a different architecture based on different assumptions and different concepts, ultimately on a different vision of the cosmos.

Medieval government provides an opportunity for us to see the lines of this architecture. Medieval kings did many things, including enforce justice and wage war. We are inclined to think of justice and war as essential and so secular. Kings are, therefore, the State, and are more often than not seen as *fundamentally* secular in nature, even if animated by sincere "religious" ideology because such ideology could transition away from its "religiousness" without doing violence to the State's *fundamental* nature. This reading is re-enforced by the terminology we find in the medieval sources, within which the kings and lords are often referred to as the "secular power." They were the "secular arm" who enforced the "secular law" with the "secular sword." This modern view is not completely wrong: kingship is without doubt an ancestor to the modern State—one branch of the State's genealogy does lead here.

The problem, however, is that in the Middle Ages the "secular" was integral to a conception of social reality that was thoroughly "supernatural" in character. "Justice" was a name for Christ, and the king was his vicar. The king's "secular" justice was a direct participation in the construction of the City of God, and his legitimacy came only through his sacramental incorporation into the Body of Christ and the office that he held within it. He wielded the secular, temporal sword that had been bestowed on the Christian people by Christ himself. The temporal sword belonged to God. The "religious" was not accidental to this world, and the kings were not the State. It was a sacramental world in which the material and the spiritual were everywhere and always present together. The spiritual power was the power of the priests to dispense the grace that sustained this society in charity and they wielded the spiritual sword of excommunication against the mortal sinner. The temporal power was the power of the laymen to organize the world of things and events, and they wielded the temporal sword against the violent.

Both powers and their swords were the power of the Church through which it worked out its salvation in time. It was an integral understanding. "Secular" simply meant "in time" or "in the world," and the Church militant operated directly in the world. Indeed, the primary dispensers of sacramental grace were the "secular" clergy and the only "religious" people were the monks and nuns. This world made sense on its own terms. It was what Henri de Lubac would have called a "complete act."[1] If we insist on reading our understanding

---

[1] Henri de Lubac, S.J., *Medieval Exegesis: The Four Senses of Scripture*, vol. 1,

of the secular and of the religious back into this world, what we see is that the government of both kings and priests were thoroughly secular—of course, they were also both thoroughly religious. Our modern categories do not hold.

One of the central arguments of this book is that we should abandon the use of "religious" and "secular," "Church" and "State," *understood in their modern senses* in our attempts to understand the Middle Ages, in this case the thirteenth century. This is not because the terms have no meaning—in our world they have a great deal of meaning. Rather, it is because one cannot get too far along in building a thick description of the thirteenth century before concluding that everything was religious or, if one is inclined to come at it from the other direction, before concluding that everything was secular. Both conclusions are correct because the thirteenth century is the common ancestor in the genealogies of both the religious and the secular. It is out of this medieval world that our conceptions of the secular and the religious slowly emerged over centuries of history—and they emerged together: the religious is a part of the secular.

It is as mistaken to read the secular and the religious back into the medieval world as it would be to describe a grandfather as a conglomeration of his grandchildren's traits. He is not a piece of this child and a piece of that child. He is a "complete act" in and of himself, and the children descend from him; before they were born, they did not exist "in him," a piece here and a piece there. Rather, it is only after their birth that we can look back at the grandfather and see whence they came. It is only after the children exist that the grandfather can be somehow "divided up." This glance back can tell us a lot about the grandchildren—it is a legitimate genealogical exercise—but it adds little to our knowledge of the grandfather. He does not need the grandchildren in order to be the "complete act" that he is. The "religious" and the "secular" are the offspring of modern history. The Middle Ages are their shared grandfather.

---

trans. Mark Sebanc, xix. "Something that existed long ago was, in its time, 'a complete act,' and it must be understood as such, in its totality."

In order to understand him, we must set the grandchildren aside because they did not yet exist.

The process through which they came into being is appropriately called secularization, but it is a very difficult process to describe without putting the cart before the horse. Peter Berger has written, "By secularization we mean the process by which sectors of society and culture are removed from the domination of religious institutions and symbols."[2] The problem, however, is that institutions and symbols are recognizable as religious only from the vantage point of the secular. This means secularization might be just as legitimately understood as being the process by which sectors of society and culture were construed *as* religious institutions and symbols. In other words, secularization is the process through which the "religious" as we conceive of it was created. Along these lines, Brent Nongbri has accurately remarked that we call religious "anything that sufficiently resembles modern Protestant Christianity,"[3] and when Charles Taylor states that the British

---

[2] Peter Berger, *The Sacred Canopy: Elements of a Sociological Theory of Religion* (New York: Anchor Books, 1967), 107.

[3] Brent Nongbri, *Before Religion: A History of a Modern Concept* (New Haven / London: Yale University Press, 2013), 18. With this in mind, we can see the circular nature of our sociological study of "religion." For example, Berger writes that the Christian Church is very unusual among human institutions because it is an institution specifically concerned with religion rather than with the institutions of society themselves. The problem, I would contend, is that we derive our definition of religion from *those things that the modern Christian Church is concerned with.* This produces ethnocentrism in the study of comparative religions and presentism in the study of history (see *The Sacred Canopy*, 123). For a good example of this problem in action, see Ernest Gellner, *Nations and Nationalism* (Ithaca, NY: Cornell University Press, 2006), 8–18. Charles Taylor defines religion as a way of thinking that posits the "place of fullness" beyond human life and the secular as a way that posits it "within" human life. This is the transcendent/immanent distinction. He writes, "The crucial distinction underlying the concept of secularity . . . [is:] what makes this group of people as they continue over time a common agent? Where this is something which transcends the realm of those common actions this agency engages in, the association is non-secular. Where the constituting factor is nothing other than such common action . . . we have secularity." The problem, though, is that Christian salvation in

were more religious in 1900 than ever before, we might consider him to be, in a sense, defining the term "religious."[4] It is no coincidence that it is precisely at this time and in this place—late nineteenth-century, Western Europe—that we can also most clearly define the "secular" (Darwin, Marxism, the factory, Otto von Bismarck, the Third Republic, etc.). It seems that historians such as Jean Delumeau, who have maintained that the people of the Middle Ages were not really Christian at all, are working within a tautology:[5] from within the categories of modern thought, the Middle Ages could not really be Christian because Christianity can only exist in a secular society. As a "religion," Christianity is a modern, dare I say "secular," phenomenon.

We live in this modern world and most of us do not believe that our concept of the secular is a historically contingent construction. Rather, we tend to believe our world to be based on the way things really are (the secular, too, has become a "complete act"): we understand "secular" and "religious" to be essential categories. And so, with these categories in hand, we go off to study the government of other cultures, other times and places, sorting whatever we find appropriately. In doing so, when we consider government, we construct sociological the-

---

the Middle Ages was not "beyond human life"; it was the fullness of human life: "On earth as it is in heaven." The Church was the "place of fullness," for it was the Body of Christ and it was both "within" and "beyond" human life. Does the Eucharist "transcend" the realm of common action that is the Mass or does the Eucharist "condescend" into history? Or conversely, does the Communist society's commitment to self-sacrifice in the service of impersonal forces of history that ultimately results in heaven on earth not count as "transcending" its common action? If so, why not? It seems to me that we are again seeing concepts that do not lead us to understanding the nature of Christianity but are rather drawn from modern Christianity. Taylor's definitions are workable for his history, but they are clearly rooted in the particular modern experience, a fact that he acknowledges; see Charles Taylor, *A Secular Age* (Cambridge, MA: Harvard University Press, 2007), 14–15, 194.

4   Taylor, *A Secular Age*, 519.

5   John Van Engen, "The Christian Middle Ages as an Historiographical Problem," *The American Historical Review* 19, no. 3 (June 1986): 521–22.

ories and historical narratives that necessarily terminate with the secular State and that posit the secular State as something that is really always there, even if nascent, not yet developed, or obscured. The discipline of political history has been practiced largely within this meta-narrative of secularization, and while the works of individual scholars are, of course, often nuanced and sensitive to potential category mistakes, it is nevertheless the case that a generalized, medieval chapter in this narrative has emerged as a synthesis of the research of the past two hundred years. This is the narrative one often finds in textbooks or in summaries of the medieval period. It is a narrative that one finds normally accepted by non-specialists without qualification.

Within this familiar story, the papacy battled the monarchs over who would have what Walter Ullmann called "monarchic functions,"[6] over whether the *imperium* or *sacerdotium* was sovereign. This was a protracted struggle, from the Investiture Controversy in the eleventh century to the Avignon papacy in the fourteenth. As Geoffrey Barraclough wrote, "It is possible to draw a straight line from what [Gregory VII] set out, but failed, to do, to the exalted claims of Innocent III and Boniface VIII."[7] Over the course of this struggle, as the popes attempted to extend their power they were forced to spend the papacy's moral capital engaging in dirty political power struggles, as well as stretch the ideology of papal monarchy into a theory of worldwide theocracy. As the papacy drifted from its properly religious and spiritual role, as it struggled to gain control of the "secular" sphere of politics, it debased the power of ecclesi-

---

[6] Walter Ullmann, *The Growth of Papal Government in the Middle Ages* (London: Methuen & Co., 1970), 451.

[7] Geoffrey Barraclough, *The Medieval Papacy* (New York: W. W. Norton & Company, 1979), 89. It is the premise of Brian Tierney's popular collection of documents that "during the period from 1050 to 1300 there took place a series of conflicts between kings and popes which merged into one another in such a fashion that we may regard them all as changing aspects of one long, continuing crisis" (*The Crisis of Church and State, 1050–1300* [Toronto: University of Toronto Press, 1988]).

astical censure and of crusade, turning them into cynical tools of statecraft; it centralized its administration, undermining the power of the episcopate, and became corrupt and legalistic. In the process, it lost the moral authority and prestige it once held. This conflict ended in an ignoble defeat of the papacy at the hands of Philip IV, from which it was a short journey to French domination of the Avignon papacy, schism, and ultimately the Reformation.[8] As John A. Watt states, "We may perhaps allow ourselves to see in the contrast between Innocent III in the authoritative splendor of Lateran IV and the bitter humiliation of Boniface VIII the measure of the decline of the papacy in the thirteenth century: a decline the popes at Avignon did little to halt."[9] The papacy's decline is to be contrasted with the rise of the monarchies, who, over the course of their struggles with the Church, achieved independence and real sovereignty. As the story goes, the renewed study of Roman law provided the State with the legal concepts needed to justify itself without religion. Theologically, Aquinas finally dispensed with Augustine's notion that the State was the consequence of sin and asserted, based on Aristotle, that the State was natural to mankind. Embracing this theoretical and legal self-sufficiency and having bested the Church, the monarchs set about building their States.

Within this narrative, the kings are certainly religious. But, it is a modern understanding of religion. It is religion as political ideology and personal piety. Because of this, "religion" remains an accident to the king's essence as the State. Ideologies can change and personal piety fade away without the essence of the State being undermined. Within the narrative, the anointed kings of the High Middle Ages were the State, and when their ideology shifted to that of absolutism in

---

[8] See, for example, R. F. Bennett's Introduction in Gerd Tellenbach, *Church, State and Christian Society at the Time of the Investiture Contest* (Toronto: University of Toronto Press, 1991).

[9] John A. Watt, "The Papacy," in *The New Cambridge Medieval History*, vol. 5, *1198–1300*, ed. David Abulafia (Cambridge, UK: Cambridge University Press, 1999), 164.

the Early Modern Period, they remained the State, and when, ultimately, the monarchies gave way to Modern secular legislatures and secular dictators, these remained the State. The State is the constant because the Modern State is really where we started.

Nevertheless, one must be careful in criticizing this narrative too harshly because the secular State most certainly does have its own history, and I suspect that a good telling of it would include many parts of the genealogy that I just laid out. That is not the problem. The problem with the accepted narrative is that within it history itself tends to become nothing but the genealogy of the secular State. In the accepted narrative, we start with the grandchildren. And so, many histories purporting to be about the Middle Ages are actually about the nineteenth century. Similar to the secularity of the State, within this narrative the Church's religiousness is conceived of as essential. The Church engaged in secular affairs throughout the narrative, to be sure, but its political activities were accidental to its essence, and when they faded away or were suppressed, when religion finally became the private, spiritual, reflective thing that it really, properly always was, the Church remained the Church and religion remained religion. The project of modern historians of the Middle Ages has often, therefore, been to show how this proper sorting happened, how we finally got to the secular State and the religious Church, and so we get the narrative of the "problem of Church and State."

Histories of St. Louis's rule have tended to be dependent on the narrative of the secular State and normally follow this pattern. In the thirteenth century, France gained territorial integrity. This newly expanded kingdom was increasingly governed by the central authority. The king worked to monopolize violence, bringing more and more "feudal" activities under his purview. To this end, Louis outlawed private war and the duel. The king's power, we are told, was increasingly the ordering principle, maintaining the peace in the face of the so-called "private violence" of the knightly class, which was previously endemic. In order to effectively exercise his power, Louis rationalized his officials into a bureaucracy complete with salaries and offices. The royal officials of this administration operated under laws, or ordinances, decreed from the center. It was under Louis that these laws were brought together and rationalized in the pursuit of justice and peace. Louis, therefore, built Parlement. Parlement was the place where the conflicts of society were worked out through the new science of law, rather than through violence. Parlement was staffed with expert officials, lawyers, the famous "New Men," who were the prototype of the middle class, a meritocracy of professionals. As Jacques Le Goff wrote, we are witnessing the "march toward absolutism," which would all come together under Louis's grandson Philip IV.[10] The French kings were building the sovereign State, and by the end of the thirteenth century this sovereignty extended to control of the Church.

In addition to the assumptions concerning the religious and the secular discussed above, I believe this reading is dependent on certain modern assumptions about how politics work; indeed, about what, in fact, they are. One of these assumptions is that sovereignty exists. Sovereignty is a difficult concept to define. But, the best place to start is probably with Jean Bodin: "Sovereignty is that absolute and perpetual power vested in a commonwealth."[11] The sovereign is that entity that wields force without reference to any other human entity: all legitimate force is ultimately a delegation from the sovereign, and the sovereign has always and everywhere the right to intervene. Like the "religious" and the "secular" in the simplified narrative of Church and State, "sovereignty" is posited as an essential part of social life. Sovereignty exists, even if it is unclear who holds it or if the apparatus to effectively wield it has not yet

---

[10] *Saint Louis*, trans. Gareth Evan Gollrad (Notre Dame, IN: University of Notre Dame Press, 2009), 235. For an extensive and nuanced articulation of this standard narrative applied to France and *mutatis mutandis* throughout Western Europe, see Richard W. Kaeuper, *Chivalry and Violence in Medieval Europe* (Oxford: Oxford University Press, 1999).

[11] Jean Bodin, *On Sovereignty: Six Books of the Commonwealth*, trans. M. J. Tooley (Oxford: Basil Blackwell, 1955), 65.

been built, and the contest, the struggle of history is about who will both claim the prize of sovereignty and be able to defend that claim. In the "problem of Church and State," sovereignty is what the popes and kings were really fighting over—a prize that by definition cannot be shared. However, it is my contention in this book that as with the "religious" and the "secular," "sovereignty" did not exist in thirteenth century France, not because the organizational technologies had not yet been invented, but because the concept of sovereignty and the attempt to build sovereign States are the products of a distinctly modern set of assumptions and institutions that was not present.

I contend that ultimately the assumption that underpins the modern understanding of politics, the assumption that leads us to see sovereignty as always historically relevant, is the same assumption that underpins the doctrine of the "secular" (and so the existence of "religion"), and this assumption is the existence of a primordial violence. The idea was articulated most directly by Hobbes: humankind is in a state of constant warfare, everyone against everyone. The sovereign power of the State is a violence so profound and so predictable in its application that everyone submits. The other founding theorists of modern political thought essentially agreed. John Locke, for example, only avoids Hobbes's natural war by positing property rights as natural. But such rights are always over and against another person. The liberalism that developed out of Hobbes and Locke conceives of human interactions as, at root, contractual actions and of contracts as a type of compromise in the face of conflict, in the face of scarcity. Because all human interactions are ultimately contractual and based on property rights and the State is that which enforces contracts and property rights, there is within liberalism itself the presupposition of the ubiquitous power of the sword—sovereignty.

I am convinced that this "ontological violence"[12] is the field

---

[12] That modern social science is predicated on an "ontological violence" is the thesis of John Milbank's *Theology and Social Theory: Beyond Secular Reason* (Oxford: Blackwell Publishing, 2006).

from which the idea of sovereignty—and so of the State—has sprouted and is cultivated because, in the face of perpetual violence, peace is possible only through the imposition of a greater violence that can suppress all other conflicts.[13] Sovereignty allows for legitimate violence. Without it, in the modern world of ubiquitous violence, you can either accept a sort of political nihilism: the strongest rule and there is no right or wrong about it—this is the route taken by many postmodern theorists. Or, you can assert that all violence is immoral and that therefore all government is crime. This is an extreme position sometimes adopted by radicals of various stripes. Or, you can maintain that sovereignty is real and has existence prior to any particular, historical political situation. The sovereign is that power that can wield violence legitimately, that is somehow morally empowered with a monopoly on violence, and who rightly wields that monopoly unchallenged; all other violence is crime. Sovereignty allows us to sort the relentless violence into two types: the legitimate and the illegitimate.

It seems to me that almost all modern political thought, from theories of the divine right of kings to theories of representative republics, are ultimately about who is sovereign and how their monopoly on violence can be realized most effectively. Because this scenario operates at the level of an assumption, history is seen as the struggle over sovereignty: who is going to

---

[13] For example, Pierre Manent has argued that the birth of the city in Greece was the politicization of the primordial warfare: "War gives way to political justice, which replaces it very advantageously. But it is important not to forget that justice is something that succeeds war." In heroic societies war is everywhere, but the modern State produces peace by pushing war to the borders; see Manent, *Metamorphoses of the City: On the Western Dynamic* (Cambridge, MA: Harvard University Press, 2013), 52–54. Robert N. Bellah recounts and endorses many anthropologists' understanding of a primordial and ever-present conflict among the men of a tribe or troop for dominance as the root of social organization. Fearing an "upstart," the men ban together to keep any one of them from gaining too much power. Thus violence is the root cause of the egalitarianism that we find in "small-scale" societies (*Religion in Human Evolution: From the Paleolithic to the Axial Age* [Cambridge, MA: Harvard University Press, 2011], 175–78).

have it and how are they going to enforce it? The right answer ideologically, of course, is the secular, democratic State—which becomes the *telos* of history and the perfect manifestation of sovereignty. It is this idea that underpins ultimately the narrative of "the problem of Church and State" because it is this idea that cannot see a way to accommodate both papal and monarchical power within a single, coherent, and stable society.

Read from within this framework, in the Middle Ages, the Church seems to have made a bid for sovereignty. It attempted a religious State, a theocracy. This attempt put it necessarily in conflict with the secular monarchies. There simply cannot be both multiple sovereigns and peace, and so we get the notion of the Church and the State in the Middle Ages as rival, parallel institutions. As one theorist of secularization has written, "the popes were to rule over the Church, and the princes were to rule over the state, and each had its own property, personnel, and politico-legal apparatus."[14] Like eighteenth- and nineteenth-century sovereigns, sometimes the two institutions formed an alliance against some common enemy, while at other times they waged war against each other, but within the confines of modern political thought, the papacy and the kings could never ultimately be anything other than rivals. The development of the secular State and the religious Church is seen as the final resolution of this struggle over sovereignty, but not without the bloodletting of the sixteenth and seventeenth centuries. The story of sovereignty, the story of Church and State, and the story of the religious and the secular are, therefore, totally bound up together as interlacing plotlines in the same meta-narrative. This whole discourse is, I believe, ultimately ideological, an explication of the modern West's legitimacy.[15]

---

[14] Philip S. Gorski, "Historicizing the Secularization Debate: Church, State, and Society in Late Medieval and Early Modern Europe, ca. 1300 to 1700," *American Sociological Review* 65, no. 1 (2000): 157.

[15] For discussions of the ideological content of the very category "religion," see William Cavanaugh, *The Myth of Religious Violence: Secular Ideology and the Roots of Modern Conflict* (Oxford: Oxford University Press, 2009); Talal

Within this reading of the Middle Ages, relations between St. Louis IX and the papacy have been largely ignored. Joseph Strayer, in an article titled "The Laicization of French and English Society in the Thirteenth Century," deals almost exclusively with Philip IV, mentioning St. Louis only once, stating that Louis was somehow resistant to the "nationalization" process.[16] The neglect of St. Louis is far exceeded, though, by the general neglect of the papacy during the second half of the thirteenth century. After the death of Frederick II in 1250 and the start of what is often called the "long interregnum" of the Empire, the history of the papacy seems to become relevant again only with the advent of its conflict with the Capetians under Boniface VIII and with the move to Avignon. Since the papacy is understood to have lost its battle with the French monarchy, and since papal power is essentially defined as its ability to dominate the antithetical power of the monarchy, it is simply assumed that the second half of the thirteenth century was a period of papal decline and monarchical ascent, even if not a period of open conflict.[17] In this emplotment the

---

Asad, *Genealogies of Religion: Discipline and Reasons of Power in Christianity and Islam* (Baltimore, MD: The Johns Hopkins University Press, 1993).

[16] The only mention of Louis reads: "Men like Saint Louis and Henry III, who believed sincerely in the old international ideals, could not follow a nationalistic policy" (Joseph Strayer, "The Laicization of French and English Society," in *Medieval Statecraft and the Perspectives of History*, ed. John F. Benton and Thomas N. Bisson [Princeton: Princeton University Press, 1971], 263).

[17] For example, Thomas Renna writes: "The power vacuum left in the aftermath of the imperial-papal conflicts was filled by a French monarch, Louis IX (1214–1270, canonized a saint in 1297). But St. Louis made no attempt to replace the universalism of Pope Innocent IV or Frederick II with his own brand of universalism. Instead, he sought to construct a particularist state, the kingdom of France. This state, a prototype of the later nation state, would serve to dismantle the Gregorian church. Ironically it was the papacy which created conditions favorable to the growth of the French national state. Indeed, nationalism, the nation might never have been realized without the drive by the holy see to forge a centralized church" (*Church and State in Medieval Europe, 1050–1314* [Dubuque, IA: Kendal / Hunt Publishing, 1977], 142). He writes further: "But the Gregorian papacy and the Holy Roman Empire had gotten Europeans accustomed to thinking in universalist terms.

seemingly cooperative relations between the papacy and the Capetian monarchy in the thirteenth century are necessarily understood in terms of realpolitik: the papacy needed Capetian support against the Hohenstaufen and their heirs and the French Crown found cooperation with the papacy to be sometimes in its interests.[18] As Elizabeth Hallam has written, "In general political dealings the king managed to remain on good terms with a papacy that could not deny his personal piety, but which he only supported when it suited his own ends: good order in the French Church, the upholding of his royal power and the recapture of the Holy Land from the infidel."[19] However, because Church and State are opposed principles within this narrative, the rise of Capetian power ultimately necessitated a corresponding decline in papal power. James Powell is so convinced of the mutual exclusivity between the power of the papacy and that of Crown that he argues that Louis IX's enthusiasm for and organization of crusades, actions to which the papacy had been exhorting monarchs since the eleventh century, were evidence of the decline of the papacy, a decline that resulted in a Church that could be characterized as "desperate" by the end of the century.[20]

I do not aspire to diminish the work of the generations of

Hence when these two monarchies depleted each other, Christians turned to the French king, the nearest thing to an 'emperor'" (ibid., 157).

[18] See, for example, the manner in which Charles Wood accounts for Louis and the papacy's agreements concerning the Provisions of Oxford while remaining within the traditional narrative: "Under the circumstances absolute proof is impossible, and yet the whole tendency of monarchical policy, at least since the reign of Philip Augustus, had been so contrary to any acceptance of papal sovereignty over matters of state that it becomes difficult to take at face value Louis' seeming acceptance of it here. . . . When Louis IX found his views in accord with the Pope's he seems to have felt no hesitation in acknowledging the pontiff's superior position" ("Mise of Amiens and Saint Louis' Theory of Kingship," *French Historical Studies* 6, no. 3 [Spring 1970]: 304).

[19] Elizabeth M. Hallam and Judith Everard, *Capetian France, 987–1328*, 2nd ed. (New York: Longman, 2001), 308.

[20] James Powell, "Church and Crusade: Frederick II and Louis IX," *The Catholic Historical Review* 93, no. 2 (April 2007): 252, 262.

scholars who have, to varying degrees, worked within the meta-narrative described above. Most have contributed greatly to
our knowledge of the medieval monarchies and of the Church,
and most nuance their own assertions in a manner that would
reduce the purchase for aggressive criticism. Nevertheless, I do
believe it to be the case that much work in this field has been
handicapped by a matrix of categories and concepts that almost
compels a certain narrative structure. The current book is an
attempt to change the terms and categories through which we
conceptualize and discuss the "problem of Church and State"
in the Middle Ages and so to free scholarship to go in a new
direction.

I argue that thirteenth-century France was built as a "most
Christian kingdom," a term that the papacy frequently used in
reference to it. I do not mean that the kingdom of France was
a State with a Christian ideology. I mean that it *was* Christian, fundamentally. There was no State lurking beneath the
kingdom's religious trappings. There was no State at all, but a
Christian kingdom. In this kingdom, neither the "secular" nor
the "religious" existed. Neither did "sovereignty." I do not mean
that the religious was everywhere and that the secular had not
yet emerged from under it. I mean *they did not exist at all*. Also,
I do not mean that the mechanisms and technologies necessary for the realization of sovereign power did not exist. Nor
do I mean that the idea of sovereignty was inchoate, that its
integrity was awaiting the development of intellectual systems
capable of giving it expression. I mean that sovereignty *did not
exist at all*. "Sovereignty," the "secular," and the "religious" have
existence only in the specific historical circumstances through
which we give them their definitions—that is, the eighteenth
and nineteenth centuries. If we approach the Middle Ages with
these categories, then really we are writing histories of these
modern centuries and not of the Middle Ages themselves. The
"State" and the "secular," like all concepts, certainly have histories, genealogies that reach back as far as one might like to go.
The people of thirteenth-century France, however, were not
trying to figure out how to build a "Sovereign State" and they

were not trying to disentangle the "secular" from the "religious." They had never heard of these things. Their world made sense, and it was a world that did not contain these concepts. This is the world that I am after.

We must abandon the assumptions of modern politics ultimately because France was a Christian kingdom and, within Christianity, peace is the primordial condition and violence is sin, an aberration, a corruption, and ultimately something that does not even have real being—it is an absence. This is a key theme of St. Augustine's thought.[21] St. Thomas Aquinas treated peace as the final end of being itself.[22] One of the things we have to allow for in order to break free from the modern construct of the "problem of Church and State" is that charity could have real content as charity, that self-sacrifice is real and not just a tactic of conflict. We have to allow for the possibility that two people can have a relationship that is not predicated ultimately on competition for power, one over the other—in effect, we have to allow for the possibility of a non-dissembling peace. If we do so, we can understand the people of the thirteenth century on their own terms, within their "complete act," because this is the language in which they speak. We can read the sources looking for their categories and concepts and we can entertain the possibility that their language is better at capturing who they were than is ours. It is this that I attempt to do.

The idea of the "complete act" is an important one. It is also very difficult to hang on to. We live in our own complete act, and we necessarily pull our language and categories from it. A history that tries to present the complete act of a distant time and place is necessarily a work of translation, and translations are always flawed: they always fail ultimately to capture all the meaning of the original. But a good translation is capable of conveying some of the meaning of the original. As people, we are capable of communicating with each other,

---

[21] Milbank, *Theology and Social Theory*, 392.
[22] ST II-II, q. 29, a. 4.

and I am convinced that this holds true in principle across the centuries. Nevertheless, translations must be very carefully made. In this work, in order to hold as closely as possible to the complete act of thirteenth-century France, I follow what must be seen as a most fundamental "complete act," the life of a single man: Gui Foucois.

Gui lived an interesting life. He was born in Saint-Gilles in the South of France sometime around 1200.[23] His father, Pierre, was an important advocate and judge under Counts Raymond V and Raymond VI of Toulouse and was involved at the highest levels in the affairs of the period.[24] Gui grew up during the Albigensian Crusade, the invasion of the South by the Northern "French." Gui went to Paris to study and returned to the South in the mid-1230s, going to work as a lay advocate. His primary task was to help figure out how the postwar region was going to be rebuilt according to the terms of the documents that ended the conflict—the task of turning theory into practice. He was very good at this, and in 1249 he went to work for Louis IX's brother, Count Alphonse of Poitiers and Toulouse. He helped build the institution of royal *enquêteurs* and wrote the rules and ordinances for the reform of secular officials. What is more, he was instrumental in the establishment of the ecclesiastical inquisition in the South. In 1254, he began his service to the king. He wrote some of the most important reforming documents of St. Louis's reign, implementing the vision of Christian kingship. He served as a royal *enquêteur* and was instrumental in the construction of the legal universe in which they would work. He became such an expert on the law of heresy that the Dominican inquisitors asked him for advice and the *Consilium* that he composed for them became one of the most important founding documents of the medieval inquisition.

Gui was a married man with two daughters. When his wife died in 1257, he took Holy Orders, and within a year he

---

[23] TNA, 2:371.
[24] See HGL, 8:428, 429, 434, 537; 7:123–24; and LTC, 1:950.

was elected to the See of Le Puy. As a bishop, he continued to work for the construction of the Christian kingdom. He served in Parlement, Louis's newly constructed royal court. He continued to serve as an investigator and delegate for royal justice but now added to it work for the pope for ecclesiastical justice. Gui constantly held both royal and apostolic commissions. After only three years, he was translated to the Archbishopric of Narbonne and was involved at the very highest levels of international affairs. In 1261 he was named a cardinal of the Roman Church and became the legal advisor to Pope Urban IV. He was sent as a papal legate to France to try to broker a peace between Henry III of England and his barons. Working with Louis IX, Gui wrote some of the most ardent defenses of monarchial power that one finds in the period.

In 1264 Gui was elected Pope Clement IV, and as pope, he continued to work closely with Louis. He helped establish the office of cardinal legate as a near permanent position in France. He pressed Louis to go on crusade and supported his efforts when he took the Cross. Clement also defended the power of the papacy. Indeed, he drafted one of the most important statements of papal primacy in the thirteenth century, a statement that was reiterated at the Second Council of Lyons and repeatedly thereafter, including in the decree of papal infallibility promulgated at the First Vatican Council.

Gui is a fascinating character. He is also a person whose life allows us to cut across so many of the lines that are normally drawn in the "problem of Church and State." He had his hand in just about everything, and his life as a "complete act" lets us get at the "complete act" that was the society in which he moved. This book is not a biography, however. Although I follow Gui and use his life as a coherent thread to reconstruct his world, I am not trying to tell Gui's story, and I diverge from him often and extensively. I am using his life to provide the backbone for my narrative, but I am not asserting that it *was* the backbone of the society in which he lived. Rather, I am trying to paint a historical picture of the span of a man's life.

The present book is divided into four parts, each of which contains multiple chapters. It progresses chronologically through Gui's life while simultaneously addressing different aspects of the dominate Church-State narrative. Part I challenges the essentialist division between the religious and the secular that underpins the modern reading of the medieval "problem of Church and State." To do so, it looks at the institutions of the ecclesiastical inquisitors and the royal *enquêteurs*. It argues that they were, in fact, two components of the same movement to institutionalize the Albigensian Crusade, which was fundamentally both spiritual and temporal in nature, a movement known as the *business of the peace and the faith*.

Chapter 1 argues that the "peace" and the "faith" were inseparable. It demonstrates how "mercenaries" were the necessary secular companion to "heretics" and how the movement against one was fundamentally a movement against the other, looking at the formation of Christian knighthood and the importance of "dualism" for understanding how the orthodox understood the world of the South of France. Within the high medieval understanding, the secular was brought up into and fulfilled in the spiritual, and so essentialist divisions between the temporal and the spiritual dissolve.

Chapter 2 develops concretely the conclusions of Chapter 1, arguing that the king stepped into the peace side of the *business of the peace and the faith*. Enemies of the peace became not only rebels against the king but also, necessarily, enemies of the Church, while, conversely, heretics became also rebels against the king. Outlawry and excommunication became united as a single sanction against a single offense.

Chapter 3 argues that the early institutional developments of the inquisitors and the *enquêteurs* shared a conceptual and legal foundation and thus cannot be separated. The *business of the peace and the faith* required reformed prelates and reformed secular lords; the inquisition was to provide the former and the *enquêteurs* the later.

Chapter 4 situates Louis IX's famous *Grande Ordonnance* within the narrative described in Chapters 1–3. The *Grande*

Ordonnance is very often seen as a crucial document in the formation of the State, and Chapter 4 argues that it cannot be divorced from the spiritual nature of what the king was up to, which was the *business of the peace and the faith*. The chapter demonstrates this thesis with concrete examples such as Gui Foucois's writing of one of the foundational documents of the ecclesiastical inquisition while serving as an *enquêteur* for the Crown. It points out how the two sides of this *business*, the spiritual and the temporal, were fundamentally relational and mutually dependent.

Chapter 5 then explores the investigations carried out by Gui Foucois and the other *enquêteurs* demonstrating that their conception of what they were doing fundamentally included the spiritual side of the business, the concern of the inquisitors. It also discusses the meaning of the *faiditi* as enemies of both Church and Crown, proving that institutional, even bureaucratic, bridges existed between the ecclesiastical and the royal. In practice, the *enquêteurs* and the inquisitors were two offices within one legal, conceptual, and organizational apparatus.

Chapter 6 concludes the first part of the book, arguing that the spiritual and the temporal (or secular) in the period under consideration were two parts of the same social architecture, which was, simply, the Church. It goes on to give a detailed look at the rite of coronation of French kings and demonstrates that this liturgy embodies the notion of the Church as the setting for both powers. The notion that the temporal was fulfilled in the spiritual and not set either in opposition nor parallel to the sacred is further developed within this context, and its connection to the four senses of Scripture is articulated. Part I as a whole demonstrates that the modern conception of the Church as the "religious" actor and the State as the "secular" actor is both theoretically and practically untenable.

Part II of the book seeks to demonstrate that medieval society was not organized around notions of sovereignty. It argues that the conviction concerning the ubiquity of violence that underpins modern political and social thought was not present in High Middle France. Rather, peace was believed to be the fundamental reality. This means that the State, or "law" for that matter, as we conceive of it had no place and did not, in fact, exist. Rather, organized force was deployed here or there in reaction to violence, but was not society's organizing principle. Society was actually organized through networks of *consilium et auxilium*, of "counsel and aid," networks of friends. Part II strikes at the heart of the dominant narrative.

Chapter 7 is an analysis of the functioning of the king's Parlement, his high court. It demonstrates that the court operated under fundamentally different assumptions concerning society and its organization than those that underpin modern justice. Peace was the conceptual norm and violence was the exception. Peace was rooted not in sameness, as are modern contractual notions, but in difference. Most conflicts took the form of rival "peaces." But this was not a static society. Change was understood as intrinsic to the peace. Sovereignty was not only non-existent in this order, it could not really be conceived of. The use of force was not monopolized by the king.

Chapter 8 posits that both the spiritual and the temporal powers operated within the social space described in Chapter 7. Spiritual powers and rights were a part of the same system of social order as were temporal powers and rights, and like the temporal, their legitimacy was rooted in the peace. The fact that clerics were capable of wielding types of power and of holding types of rights that laymen were not capable of holding does not point to a parallel "order" because this society's organization was rooted in differentiation and not sameness. The fabric of the peace could be torn anywhere, by clerics as easily as by laymen, by the misappropriation of temporal power as easily as by that of spiritual power.

Chapter 9 shows how a differentiated society that lacked the centralization of force could undertake large-scale initiatives through networks of friends. These networks of "counsel" and "aid" were united through their members' understanding of charity and through shared notions of justice, that is to say, through orthodoxies. These networks cut across clerical-lay lines, and it is precisely between the networks that we see the large-scale conflicts (and cooperation) take place. In the ideal, all of Christian society would be one such network of friends, and the king sought to make peace in his kingdom by extending his network to include more and more of the social field. Over the course of Louis IX's reign the network of the papacy and that of the Crown grew together, forming the basis of their profound peace.

Chapter 10 examines Louis IX's and Gui Foucois's involvement in the troubles of England, and especially at Louis's famous *Mise of Amiens*. The chapter argues that the papacy and Louis shared fundamentally an understanding of kingship and that this understanding was intrinsic to their conception of Christian order. The "fullness of royal power" was not only not a threat to the "fullness of papal power," but was, rather, understood as crucial to the world in which the spiritual power functioned. The chapter explores the so-called "political crusades" and shows how they fit within such an understanding. It also shows how "counsel and aid" were central to the understanding of royal power and how the network of Louis IX and that of the papacy grew even tighter through the English affair.

Taken as a whole, Part II demonstrates how a society without sovereignty actually functioned and how both the spiritual and the temporal were intrinsic to this functioning, suggesting that the conventional narrative of the Church and State as rivals for power cannot be maintained.

Through a detailed look at the office of cardinal legate, Part III explores the meaning of papal power—what was it and how did it operate? The section is focused on undermining notions of an imperial papacy or a papal monarchy bent on building a theocracy. The Crown, then, was a key player in the construction of the office of Legate and so of papal power. Through this investigation, Part III addresses questions surrounding canon law: how it was developed, what it meant, and what it actually did. This is crucial to undermining the conventional narrative because the thirteenth-century development of canon law is typically regarded as at the very heart of the formation of the papal monarchy.

Chapter 11 is a study in the canonical definition of *a latere* legates, especially with regard to what happens when the papal see is vacant. A theological understanding of papal power and a juridical understanding grew together in the mid-thirteenth century, culminating in the definitions of Clement IV (Gui Foucois). The legate was in the image of a proconsul—he held the *imperium* of the papacy, which was not *imperium* at all, but the highest *spiritualem potestatem*—the power to root up and to plant. These developments occurred in response to the reality of the office of legate as it had developed in France and in direct relation with the expansion of the power of the Crown.

Chapter 12 shows how the office of legate developed in practice as the spiritual counterpart to the temporal power of the Crown. It was through the extension of a network of *consilium et auxilium* that included both spiritual and temporal power that the government of the kingdom was built. The pope's "fullness of power" was deployed through this network as a complement to the king's "fullness of power." At the top of the network were the king and the pope (or legate), and their relationship was rooted not in juridical concepts or functions, but in ethical concepts and actions: charity.

Chapter 13 shows how canonical innovation concerning legates occurred during the papal vacancy that followed Clement IV's death. It argues that apostolic power was essential to the regular functioning of the kingdom and that the canon law surrounding the extension of and the wielding of that power was developed as a negotiation between Louis IX and the cardinals. So, formal canonical definitions arose not from "ecclesiastical" theory or institution building, but through reflection on existing law and its adaptation given the realities of spiritual-temporal government—this was as much a secular as an ecclesiastical affair. What is more, the chapter shows that the college of cardinals understood its relationship with the papacy not in terms of a juridical "constitution," but rather in theological terms centered on the notion of the "body," a notion that in the ideal would extend to all the baptized—there was no papal "sovereignty" here.

Part IV of the book articulates a theoretical description of the society of thirteenth-century France to replace traditional Church-State descriptions. Drawing on the thought of St. Thomas Aquinas, I rely on a two-tiered pattern: violence and peace, vice and virtue, sin and grace, law and charity, the historical (literal) and the spiritual, the Old and the New. I argue that this pattern existed in a dynamic of ascent from the lower to the higher, from the fallen to the redeemed, and yet everywhere and always the lower was intermingled with the upper. This dynamic of ascent was the very sacramental process of salvation, the lifting up of the lower into the higher, of conversion. The spiritual power and the temporal power operated together across this matrix and throughout society to produce this "conversion." In the lower tier they operate as swords, and in the upper tier they operate as powers, conduits of grace, and sources of organization. The "law," both canonical and civil/feudal, governed the ever-shifting boundary between the upper and the lower.

Chapter 14 articulates this vision in conversation with the thought of Aquinas, demonstrating that this conception is congruent with his thought and challenging the "whiggish" reading of Thomas as the theological founder of the "natural" State. Through the two-tiered, sacramental, and dynamic understanding of society, we can see that the traditional opposition posited between Augustine's notion of the State and Aquinas's evaporates. We can also see that the division of social life into "natural" and "supernatural" categories does not capture the heart of Aquinas's understanding. The conclusion also suggests that the secularization of the modern period might be profitably understood as the "pushing" of the upper tier of grace outside of the realm of the material and into the otherworldly realm of heaven, leaving only the lower tier, absolutized law, the realm of the temporal sword and of clerical preaching. This, it argues, is the origin of "Church and State."

Chapter 15 wraps the book up by coming back to St. Louis IX and Gui Foucois and their concrete, personal relationship by taking a brief look at two seemingly everyday documents.

It concludes simply that the two men were bound together in spiritual kinship and were engaged together in a single initiative, the construction of a sacramental order, of a "Most Christian Kingdom," of the very City of God.

PART I

The Business of the Peace and the Faith

The trouble with "peace" is that, even on the level of earthly and temporal values, nothing that we can talk about, long for, or finally get, is so desirable, so welcome, so good as peace. At any rate, I feel sure that if I linger a little longer on this topic of peace I shall tire very few of my readers. After all, peace is the end of this City which is the theme of this work; besides, peace is so universally loved that its very name falls sweetly on the ear.

—St. Augustine, *City of God* 19.11

PERHAPS NO INSTITUTION is more directly associated with the Medieval Church than the Inquisition. The popular notion of overbearing Dominicans rooting through the minds of peasants looking for an excuse to burn them at the stake is, of course, a black legend. We know that the "Inquisition" we see in Hollywood movies, the "Inquisition" that we carry around with us as a part of the mental furniture of the enlightened mind, is a creation of modern polemic—anti-Catholic and anti-Spanish—and if it can be said to bear resemblance to anything that actually happened, that thing would be the Inquisition of the early modern period and not the inquisitions of the High Middle Ages. Acknowledgement of this black legend notwithstanding, for most of us the Inquisition remains an institution of the Church that perpetuated gross violations of human rights. In the scholarly as much as in the popular imagination, it remains an example of the Church, which should be peaceful in all its ways, giving in to its characteristic medieval temptation to dominate society and coerce consciences. This basic intuition is shared even by Catholic apologists whose defense of the institution often amounts to shifting the blame for its worst offences to the "State," who, we are told, *actually* burned the heretics (thus positing the, I think, strange moral principle that the hangman is somehow more responsible for an execution than the judge).

This image of the Inquisition is profitably contrasted with that of another thirteenth-century, juridical institution, the French *enquêteurs*. The *enquêteurs* were itinerate judges, commissioned by St. Louis to travel through his domains investigating royal officials, hearing the complaints of the people, and generally seeking justice. The *enquêteurs* are almost universally presented in a positive light. They were, we are told, a huge step forward in statecraft. Through the *enquêteurs*, the king was able to divorce his officials from their offices. The officials served at his pleasure, and with the *enquêteurs* he had the mechanism to determine whether or not he was pleased. The *enquêteurs* were a centrally controlled layer of the otherwise decentralized government of the realm. In most histories that treat them, they are seen as a step toward bureaucracy—towards the realization of the State. What is more, their pursuit of justice itself was a step toward what we might consider responsible governance. No longer was the kingdom simply the personal possession of the monarch and the nobles to be exploited at their will. The king now actually sought justice, and that meant building a bureaucracy because it is bureaucracy that pursues goals unconcerned with the personal interests of the individuals of the government.

The truth, however, is that in thirteenth-century France the inquisitors and the *enquêteurs* were really the same people, and as I hope to demonstrate, the institution of the Inquisition and the institution of the *enquêteurs* cannot be understood divorced from each other. They emerge as dimensions of the same project, not the building of "States," whether theocratic or secular, but the *negotium pacis et fidei*—the *business of the peace and the faith*. The *business of the peace and the faith* was the name used for the activities of the Crown, the Roman Church, and their allies in the South of France. This very serious business, the content of which is the subject of the first five chapters of Part I of this book, included the infamous Albigensian Crusade. The *business* was directed against what was understood as a heretical and violent society in the South. The Albigensian wars were an important part of this business, but there was more to it than just military operations: in fact, the wars were the *business* in crisis.

When not in crisis, the work of the *business* went on in far less spectacular ways. The inquisitors and the *enquêteurs* were a part of this; but more than that, they were intimately connected to each other within the *business*. Indeed, as we shall see, Gui Foucois was instrumental in the construction of both offices and served in both. Gui not only helped build the institutions; he was influential in the construction of their legal and theoretical foundations. Gui viewed them as part of the same project, the project that consumed his life of service to Crown and Church. Louis shared Gui's understanding. To the king, to Gui, to the Roman Church, and to the investigators themselves, the ecclesiastical and the secular "inquisitions" were integral institutions within a complex social order that was rooted in a sacramental understanding of the cosmos that did not allow for the divorce of the spiritual from the temporal.

Ultimately, what I hope to show in the first part of this book is not only how the relationship between the spiritual and temporal powers was understood, but also in what way the emerging law and the institutions were made up of both powers in practice, not in the manner of an alliance, but rather fundamentally: the legal institutions of the *business* were a single apparatus derived from both powers, and both powers could function only through this apparatus. If either power failed in its task, the whole project would fail, rendering the other power helpless. This had serious implications: for those who worked in its service, the *business* was nothing short of the very pursuit of salvation itself.

CHAPTER ONE

ENEMIES OF THE
FAITH AND OF THE PEACE

> But the fact is, true justice has no existence save in that
> republic whose founder and ruler is Christ . . . the City
> of God.

> —St. Augustine, *City of God* 2.21

CONTEMPORARIES COMMONLY referred to the series of conflicts that we call the Albigensian Crusade (1209–1255) as the *negotium pacis et fidei*, the *business of the peace and the faith*. From the beginning, it concerned both the spiritual and the material—the faith *and* the peace.[1] The *business* began in earnest in May 1207. Gui Foucois was then a little boy in the village of Saint-Gilles in the South of France, the region in which the conflict took place.[2] The opening shot was Pope Innocent III's

---

[1] Marie-Humbert Vicaire, "'L'Affaire de paix et de foi' du Midi de la France (1203–1215)," in *Paix de Dieu et guerre sainte en Languedoc au XIIIe siècle* (Toulouse, FR: Edouard Privat, 1969), 103, 125.

[2] TNA, 2:371.

(r. 1198–1216) confirmation of the excommunication that his legates had promulgated against Raymond VI, the Count of Toulouse.[3] Given that the historiography overwhelmingly considers the conflict a crusade against heresy, it is perhaps surprising that the pope's charges against Raymond were focused on the peace side of the *business*. It is not that heresy was absent from the accusations—indeed, Innocent charged Raymond with "favoring" heretics and "receiving" them into his home as guests—but the overwhelming focus was on his failure as a Christian lord. As the pope recounted, Raymond employed Aragonese—mercenaries—devastating lands and failing to observe the times and places of truce and peace. He made war against towns and churches and pillaged the possessions of monasteries. He committed Jews to public offices and increased enormously *pedagia*, "tolls" that were really a form of extortion or protection money.[4] The crime that caused the legates to finally strike Raymond with the ultimate censure was his refusal to swear to serve the peace when his adversaries had done so.[5] This was a violation of justice.[6] And so the pope confirmed the excommunication and put all Raymond's lands under interdict. He freed all men from their oaths of fidelity to the count and anyone who gave him "auxilium"—aid—was himself excommunicated. This was the full weight of the papal office.

The pope's list of Raymond's crimes and the sanctions that he promulgated against him were not simply factual, nor were they simply arbitrary or rhetorical. Rather, they were drawn principally from five canons of the Third Lateran Council (1179).[7] The pope was making a legal as well as a moral indictment of Raymond's status as a Christian prince: to the pope,

---

3   RHGF, 19:490–92.

4   Elaine Graham-Leigh, *The Southern French Nobility and the Albigensian Crusade* (Woodbridge, UK: The Boydell Press, 2005), 97.

5   See *The History of the Albigensian Crusade: Peter of les Vaux-de-Cernay's Historia Albigensis*, trans. W. A. Sibly and M. D. Sibly (Woodbridge, UK: The Boydell Press, 1998), 20n33.

6   RHGF, 19:490.

7   Tanner, 1:221–25.

he was both wicked and criminal. The letter culminated with Innocent's mandate that Lateran III's canon 27 be applied to the count and his mercenaries.[8] This is the first indication that this conflict was to be a crusade, for canon 27 calls for the faithful to take up arms, a provision the pope was unleashing. This canon of Lateran III is key to our understanding of the fundamental connection between the spiritual and the material, between heresy and criminal lordship, which underwrote the entire *business of the peace and the faith*.

Canon 27 begins with a condemnation of the heretics who had spread through the South of France and then condemns Brabanters, Aragonese, Navarrese, Basques, Coterelli, and Triaverdini, who harassed the region—a group that are labeled by historians simply as "mercenaries" but in the sources are more often referred to as *ruptarii*, marauders. These men and their employers, "who exercised such brutality against Christians, that they honor neither churches nor monasteries, nor widows and orphans, nor the elderly and the young, neither do they spare anyone of any age or sex, but in the manner of pagans they destroy and ravage all," were subject to the same penalties as heretics. The canon exhorts Christians to take up arms against them, granting a two-year indulgence and offering the same protections granted those who visited the Lord's Sepulchre—crusaders.[9]

Historians have often been tempted to treat the canon's lumping together of "mercenaries" and "heretics" as an unfortunate bit of confusion. It is perceived as such because historians approaching the canon are almost always interested in either heresy *or* military history—seldom both—and it is bothersome that they are in each other's way. This is a mistake and we ought to recognize the conceptual unity and not confusion that underpinned the legislation. We ought to recognize that we can understand neither the heretics without the mercenaries nor the mercenaries without the heretics. It is their unity that

---

[8] RHGF, 19:491.
[9] Tanner, 1:224–25.

makes the entire *business of the peace and the faith* intelligible, and it is a unity that goes to the core of the thirteenth-century conception of society.

The "heretics" of canon 27 were those whose heresy was manifested in outward practice: they wore distinctive clothes and called themselves by distinctive names. These are the Cathars, the *perfecti*, the wandering ascetics in dark robes that personify "medieval heresy." Heresy itself, however, was a concept that went far beyond them. It included the whole society that supported such explicit "heretics," who followed them, who believed them to be holy, the *defensores eorum et receptores*—their defenders and receivers. Understanding the unity of canon 27, and ultimately that of the whole *business*, relies on the observation that to the orthodox the heretic was a type of perverted monk or priest, a distortion of the spiritual and his defender a type of perverted knight, a distortion of the secular, a violent and unjust warrior, a mercenary—the drafters of the canon understood the spiritual and the secular as always bound up together both in orthodoxy and in heresy.

The mercenaries perverted knighthood not simply because they fought for money, but because of their particular type of violence. The violent crimes enumerated in canon 27 are heavily laden with meaning. When the canon states that the mercenaries have disregard for monks, women, widows, and children, it is invoking a whole discourse on Christian knighthood and painting them as anti-knights, as dishonorable men, the opposite of orthodox laymen, as the heretics were the opposite of orthodox monks. The mercenaries had deviated from orthodoxy in their practice of secular power, and the canon's charge of paganism against them had a long history of being directed against those who preyed on the Church and peasantry.[10] The "heretics" and the "mercenaries" are treated together at Lateran III because they were two aspects of the same problem. This was explic-

---

[10] Thomas N. Bisson, *The Crisis of the Twelfth Century: Power, Lordship, and the Origins of European Government* (Princeton: Princeton University Press, 2009), 41–68.

itly understood by the fathers of the Council. The Archbishop of Narbonne, for example, when he summarized canon 27 for his prelates back home, stated simply that its provisions were directed against all those who were the source of impiety and heresy in the lands: "the heretics and their supporters and defenders, the Bravantiones, Aragonense, Cotarellos, Bascules and their servants and thieves."[11] These were the *inimici pacis et fidei*—the enemies of *the peace and the faith*: a single category.

The connection between the problem of heresy and the problem of violence was foundational, being present in some of the earliest medieval references to heresy.[12] Any attempt to untangle heresy from violence is misguided and is rooted in the modern division between the "religious" and the "secular." We need to take the opposite approach and consider their unity as our starting point. If we do, we can see that canon 27 was directed against a whole society—spiritual and temporal—that was bound together, as were other societies of the period, by personal relationships of favor and help, oaths, pacts, contracts, and friendship—connections that cut across clerical and lay, spiritual and temporal lines (such relationships are the subject of Part II of this book). To the orthodox, the heretics were the spiritual side of this iniquitous society and the criminal violence of the laymen the secular side. This secular side was most dramatically personified in the mercenaries, men totally devoid of all Christian virtue. A "mercenary" was an extreme example of a *ruptarius*, a marauder, and was an anti-knight, the negation of the ideal warrior as described not only by the theologians but by the knights themselves, the *preudomme* (worthy, valiant, prudent man) for whom Christianity was central.[13]

---

[11] HGL, 8:341–43.

[12] For example, see the canons of the council held sometime in the 1020s in Aquitaine as found in *Ademari historiarum liber III*, ed. Georg Waitz, in MGH SS, 4:148.

[13] Jessalynn Bird, "Paris Masters and the Justification of the Albigensian Crusade," *Crusades* 6 (2007): 127–28; David Crouch, *The Birth of Nobility: Constructing Aristocracy in England and France: 900–1300* (Harlow, UK: Pearson, 2005), 35–79.

This Christian knighthood had deep roots. In 881 Hincmar of Reims wrote of ideal warriors: "They should protect and assist orphans and widows and other poor folk, and they should hold the Church and its servants in respectful deference, as far as they are capable. By constant effort and repression they should restrain those who, in their arrogance and violence, seek to undermine the common peace of the people by theft and brigandage."[14] Hincmar was here extending the Davidic conception of royal power as it was developed by the Carolingians to all those who wielded the sword.[15] The protection of widows and orphans in particular was biblical shorthand for Christian compassion and justice—the duty of the material sword. No longer was the warrior's only hope to be found in the vicarious merit of the monks and the economy of penance that they managed. A knight could find God's favor in his knighthood.[16]

Through the peace and crusade movements of the tenth, eleventh, and twelfth centuries, this conception of ideal knighthood was steadily adopted into the mentality of the warrior class, especially in France, becoming the core of *chevalerie*, chivalry—the knights' own ethos. For example, when the vernacular *Gaydon* (ca. 1230) wanted to describe an evil family, it had its members on the occasion of their knighting swear a wicked oath to never keep one's word or one's loyalty to one's liege lord, to betray honest men for money, to exalt the evil and trample the good, to flatter and to slander, to humiliate the poor, to steal from orphans and widows, to take the part of murderers and thieves, to disgrace the Church and shun the clergy, to rob from monks and religious, to push children

---

[14] Crouch, *The Birth of Nobility*, 72.

[15] For a thorough articulation of Charlemagne's Davidic conception of kingship, see *Capitulare missorum generale* (AD 802), in MGH *Leges Capit.* I, 1:91–99; see also Warren C. Brown, *Violence in Medieval Europe* (Harlow, UK: Longman, 2011), 69–96.

[16] John Baldwin, *Masters, Princes, and Merchants: The Social Views of Peter the Chanter and His Circle* (Princeton: Princeton University Press, 1970), 1:162–222.

in the mud and even strangle them, to rough up the old and spit in their faces, to devastate abbeys and leave nuns without protection, to lie and to perjure one's self, and so on.[17] This list, coming from the vernacular literature of the knightly class, is a near perfect parallel to the crimes of the mercenaries as described by the bishops of Lateran III. The priests and the knights here agreed on the content of secular power.

In fact, the fathers of Lateran III were clearly invoking the well-known discourse on the Christian use of the sword, a discourse they shared with the laity, who were, after all, their fathers, brothers, and nephews, not to mention their patrons and protectors. We can see, then, that the council's use of "mercenaries" is parallel to its use of the label "Cathars" for heretics, which it did to invoke a long-running discourse on heresy. What this means is that a fixation on the literal meaning of "mercenary," a temptation of some historians, obscures the nature of the *business* as much as does other historians' fixation on the actual doctrine held by the heretics.[18] Rather, "mercenaries" was shorthand for the secular, military side of that society made up of those people that the 1195 Council of Montpellier referred to as "pestilent men": Heretics, mercenaries, supporters of Saracens, pirates, usury-charging Jews, and so on.[19] There was a Christian way of being a knight, of wielding the sword, and to behave otherwise, to behave as if one was a "mercenary," was to behave in the realm of mortal

---

[17] *Gaydon: Chanson de geste du XIIIe siècle*, ed. and trans. Jean Subrenat (Louvain, BE: Peeters, 2007), 411–12.

[18] Monique Zerner, "Le negotium pacis et fidei ou l'affaire de paix et de foi, une désignation de la croisade Albigeoise á revoir," in *Prêcher la Paix et Discipliner la Société* (Turnhout, BE: Brepols, 2005): 63–102; Zerner, "Le déclenchement de la croisade Albigeoise retour sur l'affaire de paix et de foi," in *La Croisade Albigeoise, Actes du Colloque du Centre d'Études Cathares Carcassonne, 4, 5 et 6 octobre 2002*, ed. Michel Roquebert (Carcassonne, FR: Centre d'Études Cathares, 2004), 127–42; Philippe Ménard, "Rotiers, soldadiers, mainadiers, faidits, arlots, Réflexions sur les diverses sortes de combattants dans la Chanson de la croisade albigeoise," *Perspectives Médiévales* 22 (1996): 157–62.

[19] Mansi, 22: 668.

sin, a realm whose border with heresy, if it existed at all, was ill-defined and most certainly porous.

The discourses on the correct secular life and on the correct spiritual life were thoroughly intertwined and subsumed into a larger discourse concerning Christian order itself as something both spiritual and material.[20] The famous theologian Alan of Lille (d. 1202) explained that just as man is made up of both body and spirit, so there are two swords with which to protect humanity: the material, which repels injury, and the spiritual, which repels molestations of the mind: "Externally let knights take up violence, therefore, for the reformation of peace in time; internally, though, with the sword of the word of God, let them seek the restoration of peace in their own hearts." He goes on to contrast true knights, who protect their homelands and defend the Church, from those who steal and oppress the poor. These last were not knights at all, "but robbers and plunderers; not defenders, but invaders" who thrust their swords "into the gut of Mother Church." They were in direct opposition to Christian society from the inside, both corporally and spiritually. The exercise of knighthood, Alan tells us, was bound up with warfare against the devil himself, in both its spiritual and temporal dimensions.[21] Far from attacking "knighthood" or the "lay life" as some would have it,[22] clerics such as Alan of Lille were participating in a discourse with the lay warriors, constructing holy knighthood as a necessary vocation within the Church.[23] This was orthodoxy.

---

[20] For a classic formulation, see Hugh of St. Victor, *De sacramentis* 2.2.2–9.

[21] Alan of Lille, *Summa de arte praedicatoria* (PL, 210:185–87).

[22] See, for example, Richard W. Kaeuper, *Holy Warriors: The Religious Ideology of Chivalry* (Philadelphia: University of Pennsylvania Press, 2009), 9–16. Kaeuper, *Chivalry and Violence in Medieval Europe*, 77.

[23] For a thorough discussion of the moral and "religious" content of *chevalerie*, see Richard W. Kaeuper, *Holy Warriors: The Religious Ideology of Chivalry* and *Chivalry and Violence in Medieval Europe.* Kaeuper's work is of value primarily for its masterful ability to reveal to the reader the content of a wide range of sources, especially the vernacular literature aimed at knights themselves. Unfortunately, Kaeuper approaches these sources with a standard matrix of

Lateran III and Pope Innocent III's 1207 letters against
Count Raymond VI initiating the *business of the peace and*

modern categories—religious/secular, church/state, clergy/lay—and with
an evident deep suspicion of the "clergy." For example, he sums up the guiding
question of his work with regards to knights' reforming efforts: "Was the clerical ideology of reform absorbed by the knights themselves; in other words,
was this external ideology to any significant degree internalized by knights,
who (as we have already noted) displayed a high degree of independence of
thought?" [Kaeuper, *Chivalry and Violence in Medieval Europe*, 84]. That it
was an "external ideology," that somehow "independence of thought" means
resistance to the clergy, that ultimately the clergy and knights somehow occupied different, coherent societies that sat uneasily with each other, seem
to be the starting assumptions of his interpretation of the sources. Kaeuper
sees the knights appropriating "selected principles of medieval Christianity," [*Chivalry and Violence*, 50] as if Christianity was somehow something
that they observed from a distance rather than the framework for their
very lives—can we even talk about "medieval Christianity" and not include
integral to it chivalry? Because of this interpretative framework, Kaeuper
sees paradoxes everywhere; for example, the knights seem to think for themselves, and yet they acknowledge the essential role of the priesthood. This is
a paradox only if we assume a certain stereotypical liberal approach to the
medieval Church and its members. Similarly, the implicit assumption that
Christianity is by rights something resembling modern liberal Protestantism
leads Kaeuper to see a certain incoherence or at least tension in the clergy's
approach to the sword, as if their condemnation of bad knights and praise of
good knights is somehow problematic. As if their condemnation of corrupt
knighthood was really a condemnation of knighthood itself, because, after
all, in the real world it did not live up to the ideal. And so, he sees the clergy
speaking of the "evils of knighthood" when in reality they are speaking of
"evil knights." Kaeuper writes of the tenuous clerical support of knighthood:
"We have seen that the clerical theory accepted violence for right causes and
not for wrong—a distinction that is tricky to make at the best of times, and
especially so in an imperfect world." But, of course, this "problematic" is at
the very core of Christian moral thought. "Violence" could be replaced with
any number of legitimate human activities, for example, sex, speech, prayer,
social organization, and the statement would hold true. The existence of the
problematic does not point to clerical ambivalence toward the sword in the
abstract. That the sword, and with it power, was surrounded especially by
the temptations of the world, as was sex and money, and was therefore dangerous was, of course, a basic assumption of religious flight from the world
to the relative safety of the cloister. But, the clergy's exhortation of knights
to use their swords in the cause of righteousness simply cannot, I believe, be
used as evidence that the clergy ultimately, at some deep level, disapproved

the faith in the South of France were participations in this long-running discourse, a discourse that must be read from within a cosmology that was profoundly sacramental, within which the immanent and the transcendent were in constant contact and human actions had direct spiritual significance, the implications of which could be understood only within an allegorical and incarnational hermeneutic.[24] The literal, the empirical, derived its ultimate significance not from being fact, as modern historians who are searching for the "true" heretics and "true" mercenaries would have it, but from what it meant in the context of the larger narrative of the pursuit of salvation.

This does not mean, however, that what was said about the situation in the South of France had no bearing on reality or that there were no heretics or mercenaries. Rather, we must read the situation in the South through this symbolic discourse, for the historical was not destroyed by the spiritual, but brought up into it and fulfilled by it. When we do so, we can see that the orthodox perceived there to be, in the South, a heretical society that manifested itself both in heretics who lived a life of extreme austerity and pacifism and in laymen who lived a life of extreme violence.

---

of knighthood itself—which seems to be one of Kaeuper's points. His argument, if simplified, seems to be along these lines: the clergy did not approve of certain behaviors, such as blood feuds, and many knights were especially prone to participate in blood feuds; therefore the clergy did not approve of knighthood. If this argument holds together, we would have to conclude that this same reforming clergy disapproved of, or was at least ambivalent toward, the clerical *ordo* itself because they reserved their most vitriolic criticisms for corrupt monks and priests. Pope Innocent III, for example, proclaimed that all evils entered the world through corrupt clergy. Rather, we should see that the high medieval reformers perceived deep tendencies within chivalric culture that were especially dangerous in a way directly parallel to the manner in which they perceived deep tendencies within clerical culture that were especially dangerous. The reformers sought to mitigate such dangers wherever they found them.

24 See, for example, Henri de Lubac, S.J., *Medieval Exegesis: The Four Senses of Scripture*, vol. 1, 103.

For the orthodox, dualism accounted for this odd combination. After all, dualists believed, as the orthodox understood them, that the material world was the realm of the evil principle, that it could not be redeemed. In such a world the very notion of moral temporal power was an absurdity akin to talking about moral devil worship. The world was violent and disordered. Those who lived in it were violent and disordered, and there could be no "morality" that would suggest they be otherwise. Only the spiritual men—the Cathars and *perfecti*—who gave up as much interaction with the material world as possible, offered even a glimmer of good in the world. The orthodox observed these men preaching against the visible Church and her sacraments, giving up property, condemning marriage, eating as little food as possible (which they believed to defile a man), condemning worldly dignity and all power. And the orthodox observed violence; they saw that a society of violent men supported the spiritual men. For the orthodox, dualism—the denial of the sacramental and the incarnational, of the efficacy of grace, of the fulfillment of the Old in the New, of the goodness of the material world—made sense of this; it was what the southerners' way of life meant. It was the reason for both the "mercenaries" and the "heretics."

But were there really dualists in the South of France? Or are we just witnessing the extrapolations of Parisian theologians who had read too much St. Augustine, as many historians have maintained? Was the region really torn apart by nihilistic mercenaries? What was the reality that Lateran III and the whole *business of the peace and the faith* were responding to? This is a hard question to answer because the majority of our sources come from the orthodox. Nevertheless, it seems to be the case that it was a very violent region indeed. By all accounts, it was rent by near constant low-scale conflict.[25]

---

[25] Graham-Leigh, *The Southern French Nobility*, 92–97; Thomas N. Bisson, "The Organized Peace in Southern France and Catalonia, ca. 1140–ca. 1233," *The American Historical Review* 82 (1977): 290.

Passing through the region in the 1180s, Stephen de Tournai[26] recounted constant dangers such as bandits and the burning of towns and fields—nothing was safe from the mercenaries. It was a region of dread, comparable to hell itself, full of death and heresy.[27] But what of the lives of those who lived there? Does the orthodox polemic fit?

Recently, Mark Pegg has attempted to reconstruct their world using the categories of anthropology. He paints a vivid picture of the lives of the "good men" and "good women" (the "heretics"), lives that were integral to the conceptual and social world in which they moved, a world organized around the concepts of honor and *cortezia* (courtesy).[28] In this society, honor and *cortezia* were the basis of the order of the universe, and the "good men" were the masters of its holiness. Within their understanding, Christ "saved the world by showing how He mollified His humanity," and so all sacramental or corporal elements of "orthodox" religion made no sense.[29] Honor and *cortezia* were the organizing concepts that provided the shared social space in which the holy "good men," the prominent men of the community, the knights and lords, and even the clergy lived. The hundreds of small wars that occurred every spring and summer in the region, the conflicts witnessed by Stephen de Tournai, were integral to this world, occurring within the social space governed by honor and *cortezia*.[30] Pegg's work is very interesting and shines a great deal of light on an otherwise dark time and place. It is especially significant, I think, that what Pegg does with modern categories drawn largely from anthropology is very similar to what the orthodox churchmen in the period were doing with categories drawn from the discourses of heresy and violence, and that he reaches, it seems,

---

[26] He was Abbot of Sainte-Geneviève at the time.

[27] RHGF, 19:283–84.

[28] Mark Gregory Pegg, *A Most Holy War: The Albigensian Crusade and the Battle for Christendom* (Oxford: Oxford University Press, 2008), 28–49.

[29] Ibid., 48.

[30] Ibid., 55.

some of the same conclusions: to both the southerners' spirituality and their violence were bound up together in a single social "space." Pegg writes about "methods for organizing time and space" or "modest variations and improvisations of quotidian courtliness" in describing the way of life in the troubled regions.[31] The orthodox talked about the "two principles" and the "denial of the sacraments" when they described the same society. In neither case are these concepts that the people of the South would have applied to themselves. But this is not, I think, a problem. Within modern discourse, Pegg's description of the world of the South can be quite accurate, and the same can be said of that of the orthodox theologians within their discourses. Regardless of what the heretics would say of themselves, within orthodox discourse the region's violence and its heresy could be accurately described as rooted in "dualism." And it is clear that the orthodox perceived what was happening in the South of France to be a direct threat to Christianity.

The connection between dualism and the two swords is perhaps easy for us to overlook, as used as we are to a division between worldly and spiritual concerns. But, it was, as we have seen, a central component to orthodox concerns surrounding heresy. The swords were integral to a thoroughly unified, sacramental understanding of society, of history, and of man's origins and his final destination. This understanding is nowhere more clear than in the pontificate of Pope Innocent III, the man who launched the Albigensian Crusade. For example, Innocent opened the Fourth Lateran Council (1215) with a sermon on Luke 22:15: "I have earnestly desired to eat this Passover with you before I suffer." Innocent explained that just as King Josiah, in the eighteenth year of his reign, restored the temple and celebrated the Passover, so he—Innocent—in the eighteenth year of his reign, would restore the "Temple of the Lord" that was the Church, and the Passover, which he identified as the Council and its work, would be celebrated.

---

[31] Ibid., 28.

Josiah was the last of the good kings of the line of David who attempted to restore the right worship of God in the Temple and to enforce the law of Moses. When he had completed far-reaching reforms, he held a massive Passover celebration: "No Passover like it had been kept in Israel since the days of Samuel the prophet; none of the kings of Israel had kept such a Passover as was kept by Josiah" (2 Chron 35:18). This Passover was an attempt at renewing the covenant between Israel and the Lord. Innocent was placing himself as Josiah and the Church as the Temple, the very dwelling place of God. The Passover, which was the council and its work of reform, would be the context for a renewing of the covenant with God. To Innocent, the meaning of Christendom, what it was and where it was going, was found in the Old Testament read through the New Testament. Innocent, the new Josiah, would lead the new Israel to the proper observance of the New Covenant through the New Passover, which was, of course, the very Paschal Mystery of Christ.

Innocent went on to explain that this Passover that they celebrate must be understood in three senses: the physical—the liberation of Jerusalem—the Crusade; the spiritual—the reform of the Church; and the eternal—salvation itself. These are, of course, the familiar senses of Scripture. He then proceeded to expound on each of these, demonstrating how each task was bound up with the Paschal Sacrifice of Christ itself. The sermon culminated in Innocent's treatment of salvation, "the eternal Passover." It was this pasch above all that Innocent desired to eat with the fathers, and the meal could be understood either spiritually or corporally. Both meanings come together in the Eucharist: "Of the Eucharist it is said, 'He that eats me shall live because of me'; of eternal glory it is read, 'Blessed is he who will eat bread in the kingdom of God.'" [32]

---

[32] Pope Innocent III, *Sermo in concilio generali lateranensi habitus* (PL, 217:673–80, at col. 673); in English in Pope Innocent III, *Between God and Man: Six Sermons on the Priestly Office*, trans. Corinne J. Vause and Frank C.

In this sermon, Innocent demonstrated how the temporal sword (here in the context of the crusade) was integral to a profoundly theological understanding of society, as integral as the Old Testament was to the New. The movement from the historical to the allegorical, to the tropological, and on to the anagogical was not simply a movement of scriptural exegesis, as if the senses were parallel glosses to the biblical text. Rather, the historical was fulfilled in the allegorical, the allegorical in the tropological, and all in the anagogical, and this sequence was nothing short of the very path of salvation, for society as a whole as much as for each of its individual members.[33] Revelation was read this way because reality was, in fact, understood this way. Both swords, the spiritual power's excommunication (which Innocent evokes in the context of "reform") and the secular power's iron, then, performed the function of the law, which functioned within the allegorical sense to those with faith and the historical or literal sense to those without—a sense that was not simply dispensed with or rendered void by the spiritual senses, but was rather elevated into them through grace: the allegorical sense gave the historical meaning through the revelation of Christ, the tropological sense fulfilled it in the law of charity, and all was fulfilled in the final peace of anagogy.

Innocent did not divide society into a static scheme of those who prayed, those who fought, and those who worked.[34] Rather, he emphasized the distinctions between the ordained, the celibate, and the married. In an Easter sermon he stated that Mary Magdalene, Mary the Mother of James, and Salome represented the three lives—lay, regular, and clerical: "The lay life should anoint the feet of Jesus, the regular life the head,

---

Gardiner (Washington, DC: Catholic University of America Press, 2004), 55–63.

[33] For a thorough explication of this dimension of the senses of Scripture, see Henri de Lubac, *Medieval Exegesis: The Four Senses of Scripture*, vol. 2, trans. E. M. Macierowski (Grand Rapids, MI: Eerdmans, 2000).

[34] See John C. Moore, "The Sermons of Pope Innocent III," *Römische Historische Mitteilungen* 36 (1994): 81–142, at 104.

and the clerical life the body. For the feet of Christ are the poor, the head is the divinity, and the body is the church." The laity supported the Church through the corporal works of mercy, the regulars through prayer, and the clergy through word and example.[35] This conception reached perfection in the Mass. There were three orders of guests to the wedding feast, *praelati, continentes,* and *conjugati,* and three types of people participated in the Mass: *celebrantes, ministrantes,* and *circumstantes.*[36] Together, these orders constituted the Body of Christ and each was perfect in its own way.[37] Innocent's view of all of society was, therefore, essentially ecclesiological and liturgical, with its various orders striving after unity in Christ through faith and charity, a unity that would be perfectly achieved only at the eschaton. No one was left out, and no function of Christian society fell outside this vision, even the use of force—the society of Innocent III was a "complete act."[38]

Within it, where faith and charity failed, one found oneself back in simple history, in the realm of the sword. But, this was not a realm that fell outside of Christianity. It was the foundation on which the Church was built. It was the Law, the Old Testament, the literal sense. This foundation had not been abolished. Rather, it was being fulfilled as the society of the baptized became more closely united in grace as the Body of Christ. And so the swords' validity in Christian life directly implicated the validity of the Old Testament and vice-versa. Pope Innocent III argued that all the orthodox doctors taught that both the spiritual sword, wielded by the priests, and the material sword, wielded by the laity, were necessary for the

---

[35] *Sermon for the Resurrection of the Lord,* in Moore, "Sermons," 138–42.

[36] *De Quadripartita Specie Nuptiarum* (PL, 217:948); *De Sacro Altaris Mysterio* (PL, 217:774).

[37] See André Vauchez, "Innocent III, Sicard de Crémone et la canonisation de Saint Homebon (†1197)," in *Innocenzo III: Urbs et Orbis* (Rome: Roma Istituto Storico Italiano per il Medio Evo, 2003), 1:443–44.

[38] For more on Innocent's understanding of the different orders of society and their roles, see Andrew W. Jones, "The Preacher of the Fourth Lateran Council," *Logos* 18, no. 2 (Spring 2015): 121–49.

defeat of evil-doers and that both were praiseworthy. We can, therefore, understand why the pope explicitly singled out the heretics' denial of this principle as one of their major errors, a denial wrapped up in their dualism.[39] The author of the early thirteenth-century *Summula contra hereticos* devoted a whole chapter to the heretics' mistake on this point, arguing that the two swords of the Gospel (Luke 22:38) signified the two swords wielded in the Church, the material and the spiritual, and that both were granted by God and so good. The heretics, he asserted, could not avoid this conclusion by arguing that the two swords referenced rather the two testaments, as did the *glossa ordinaria*, because they denied the goodness of the Old Testament.[40] Denying the goodness of the Old Testament and denying the goodness of the temporal sword were two dimensions of the same error, an error that was ultimately dualist. Within our modern conceptions, we can perhaps easily understand why the heretics would deny the power of the spiritual sword and why the orthodox clergy would defend it. But, we ought not fail to see that the heretics likewise (and in the same breath) denied the power of the temporal sword and that the orthodox clergy likewise defended it: they rose or fell together, to both sides.

To the orthodox Christian inhabiting a sacramental cosmos, the heretics and the violent men—mercenaries at the most extreme—were two sides of the same coin, just as the divine and the human, the soul and the body, the spiritual and the temporal, the doctrinal and the practical, the allegorical and the literal, and the New and the Old Testaments remained entirely bound up together; this was at the very core of orthodoxy. And from within orthodoxy, the use of "Manichaeism" to describe the heretics' approach to the world—an approach

---

[39] PL, 216:76–77.

[40] *Summula contra hereticos: un traite contre les cathares du XIIIème siecle*, Manuscrits Doat XXXVI de la B.N. de Paris, 379 de la B.M. de Toulouse, ed. Jean Duvernoy (1986), 64–66, accessed September 24, 2016, http://jean.duvernoy.free.fr/text/pdf/summula.pdf. *Biblia cum glossa ordinaria. Pars IV* (Rusch, 1480/81); also found in PL, 114:340.

that denied that the temporal was integral to the Church, that denied that the secular and the spiritual could be ultimately in harmony—was accurate. It was against this violent heresy that canon 27 was written and against which the *business of the peace and the faith* was directed. Pope Innocent III spent most of his letters against Raymond expounding upon his status as a violent and unjust lord because they were written about a lord and to arouse other laymen to action against him. But the pope's writings were as much about heresy. The peace and the faith cannot be separated; they were intrinsic to orthodoxy, to heresy, and to the war that finally erupted between the two in 1209.

Just how unified the peace and the faith and the two swords that defended them were perceived to be can be further appreciated through the work of the great canonist Hostiensis (Cardinal Henry of Susa). Writing in the mid-thirteenth century, Hostiensis argued that the laity were similar to the Father through their power, and theirs was the civil law; the religious were similar to the Holy Spirit through their holiness, and their law was theology; and the secular clerics were similar to the Son through wisdom, and they were the masters of canon law: as the three types of men where a trinity that formed a unity in the holy Church and the Catholic faith, so the three Persons of the Trinity found unity in their essence and divinity.[41]

This Trinitarian reading of the orders of the church and their respective jurisdictions should be seen as complementary to that of Innocent III. It was normal in the period, after all, to see the stages of salvation history through a Trinitarian lens, with the age of the Father as the age of the Law, the age of the Son as the age of the sacramental Church, and the age of the Holy Spirit as the spiritual age to come, all of which was, of

---

[41] Henry of Susa, *Summa aurea* (Venice, 1574), 8: "In his generibus, scilicet laicorum, clericorum secularium, et religiosorum, est trinitas: sed in sacra conjunctione ecclesiae, et fide catholica unitas. Item in personis patris et filii, et spiritus, trinitas: sed in essentia et deitate, unitas."

course, a complement to the progression of the senses of Scripture.[42] The material sword was wrapped up in an ecclesiology and a soteriology that were themselves wrapped up in the doctrine of the Trinity. To deny the sword's validity was to attack the doctrine of the Trinity and the understanding of salvation that it underpinned. To the orthodox, it was manifest heresy.

The war that was launched in 1209 was directed against the *inimici pacis et fidei,* the enemies of the peace and the faith. It was over the course of this long conflict that the ideas that we have just explored were put into practice and that the *business of the peace and the faith* steadily became a program for government and the basis of extensive legal developments and for the construction of institutions such as those of the inquisitors and the *enquêteurs.* As this happened the "enemies of the peace and the faith" became the "enemies of the king and the Church." It is to this dynamic that we now turn.

---

[42] See Brett Edward Whalen, *Dominion of God: Christendom and Apocalypse in the Middle Ages* (Cambridge, MA: Harvard University Press, 2009), 170–203.

CHAPTER TWO

Enemies of the King and the Church

The wicked war with the wicked; the good also war with
the wicked. But with the good, good men, or at least
perfectly good men, cannot war; though, while only
going on towards perfection, they war to this extent, that
every good man resists others in those points in which
he resists himself.

—St. Augustine, *City of God* 15.6

IN 1208 THE PAPAL LEGATE in the South of France, Pierre
de Castelnau, was murdered, and we can see in Pope Innocent
III's subsequent letters how profoundly the *business of the peace*
and the *business of the faith* were one and the same business—
the basis of orthodox action. Pierre had been sent to "preach
peace and secure the faith," the pope wrote. The Count of Toulouse, Raymond, whom Innocent blamed for the murder, was
the minister of the devil, "a shape-shifting and crafty man, slip-

pery and fickle."[1] Innocent again excommunicated Raymond and his followers and promised the remission of the sins of all those who, inspired by zeal for the orthodox faith, avenged the spilling of this just blood by pestilent men, men "who fought against peace and truth at the same time," who kill "not only the soul but the body."[2] All those bound to Raymond through oath or fidelity were freed, and his lands were to be occupied—this was the calling for crusade.

Innocent exhorted King Philip II, who had nominal dominion over the South, to take up his sword and seek vengeance against the "inhuman malefactors." The pope explained to the king that the two swords existed united within the Church of Christ, who was both priest and king in the order of Melchizedek. One was wielded by a priestly king and the other by a royal priest. They were united as the two Testaments were united. And they were to work together, giving each other help, to protect the Church; and the Church was under attack: peace perished and heresy spread. The pope exhorted Philip, "in the image of King Solomon," to suppress both those who destroyed the peace and heresy in his kingdom.[3] From within a

---

[1] PL, 215:1354. He instructed the bishops: "verbum pacis et fidei seminatum ab eo vestrae praedicationis irriguis coalescere facientes, et ad expugnandam haereticam pravitatem ac fidem catholicam confirmandam, exstirpando vitia et seminando virtutes, indefessae studio sedulitatis instantes, jam dictum Dei famuil occisorem et universos quorum ope vel opera, consilio vel favore tantum cacinus perpetravit, receptatores quoquo ver defensores ipsius ex parte omnipotentis Dei Patris at Filii et Spiritus sancti" (PL, 215:1356).

[2] PL, 215:1356.

[3] PL, 215:1359: "Attende per Moysem et Petrum, patres videlicet utriusque Testamenti, signatam inter regnum et sacerdotium unitatem, cum alter regnum sacerdotale praedixit, et reliquus regale sacerdotium appellavit; ad quod signandum rex regum et Dominus dominantium Jesus Christus secundum ordinem Melchisedech sacerdotis et regis de utraque voluit stirpe nasci, sacerdotali videlicet et regali. Et princeps apostolorum: *Ecce gladii duo hic* (Luke 22:38), id est simul, dicente demum Domino: *Satis est*, legitur respondisse, ut materiali et spirituali gladiis sibi invicem assistentibus, alter per alterum adjuvetur. Cum igitur post interfectionem praefati justi Ecclesia quae in partibus illis est absque consolatore in tristitia et moerore sedente fides evanuisse, periisse pax, haeretica pestis et hostilis rabies invaluisse di-

Christian understanding of the cosmos, the peace and the faith rose or fell together, and the *business of the peace* was Philip's duty as a Christian king, a duty rooted in Christ's kingship as the fulfillment of the kingship of the Old Testament, a duty rooted in the intrinsic temporality of Christianity. It was this very duty, the pope reminded the king, that Raymond was failing to perform, not through weakness, but through pride and contumacy, and so he was in league with the heretics. The king, as a Christian, must act!

Philip and Innocent had a rather checkered past that need not delay us here, but one that clearly disinclined Philip from working closely with the pope. Nevertheless, with the king's limited support, but without his direct involvement, a crusading force was raised under the papal legate and eventually Simon de Montfort, a relatively minor French noble. At the 1209 council held at Avignon launching the expedition, the papal legate articulated the mission of the crusade, a reiteration of the entire Lateran III program.[4] In 1212, with the war entering its third year, Simon de Montfort called together the expedition's lay and clerical leadership and promulgated what has become known as the Statutes of Pamiers. Like the council of 1209, the statutes articulated a comprehensive vision of reform, targeting heresy as much as violent and exploitive lord-

---

cantur, ac nisi potenter in hujus novitate procellae succurratur eidem, pene penitus videatur ibidem navis Ecclesiae naufragari, regalis mansuetudinis pietatem monemus attentius et propensius exhortamur, ac in tanto necessitatis articulo in virtute Christi confidentes injungimus, et in remissionem peccaminum indulgemus, quatenus tantis malis occurrere non postponas, et attendens quod usque adeo regium sit officium in regno suo pacis negotium promovere quod regum sapientissimus Salomon in figura Regis aeterni fuit pacificus appellatus, ad pacificandum gentes illas in eo qui est Deus pacis et dilectionis intendas, et quibuscunque modis revelaverit tibi Deus, haereticam tamen studeas perfidiam abolere, sectatores ipsius eo quam Saracenos securius quo pejores sunt illis, in manu forti et extento brachio impugnando."

4 Mansi, 22:783–92. See also Mark Gregory Pegg, *A Most Holy War: The Albigensian Crusade and the Battle for Christendom* (Oxford: Oxford University Press, 2008), 95.

ship, only from a decidedly lay perspective.[5] This conflict was truly the *business of the peace and the faith.* This *business* aimed to defeat the existing heretical and violent society—whose defenders were labeled the *inimici ecclesiae,* the "enemies of the Church"—and to replace it with an orthodox and peaceful society.

The crusade was a success. By 1214 the major nobles and towns of the South were capitulating. The oaths of peace that they swore to the papal legate clearly illustrate the objectives of the war—the dismantling of a whole heretical and violent society and all the social structures that supported it. They swore that they were not "believers, favorers, helpers, defenders, or receivers" of heretics, nor of exiled people, and that they would not give "aid, counsel," or "favor" to "marauders" who fight against the Roman Church or her allies. Rather, against all these "enemies of the Church," they swore to give "aid, counsel, and favor" to the Roman Church and to observe and make to be observed the statutes made by the Church against all violators concerning "the business of the orthodox faith and the establishment of peace." Finally, they swore that they would not give "aid or counsel" to anyone as of yet not reconciled to the Church and that they would treat anyone who made war by the authority of the Church (the crusaders) as the Church herself.[6]

The structure of *aid and counsel*—of honor, oaths, and friendships—which governed this society and within which the "heretics" and the "mercenaries" were integral was to be dismantled and replaced with one centered on the legate and orthodoxy.[7] The entire project in both its secular and spiritual

---

5   G.E.M. Lippiatt, "Implementing the *Negotium Pacis et Fidei:* The Statutes of Pamiers, Heresy, and Social Order, 1212." Paper given at the International Medieval Congress at Leeds, UK on July 3, 2013 (I give thanks to Gregory Lippiatt for making the paper as well as his yet unpublished critical edition of the statutes available to me). The statutes can be found in HGL, 8:625–635.

6   LTC, 1:1068, 1072.

7   The different dimensions of this project were laid out in great detail at the 1215 council held at Montpellier (Mansi, 22:935–50).

dimensions was *negotium Christi*—the "business of Christ"—
and those who served it received the same benefits as those
who fought in the Holy Land.[8] It was a crusade, but one
very different from the campaigns against the Muslims. This
crusade included the reform of a whole society.

This project ended up being more difficult than had
been expected. It involved more than the simple replacing of
bad nobles with good ones or the prosecution of manifest
and unrepentant heretics. Rather, new networks of personal
relationships had to be constructed, for it was through such
networks of aid and friendship that all power, temporal as
much as spiritual, was directed and controlled, as we will
explore in depth in Part II. The old networks had to be re-
lentlessly dismantled and the new ones steadily grown.[9] This
proved exceedingly difficult. By the early 1220s the region was
in disarray and the crusaders were steadily losing ground to the
regrouped forces of the Count of Toulouse and his allies. The
pope needed help.

As we have already seen, to the papacy it was the monarch's
duty to maintain and defend the peace and the faith. Accepting
the papal rationale, in 1224 Philip II's son Louis VIII agreed

---

[8] RHGF, 19:664.

[9] For example, it is this effort that can be seen behind Pope Honorius III's letter
of 1217 to the prelates of the region, in which he writes: "Quantis autem personarum et rerum laboribus et dispendiis fuerit laboratum, ut fides, quae mortua
fuerat in illis partibus, revivisceret, et pax, quae de terra sumpta fuerat, tandem
desiderata rediret, sic legistis et legitis jamdiu in vestris periculis, ut necesse
non sit ea explicare latius scriptis nostris: . . . cum per studium apostolicae sedis
et vestrum, ac maxime per sudores et pericula nobilis et strenui viri S. Comitis
Montisfortis, discussis errorum tenebris, et bellicis cladibus propulsatis, jam
pacis et fidei viderentur tempora rediisse, . . . Quoniam igitur melius est in
tempore occurrere quam sera post tempus remedia mendicare, universitatem
vestram rogamus, . . . in virtute obedientiae stricte praecipiendo mandantes ac
injungentes in vestrorum remedia peccatorum, quantenus, communi pericu-
lo communiter obviantes, praefato Comiti succursum personarum et rerum
et etiam terrarum vestrarum, cum opus fuerit, fideliter impendatis, et ei per
vos ac subditos vestros assistatis viriliter et potenter, turbatoribus pacis et
fidei omnem omnino favorem, consilium et auxilium subtrahantes" (RHGF,
19:644).

to the monarchy's direct intervention in the southern struggle. This involvement of the Crown had serious implications. Louis's expedition was a "feudal" crusade,[10] not an act of supererogation like those that had preceded it. Rather, holy war and the duties of Davidic lordship were revealed to be one and the same: the temporal power and the spiritual power became intrinsically united in a single project, a project that was demanded of them because of what they were in themselves. This crusade was not presented as voluntary. This crusade was not the king responding to the entreaties of the pope because of his personal devotion. Rather, the king was fulfilling his own office, but this fulfillment required the spiritual power which was itself also fulfilling its office and needed the temporal power to do so. Louis was campaigning not as an individual pilgrim, but as the king in his own kingdom.

Because the war was demanded by his office, his vassals were obliged to participate, and the king issued a general summons to all who owed him military service,[11] a summons that was enforced by Cardinal Romano, the legate, with excommunication if necessary. The muster was justified, the king argued, accepting the papacy's logic, because his vassals were bound by oath to conquer the enemies of the kingdom and no enemies were greater than the enemies of the faith.[12] The vernacular *Chronique Rimee* recounted that "everyone" was forced to participate and to pay their own way, just as in the host.[13] The king wielded the temporal sword and the papal legate the spiritual, and together they would lead the crusade: "So that as much through fear of the king as through the preaching of the legate, around one hundred thousand men set out into those

---

[10] For example, the great barons, having taken counsel with Louis, recommended that he take up the Albigensian business, and they promised to help him in good faith according to the fidelity that they owed him as their liege lord (LTC, 2:1742).

[11] *Chronicon Sancti Martini Turonensi*, in Kay, *The Council of Bourges, 1225*, doc. 3:302–03.

[12] Kay, *The Council of Bourges, 1225*, doc. 7:326–29; LTC, 1:1534.

[13] Ibid., doc. 4:315.

parts from the Crown of France, with an infinity of treasure and machines."[14] Through this move, monarchical government itself became an intrinsic component, not just in theory but in practice, to the *business of the peace and the faith*. The enemies of the peace and the faith—who, through the first round of conflict, had already become the "enemies of the Church"— became also the *inimici regis*, the enemies of the king. This was one expedition with two natures—*the business of Christ*— directed against a society that was perceived as denying the incarnational and sacramental nature of reality and the immediate and ultimate peace that this nature made possible.

Louis VIII's campaign was a great success, and in the numerous oaths the southerners swore to the king and legate after having capitulated, we can see its spiritual-temporal nature. Indeed, within most of these oaths it is simply impossible to untangle the spiritual from the temporal; the southerners were making themselves men of the king and men of the Roman Church in one and the same act. The oath of Poncius de Tesano was typical. He swore to observe all the mandates of the legate and, equally, all the mandates of the king in whatever was his will. He swore not to receive any "enemies of the Church" or their "protectors" and "helpers," and not to give them "counsel" or "aid," "against the will of the lord king and the lord cardinal." He would receive the king and the cardinal and be prepared to obey them in all things and to serve them with devotion and with faith, placing in their power his person and all his lands. If he contravened the oath, all his men would be absolved of the homage and fidelity they owed him.[15] The nobles swore to follow the mandates of the Church and the monarch as if it were inconceivable that they might be in conflict and to fight the "enemies of the Church and the lord king" as if it was obvious that these were the same.[16] Over and over, the oaths

---

[14] *Annals of Dunstable*, in Kay, *The Council of Bourges, 1225*, doc. 3:294.

[15] LTC, 2:1752.

[16] See, for example, LTC, 2:1747, 1767, 1776, 1791, 1794, 1796, 1799, 1800, 1804, 1809.

demonstrate that the new "lord" of the South was the king *and* the Roman Church. Submission to the king was simultaneously submission to the Church, and vice versa.[17] The enemies of *the peace and the faith* had become definitively the *enemies of the king and the Church.* This was a reality that not even these enemies denied.[18]

In 1226 the king and Cardinal Romano made an innovation in the juridical relationship between the secular and spiritual powers as they related to the censure of excommunication, an innovation that was an appropriate legal manifestation of this reality and that would have far reaching implications for the relationship between the two powers. Having seen how many "pernicious laymen" there were in the province of Narbonne and how they "held the sentence of excommunication in contempt," the king decreed that if anyone remained contumaciously in a state of excommunication for one year, all his goods were forfeit.[19] The "enemies of the king and the Church," pernicious laymen, as a single category of criminal, were subject to a single sanction, both spiritual and temporal in character: excommunication followed by confiscation.

While this decree was an innovation, it was an innovation with a dual secular-ecclesiastical history. On the ecclesiastical side, Lateran III (1179) had stipulated that those who sold arms or in other ways aided Saracens against Christians were to be excommunicated and have their goods confiscated and called for the same sanction against heretics and mercenaries. It also stipulated that such men could be reduced to slavery by Catholic princes.[20] These were cases of outright warfare against Christian society, and the sanction was severe and immediate: expulsion from the Church and expulsion from the

---

17   See, for example, LTC, 2:1760.

18   See, for example, LTC, 2:1928.

19   Mansi, 23:21; Charles Petit-Dutaillis, *Étude sur la vie et le règne de Louis VIII, 1187–1226* (Paris: Librairie Emile Bouillon, 1894), 504–05; HGL, 8:855–62.

20   Tanner, 1:223–25.

society of freemen, which included the ability to hold property.[21] This line of thinking was developed in Pope Innocent III's
famous 1199 decretal *Vergentis in Senium,* in which he asserted
that heretics should have their goods confiscated because, in
civil law, this was the punishment for *lèse majesté* and heresy
was *lèse majesté* against God himself.[22] Innocent's bridge
between canon and civil law applied equally to feudal law, in
which rebellion—the felony par excellence—was grounds for
confiscation of all a vassal's fiefs and the disinheritance of his
children.[23] In 1215 Lateran IV had decreed that the goods of
all heretics were forfeit but added that those who were only
suspect of heresy were to be excommunicated. If they persisted
in this state for a year and a day, they were to be condemned
as heretics and treated accordingly.[24] The willingness to forgo
the sacraments for a year suggested contempt for them, which
was sufficient for the legal presumption of heresy.[25] By 1215,
then, on the ecclesiastical side, heresy and excommunication
had grown together and they had been directly compared to
rebellion in secular law.

There was a parallel development on the secular side. In
1188 Frederick I issued his *Constitutio de incendiariis et pacis
violatoribus* (*Constitution Concerning Arsonists and Violators of
the Peace*)—which was subsequently added to the *Liber feudorum* and so studied as a part of *Corpus juris civilis* from the
beginning of the thirteenth century.[26] This constitution was

---

[21] There were other crimes, however, for which only excommunication was
prescribed—such as breaking the truce and peace or charging unjust
pedagia—and others for which excommunication and limited secular action
was demanded to ensure that restitution was made, such as usury or the
favoring of Jews (Tanner, 1:222–24).

[22] X 5.7.10.

[23] Jean Dunbabin, *France in the Making, 843–1180* (Oxford: Oxford University Press, 1985), 361.

[24] Tanner, 1:233.

[25] Elisabeth Vodola, *Excommunication in the Middle Ages* (Berkeley: University
of California Press, 1986), 32, 179.

[26] *Consuetudines Feudorum* 5.5.10, in *Corpus Juris Civilis,* ed. Giovanni Calza
(Turin: Edid. heredes S. Bottae, 1829), 2:1191–12; MGH *Leges Capit.* I,

aimed at "the reprobate and criminals," and sought to temper the violence of society.[27] Imperial judges were to proscribe all violators (and their "receivers" and any who gave them "counsel or aid"), and the local bishop was to eject them "from the communion of the Church of God and the faithful of Christ." If the judge acted first, the bishop was to follow his lead, and vice versa. It was a dual spiritual-temporal sanction under imperial authority. If one remained in such a state for a year and a day, he was to lose his fiefs, all his honors and rights, and the ability to offer testimony in court—the sanctions for rebellion.[28] Frederick I was here asserting that felonies ought to also be grounds for excommunication and, to the extent that he controlled the bishops, mandating that they be treated as such.

In 1220 the spiritual and secular sides of this dynamic moved even closer together. On the occasion of Frederick II's coronation in Rome by Pope Honorius III, the young emperor promulgated a law known as the *Lex edictalis*. Sections of the

---

2:183–85; Kenneth Pennington, "Law, Feudal," in *Dictionary of the Middle Ages: Supplement 1* (New York: Charles Scribner's Sons-Thompson-Gale, 2004), 320–323; See also *Consuetudines Feudorum* 2.27–28.

[27] MGH, *Leges Capit. I*, 2:184.

[28] Ibid. Throughout the *Consuetudines Feudorum*, one year is treated as the duration after which one's decisions are to be considered definitive. So, after one year, a fief cannot be confiscated by a lord without cause, and after one year, a vassal's disobedience to his lord becomes outright rebellion; see, for example, *Consuetudines Feudorum* 1.1.1, 2.55, 4.97. The *Sachsenspiegel* states: "Any person who has been in royal outlawry for a year and a day [permanently] loses his legal rights and forfeits his allod and his fief by court decision. The fief reverts to the lord's free disposal and the allod to the royal domain. If the heirs do not claim it from the royal domain within a year and a day with their oath, they forfeit it together with the outlaw unless legitimate exigency prevents them from appearing.... A man without legal capacity cannot have legitimate children afterwards. If a person is outlawed by the realm for a year and a day, and if after that year his rights and legal protection are withdrawn [permanently], his outlawry can be commuted only to the extent that no one can take his life. He cannot, however, be reinstated into the law unless he fights a joust before the emperor's retinue and prevails over a foreign king. He can regain his rights in this way, but not the property that was confiscated from him" (*The Saxon Mirror*, trans. Maria Dobozy [Philadelphia: University of Pennsylvania Press, 1999], 80).

law followed Lateran IV's decree on heresy closely; it was, in fact, the secular side of Lateran IV's legislation, calling for the imperial ban at precisely those points where the Council called for secular action in the face of manifest heresy or contumaciousness in excommunication. It prescribed that the imperial ban be applied to all heretics of whatever name and that their goods be confiscated. It decreed that those suspected of heresy were to be banned if they did not respond to the mandates of the Church; and, if they remained in this state for a year and a day, they were to be condemned as heretics. It banned also all those believers, receivers, or defenders of heretics who remained in a state of excommunication for a year and a day. The *Lex edictalis* was the imperial acceptance of the papacy's logic. Heresy was indeed simultaneously a felony. It also extended this logic beyond Lateran IV, which had focused on heretics and their supports, in that the law prescribed the ban not only for those contumacious excommunicates who were suspect of heresy but also for all who had been censured for any violation of the liberty of the Church. However, it did not go so far as to extend the ban to all contumacious excommunicates without exception. This law was also added to the *Corpus juris civilis*.[29]

And so we can see that over the course of the years of the *business of the peace and the faith*, the two sides of the excommunication-heresy-*lèse majesté*-rebellion logic, the ecclesiastical and the secular steadily came together, culminating in the statute of 1226, according to which all excommunicates became rebels.[30] The popes had tried unsuccessfully to con-

---

[29] MGH *Leges Const.*, 2:106–10. For an extended discussion of the law and the circumstances of its promulgation, see Stephan Kuttner and Antonio García y García, "A New Eyewitness Account of the Fourth Lateran Council," *Traditio* 20 (1964): 167–71.

[30] This final move had been anticipated. In 1203, Philip of Swabia had promised Pope Innocent III that he would extend the imperial ban to all those who had been excommunicated by the Holy See, but it is not clear that he ever made good on his promise (MGH *Leges Const.*, 2:9). In 1212, Peter of Aragon had promulgated a statute similar to that of 1226 for his kingdom, but it is framed in such a way that it is the extension of royal power in the

vince Philip II to make this final move, to align his kingship with the Church within this logic.[31] But it was when his son Louis VIII stepped into the peace side of the *business* that the rebellion-heresy-excommunication identification became a reality.[32] It became in effect a matter of definition that heretics were rebels and rebels were heretics and both were excommunicated.

Lateran IV had stipulated that if someone suspect of heresy remained excommunicated for a year, he was to be condemned as a heretic and so lose his property.[33] The excommunication statute of 1226, however, extended this to include all excommunicates, not just those somehow directly implicated in heresy. Furthermore, the statute was the king's, acting with the *counsel* of the legate, and not that of a papacy attempting to bend a secular prince to its will. And it was promulgated within the context of the king and the legate's systematic subjugation of rebellious lords—all of whom had been, of course, excommunicated. For Louis, spiritual power was far from being a rival. In fact, it had become integral to the legitimacy of his actions as king: contempt for the sentence

---

aid of ecclesiastical power—the king bending to the demands of his bishops; see *Pedro el Católico, Rey de Aragón y Conde de Barcelona (1196–1213): Documentos, Testimonios y Memoria Histórica,* ed. Martín Alvira Cabrer (Zaragoza, ES: Institución "Ferdando el Católico," 2010), 1199–202, no. 1136. In a similar vein, the Archbishop of Sens promulgated in 1216: "Si aliquis per annum et diem excommunicationem publicam sustinuerit, compellatur potestas saecularis, ut excommunicatum ad unitatem ecclesiae per suam postestem venire compellat, mittendo manum in ipsum et res eius" (*Acta Conciliorum Epistolae Decretalies, ac Constitutione Summorum Pontificum,* ed. Jean Hardouin [Paris, 1714], 7, 85). In these cases, the pope and bishops clearly want the king to enforce excommunications—this is not surprising. In the act of 1226, though, there is no such unilateralism or tension because the king was not doing the bishops a favor, but rather defending the legitimacy of action that the Crown was taking in its own right.

[31] RHGF, 19:646–47.

[32] In fact, the rebels' excommunication was a key component in the propaganda that defended the "feudal" confiscation of their lands (Kay, *The Council of Bourges, 1225,* doc. 7: 326–29).

[33] Tanner, 1:233–34.

of excommunication became rebellion against the king, and rebellion against the king was grounds for excommunication. The 1226 statue was the legal codification of realities on the ground. The rebels were rebels simultaneously both against the king and against the Church.[34]

In late 1226, Louis VIII died and Louis IX, then twelve years old, with the help of his mother, Blanche, and Cardinal Romano, took command. By 1229 victory was secure. After the final surrender of the Count of Toulouse, the legate announced his absolution in this manner: "The son of Raymond the former Count of Toulouse, persisting for a long time excommunicate, for a long time contumacious and a rebel against the Church of God and the king of the Franks, having been made by the Lord to have a change of heart, came humbly and devoutly to the mandate of the Church and the king, seeking absolution and the grace and mercy of the Church and the king." Raymond went on to swear devotion to the Church of Rome and to the king.[35] They were a single authority, both spiritual and temporal.

When the war ended in 1229, its spiritual and temporal natures were codified in three important legal acts: the royal ordinance known as *Cupientes*,[36] the Peace of Paris,[37] and the canons of the Council of Toulouse.[38] All three were written by the legate Romano in conjuncture with the young Louis IX and his mother and borrowed heavily from Simon de Montfort's *Statues of Pamiers* of 1212.[39] Together, these acts provided the

---

[34] See, for example, the canons of the 1227 council held in Narbonne (Mansi, 23:25).
[35] LTC, 2:1991.
[36] RGALF, 1:230–33.
[37] HGL, 8:883.
[38] Mansi, 23:193–204. These canons restated many of those of the 1227 Council of Narbonne (Mansi, 23:21–25).
[39] It is clear from internal references that *Cupientes* and the Peace of Paris were written at the same time and place. The latter is explicitly written to Cardinal Romano, and in it Raymond VII swears: "et fieri faciemus per ballivos nostros, viriliter et potenter inquiri faciemus et inquiremus diligenter de

legal foundation for the construction of the social order that was to perpetuate the mission of the crusade, which was ultimately the expansion of orthodox Christian faith and peace. It was in this project that Gui spent most of his career, and both the *enquêteurs* and the inquisitors based their operations on the documents of 1229. Within the legal world for which these documents would form the foundation, the temporal and the spiritual remained totally bound up together; through them, the *business of the peace and the faith* pressed on, though now in the humdrum arena of statute and governance.

According to its preamble, the purpose of *Cupientes* was to preserve the peace and liberty of the Church.[40] It paraphrased large sections of Lateran IV, Lateran III, and even Lucius III's *Ad Abolendam*, which concerned heretics and the secular power's responsibilities towards them.[41] What the ecclesiastical canons had called on the secular power to do, Louis now

---

inveniendis hereticis, credentibus, fautoribus, et receptatoribus eorumdem secundum ordinationem, quam super hoc faciet dominus legatus" (HGL, 8:884). The canons of the Council of Toulouse are prefaced with a declaration that their purpose is to promulgate and make to be observed the many acts of the legates of the apostolic see, after which preface, the canons closely follow *Cupientes* and the Peace of Paris; see Guillaume de Puylaurens, *Chronique, 1145–1275: Chronica Magistri Guillelmi de Podio Laurentii*, ed. Jean Duvernoy (Paris: Le Pérégrinateur, 1996), 144. Cardinal Romano was intimately involved in the final stages of the crusade and the victory of the young Louis; see, for example *E Mari Historiarum, Auctore Johanne de Columna, O.P.* (RHGF, 23:107). Especially with reference to the regulation of "secular" matters such as petty violence and the positive vision of Christian lordship, the documents follow closely the 1212 *Statutes of Pamiers*, HGL, 8:625–635 (I would like to thank Gregory Lippiatt for bringing the correlation between these documents to my attention).

40 RGALF, 1:231.

41 *Ad Abolendam* (PL, 201:1297–300) was issued by Pope Lucius III in 1184 in conjunction with Emperor Frederick Barbarosa. It anathematized a variety of types of heretics and laid out the basic procedure of investigation that bishops should follow to find and eliminate heretics from their dioceses. The document is often understood as the founding charter of the Inquisition. This is to overstate the case. However, it was reiterated in a variety of forms in the documents that did indeed "found" the Inquisition, such as those of 1229 under discussion here.

mandated as king: after a heretic was condemned by his bishop or another cleric with authority, he was to be punished without delay; receivers, defenders, and favorers of heretics were to have their goods confiscated and were to be intestable, barred from court, and incapable of holding office, and the king's barons, bailiffs, and subjects, "solicitous to purge the land of heretics," were to investigate and capture them, delivering them to the Church for judgment. Then, following closely canon 27 of Lateran III, *Cupientes* decreed that the bailiffs were to expel all "ruptarii," marauders, from the land and to make the peace to be observed. Louis VIII's 1226 statute dealing with excommunication (discussed above) was reiterated, but with the added emphasis that because they had contempt for the keys of the Church, excommunicates were to be shunned according to the canons, and that if someone contumaciously persisted in a state of excommunication, the king's men were to compel them to return to unity through confiscation of all their goods, both mobile and immobile. The tithe was to be restored everywhere to the churches. And finally, as was demanded by Lateran IV, Louis ordered that his barons, vassals, and bailiffs swear publicly and on a solemn day to serve these statutes in good faith and that if they did not they would be deprived of all goods and their bodies punished.[42] With *Cupientes*, the monarchy committed itself to fulfilling the role of the ideal orthodox ruler, making the ecclesiastical canons that touched on the responsibilities of such rulers its own law. The canonical and civil/feudal had become one and the same. Heretics, marauders, and their associates, as well as corrupt secular officials, were now in violation of the king's laws as much as those of the Church.

The Peace of Paris was the treaty reconciling Raymond VII with the king and Church, and the first part of the treaty was largely a duplicate of *Cupientes*. Raymond was promising to both legate and king that he would perform the duties of a faithful and orthodox vassal as spelled out in the document.

---

[42] RGALF, 1:232–33.

He also agreed to enforce whatever was ordained by Cardinal Romano with regards to heresy, which was a reference to the legate's forthcoming council to be held at Toulouse. He further swore not to appoint Jews or anyone in suspicion of heresy as bailiffs, a condition which harkened back to Lateran III and to the pre-crusade excommunications of his father. He also swore to make restitution for all the damages he had caused.[43] The document moved on to deal extensively with the dismantling of his military capabilities, the handing over of castles to the king, the establishment of men who had remained loyal to the king and the Church as castellans, and the establishment of the Templars and Hospitallers in other fortified positions.[44] The provisions of the Peace of Paris must be understood as a specific application of *Cupientes* with the intent of reforming Raymond into the ideal secular lord and integrating his power with the monarch and Church's networks of *counsel and aid*. Throughout the document, the Church and king were treated as a single party and the serving of the peace and the faith were inseparable.[45]

More than either *Cupientes* or the Peace of Paris, however, the canons of the Council of Toulouse offered a codification of the objectives of the crusade, of the *business of the peace and the faith*, in both its destructive and constructive aspects.[46]

---

[43] HGL, 8:883–86.

[44] Ibid., 8:886–92.

[45] See also the document written by Roger-Bernard, Count of Foix, who was seeking reconciliation after Raymond made peace (LTC, 2:2003).

[46] Cardinal Romano prefaced the council with these words: "Licet a diversis apostolicae sedis legatis diversa emanaverint instituta contra haerticos, credentes, fautores, et receptatores haereticorum, et super pace conservanda in Tolosana dioecesi, et Narbonensi provincia, et circumadjacentibus dioecesibus, et terris vicinis, et super aliis quae ad bonum statum terrae pertinere noscuntur: nos tamen attendentes, terras praedictas, post longae ac miserabilis turbationis discrimina, nunc quasi miraculose, pace, de assensu et voluntate majorum, gaudere: ordinandum duximus et statuentdum de consilio archiepiscoporum, episcoporum, et praelatorum, et baronum, et militum, quae ad purgationem haereticae pravitatis, conservationem pacis, necnon et terrae quasi neophytae, novimus expedire" (Mansi, 23:194).

When read as a coherent whole, the canons reveal both how the victors in the war understood the society that they had defeated and how they envisioned both the final dismantling of that society and the construction of a new one. The council can roughly be divided into two sections: one dealing directly with heresy and another with the peace—though they are completely mutually-dependent, especially through the duties of the prelates and the secular authorities.

Following *Cupientes* and the Peace of Paris, the council stipulated that the lords of the land were required to proactively investigate heretics, delivering them to ecclesiastics for judgment.[47] Anyone who allowed a heretic to remain on his lands, even if it was for money or through negligence, would lose his lands and be subject to corporal punishment.[48] Bailiffs, in particular, were to work against heresy and to give "aid" and "favor" to others who were doing likewise, especially if they were officers of the king.[49] There was a clear effort to eliminate heretics from quotidian society.[50]

A thoroughly orthodox religion was to replace the heretical aspects of this society. Everyone was to swear an oath to abjure all heresy and anyone censured by name and to serve the Catholic faith that the Roman Church preached. If they refused the oath they were to be suspect of heresy themselves.[51] Everyone was to make a confession and receive the Eucharist three times a year or they were suspect of heresy, and everyone was to attend Mass and hear the preaching and Divine Office on Sundays and major feast days.[52] The religious life of the society was to be public, focusing on the liturgy and the sacraments. The council was not concerned only with rooting out the black-robed heretics hiding in the woods,

---

[47] Canons 1, 3, 8 (Mansi, 23:194–95).
[48] Canons 4, 5 (Mansi, 23:195).
[49] Canons 7, 9 (Mansi, 23:195).
[50] See Canons 6, 10, 11, 15, 17, 18 (Mansi, 23:195–98).
[51] Canon 12 (Mansi, 23:196–97).
[52] Canons 13, 25–77, (Mansi, 23:197–200).

but also with up-rooting the entire heretical social order and replacing it with a Catholic social order. This objective was to be met through the concerted effort of both ecclesiastical and lay authorities, working together as much through censure and coercion as through preaching, the sacraments, and good government.

The council followed closely the conception of secular lordship as described in *Cupientes* and the Peace of Paris, but in much greater detail, borrowing heavily from Simon de Montfort's *Statutes of Pamiers*, which had been promulgated at the start of the *business*. As was standard, the "liberty of the Church," meaning her tithes and revenues, were to be protected and the clergy were to be free from talliage and to be judged in ecclesiastical courts.[53] But it was not just the clergy who were to be free from unjust extractions. No one was to be subject to *pedagia*—tolls—on the roads except merchants, and even these only in the case when the lord could demonstrate his right, a condition that struck at the very heart of the nobility's way of life. If a lord justly received a toll, he was to protect all travelers from violence, making restitution for their losses if he failed. This was to be enforced through ecclesiastical censure and, if necessary, by the superior lord.[54]

The secular power generally was to be controlled and organized through the peace, and what it meant to be inside the peace and outside the peace was defined in great detail. Everyone fifteen years and older had to swear to uphold the peace every three years. The bishops were to force them through censure if they were reluctant, and if this failed, they were considered to have broken the peace. Anyone who broke the peace or made war was to be excommunicated and everyone was to make war on them and their lands. Cities and towns were to expel them and their men even if they owed them fidelity. Their goods were to be confiscated and their superior lord was to "do with their bodies as he ought." Furthermore, anyone,

---

[53] Canons 19, 20, 24 (Mansi, 23:198–99).
[54] Canons 21–23 (Mansi, 23:199).

including parents and relatives, who gave such a breaker of the peace "aid, counsel, or favor" or received them were to suffer the same penalties.[55] Vassals who rebelled against their lords were defined as breakers of the peace. No one was to have a friendship or be familiar with or make a treaty with *faidits*[56] or others who make war, or they too were to be treated as breakers of the peace. No one was to accept "thieves" or "plunderers" or they were breakers of the peace.[57] What is more, anytime someone broke the peace, a new oath *contra inimicos fidei atque pacis*—"against the enemies of the faith and the peace"—was to be sworn against them, and they were excommunicated and perpetually disinherited.

That these canons surrounding the peace were not aimed at simple criminals or renegade knights, but rather at an entire social order, becomes even clearer in the final series of canons. The constant petty wars that had characterized secular life within that order would not be suffered. The council forbade the formation of sworn associations among barons, castellans, and knights. If one took a castle or town from one who held it from the king or Church, his goods were forfeit and he was excommunicated.[58] No one was to violently seize goods or hostages for their lord. Rather, if one believed something to be owed to him, he was to seek it through judges, who would determine who had "ius." If one did otherwise, he was a breaker of the peace. And all justice was to be free. For the conservation of the peace, no new fortifications were to be built, none that had been demolished were to be rebuilt, and women who held fortifications were not to marry "enemies of the faith and the peace," or their lands would be forfeit.[59]

Read together, the documents of 1229 aimed at disman-

---

[55] Canons 28–30 (Mansi, 23:201).

[56] We will discuss *faidits* in much greater detail in a later chapter. In 1229 the meaning is very unclear. Generally, though, *faidits* were anyone who was known to have fought against the king or the Church.

[57] Canons 32–36: "latrones, ruptarios, vel lacionones" (Mansi, 23:202).

[58] Canon 37–39 (Mansi, 23:203).

[59] Canons 40–43 (Mansi, 23:203–04).

tling an entire way of life and replacing it with another. They were directed against a society of small-scale warfare and vendetta. As the orthodox saw it, it was a world in which vassals had little obligation to their lords, and in which lords fought their wars with mercenaries, a world of castles and fortified villages and near perpetual violence. Within the orthodox sacramental cosmos, the society of the South was understood to be as intrinsically spiritual as it was temporal. To the orthodox, the "heretics" of the documents were not isolated dissidents; they were the holy men of a deeply unholy society, the pacifist counterparts to the violent lords and knights, a dependency that made sense only within the doctrinal framework of dualism, and which shows how foreign the "complete act" of the south was to that of the orthodox. The documents describe the personal networks that sustained this society in the language which was used to describe how all power was wielded: through *aid, counsel,* and *favor* (subjects of a later chapter). These networks were clearly understood as practically uniting the heretics and the violent laymen. Both the discourse surrounding the peace and that surrounding heresy were long-running, and the *business of the peace and the faith,* as both a theoretical and a practical undertaking, was incorporated into them and was understood through them.

A Catholic order, by definition as much temporal as spiritual in nature, was to replace this heretical one. Its worship was focused on the sacramental system, and its conception of secular power was modeled on the Davidic ideal. The material, practical realm and the spiritual realm found their unity not in contradiction, as for the dualists, but in essential compatibility and coexistence. The spiritual and temporal aspects of this order were inseparable. One was ejected from the spiritual order, from the sacramental system, by excommunication and from the temporal order through the loss of one's legal life, most clearly expressed through the inability to hold property or swear a binding oath. By 1229, these two sanctions became different aspects of the same sanction. Persistence in excommunication became a felony, and felonies became grounds for excommunication. The pope, his legates and delegates, and bishops excommunicated, and the king and his officers confiscated property: the "enemies of *the peace* and *the faith*" had become interchangeable with the "enemies of the king and the Church." A man who rebelled against the king and a man who adored a Cathar *perfectus* would ultimately be subject to the same sanction, a sanction dependent on both spiritual and temporal powers for its application and enforcement. The inquisitors into heresy and the secular *enquêteurs* would emerge and work in the South of France within this conceptual and legal framework, and they must be understood together.

For the Extirpation of Heretical Depravity and for the Conservation of the Peace

In this wicked world . . . there are many reprobate mingled with the good.

—St. Augustine, *City of God* 18.49

THE ALBIGENSIAN CRUSADE was the context for Gui Foucois's childhood and adolescence in Saint-Gilles.[1] His father, Pierre, was an important advocate and judge, involved at the highest levels in the affairs of the period.[2] It is certainly an indication of Pierre's orthodoxy that he joined la Grande Chartreuse late in life, dying as a Carthusian.[3] Gui himself likely spent the later part of the first phase of the war in Paris pursuing his studies, returning to the South in the 1230s.[4] He had a

---

[1] TNA, 2:371.

[2] HGL, 8:434 (see also HGL, 7:123–24; 8:428, 429, 537; LTC, 1:9500).

[3] HGL, 7:123.

[4] TNA, 2:431; *Chronica S. Petri Erfordensis moderna*, ed. Oswald Holder-Egger, in MGH SS, 30:402; LTC, 2:2582.

foot in both the world of the South and the world of Paris and would have been as conversant in the arguments of the counts of Toulouse as he was in those of the papal legates, and as knowledgeable concerning the world of honor and *cortezia* as he was about the thought of Parisian intellectuals. He would have surely had personal experience with crusaders, heretics, and mercenaries. Gui's life took place within the *business of the peace and the faith*, and he would become a master of the legal world that grew out of the documents of 1229. As we shall see, he had a direct and important role in the construction of a legal apparatus that sought to enforce this body of law.

As we saw in the previous chapter, the *business* called for complete cooperation between the ecclesiastical and secular authorities. What is more, it demanded clerics and lords of a certain type. These men had to be reliable and moral, wielding the two swords together toward the necessarily united spiritual and temporal reform of society. How to make this a reality was the principal problem of the 1230s–1250s, the problem on which Gui worked. This was a great challenge, and as problems arose, both the secular and the spiritual authorities attempted solutions, adding pieces of law here and there or forming new offices or new procedures where needed. These additions made constant reference to each other as parts of the same project. With each addition or innovation by either power, the entirety of the *business* was evoked and reiterated. The law and institutions that were built in this period, therefore, were the result of the actions of both spiritual and temporal powers within a legal framework that was fundamentally both spiritual and temporal and without either power being the sovereign or architect over the whole. The ultimate solution to the problems faced, as we will see, was the long-term moral reform of clerics and nobles, coupled with an apparatus of oversight and appeal that intrinsically included both the spiritual and the secular realms—the inquisitors and the *enquêteurs*.

The documents of 1229 laid out the program of the *business* and attempted to provide the legal backbone that it required. The immediate problem, however, was that the spiritual and temporal authorities that the program's implementation relied on were just as likely to be the source of disorder—the breakers of the peace and the protectors of heretics—as its solution. While Count Raymond VII of Toulouse made an initial show of abiding by and enforcing the reform, it was predictably halfhearted.[5] But he was not alone in his passive resistance. Unsurprisingly, there seems to have been widespread lack of enthusiasm for the prosecution of the *business* among the lords and knights who had just been defeated.[6] King Louis IX and the papal legate acted together to try to motivate Raymond. In 1232, the legate and a representative of the king held a council at Béziers with the Archbishop of Narbonne and all the suffragans,[7] a council that reiterated the provisions of 1229, stressing the obligations of the secular powers[8] and drafted a series of articles that Raymond was compelled to promulgate in 1233 as his own statutes.[9]

These statutes, promulgated "for the extirpation of heretical depravity and for the conservation of the peace and for the conservation of the good status of all the land," described in great detail the obligations of the secular power in eradicating heresy, and particularly the count's obligation to ensure that all his barons, knights, and officials comply.[10] They were obligated not only to persecute heretics but also to cooperate completely with inquisitors into heresy, offering them "aid" and "favor" and enforcing their sentences. The statutes stipulated that the count was to have inquisitions made into anyone suspected of not doing so.[11] With a reiteration of the statute from the documents of 1229, which stipulated that excommunicates who were contumacious for a year were to be compelled to return

---

[5] Guillaume Pelhisson, *Chronique (1229–1244), suivie du récit des troubles d'Albi (1234)*, ed. and trans. Jean Duvernoy (Paris: CNRS, 1994), 148, 154.

[6] Ibid., 48.

[7] Ibid., 154.

[8] Mansi, 23:269–70.

[9] Guillaume de Puylaurens, *Chronique*, 154; HGL, 8:963–69.

[10] HGL, 8:963.

[11] Ibid., 8:963–96.

to the Church, Raymond's statutes transitioned to deal with breakers of the peace. He ordered that all marauders, thieves, and traitors, as well as their receivers, be expelled from his lands. He would seize the goods of all breakers of the peace and all who give them "aid." He ordered inquisitions into all clandestine malefactors who stole or destroyed property or who offended religious houses. He forbade all unjust extractions and tolls and ordered inquisitions to be made into those barons and knights who concealed or helped thieves or brigands, as well as those who broke their oaths.[12]

Throughout the document, whether with regard to heresy or to the peace, the primary means of enforcement was inquisition followed by confiscation. Heretics, breakers of the peace, and all those who either helped them or failed to persecute them were together expelled from Christian society, both temporally and spiritually. In the numerous inquisitions called for in Raymond's statutes of 1233 we clearly see the tasks of those who would become the *enquêteurs* of the 1240s. This was the first major step toward their legal definition as the "inquisitors" charged to enforce the secular side of the *business of the peace and the faith*.

The secular and ecclesiastical sides of this *business* cannot, however, be separated. The *business* required not only a certain type of lord but also a certain type of prelate. Both excommunications and confiscations had to be just or the whole project failed. And so, it makes sense that the same council that promulgated Raymond's "secular" statutes also read into its canons Lateran IV's constitutions against unjust excommunications, *Sacro Approbante* and *Sub Interminatione*,[13] because "where there is not government the people fall, and a Church without a proper guide is in spiritual and temporal defeat."[14] In fact, the vast majority of the council's canons dealt with the

---

12 Ibid., 8:966–69.
13 Lateran IV, canons 47 and 49 (Tanner, 1:255 and 257).
14 Mansi, 23:272.

reform of the clergy in every detail of their lives.[15] The clergy needed not only to be fair judges; they were also to be holy, dispensing the sacraments and caring for their flocks, just as the secular authorities were to be Davidic. The reform of the clergy was therefore as much a component of the *business* as was the reform of the lords, and the numerous councils held through the 1230s and 1240s that dealt predominantly with the reform of the clergy should be read as a part of this project.

In the case of heresy, ideally the local bishop would investigate and pass judgment on suspect heretics and the local lord would enforce the sentence.[16] Pope Gregory IX's initial commissioning of Dominican inquisitors must be seen as a supplement to this ordinary model and not a replacement. The two papal bulls most often discussed in the establishment of the "Inquisition" are the 1231 *Excommunicamus* and *Ille Humani Generis*.[17] *Excommunicamus* extended *Ad Abolendam* to include the anti-heresy provisions of Lateran IV (the basis for the documents of 1229). It was basically an extended definition of the crime of heresy and the appropriate punishments, a necessity for ecclesiastics to judge in the matter. *Excommunicamus* also took for granted the direct involvement of the secular powers as a necessary component in such action. It was, in fact, promulgated along with a secular counterpart: the Roman senator and people had simultaneously promulgated an edict that was the secular mirror image of *Excommunicamus* committing the municipality to enforcing its provisions.[18] And Gregory promulgated these statutes together, commanding the bishops to have both written into local statutes, secular

---

[15] Mansi, 23:269–78.

[16] This was the vision of *Ad Abolendam* that was reiterated throughout the *business of the peace and the faith.*

[17] *Corpus Documentorum Inquisitionis Haereticae Pravitatis Neerlandicae,* ed. Paul Fredericq (Gent, BE: J. Vuylsteke, 1889), 1:79, 89; Yves Dossat, *Les crises de l'Inquisition toulousaine au XIIIe siècle,* 1233–1273 (Bordeaux, FR: Bière, 1959), 111–18; Edward Peters, *Inquisition* (Berkeley: University of California Press, 1989), 55–57.

[18] *Corpus Documentorum Inquisitionis Haereticae Pravitatis,* 1:80.

and ecclesiastical, and enforced.[19] When *Ille Humani Generis* established the Dominicans as inquisitors in Languedoc in 1233,[20] that "they might proceed against [heretics] according to our newly promulgated statutes against heretics," Gregory was inserting them into this complex of secular-ecclesiastical law—from the beginning they were envisioned as a component in a business as much secular as spiritual.[21]

The *business of the peace and the faith* was aimed at both spiritual and temporal corruption, and it required the symbiosis of the spiritual and temporal powers for its prosecution. This was, as we have seen, clearly expressed in the documents of 1229. In order for the office of the secular lord to be fulfilled in accord with Raymond's statutes, it was necessary that condemnations for heresy and excommunications be forthcoming and just. He could move against only those condemned by the Church,[22] and the Dominican inquisitors were to provide such reliable ecclesiastical judgment. The converse was equally true: the prosecution of heresy required, at its very legal foundations, the reliable wielding of the material sword.[23] The various inquisitions called for in Raymond's statutes were supposed to ensure such reliable secular power. We can see just how en-

---

[19] Ibid., 1:81.

[20] A version of the bull had first been sent to the Dominicans of Regensburg in 1231, and in 1233, versions were also sent to Mainz and Strasbourg (Dossat, *Les crises de l'Inquisition*, 113, 329 no. a).

[21] "Procedant contra eos [heretics] juxta statuta nostra contra hereticos noviter promulgata." *Ille humani generis* is printed in (Dossat, *Les crises de l'Inquisition*, 329). It is important also to note that they were not replacing the episcopal recipients of *Excommunicamus*, but coming to help them fulfill their duties, that the burden might be shared. See Dossat, *Les crises de l'Inquisition*, 326; Walter L. Wakefield, *Heresy, Crusade and Inquisition in Southern France, 1100–1250* (Berkeley: University of California Press, 1974), 140.

[22] HGL, 8:965–96. See also the 1234 Council of Arles (Mansi, 23:337).

[23] Indeed, there was a "crusading" component to the friars' commission: those who gave the Dominicans "aid," "counsel," or "favor" would receive the relaxation of three years of penance, and those who died in such fighting as may occur would receive the plenary indulgence (Dossat, *Les crises de l'Inquisition*, 329).

twined these two dimensions of the *business* were by looking at the instructions given to the Dominicans by a 1235 council held at Narbonne. The bishops included as "protectors of heretics" those who failed to look into suspect heretics, those who had temporal jurisdiction but neglected to persecute heretics or rebels denounced by the Church, and those who let pass an unexpected opportunity to capture heretics or rebels.[24] Rebels and heretics were lumped in together, and someone negligent in the prosecution of either was in violation of both canon and secular law and could quickly find himself the object of an inquisition that was both ecclesiastical and secular—this was one "apparatus," not because it came from one "sovereign," but because it grew out of a single initiative, a single *business*.

The Dominican inquisitors of the 1230s faced serious opposition. Not only did the local population resist them, outraged as they were with the friars' often excessive and probably unjust (by their own criteria) persecution of suspected heretics and their disregard for local custom, but they found Raymond and the nobility in general to be of little help, and sometimes to be violently opposed to their operations.[25] In addition to problems with the secular lords, the Dominican inquisitors often had problems with the bishops, under whose authority they remained and who were inclined to use the inquisitions in local contests for power.[26] In all, the friars's inquisitions were not very successful, and they were suspended in 1238.[27] Raymond's secular inquisitors, for their part, do not seem to have ever really materialized in practice. Nevertheless, the conceptual and legal foundation for both the inquisitors into heresy and the *enquêteurs* was in place.

The ultimate problem, of course, was that the society of the South had been beaten but not broken. Indeed, by 1240

---

[24] Mansi, 23:360.
[25] See, for example: HGL, 8:1014–17; Wakefield, *Heresy, Crusade and Inquisition*, 142–43; LTC, 2:2445; Guillaume Pelhisson, *Chronique*, 72–84.
[26] Wakefield, *Heresy, Crusade and Inquisition*, 143–46.
[27] LTC, 2:2711.

the *business* was in crisis and from 1240–1243 there were large scale rebellions in the South. The monarchy's eventual defeat of these rebellions finally broke the back of noble resistance.[28] Within the context of these rebellions, the Church and the Crown, the faith and the peace, remained bound up together. For example, when Raymond abandoned peace and again took up arms against the king in 1242, the friar inquisitors in Avignonet were attacked and murdered, demonstrating that to much of the population the inquisitors and the king were understood as together the enemy.[29] In response, Raymond was excommunicated. He was a "protector, defender, and receiver" of heretics because, when the inquisitors had determined some of his men to be heretics, he did not enforce their mandates, as was stipulated in his statutes, but instead received the condemned with familiarity. What is more, like a "marauder and violator of the peace," Raymond violated the rights of the Church and committed perjury against the Church and the king of France.[30] In this rebellion, Raymond and his followers were condemned on all counts; they violated the 1229 Peace of Paris, article by article. And when they had been defeated, it was to the Peace of Paris that they again had to swear.[31] Heresy and bad lordship, like the Church and the Crown, remained inseparable both legally and in practice.[32] These wars were a continuation of the crusade concluded in 1229; they were the *business* again in crisis.

---

[28] See Wakefield, *Heresy, Crusade and Inquisition*, 153–65.

[29] Mark Gregory Pegg, *A Most Holy War: The Albigensian Crusade and the Battle for Christendom* (Oxford: Oxford University Press, 2008), 184–85.

[30] HGL, 8:1090–91.

[31] HGL, 8:1053, 1066, 1097; LTC, 2:2995, 2996, 3000, 3011, 3013, 3029; John H. Mundy, *Society and Government at Toulouse in the Age of the Cathars* (Toronto: Pontifical Institute of Mediaeval Studies, 1997), 3:369 (Appendix).

[32] For the very real centrality of the problem of heresy in the thinking of the Crown, see Raymond's letter to Queen Blanche of 1243, wherein he attempts to put her mind at ease by promising to purge his lands of heretics and their supporters and to support the Church in its condemnation of heretics (LTC, 2:3012).

The defeat of these rebellions meant the end of large-scale southern resistance. The will of the nobles had been largely broken and the construction of the social order envisioned by the *business* was well underway. These wars had a large impact on Louis IX. The conflict of 1242–1243 with Raymond VII and the barons of the South was actually the final phase of a larger rebellion of nobles, initially led by Hugh X, Count of la Marche, and King Henry III of England, testing the young king.[33] Then in his late twenties, Louis often led his armies into battle personally, and the wars were crucial to the consolidation of his rule.[34] These wars were, therefore, formative both for Louis's understanding of his rule and for the reality of that rule. It has been argued by William Chester Jordan that it was over the course of these conflicts that Louis came out from beneath his powerful mother, Blanche of Castile, and into his own as a ruler, a process that culminated in 1244 when, against his mother's wishes, he took the vow to go on crusade in the Holy Land.[35] Jordan suggests that his crusade vow was an assertion of adulthood: Louis was now in charge. We should add to this analysis, however, that Louis's fight against the rebellious barons led him to refine his understanding of his own *officium*, of what it meant to be king. This understanding, as clearly expressed in the oaths he imposed on the rebels of 1242–1243, was that of 1229, the Davidic conception, the conception of the *business of the peace and the faith*. There was nothing more consistent with this "orthodox" understanding of secular power than the idea of crusade, as we saw in the case of Louis's father and the Albigensian Crusade. Louis's taking of the Cross was, therefore, the logical culmination of this "coming into his own" as an orthodox monarch.

---

[33] Jacques Le Goff, *Saint Louis*, trans. Gareth Evan Gollrad, 103–08.

[34] William Chester Jordan, *Louis IX and the Challenge of the Crusade: a Study in Rulership* (Princeton: Princeton University Press, 1979), 16.

[35] Ibid., 3–7. See also *The Memoirs of the Lord of Joinville: A New English Version*, trans. Ethel Wedgwood (New York: E. P. Dutton and Company, 1906), 45.

What this means is that while it is clearly the case that the last few years of the 1240s were consumed with preparations for the crusade overseas, it is not necessary to subordinate all Louis's activities to some perceived utility for the war effort, as has been the temptation of some historians. Rather, his actions of the 1240s can be seen both as manifestations of his understanding of what a good king did and as a part of his preparations for the ultimate display of what such a good king did: go on crusade—they are perfectly congruent motives. Louis sought to reform his officials and cleanse his kingdom of sin not just because that would help him gain the favor of God and so win a war. Rather, he was engaging in the crusade because he moreover intended to be the type of king who also reformed his officials and cleansed his kingdom of sin—they were multiple sides of the same *business*, a business to which Louis was committed as a Davidic monarch. It is not surprising, therefore, that his preparations were as much spiritual as they were material.

We have already seen how the *business* in the South of France had set the legal and conceptual stage for the *enquêteurs* work concerning the affairs of secular officials. The documents from 1229 through the 1230s repeatedly called for such investigations to be made. However, they had always envisioned these investigations to be ad hoc, focusing on specific officials in specific circumstances. What Louis did in 1247 was different, although built on the same foundations. He sent the first royal *enquêteurs* to make a grand tour through the kingdom, righting any wrongs that he or his ancestors might have done.[36] These *enquêteurs* were not responding to specific complaints concerning specific officials. Rather, they went out and actively sought instances of abuse by secular power. They conducted thorough investigations of whatever they found and compelled the royal officials to make restitution.

These *enquêteurs*, or *inquisitores*—inquisitors—as the Latin sources call them, were virtually all clerics, and most

---

[36] RHGF, 24:4.

of them were Mendicant friars bearing licenses from their provincials and priors. Historians have sometimes speculated about the significance of professed religious acting as secular judges—whether or not they perceived something "religious" in what they were doing—but I would hope that at this point in our investigation it is clear that there was nothing "secular" (in the modern sense) going on here. The clerics and friars were working for peace and justice, and such things were understood to be as much a part of the "religious" world in which they lived as were questions of doctrine or right worship—the concern of those other mostly Mendicant friars, the "inquisitors" into heresy. Indeed, the subject matter of the cases that these secular inquisitors dealt with overlapped directly with that of the ecclesiastical inquisitors, especially in the South. Was a confiscation predicated on account of heresy justified? Well, the inquisitors had to figure out whether the person was really a heretic.[37] The line between the secular "enquêteurs" and the ecclesiastical "inquisitors" was not clear. Also in 1247, Louis IX was paying for the activities of the Dominican inquisitors into heresy and ordering his men to cooperate with them.[38]

We will have an opportunity to look deeply into the work of royal *enquêteurs* and its connection with that of the inquisitors and the *business* in general in the next chapter when we explore Gui Foucois's later career as a royal *enquêteur* and judge. In order for that investigation to be fruitful, however, we need to return to the South of France and the earlier career of Gui because this work provided the foundation for much of what Louis would do after his return from the Holy Land in 1254, at which point his "construction" of the French monarchy would enter its most important and dramatic phase.

Count Raymond of Toulouse died in 1249. His son-in-law, Alphonse of Poitiers, brother of Louis IX, was heir to the county. Alphonse had left with Louis on crusade and was in Egypt when news of Raymond's death reached him. He im-

---

[37] See, for example, RHGF, 24:362.
[38] HGL, 8:1206.

mediately left for France to successfully defend his somewhat
disputed claim. Alphonse's investment with the county of
Toulouse made it possible to pursue the *business* in the region
in earnest, as Alphonse was at least as committed to it as his
brother. The secular power in the South was now effectively
the Crown itself.

It was at this point that Gui Foucois rose to prominence.
He had been working as a lawyer in the region since 1237 in
a number of minor capacities.[39] When Alphonse took power,
however, he assumed a much more prominent role, no doubt
because of his unquestionable orthodoxy. He could be trusted,
and Alphonse needed help. Gui went to work immediately as
a legal advisor and a judge as the new count sought to sort
out Raymond's testaments and charters.[40] Like his brother,
Alphonse was committed to fulfilling the obligations of orthodox secular power. In 1251, with Gui Foucois as his legal
counsel, Alphonse swore an oath to the Bishop of Avignon
that he and his men would perform the secular office justly.
Such an oath was demanded by Lateran IV and the documents of 1229, and it covered every aspect of the secular office
as described therein (as well as in the councils of the 1230s
and 1240s).[41]

Alphonse's first responsibility and chief problem was ensuring that his officials fulfilled their duties justly. Part of the
difficulty that Alphonse faced was that the officers' powers and
responsibilities were not clearly defined. There was, as we have
seen, a mass of ecclesiastical and secular legislation that dealt
with secular power, but this had to be translated into practical statute and procedure and applied to specific situations
if the secular offices envisioned in 1229 and 1233 were to be
constructed. From 1251 to 1254, Gui Foucois was largely re-

---

[39] LTC, 2:2486, 2693, 2708, 2787, 2793, 2794; HGL, 8:1029–31.

[40] LTC, 3:3829, 3939, 3943, 3962; HGL, 8:1262–5.

[41] *Gal. Christ.*, 1:Instrumenta, 144; LTC, 3:3938. See, for example: Council
of Arles (1234) (Mansi, 23:337); Council of Narbonne (1235) (Mansi,
23:360–62); Council of Béziers (1246), (Mansi, 23:694, 722).

sponsible for performing this task and the results of his labors, as we shall see, would significantly impact the governance of the whole kingdom.

Sometime between 1251 and 1253 Alphonse's seneschals, bailiffs, and judges began swearing oaths to uphold a set of *constitutiones* concerning their administration upon taking office. It is very likely Gui had a hand in writing them.[42] The constitutions paint a picture of the ideal secular officer, and the two overriding considerations are justice and accountability. The count expected his officers to live up to their obligations, and in order to make this more likely, care was taken to isolate their offices from local interests. The officers were not to accept gifts from anyone or payments from litigants or to sell lesser offices to their family members, being content with their stipend. They were to make condemnations of *maleficium*— evil deeds—based on law and the customs of the country, not on their own will. They were to render the same justice to knights as they did to everyone else, and their punishments and fines were to be moderate. They were not to use their office to impose themselves in matters not under their jurisdiction or to attempt anything in prejudice to someone else's rights. The constitutions also established means of accountability. A detailed process of appeals was determined by which a litigant could press his case all the way to the count's court, and the officers were warned not to molest men who did so. After the termination of their administrations, the count's officers were to stay in place for a certain period of time during which, now powerless, they could be sued for extortion and, if found guilty, forced to make restitution. Having been investigated, if the officers were found to have been excessive, they were to be punished publicly as an example because "restitution was

---

[42] This judgment is based on these facts: Gui was an important legal advisor to the count; he would start in 1253 to actively investigate the count's officials and produce statutes to govern them that followed the *constitutiones* closely, and the *constitutiones* would become the model for parts of Louis IX's *Grande Ordonnance*, which it is very likely Gui had a hand in writing.

not sufficient for illicit gains."[43] In short, the constitutions forbade the exploitation of offices for personal gain or power, and to this end they stipulated that the count would actively investigate his own men. All of this was to be implemented and enforced by *enquêteurs* who answered to the count directly. Having returned from the clearly failed crusade, Alphonse was serious about the reform of the secular power.

Gui Foucois not only likely drafted the *constitutiones*, he also was one of the first of the *enquêteurs* that they established. In 1253 he and several others traveled through Alphonse's lands hearing complaints, reforming whatever needed to be reformed and promulgating *ordonnances* as necessary to ensure adherence to the *constitutiones*.[44] The *constitutiones* provided a point of departure for the particular ordinances that Gui promulgated to deal with situations as they arose. These ordinances demonstrate that the secular officers were envisioned as definitively part of the *business of the peace and the faith* and its now long-running legal tradition. The ordinances reiterate sections of the documents of 1229, the statutes of Raymond VII discussed above, Alphonse's oath of 1251, and canons from various Church councils: the bailiffs were not to be clerics, suspect of heresy, or infamous in any way; they were to remain within the confines of their jurisdictions; they were not to oppress the Church, to implement new extractions or exploitive customs; they were not to build or condone the building of new fortifications; there was to be only one bailiff in each jurisdiction; and they were generally to be the enemies of *maleficium*, not its agents.

They were to pursue this enmity against "evil deeds" by diligently, with good counsel, and according to the customs of the region and the statutes of the land, conducting "inquisitions" into the truth. If a crime was proved, they were to do what the "divine honor and the statutes of the land" demanded of them. The ordinances then spelled out what some of these demands

---

[43] EAAP, 59–62.
[44] Ibid., 64, 71.

were—many of them directly dependent on ecclesiastical judgment. For example, because contempt for the keys of the Church "prepares the way for heretical depravity," they reiterated that contumacious excommunicates were suspect heretics and that their goods should be confiscated. Falling under this legislation would be anyone directly associated with heretics, breakers of the peace, oppressors of the Church, bad lords in general, usurers, and even those who did not attend Mass regularly—anyone who fell into crime or public mortal sin and persisted in their error. The ordinances spelled out many distinctions between when confiscations of goods for heresy, breaking the peace, and other crimes were called for and when they were not, for whether wives of heretics had rights to their dowries, for whether creditors of heretics were to be paid out of their confiscated goods, and for whether the fiefs of heretical vassals reverted to their lords. Gui was developing statutes and procedures not to build a secular "State," as we might be tempted to think, but rather, in order to enforce the secular side of the *business*, to construct the type of secular power it demanded, and they were built upon a conceptual and legal foundation that was as much secular as spiritual.[45]

The legal world of the inquisitors into heresy was being constructed at the same time and on the same foundations. For example, in 1246 at a council in Béziers, the bishops promulgated an extensive body of canons and a lengthy *consilium* to the Dominican inquisitors in response to a papal mandate that they cooperate with the inquisitors and provide solutions to tricky legal problems.[46] A great many of the canons dealt with what we might consider ecclesiastical issues: the morality of the clergy, their praying of the Office, churches having the proper books and vestments, and the like. These canons can be compared to the seemingly "secular" aspects of Alphonse's legislation concerning his officers, such as the protocols to ensure accountability or the procedure for appeal. Both the

---

[45] Ibid., 64–71.
[46] Mansi, 23:691–704, 714–24.

spiritual and the secular sides needed to ensure that their personnel were fulfilling the demands of their offices. The council at Béziers, however, was also concerned with the functioning of inquisitions into heresy—that is, with their procedure and definitions—and it is here that we can see that there was no hard line between the spiritual and the secular. For example, excommunication was the ubiquitous censure for infractions, and the canon on excommunication restated the 1226 statute promulgated by Louis VIII and Cardinal Romano. This same statute, as we have seen, was reiterated by Alphonse in his statutes. Excommunication and felony had a fundamental identification shared by both aspects of the *business*, the *peace* and the *faith*. As with Alphonse's secular legislation, the ecclesiastical legislation was integrated fundamentally into a body of law that was as much secular as ecclesiastical.

However, the two swords were distinct, even if united in a single *business*, and in both the secular and the ecclesiastical legislation we can see clearly that corruption on the part of the other side was feared. The council in Béziers stated not only that the goods of heretics and breakers of the peace were to be confiscated but also that *only* those appropriately condemned were to be subject to the penalty, and the council forbade secular powers from using an excommunication simply as a pretext for confiscation.[47] Similarly, Alphonse's ordinances stipulated that his seneschals were not to enforce excommunications promulgated in the course of disputes over money.[48] The two swords needed each other to behave properly, and they built checks into their internal procedures to make sure that the one sword's failure would not lead the other into sin. Neither excommunication nor confiscation was to be used as a means toward self-aggrandizement by either churchmen or secular officials.

But the overlap between secular and ecclesiastical law was far more extensive than the ultimate censure (excommu-

---

[47] Ibid., 23:695, 699.
[48] EAAP, 69.

nication and confiscation). As we have already seen, secular power was intrinsic to the attempt to root out heresy, and in the canons of the 1246 council, a picture of the ideal secular officer was painted and his legal obligations were spelled out. This officer was basically identical to that presented in Alphonse's statutes—though viewed from a different perspective. And counterwise, Alphonse's statutes presupposed the ideal churchman and so the just promulgation of ecclesiastical censures. The *consilium* to the inquisitors that the bishops composed in 1246 was written in order to help them become these ideal ecclesiastical judges. In law, the secular power could not perform its function without the ecclesiastical performing its function and vice versa. But beyond this, their functions were defined by each other's functions: the law that defined the office of inquisitor into heresy made no sense without the secular power, and the law surrounding the duties of the secular powers made no sense without the spiritual power.

A large body of law was being constructed in order to prosecute the *business of the peace and the faith.* This law had secular and ecclesiastical sources, but it was one body of law, growing out of the crusade and the legislation of 1229 with influences and adaptations from both sources. The 1246 council at Béziers was called "because the Catholic faith and secure peace are proven to be the foundation of all Christian religion," and it mandated that the peace oath be sworn by all according to the Council of Toulouse because only in a time of peace could the faith be freely preached, heretics be persecuted, and the sacraments be ministered.[49] That heresies might be better extirpated and the faith planted, the bishops ordered the inquisitors to observe fully the statutes and laws of the apostolic see, its legates, *and* the princes of the land.[50] Gui Foucois and Alphonse's other *enquêteurs* made ordinances "to the honor of God and to the benefit and quiet of the lands of our lord the

---

[49] Mansi, 23:691, 695.
[50] Ibid., 23:722.

count."[51] This was a single legal universe—neither the secular power nor the spiritual power controlled or made this law as a "sovereign," somehow standing outside or above it. Rather, they both worked within it, making changes or explications as necessary in the course of practice and in constant negotiation not only with each other but also with different sources of authority from within the secular and spiritual powers broadly understood. The law flowed out of the practice of orthodoxy, the *business*, when necessary, and the papacy, like the Crown, was only one source of this law. We will explore this dimension of the functioning of law much more extensively in the second part of this book.

The development of the spiritual and the secular sides of this *business* were in no way sealed off from each other, in theory or in practice, and in the formative period of the 1250s, Gui Foucois was situated right in the middle of it, a crucial personality in its development. For example, in 1249 the Dominicans were frustrated with episcopal and papal oversight and had again retired from investigating heresy, a task that had reverted to the local ordinaries. This was a setback for the *business* to which Gui and Alphonse were committed, and so, it is perhaps not surprising that Gui was instrumental in bringing the Dominicans back. Indeed, while it is well known among scholars of the Inquisition that in 1251 Pope Innocent IV called on the Dominicans of Provence to once again take up the office of inquisitor, what is less well known is that this was done only after Alphonse had made an agreement with the local bishops. The bishops agreed to cooperate fully with Dominican inquisitors so long as the individual friars were chosen personally by Gui Foucois, the count's *enquêteur*.[52] Gui, it seems, was a trusted man who had a reputation for fair-dealing and a reputation for commitment to the ideals of justice and

---

[51] EAAP, 64.

[52] "Une lettre addressée à Alfonse de Poitiers (24 mars 1251)," ed. Ch.-V Langlois, in *Bibliothèque de l'Ecole des Chartes*, vol. 46 (Paris, 1885), 389–93; HGL, 8:1313.

not self-aggrandizement. It was only after this agreement was made that papal commissions to the Dominicans were granted.

Far from being an "extension" of papal power, Innocent IV's commission was the final step in an arrangement wrought primarily between Alphonse and the local ordinaries. As per their agreement with Alphonse, the ordinaries granted the friars named by Gui their *vices* (their personal authority) in their dioceses provided that they in no way prejudiced episcopal rights and that they acted always with the ordinary's consent.[53] These same limitations were present in the papal commissions, which emphasized that the local ordinaries' authority was not to be derogated and that the friars were to work with their "counsel" and "assent."[54] The apostolic mandate was the cap on this arrangement, providing the friars the approbation necessary to travel freely and warning both the bishops and the friars to uphold their ends of the bargain, but the arrangement itself was the product of a negotiation between temporal and spiritual powers within the legal world discussed above and in pursuit of the *business*.

It is interesting to note that the inquisitor friars who were the product of this negotiation were chosen by Gui, a lay official of the count, that they bore the *vices* of the local bishops, that they were commissioned by the papacy, that they relied on the local secular officials for the prosecution of their office, and that they worked within a legal world as much secular as ecclesiastical. The two sides of the *business* remained inseparable, not just in abstraction but in practice: Alphonse and Gui worked through their influence to produce in the Dominicans the type of ecclesiastical judge that the *business* demanded, even as they worked to produce the reformed secular officials it also demanded. They were building the social order sketched out in 1229, and both the papacy and the count understood the spiritual and the temporal as two aspects of the same social reality: orthodoxy. The construction of the social architecture

---

[53] HGL, 8:1313.
[54] LTC, 3:3946, 4000, 4001.

of orthodoxy required certain institutional tools, and among these were the inquisitors into heresy and the *enquêteurs*, and so the spiritual and temporal powers built them together.

CHAPTER FOUR

From the Duty of Royal Power

But there could be nothing more fortunate for human affairs than that, by the mercy of God, they who are endowed with true piety of life, if they have the skill for ruling people, should also have the power. But such men, however great virtues they possess in this life, attribute it solely to the grace of God that He has bestowed it on them—willing, believing, seeking. And, at the same time, they understand how far they are short of that perfection of righteousness which exists in the society of those holy angels for which they are striving to fit themselves.

—St. Augustine, *City of God* 5.19

Louis IX left for Egypt in 1248 and was gone for nearly six years. The details of his adventure need not concern us here; it suffices to say the crusade was not a success. Louis returned in 1254 more committed than ever to the Davidic conception of Christian kingship, and historians have paid a great deal of attention to his reforms during the 1250s and 1260s. His establishment of itinerant *enquêteurs* as regular aspects of his governance and his so-called *Grande Ordonnance* of December 1254 are widely understood as major steps (along with the formalization of Parlement—the subject of a later chapter) toward the centralization of the nascent French State. Louis, they tell us, was constructing the foundations of absolutism.[1] William Chester Jordan has recognized three reform initiatives undertaken by the king upon his return: the curtailment of certain activities of the Jews, the establishment of the Dominican inquisition into heresy across the whole kingdom, and the reform of his secular officials.[2] When situated within the context of the *business of the peace and the faith*, as they ought to be, these three initiatives are revealed to be, in fact, components of a larger initiative within which any perceived "gap" between the temporal and the spiritual collapses. The reality of this collapse can be demonstrated not only in a detailed reconstruction of the legal and practical manifestations of the king's initiatives but also in the coherence of the life of Gui Foucois, who, having gone to work for the king in 1254, was (as he had been in Alphonse's efforts) front and center at the inception of these initiatives and continued in their prosecution through the various phases of his career.

Louis's *Grande Ordonnance* was one of his first acts after his return.[3] It was in large part an elaboration on Alphonse's *constitutiones* and *ordonnances* discussed in the previous chapter. Louis anticipated it with two smaller acts as he passed through the South on his way to Paris, acts by which he sought to remedy the abuses of his men and improve the peace and quiet of his subjects.[4] Louis Carolus-Barre has

---

[1] For example, Le Goff, *Saint Louis*, trans. Gareth Evan Gollrad, 569.

[2] William Chester Jordan, *Louis IX and the Challenge of the Crusade: a Study in Rulership*, 154–59.

[3] *The Memoirs of the Lord of Joinville: A New English Version*, trans. Ethel Wedgwood, 365.

[4] HGL, 8:1337–39.

argued convincingly that in view of the obvious influence of Alphonse's *ordonnances* both on these two acts and on the *Grande Ordonnance* (whole articles, for example, are repeated or closely paraphrased), and in view of the fact that Gui came into Louis's service as he passed through Alphonse's lands, it seems very likely that Gui had a personal hand in their drafting.[5] This likelihood is increased when we consider that Gui went immediately to work in promulgating and enforcing the *Grande Ordonnance* as a royal *enquêteur* in the South, as we will consider in depth below.

Everything about the *Grande Ordonnance* places it within the narrative of the *business of the peace and the faith*. The preface states: "From the duty of royal power, the peace and quiet of our subjects, in the quiet of whom we rest, desiring with our heart, and against the injurious and the wicked, who begrudge the tranquility and quiet of them, having the zeal of indignation, to repel injuries of these kind, and to reform to a better condition the state of our kingdom, these which are contained below we ordain."[6] It then goes on to articulate the content of the oath to which all royal officials were to swear publicly. This oath followed closely that of Alphonse's men discussed in the previous chapter. The officials swore to deliver justice without regard to persons (but with full regard for local uses and customs) and to serve the king's *iura* (rights) in good faith and without in anyway diminishing or impeding the rights of others. Like Alphonse's officers, Louis's

---

[5] Louis Carolus-Barre, "La grande ordonnance de reformation de 1254," in *Septième centenaire de la mort de Saint Louis: Actes des colloques de Royaumont et de Paris (21–27 mai 1970)* (Paris: Société d'édition "les belles lettres," 1976), 92–94.

[6] *Recueil Général Anciennes Lois Françaises*, ed. A. J. L. Jourdan et al. (Paris: Belin-Le-Prieur, 1822), 1:267; HGL, 8:1345. "Ex debito regiae potestatis, pacem et quietem subditorum nostrorum, in quorum quiete quiescimus, praecordialiter affectantes, ac adversus injuriosos et improbos, qui tranquillitati eorum invident et quieti zelum indignationis habentes, ad huiusmodi propulsandas injurias, et statum regni nostri reformandum in melius, haec quae continentur inferius, duximus ordinanda."

were to swear not to receive gifts; but Louis expounded upon the prohibition, listing in detail types of prohibited gifts and extending the prohibition to include wives and *familia*. What is more, the king's officers were not to give gifts to anyone in the king's service or their families or servants. Also, they were not to acquire any land or possessions in the lands they served.

Like those of Alphonse, Louis's *ordonnances* were designed to separate the royal officers from local contests of lordship, and the officers were, indeed, forbidden from treating their offices as positions for exploitation. They were forbidden from all sorts of activities often associated with "exploitative lordship"[7]: seizing men or their property without license, taking horses from laymen or churchmen, or imposing new extractions, customs, or burdens. The provisions for accountability were nearly identical to those promulgated by Gui for Alphonse. And like Alphonse's men, Louis's were to conduct inquisitions into all crimes.[8] We can read in Louis's *Grande Ordonnance* the whole history of the *business of the peace*—back through the work of Alphonse, the statutes of Raymond VII, the legislation of 1229, the Albigensian Crusade, the Lateran councils, and to the *pax* movements. The statutes are heavy not only with practical but also with symbolic importance.

It is true, as historians frequently point out, that royal offices were being professionalized and in a sense bureaucratized. What is incorrect is the placement of these facts within the context of the narrative of the construction of the "State," unless, of course, one is writing a genealogy of the nineteenth century. Regardless of what these offices eventually evolved into, Louis was not building an absolutist State, let alone the foundations of a secular one. In the thirteenth century the *Grande Ordonnance* was a part of something that had nothing to do with absolutism, "divine right of kings," the separation of

---

[7] Thomas N. Bisson, *The Crisis of the Twelfth Century: Power, Lordship, and the Origins of European Government*, 41–68.

[8] RGALF, 1:267–74.

Church and State, or the construction of the modern State. It was a part of the construction of a Christian kingdom.

Even the articles in the *Grande Ordonnance* against Jews must be understood not as a separate legislative initiative, distinct from the professionalization of the officials—as some historians have posited—but as integral to the rest of the program.[9] It should be remembered that one of the charges repeatedly made against Raymond VI and Raymond VII was the favoritism toward Jews. Showing favor to Jews at the expense of Christians was a mark of bad lordship.[10] Anti-Jewish statutes were shared between secular and ecclesiastical legislation: the Jews were a common "other" by which both the spiritual and the temporal protagonists of the *business* oriented themselves.[11] Louis's anti-Jewish statutes remain solidly within this tradition, being largely a restatement of Alphonse's statutes and those of any number of Church councils.[12] Louis's officials were to expel Jews who practiced usury, of course, but also those who blasphemed or practiced fortune-telling. Jews who did not commit these crimes, however, were to be protected.[13] It is not Jews as Jews that Louis was primarily concerned about in the *Grande Ordonnance*, but Jews as manifest sinners—such manifest sinners, be they Jewish or Christian, wayward knights, or the king's own officers, were the *improbi*, the "wicked," to be removed from the land.

When they are read as a secular action within orthodoxy, we can see that the articles of the *Grande Ordonnance* that not only forbid royal officers from swearing, playing games of chance, fornicating, and visiting taverns, but actually forbid *all* gambling, prostitution, and frequenting taverns (by any

9 Jordan, *Louis IX and the Challenge of the Crusade*, 154.

10 See Solomon Grayzel, "Jews and the Ecumenical Councils," *The Jewish Quarterly Review*, n.s., 57 (1967): 287–311.

11 See, for example: Mansi, 23:710–2; EAAP, 62.

12 Most notably canon 26 of Lateran III and canons 67–71 of Lateran IV (Tanner, 1:223–24, 265–70).

13 RGALF, 1:272–3; HGL, 8:1358.

except travelers) in the king's domains are not some moralizing or puritanical gloss to legislation otherwise notable for its establishment of official and bureaucratic government; they rather point to the very core of the *Grande Ordonnance*'s significance.[14] In the pursuit of the fulfillment of the "debt of royal power," Louis brought together the long-running discourse on right rulership with that on the moral life itself, and in doing so he provided a convergence between the lay and the clerical. For, this "moral" legislation was largely lifted from Church canons prescribing the correct life of the clergy.[15] To Louis in the *Grande Ordonnance* the moral life of the laity was the same as that of the clergy. And this convergence was not limited to their "personal" life but extended to their official capacities—the offices of the *Grande Ordonnance* often have a "canonical" ring to them.[16] Far from laying the groundwork for the "secular" State, the *Grande Ordonnance* was a proposal to bring the spiritual and the temporal powers further into each other. It expanded the domain in which they overlapped and strengthened their unity within an orthodoxy that included the lay and clerical estates intrinsically and that recognized through its sacramental understanding of reality that fundamentally the spiritual and the material were not only not in conflict—rather, they interpenetrated each other at every level.

This reading of the *Grande Ordonnance* is further strength-

---

[14] RGALF, 1:260, 273–74.

[15] See, for example, canon 16 of Lateran IV (Tanner, 1:243). For a thorough restatement of the moral strictures canonically placed on the clergy in France, see *Constitutione Bonfilii Senensis Episcopi* (1232), in Mansi, 23:243–46.

[16] Compare, for example, article 25 of the *Grande Ordonnance*—"Porro viam maliciis volentes precludere quantum possumus, firmiter inhibemus, ne senescalli, aut inferiores bailivi in cuasis criminalibus, vel civilibus, subditos nostros locorum mutatione fatigent, sed singulos in illis locis audiant ubi consueverunt audiri, ne gravati laboribus et expensis, cogantur cedere juri suo" (RGALF, 1:271)—with canon 37 of Lateran IV—"Nonnulli gratia sedis apostolicae abutentes, literas eius ad remotos iudices impetrare nituntur, ut reus fatigatus laboribus et expensis liti cedere vel importunitatem actoris redimere compellatur" (Tanner, 1:251).

ened when its promulgation is considered, which occurred in the context of Louis's post-crusade, multi-pronged strategy of reform. It was the "statutory" component of Louis's concerted effort to make just rulership a reality. Just as the statute made provisions for accountability in the form of inquisitions to be conducted at the end of the terms of royal officers, so Louis's post-crusade efforts began with an exercise in accountability in the form of inquisitions into the justice of his holdings and acquisitions. In the South, he charged his seneschals to begin looking into complaints and making amends and to settle outstanding conflicts, and he dispatched special inquisitors, or *enquêteurs*, with the same charge.[17] These *enquêteurs* were Gui Foucois; Philip, Archbishop of Dax, the Dominican Poncius of Saint-Gilles; and the Franciscan William of Beaucaire. They were commissioned by the king to investigate and make restitution for any possessions the king held unjustly in the seneschalcies of Beaucaire and Carcassonne[18] and were at work in Nîmes by October of 1254.[19] It was they who promulgated the *Grande Ordonnance* in the region, fully within the context of continuing and strengthening the *business of the peace and the faith*.

In the spring of 1255 a royal force led by Peter de Antolio, the seneschal of Carcassonne and Béziers, was seeking to reduce the Château de Quéribus, a pocket of resistance outside Carcassonne. Peter sought the aid of the prelates of the region and invoked the full tradition of the *business* in doing so. He was fighting against "the enemies of the peace and the faith" and currently engaged in a siege of "a place of refuge for heretics, murderers, and thieves," and so he asked for the "aid" of the Church.[20] The Archbishop of Narbonne called a council at Béziers to consider the request. Gui Foucois himself arrived at the council and read aloud the *Grande Ordonnance*, no doubt

---

[17] HGL, 8:1356–66.
[18] RHGF, 24:530; HGL, 8:1358.
[19] RHGF, 24:531.
[20] CGN, 65–66.

also explaining to the prelates the king's commitment to the *business* and the commissioning of himself and his fellow *enquêteurs*.[21] In response, the prelates agreed to the seneschal's request, although pointing out that in the past the Church's participation had always been under a papal legate. They acted now, therefore, not out of obligation but freely for the honor of the king, and because "it seemed to be the business of the peace and of the Church."[22] The promulgation of the *Grande Ordonnance* was explicitly, and not just in theory, connected to the *business of the peace and the faith*.

What is more, the *Grande Ordonnance* and the commissioning of the royal *enquêteurs* were complemented with a simultaneous extension and reorganization of the inquisitions into heresy: the Parisian Dominicans were commissioned with the office in the lands of Alphonse and throughout Louis's kingdom. In the winter of 1254–1255 Louis had asked Pope Alexander IV to commission the Parisian Dominicans because he believed they would be "especially efficacious in the promotion of the business," and the pontiff quickly complied with the king's request.[23] The king had a very close relationship with the Dominicans of Paris, and we should see in the commissioning of the Parisian friars a clear continuation of the strategy pursued by Gui and Alphonse and the understanding that underwrote it: the reform of the secular officers was an essential part of the *business* and it had to be complemented with ecclesiastical judges who sought similar goals—and the Dominicans were ideal for the job. Louis was clearly following the lead of his brother and taking the advice of his experienced *enquêteur*, Gui.

As we saw in Alphonse's statutes and in the *Grande Ordonnance*, a persistent reforming strategy attempted to separate secular authorities from the contingencies of local power

---

[21] Ibid., 68.

[22] Ibid., 67.

[23] *Corpus Documentorum Inquisitionis Haereticae Pravitatis*, 1:130, 132; *Annales Minorum*, 3:385.

dynamics. We can see the same imperative in play when, in great contrast to past commissions,[24] the pope now granted the inquisitor friars the power to coerce with ecclesiastical censure the ordinaries and revoked all the apostolic letters and privileges those ordinaries might hold that could compromise the *business* in any way.[25] The pope was commissioning inquisitors into heresy with a mandate that allowed them to bypass the local problems that had continuously plagued the *business* and to work directly with the king, who was himself setting about eliminating the problems of local secular power. This was a two-pronged development within the *business*. Indeed, the pope invoked the 1229 Council of Toulouse and the Peace of Paris by name as the inquisitors' guiding documents, and he instructed them to enforce all these statutes, which "are recognized as bearing on the business of the faith."[26] At the same time, Louis mandated that his officers enforce the 1229 documents "against heretics and marauders and those who stay contumaciously excommunicate for a year."[27] The spiritual and the secular sides were explicitly working to enforce the same body of law and to advance the same mission. The sources themselves make direct and explicit reference to its reality.

This dynamic was a mirror of that spearheaded by Gui a few years earlier for Alphonse, and so it is no surprise that he was again front and center in this extension of the *business*. Gui, in fact, had a direct and very important role in the legal definition of inquisitorial power. It was on the occasion of the commission of the Parisian Dominicans that Gui Foucois composed one of the most important works of the Middle Ages having to do with the procedure and functioning of inquisitions into heresy, his so-called *Consilium* to the inquisitors.[28]

---

[24] For example, Innocent IV's 1251 commission discussed in Chapter 3 above.

[25] *Corpus Documentorum Inquisitionis Haereticae Pravitatis*, 1:132; *Annales Minorum*, 3:385.

[26] *Corpus Documentorum Inquisitionis Haereticae Pravitatis*, 1:130.

[27] HGL, 8:1360.

[28] *Consilium* is printed in C. Carens, *Tractatus de Officio sanctissimae Inquisitionis et modo procedendi in causis fidei* (Lyon, FR, 1649), 322–47. It was

Gui wrote this work in either 1255 or 1256 during his time as an *enquêteur* for the Crown.[29] Given the role played by Gui in the development of the law that surrounded the *business of the peace and the faith*, the fundamental connections between the work of the *enquêteurs* and that of the inquisitors (to be explored more extensively in the next chapter), and the importance Gui played in getting the Dominicans to once again take up the office of inquisitor, it is not surprising that the Parisian Dominicans would have sought out his advice.[30] They, after all, were more or less new to this *business*, and he was not only the foremost expert on the law surrounding it but also thoroughly reliable, for his motivations were congruent with those of the papacy, the Crown, and the Dominicans themselves.

Indeed, not only was Gui's whole professional and intellectual career wrapped up in the *business of the peace and the faith*, but he had a special relationship with the Dominican order. In fact, his first extant writing is a letter found in the *Lives of the Brethren of the Order of Preachers*. In it he recounts how his sister had a great devotion to the friars and had visions of the Holy Spirit descending upon them and of the Blessed Virgin interceding for them. Gui refers to the friars as being sent by the Holy Spirit to preach as the apostles themselves had.[31] As a young man, he had written a song on the seven joys of the Virgin, a devotion that would be adopted and spread

---

included more often than any other in the many handbooks for inquisitors that were compiled in the thirteenth and fourteenth centuries (see Antoine Dondaine, "Le Manuel de L'Inquisiteur (1230–1330)," *Archivum fratrum praedicatorum* 17 [1947]: 85–194).

[29] For the *Consilium*'s dating see Yves Dossat, "Gui Foucois, enquêteur-réformateur, archevêque et pape," *Cahiers de Fanjeaux* 7 (1972): 23–57, at 33.

[30] On the occasion of their commission in the South in 1255, the Dominicans from Paris asked Pope Alexander IV for permission to seek legal counsel, and he granted it. The result was most likely Gui's *Consilium*; see *Regesta Pontificum Romanorum*, ed. August Potthast (Berlin: Rudolf de Decker, 1874), 2:15805.

[31] *Lives of the Brethren of the Order of Preachers, 1206–1259*, trans. Fr. Placid Conway, O.P., ed. Fr. Bede Jarrett, O.P. (London: Burns Oates and Washbourne Ltd., 1924), 44–48.

throughout Europe by the friars,[32] and as Pope Clement IV, he would introduce aspects of the Dominican liturgy into that of the papal court.[33]

Indeed, the affinity between Gui and the Dominicans was such that some historians have mistakenly assumed that he was himself a Dominican.[34] He had an obvious affinity for the way Louis and Alphonse thought, and the royal family's affection for the Mendicant orders is well known.[35] Gui and the Dominicans of Paris were members of the same network of *consilium et auxilium*—counsel and aid (the topic of the second part of this book)—and they viewed the world in basically the same way and sought to direct it toward the same goal. And so, it is not surprising that the Dominicans would ask his advice, layman or no. Nor is it surprising that Gui would have felt perfectly competent to give them counsel or that the contents of his *consilium* would make sense. These require some attention.

One of the chief issues dealt with in the *Consilium* was the relationship between the inquisitors and the local ordinaries. The first question the Dominicans posed to Gui was whether the ordinaries could continue in the business of the Inquisition after the friars had been commissioned.[36] His answer was a definitive No. He argued that the pope seemed to have recalled the *business* to his own curia, making it no longer the office of others. The inquisitors were therefore the legal equivalent of papal judges delegate, meaning that they had, in the cases com-

---

[32] *Les sept joies de la Vièrge par Guy Folqueis*, ed. C. Fabre (Le Puy, FR: Impr. Marchessou, 1920).

[33] See Stephen J. P. van Dijk, O.F.M., *The Ordinal of the Papal Court From Innocent III to Boniface VIII and Related Documents* (Fribourg, CH: Fribourg University Press, 1975).

[34] Quentin Griffiths, "New Men among the Lay Counselors of Saint Louis' Parlement," *Mediaeval Studies* 32 (1970): 259.

[35] See Lester K. Little, "Saint Louis' Involvement with the Friars," in *Church History* 33, no. 2 (June 1964): 125–48; Sean L. Field, *Isabelle of France: Capetian Sanctity and Franciscan Identity in the Thirteenth Century* (Notre Dame, IN: University of Notre Dame Press, 2006).

[36] *Consilium*, 324.

missioned to them, power greater than even general legates. The inquisitors, Gui contended, had the ability to absolve those excommunicated by the ordinaries or to excommunicate those absolved by them, for "the lesser has no *imperium* against the greater."[37] Indeed, the inquisitors, like judges delegate, received their jurisdiction directly from the pope, their provincial priors providing only the permission to exercise it. This meant that they had the power to sub-delegate, to commission others with their *vices*, others to whom, just as to themselves, the bishops must defer in the business.[38]

But, the inquisitors were not normal judges delegate. They did not impose judicial punishments or sentences, Gui argued. Rather, they enjoined penances.[39] They were more like confessors than civil or criminal judges. One of the implications of this was that their jurisdiction over those on whom they imposed penances expired only when the penance was completed, unlike those of judges delegate, whose jurisdiction ended with the expiration of their commission.[40] And so, the ordinaries did not have the power to commute penances imposed by the inquisitors, not even after the inquisitors' commission had expired. Gui was arguing for the creation of a new office in the hierarchy of the Church, one designed specifically for the prosecution of the *business of the peace and the faith*, one that was like the office of judge delegate but whose charge was equally as in the internal forum of the confessional as it was in the external forum of the court (if not more). Within the bounds of their commissions these inquisitors were rightly independent from and superior to the local hierarchy.

The office of inquisitor in Gui's *Consilium* was totally bound up with the office of the secular power. The normal

---

[37] Gui was here in total agreement with Pope Alexander IV, who wrote to the inquisitors granting them directly the power to overturn excommunications or absolutions of the ordinaries; see *Regesta pontificum romanorum*, letter no. 15805.

[38] *Consilium*, 328, 332.

[39] Ibid., 343, 345.

[40] Ibid., 343.

punishment for heresy was the confiscation of one's goods. This was a separate event, however, from the inquisitors' imposition of penances. Indeed, confiscations, Gui asserted, "do not pertain to the investigation of the friars." Rather, citing both Innocent III's *Vergentis in Senium*—which stated that heresy was treason against God—and civil law, he argued that confiscations were a consequence of the crime of *lèse-majesté* and so pertained to the prince. Essentially, Gui was asserting that heresy was simultaneously a civil and canonical offense: treason simultaneously against both God and king. And so by necessity heretics were to be dealt with through cooperating secular and spiritual authorities who had *consilium*—counsel—with each other.[41]

But, while enforcing sentences against heretics may have pertained to the prince, it was not a matter of his prerogative. Rather, those who had the power of the sword, those who exercised *potestas* were to be considered *fautores*—protectors—of heretics and to be proceeded against accordingly if there was a single omission in their duty to drive out of their lands or to punish appropriately those condemned by the Church.[42] To Gui, the prosecution of heretics as condemned by the Church was intrinsic to the offices of secular power, and negligence in this duty should be met with an immediate, severe, and canonical sanction, to be enforced by the inquisitors. Of course, such *fautores* of heretics were simultaneously guilty of the crime of *lèse majesté*, which justified action against them by other secular powers.

Gui's *Consilium*, as much in the context of its production as in its content, demonstrates the institutional and conceptual unity of the *business of the peace and the faith*. The mutual dependence between the secular and the spiritual powers is clear: the powers were fundamentally relational. Louis's reformed officers and the inquisitors relied on each other both practically and theoretically. Gui's primary focus was on the king's men,

---

[41] Ibid., 345.

[42] Ibid.

but clearly neither he nor the Dominicans understood that focus as categorically distinct from that of the inquisitors into heresy. Rather, his secular initiatives required reliable spiritual power in order to be successful. Indeed, his conception of secular power included within it the spiritual power, and vice versa. His involvement with the inquisitors was therefore a part of his efforts on the secular side of the *business*, or perhaps we should say that his efforts were simply not divided into the categories that we are trying to impose.

This interdependency between the spiritual and the secular was not simply a matter of theory or legal abstraction. Rather, it was felt immediately by the men in the field. In 1256 or 1257 the seneschal of Carcassonne Peter de Autolio sent to the king his responses to a list of complaints that had been leveled against him by the prelates of the region.[43] These responses clearly demonstrate the codependency of the two sides of the *business* as an aspect of their very definitions. Essentially, Peter acknowledged that, as the prelates accused, he had not sworn to uphold the 1229 royal statute *Cupientes*, an oath that was mandated by the king. His reason for this obvious deviation from the laws of the *business* was, as he explained, that the prelates were not themselves properly committed to it. Rather, they were attempting to use the *business* to augment their own power by using ecclesiastical censure as a weapon. In doing so, they rendered it impossible for the seneschal to fulfill his duties as stipulated in the documents of 1229.

In fact, if he did swear to the documents of 1229, he feared that it would be impossible not to sin and so threaten his eternal soul. The seneschal offered the following example: the prelates often unjustly excommunicate the king's men based on movements of their own will and in diminution of the king's rights and then refuse to absolve these men unless they comply with their wishes. Now, if the seneschal were to seize the goods of these men, as he would be held to do if he swore to *Cupientes*, he would clearly sin; but if he failed to do so, having sworn,

---

[43] HGL, 8:1419–27.

he would commit perjury. Because the prelates were unjust, justice on the part of the royal official would paradoxically require that he act criminally.[44] Sinning prelates rendered his office in the *business* impossible, and he gave multiple examples of this problem, a problem that penetrates to the very core of the *business*.

As Peter pointed out, the prelates frequently attempted to extend their rights to the first fruits and tithe beyond what was customary and excommunicated anyone who resisted them. If the goods of these excommunicates were seized, the result would be turmoil and scandal among the barons and through all the land, which would contradict the very purpose of *Cupientes*, which was the peace.[45] What we must recognize is that what this conflict between the bishops and the seneschal reveals is not some fundamental divide between the temporal and the spiritual powers, but rather the opposite: their profound mutual dependence. The *business* was constantly threatened by self-serving parties who attempted to use it in their contests for power, and this was recognized by everyone involved.

Neither the spiritual nor the secular could fulfill its obligations unless its counterpart did so. In 1257 the Dominican inquisitor in Toulouse Rainaud de Chartres wrote to Alphonse of Poitiers.[46] He informed the count that when he and his companion arrived in Toulouse, they learned that the inquisitors who had preceded them had sentenced some relapsed heretics who abjured their heresy to perpetual incarceration and then handed them over to the secular judge. The judge, with disregard for the inquisitors' sentence, had the prisoners burned. Rainaud was struggling with doubts of conscience: could he look past the secular judge's actions without danger to his own soul, or was he obligated, rather, to promulgate ecclesiastical censure against him? Some people, he stated, argued that unless the sentences of the inquisitors were fol-

---

44 Ibid., 8:1420.
45 Ibid., 8:1422.
46 Ibid., 8:1409–10.

lowed, the entire cause of their labors against heresy would be overthrown. Others, however, argued that he threatened the "business of the inquisition" if he acted against the overly zealous secular judge. What course Rainaud should take might have been unclear to him, but what was very clear to him was that for an inquisitor to continue in his office when the secular power was not acting congruently with him threatened the whole *business* and (just as in the case of the seneschal above) actually threatened his soul.[47] The stakes were very high.

In order for the *business* to advance, the ordinary holders of both the temporal and the spiritual powers had to commit themselves to it, be compelled by a higher power to enforce it, or be simply sidestepped through the establishment of "extra-ordinary" offices. We can see in 1254 a concerted effort on the part of Louis IX and the pope to use all three of these options. The *Grande Ordonnance* was aimed largely at the first option, at reforming the ordinary officials. The friar inquisitors into heresy were clearly, by 1255, an example of the latter option, that of sidestepping the ordinaries, so to speak. And the secular *enquêteurs* were a combination of the last two options. It is indicative of the relationships between these various layers of the *business* that in his dilemma discussed above, Friar Rainaud ultimately sought the counsel of two royal *enquêteurs*, Stephen of Bagneux and Stephen of Béziers,[48] and they advised him to ask for clarification from the pope.[49] How are we to draw lines between Church and State, either in theory or practice? Unfortunately, we do not have the pope's response.

The three reform initiatives of Louis after 1254 find a unity within the *business*, and they were wrapped up fundamentally with the spiritual power. Louis was not laying the foundations for a secular "State"; he was pursuing the program of orthodoxy. Gui Foucois and the Dominicans, and more

---

[47] Ibid.

[48] Ibid., 8:1410; EAAP, xxxv, xxxvn4, 310n1, 334, 349n2.

[49] HGL 8:1410.

distantly the pope, were likewise pursuing this program, and together they were building the social architecture it required. The *enquêteurs* and the inquisitors were part of this architecture: two pillars of the same structure.

CHAPTER FIVE

Desiring That the King Not Gain Some Advantage from This Violence

> David therefore reigned in the earthly Jerusalem, a son of the heavenly Jerusalem.
>
> —St. Augustine, *City of God* 17.20

THE MISSION OF GUI FOUCOIS and the other royal *enquêteurs* of 1254–1262 was broadly to clean the slate, to right all wrongs committed by royal officials in the past, and to start holding the current officials to the high standards demanded by the king, to the standards of "Davidic" lordship.[1] The subject matter of their investigations, therefore, was simply everything that touched the secular power. Because the primary way in which secular power was manifested was the confiscation of rights and property, the *enquêteurs'* investigations focused on the propriety of such confiscations. But, like the regular royal officials, they were also concerned with the maintenance and

---

[1] Most of the surviving records of this mission are found in RHGF, 24:530–691.

enforcement of people's rights, especially those of the king.[2] Essentially, any change in the status of the land that was not precipitated by a crime was unjustified: in direct opposition to the modern and postmodern understanding, peace was the assumed status quo. Thus the distinctions between *lex, ius,* and *usus* are unclear, with what was law, what was established, and what was right all being understood as the same when peace reigned.[3] Since peace, the fruit of justice, was the objective of the secular power, only the fracturing of this "peaceful" status quo could justify intervention; otherwise, the secular power itself fractured the peace and was criminal.

The same considerations applied to matters of the faith: the temporal powers could intervene in cases of heresy and contumaciousness in excommunication only because these were understood as felonies of the same caliber as homicide or rebellion.[4] Because the fracturing of the peace was hardly rare (it was a fallen world, after all), the potential scope of royal action was great; there were no "constitutional" limits. But this is not absolutism: royal power was not the "ordering principle," the source of all legitimacy; it was, rather, force countering force.[5] (This

---

[2] Sometimes they worked directly with the seneschals in the enforcement of royal rights. For example, Louis sent Gui Foucois and Guillelmus de Autono, the seneschal of Beaucaire, to investigate his rights over the monastery at Crasse and the authenticity of certain charters and privileges that the abbot held (LTC, 3:4282, 4317). See also the work establishing the king's rights in Maguelonne (LTC, 3:4156, 4312).

[3] See Warren C. Brown, *Violence in Medieval Europe,* 10–11. Alasdair MacIntyre has written of this aspect of medieval law and ethics: "To say what someone ought to do is at one and the same time to say what course of action will in these circumstances as a matter of fact lead toward a man's true end and to say what the law, ordained by God and comprehended by reason, enjoins," see *After Virtue* (Notre Dame, IN: University of Notre Dame Press, 2007), 53.

[4] HGL, 8:1379; X 5.7.10.

[5] The prologue to the so-called *Établissements de Saint Louis,* the codification of law and procedure around Paris promulgated sometime in the 1260s, states: "Looys, roy de France par la grace de Dieu, à tous bons cretiens habitanz u reaume et en la segnorie de France, et à touz autres qui I ssont present et à venir, salut en nostre Segneur.

aspect of secular power will be explored in detail in connection to Parlement in Part II.)

What this meant was that the activity of the secular power was ultimately prohibited from being "proactive." It had to be justified as a reaction to prior violence. A "new" custom was basically synonymous with a "bad" custom, both of them subjecting victims to an arbitrary will and so reducing them to servitude.[6] And so, inquisitions into the status and customs of the land were prerequisite for any secular action, and in the case of the *enquêteurs*, such inquisitions were the first step in absolving the Crown of any criminal guilt from past "proactive" (illegal, unjust, or contrary to the status quo) actions—that is to say, violent actions.[7] The inquisitions of the *enquêteurs*,

---

Por ce que malice et tricherie est si parcreüe etre l'umein lignage que les uns font souvent aus autres tort et ennui et meffeiz en maintes manieres contre la volenté et les coumendemenz de Dieu, et n'ont li pleuseur peor, ne espouvantement de cruel jugement Jhesu-Crist, et por ce que nos voulons que le pueple qui est desouz nos puisse vivre leaument et em pes, et que li uns se gart de forfaire à l'autre par la peor de la decepline du cors et de perdre l'avoir, et par chastier et refrener les maufeteurs par la voie de droit et de la reideur de jostice, nous en apelons l'aide de Dieu qui est juge droiturier seur touz autres, avons ordené ces establissemens selone les quels nos voulons que l'en use es cours laies par tout le reaume et la segnourie de France"; see *Établissements*, 2:474.

In English, this reads: "Because evil and deception have grown so much among the human race that some men often do other men wrong and harm, and commit crimes against them against the will and commandments of God, and many have no fear nor dread of the severe judgment of Jesus Christ, and because we wish the people beneath us to be able to live honestly and in peace, and so that one will refrain from doing harm to another through fear of bodily punishment or the confiscation of property, and in order to punish and control offenders by means of law and rigorous justice we call upon the help of God, who is a just judge above all others, and we have set out these laws which we want to be put into practice in the secular courts in the whole kingdom and lordship of France" (*The Établissements de Saint Louis: Thirteenth-Century Law Texts from Tours, Orléans, and Paris*, trans. F. R. P. Akehurst [Philadelphia: University of Pennsylvania Press, 1996], 3–4).

[6]   See, for example, article 26 of the *Grande Ordonnance* (RGALF, 1:271). See also the case of the men of Laurano (RHGF, 24:687, 561–62 [244]).

[7]   See, for example, the typical ruling in RHGF, 24:677.

therefore, should not be seen as something substantively distinct from the inquisitions of the ordinary royal officials or the multitude of inquisitions launched by the king's Parlement. Rather, they were an additional "layer" of secular power who were charged with clearing the backlog of cases and providing accountability to the ordinary officials.

This point is important because what we see in the work of the *enquêteurs* is that, in their attempt to enforce "Davidic" power, they operated within the body of law that had grown up around the *business of the peace and the faith*, a body of law that was, as we have seen, integrally both spiritual and temporal. Because of this, their work was contiguous in one direction with that of the ordinary secular officials, such as those in Parlement, and in the other direction with that of ordinary ecclesiastical officials, such as the papal judges and bishops. In neither direction do we encounter hard theoretical, institutional, or legal breaks. The ecclesiastical judges operated under the same principles as did the secular judges; peace was the assumed status quo.[8] Men such as Gui Foucois (as well as the Dominican order generally), as we will see, moved between the two extremes of the continuum without apparent difficulty. Far from being two "parallel" legal systems or competing "absolutisms," they were a single legal universe that "floated" between two poles of authority without descending from either—this was the very nature of the *business*.

Gui Foucois was an *enquêteur* for the king in the seneschalcies of Beaucaire and Carcassonne from 1254 through 1257. During this nearly four years, the *enquêteurs* conducted scores of inquisitions and listened to untold complaints against the king's men. While they ruled in many cases,[9] it seems their major achievement was the investigation of the complaints and

---

[8] Charles Duggan, "Papal Judges Delegate and the Making of the 'New Law' in the Twelfth Century," in *Cultures of Power*, ed. Thomas N. Bisson (Philadelphia: University of Pennsylvania Press, 1995), 195.

[9] RHGF, 24:530–41; LTC, 3:4202, 4207, 4208, 4244, 4269, 4272, 4278, 4320, 4321, 4367, 4376.

the interrogation of witnesses.[10] This evidence was then used by the *enquêteurs* who succeeded them in 1259–1262 to make formal rulings.[11] In order to assess whether a secular official had acted properly in a certain situation, an *enquêteur* had to first assess whether the crime that justified his action had actually been committed, and if so, whether the punishment applied by the secular official was the proper one. Within the context of the *business of the peace and the faith*, this meant making investigations and judgments not only concerning "civil" or "feudal" matters but also concerning heresy and excommunication and all the canon law connected to them, as well as the precise relationships between these canonical situations and secular power.

A great deal of their work was "feudal" in character, dealing with questions of jurisdiction, custom, exploitation, and violence. For example, the men of the fortified village of Redorta complained that the bailiff of the king compelled them, against their ancient liberty, to carry the "returns" of the king from the village to Carcassonne or Narbonne (the *enquêteurs* ruled in their favor).[12] The men of Asellanus claimed that the bailiff of the king, against their ancient liberty, forbade them from grazing their animals in a certain wood, forced them to pay a new *pedagia* when their merchants passed through certain regions, reduced them to servitude in multiple other ways. The *enquêteurs* investigated each claim, determining some to have merit and others to be frivolous, and ordered the bailiff

---

[10] RHGF, 24:541–614.

[11] Ibid., 24:618–91. The most complete study of these records is Joseph R. Strayer, "La Conscience du Roi: Les Enquetes de 1258–1262 dans la sénéchaussée de Carcassonne-Béziers," republished in *La Faculté de droit et des sciences économiques*, ed. Mélanges Robert Aubanas (Montpellier, FR: La Société d'Histoire du droit et des institutions des anciens pays de droit écrit, 1984), 725–36.

[12] Ibid., 24:634. We cannot tell what the king's "returns" were. They were certainly revenues and produce that the villagers were obliged to pay to him, but the documents are not specific.

to return the town to its customary liberty.[13] Such examples could be multiplied.[14]

Often, such petitions were long lists of complaints in which heresy might figure in some but not in others. Heresy is not presented as anything exceptional, but as simply the circumstances surrounding certain actions of the king's men and not substantively distinct from other "feudal" matters. B. Faber de Pesincho and Peter Raymond Vitalis claimed that their entire village had been reduced to servitude when the king's seneschal and bailiff imposed upon it the obligation to deliver to Carcassonne the king's "returns" from the village. They also claimed the seneschal fined the villagers sixty pounds when they burnt down a house that by rights belonged to the king on account of the heresy of the occupants. They asked that the money be returned and the servitude lifted. The *enquêteurs* ruled that the king was right to fine them for the house but that the old customs were to be restored and the servitude lifted.[15] The Hospital of Saint John de Ulmis had multiple claims against the seneschal who, they said, despoiled them unjustly, for example, in the confiscation of a vineyard predicated upon the heresy of the women who held it, even though the women had converted. The *enquêteurs* denied the petition concerning the vineyard but ordered restitution made concerning others.[16]

Whenever confiscations had been predicated on heresy, the *enquêteurs* needed to determine whether the person from whom a confiscation was made was really a heretic or somehow associated with heresy. We can see in the surviving records of their interrogation of witnesses and their rulings that they

---

[13] Ibid., 24:655.

[14] See, for example, RHGF, 24:629, 631, 636, 638, 643, 653, 659, 667, 670, 672, 674, 675, 683, 688, 690. See also the 1259 records of Alphonse's *enquêteurs* for numerous examples; in *Correspondance administrative d'Alfonse de Poitiers*, ed. Auguste Molinier (Paris: Imprimerie Nationale, 1895), 1:1909–23. These are the types of cases that constituted the bulk of Parlement's work, to be considered in a later chapter.

[15] RHGF, 24:634.

[16] Ibid., 24:659.

made very subtle distinctions within the various categories of heretical activity and association, as well as the categories of other crimes.[17] Were the subjects of confiscation "thieves," "marauders," or "evil doers"?[18] Could a person be considered a defender of heretics?[19] Had a heretic ever been seen in his home? Was a person themselves a heretic? Had he fled an inquisition out of fear? Had he broken out of a prison? Had he been convicted or immured by an inquisition? Was he "signed with the cross for heresy"?[20] Was he a *faidit* (a term discussed in detail on pp. 128–136)?[21] A *faidit* and a heretic, perhaps?[22] Was he excommunicated? If so, for how long?[23] If a woman was seeking a confiscated dowry, had she married a heretic or *faidit* knowingly?[24] Was she a "believer" in her *faidit* or heretic husband?[25] Was the marriage even valid to begin with?[26]

A few detailed examples allow us to see the type of investigations that the *enquêteurs* were carrying out. A certain Bernardus claimed that a woman, Guilhelma, owed him thirty-one *sous* for some bread that he had sold her. Because Guilhelma had subsequently been convicted of heresy and her property confiscated, Bernardus asked the king for his money.

---

[17] Because the examples are so numerous, my list below is not exhaustive and is drawn from the interrogation of only one witness, Dominus Arnaldus de Laurano (RHGF, 24:545–64).

[18] RHGF, 24:553 (124), 556 (161), 558 (189), 559 (207).

[19] Ibid., 24:546 (15), 556–57 (171).

[20] Ibid., 24:545 (6) (7), 546 (18) (25), 547 (31) (38), 548 (45) (48), 549 (63), 550 (71) (73), 551 (93), 552 (107), 555 (152), 557 (184), 558 (193), 559 (203) (204) (207–10), 560 (214) (219) (226), 563 (268).

[21] Ibid., 24:678. The examples of *faiditi* in the records are far too numerous to cite. Indeed, *faidimentum* was an issue in the vast majority of cases, and the problem of the *faiditi* is discussed in detail on pp. 128–136.

[22] In the majority of cases where the heresy of a man was in question, so too was his *faidimentum*. For example, see Ibid., 24:557 (174), 559 (207–10), 561 (232) (235) (236) (241) (242), 562–63 (254), 564 (271).

[23] Ibid., 24:546 (16), 549 (49) (66), 559 (204), 563 (268), 564 (271).

[24] For example, Ibid., 24:545 (8), 546 (19) (20), 549 (60), 551 (90) (91) (98), 552 (111) (112) (113), 553 (117), 554 (138), 555 (146), 561 (233).

[25] HGL, 8:1443.

[26] RHGF, 24:548 (43), 550 (75) (80).

The *enquêteurs* instructed the seneschal to make an inquisition: had the transaction occurred after Guilhelma was in manifest heresy, was already cited for heresy, or her heresy known publicly? If the answer was no, restitution was to be made; if yes, Bernardus, in fact, opened himself to prosecution.[27] In another case, Guiraudus Trepati asked for the inheritance that had been given to him by Amblardus de Villa Longa but was being held by the king's men on account of heresy. This was unjust, Guiraudus argued, because Amblardus had never been condemned for heresy. Through their inquisition, the *enquêteurs* determined that Amblardus had in fact fled for fear of the friar inquisitors. He had indeed later been absolved, but this was not the crucial point. Rather, the case turned on whether or not he had been a fugitive and therefore excommunicated for more than a year. If he had been, the confiscation stood, but if not, restitution was to be made.[28]

In a third case, the abbess of the monastery of Anonensis petitioned for the restoration of the returns and revenues that her mother had given to her that were being held by the king. In their inquisition the *enquêteurs* determined that while the abbess's mother was "immurata" (convicted of heresy) after the said donation, the crime of heresy had long preceded it. Nevertheless, the *enquêteurs* could find nothing in the papal decretals stating that a heretic's prohibition from alienating their property began at the commission of their crime (rather than at their conviction for it), even though there were certain customs that maintained this to be the case. The *enquêteurs*, therefore, decided that it was an open legal question and that until the king might try it in his court, the abbess was to have possession of the revenues.[29]

The *enquêteurs'* investigations into heresy often mirrored those of the ecclesiastical inquisitors because, in order to get to the bottom of the propriety of a secular action, they had

---

[27] Ibid., 24:685.
[28] Ibid., 24:683.
[29] Ibid., 24:685. See also HGL, 8:1441.

to determine the "canonical" status of the object of the action, even when there had been no ecclesiastical involvement in the original action, as was common in the early years of the *business* and in the aftermath of the wars of 1240–1243.[30] If the *enquêteurs* could determine that someone had been a heretic through the testimony of witnesses, the confiscation could stand, even if there had never been an ecclesiastical condemnation for heresy.[31] For example, the *enquêteurs* restored to Pagana Guerina d'Onos and Aladaicis, sisters, the lands and home of their father, Bernard, which had been confiscated by the castellan of Monreale on account of heresy, because Bernard had been neither cited nor condemned for heresy and the *enquêteurs* could find no witnesses to his supposed heresy.[32] At the same time, however, ecclesiastical condemnation was accepted as definitive evidence of heresy or other legal liability and was clearly preferred.[33] The preference for ecclesiastical condemnation was such that in 1259 Louis limited the legal liability of suspicion of heresy without ecclesiastical censure—allowing such "suspect" persons the right to at least present their petition.[34]

---

[30] An item from the testimony of Leo de Rebentino is demonstrative of the type of information the *enquêteurs* were after and the type of questions they put to the witnesses: "Item contra petitionem dominae Ermengardis de Riuterio, uxoris condam B. de Pomars, dixit se audivisse dici quod dicta Ermengardis fuit immurata pro haeresi. Item dixit se vidisse Bernardum de Riuterio, patrem dictae Ermengardis, et B., Fratrem eiusdem Ermengardis, faiditos tempore comitis Montis Fortis, et dictus Bernardus pater fuit interfectus per Gallicos in guarnisione de Vaure, ubi se miserat contra comitem Montis Fortis. Item interrogatus super facto dominae Cavaiers, si fuit haeretica, dixit quod non, immo dixit magnum mendacium ille qui dixit, sed fuit bona et catholica et fuit monacha Pruliani, ubi cum habitu moniali decessit ut bona domina" (RHGF, 24:592 [654]).

[31] HGL, 8:1441–42.

[32] RHGF, 24:642.

[33] So, for example, cases in which evidence was collected as to whether someone was excommunicated when they contracted a marriage, for example, RHGF, 24:569 (333) (344). After the *enquêteurs* pressed a certain witness on the point, he admitted to not remembering if a certain woman wore one cross or two (RHGF, 24:575, [415]).

[34] HGL, 8:1440.

The *enquêteurs* worked definitively within both the "ca-nonical" and the "secular" aspects of the body of law which had grown up around the *business of the peace and the faith*. Take, for example, the cousins Bernard and Roger Durfort. Their fathers Sicardus and Peter, respectively, had fought against the northern crusaders, as was attested to by several witnesses, but had ultimately sworn homage to Louis VIII in the late 1220s.[35] Bernard and Roger asked for the lands that their fathers had possessed at the time of these oaths and that had later been confiscated because the vassals who held them were condemned for heresy.[36] However, witnesses reported that Si-cardus had been a *faidit* in the war of 1240,[37] and, after the war, Bernard had married a woman whose parents were manifest heretics and was seen staying with other heretics.[38] While we are not given an explanation, the *enquêteurs* ruled in favor of Roger and against Bernard. In this ruling, heresy and rebellion, the "feudal" and the "canonical," are thoroughly intertwined and are both considered by the *enquêteurs* to be intrinsic to the performance of justice.

But how the "feudal" and the "canonical" aspects of the law interacted with each other was not always clear, and the *enquêteurs*, sometimes taking counsel with the king himself, had to make interpretations as circumstances arose. For example, it had been established that a lord did not lose his lands on account of vassals who held them being condemned for heresy,[39] but what about the reverse situation? Was it just that a vassal be deprived of his fiefs because of the heresy of his lord? The *enquêteurs* said no.[40] That it was generally

---

[35] RHGF, 24:554, 567, 597, 623–24.

[36] Ibid., 24:623–24.

[37] Ibid., 24:597.

[38] Ibid., 24:587.

[39] See, For example, Ibid., 24:633, 634, 637, 640, 676, 679, 684

[40] Ibid., 24:630. If a lord's property was confiscated *occasione criminis*, a vassal was likewise not to be deprived of his fief (Ibid., 24:629). Similarly, a prop-erty owner was not deprived of his property if the leaseholder was a heretic (Ibid., 24:654, 660).

unjust for one to be punished for the crime of another was the principle behind Louis's and his *enquêteurs'* careful treatment of the wives of heretics or *faidits.* The central question concerned the wives' dowries: could the king retain them when he had confiscated them as a part of the lands and goods of their heretical husbands? Writing to his *enquêteurs* in 1259, Louis stated that he wanted the wives of heretics to have their petitions heard unless they had fled for fear of the inquisition, they had persevered in contumacy after being cited, they had heretics discovered in their houses, they had been imprisoned, or they had been relaxed to the secular court.[41] However, restitution of their dowries was to be made only if it could be demonstrated that they married before the man had become a heretic or if his heresy was not publicly known.[42]

Within these guidelines, the *enquêteurs* ruled overwhelmingly in favor of widows seeking their dowries or orphans seeking those of their mothers.[43] But here too, circumstantial judgments had to be made. When three brothers petitioned to have returned to them some goods confiscated from their father when he fled for fear of the inquisition, goods that had originally come from their maternal grandfather, their request was denied.[44] And when a woman sought the dowry of her mother in addition to the amount added to it by her father, who had been condemned for heresy, the *enquêteurs* restored the original dowry but denied the augmentation.[45] Ermenjardis de Leuco was signed with the cross for heresy, and her

---

[41] HGL, 8:1440–41. While the records do not seem to exist, it would be interesting to know how the *enquêteurs* ruled in the case of Rixenda de Rivo Vallis Daniae. According to one witness, her father had been a *faiditus* against Simon de Montfort, she was infamous for having her husband killed in bed on their wedding night, as well as for committing adultery with the chaplain de Rivo (RHGF, 24:571 [369]).

[42] HGL, 8:1441.

[43] For example, see RHGF, 24:629, 630, 632, 634, 635, 643, 646, 652, 654, 659, 661, 668, 687. See also, Strayer, "La Conscience du Roi," 731–32.

[44] Ibid., 24:631.

[45] Ibid., 24:659.

husband was "immurati," and when she sought her dowry, which had been confiscated along with the rest of her husband's property, the *enquêteurs* restored it.[46] The children of Raymund Berengarii de Muro Veteri asked that their father's property be returned to them. When Raymund had died, his wife held their inheritance and it was confiscated from her by the king's men on account of her being condemned for heresy. Raymund, though, had been a Catholic and faithful man, and the *enquêteurs* granted their request.[47]

A certain P. Guilhelmi asked for some property and rights of his late father that had been set aside as a dowry for his sister but then confiscated on account of his father's heresy. He was denied because he and his late father were *faidits*, his father having fought against Simon de Montfort (or his son, Amalric) and he himself against the king. The king, though, proceeded to grant his sister, Mabilia, her dowry directly, sidestepping her brother.[48] The *enquêteurs*, with the direct input of the king, adapted the law at the point of intersection between the "ecclesiastical" and the "secular" in order to fulfill the requirements of justice. The emphasis on the weak, on widows and orphans, allows us to see how this justice was intrinsic to Davidic lordship, which was itself integral to the *business*.

It was during his time as an *enquêteur* that Gui Foucois wrote his *Consilium* to the Dominican inquisitors (discussed in the previous chapter). And given the content of the *enquêteurs'* work, we can clearly understand how he was qualified—in fact, probably the most qualified man—to give to the Dominican's working definitions of *credentes*, *fautores*, *receptatores*, and *defensores* of heretics, to explain to them relationships between the prince and the inquisitors and those between the inquisitors and the bishops, to give them advice concerning the number of witnesses to call and when to be lenient and when to be severe, and to advise them about the time of grace, about

---

[46] Ibid., 24:660. See also Ibid., 24:668.
[47] Ibid., 24:683.
[48] Ibid., 24:660–1, 594.

simple people who are easily led astray, and about the confiscation of heretics' goods.[49] This was not mere theory (though the *Consilium* is full of citations of canon and civil law), but the fruit of experience. Gui had been intimately involved in every stage of the *business of the peace and the faith*, one of its chief architects as it transitioned from crusade to governance. The fact that he was a layman and a servant of the Crown certainly did not compromise his ability to give good advice to churchmen, nor did it introduce any tension in his relationship with the inquisitors. Far from it, the inquisitors and the *enquêteurs* seem to have seen each other as engaged in different dimensions of the same task—the task of orthodoxy.

A "Davidic" lord's charge to protect the weak included the responsibility to protect the Church's rights, properties, and privileges. In 1259 Louis wrote to his *enquêteurs*, instructing them concerning how he wanted them to proceed in certain tricky situations. In addition to outlining the treatment of widows and orphans, he told them that he had neither the desire nor the ability to confiscate the goods of churches and give them to others. So, if ecclesiastical persons petitioned for the restoration of their goods, the *enquêteurs* were to see to it that justice was served quickly.[50] We can see in the records of the *enquêteurs* that this instruction was followed. In multiple cases, the *enquêteurs* returned goods and rights to ecclesiastical persons or institutions, citing Louis's letter directly. There is a clear, indeed explicit, bias in favor of ecclesiastical institutions.[51]

Joseph Strayer's contention that the *enquêteurs* were especially hard on bishops and that in being so they were acting in accordance with the king's suspicion of a temporally endowed clergy is therefore doubly puzzling.[52] Not only is there little evidence for this position in the actions of the *enquêteurs*, but

---

[49] *Consilium*, 322–47.
[50] HGL, 8:1443.
[51] See, for example, RHGF, 24:663, 665, 669, 672, 673, 674, 679.
[52] Strayer, "La Conscience du Roi," 734–35.

it takes only a cursory look at the records of Louis's Parlement to become convinced beyond a doubt that he applied equal vigor to the protection of the temporalities of ecclesiastical persons and institutions as he applied to the protection of all established rights.[53] Louis's concern with all abuses of power was rooted in the scandal and the fracturing of the peace they caused. Indeed, ecclesiastical abuses rendered the *business of the peace and the faith* as impossible as did secular abuses.

In an attempt to buttress his laicization thesis, it seems Strayer has projected onto Louis a position similar to that of the baron's league of 1246.[54] The league challenged the jurisdiction of the clergy over all things except heresy, marriage, and usury, and they suggested that the clergy return to the condition of the primitive Church as they saw it, a purely contemplative Church, leaving the active life to the lay nobility. The barons believed the clergy had derogated their temporal rights and their wealth in an apparent zero-sum contest over temporal power wherein the clergy abused the censure of excommunication.[55] (The barons were clearly influenced by the propaganda of Frederick II[56]—something Matthew Paris

---

[53] The examples are far too numerous to cite. Nevertheless, by looking at just one Parlement, that of February 1261, the point can be demonstrated: There were nine *arrêts* in favor of the claims of ecclesiastical persons and four against. The court declared itself incompetent to hear one case because it fell under ecclesiastical jurisdiction, and declared in another case that a prior's claim to ecclesiastical immunity was unfounded. A bailiff was also suspended for slapping a cleric. What is more, the king overturned the ruling of an earlier Parlement against the Abbot of Saint Vincent in a dispute over rights to a certain wood because "he did not want churches to lose through such a ruling, nor did he want such rulings made against churches"—a paraphrase of what Louis wrote in 1259 to his *enquêteurs* and repeated often in the *enquêteurs'* rulings; see *Actes*, 1:513–57.

[54] Joseph Strayer, "The Laicization of French and English Society," in *Medieval Statecraft and the Perspectives of History*, ed. John F. Benton and Thomas N. Bisson (Princeton: Princeton University Press, 1971), 251–65.

[55] *Hist. Frid.*, 6.1:467–69; LTC, 2:3569.

[56] See, for example *Hist. Frid.*, 6.1:391–93.

pointed out.)[57] The truth is that neither Louis nor his *enquê-teurs* had a problem with the temporal power of prelates; they did however have a problem with the abuse of that power. This position was not substantively different from the one they held toward all power, secular as well as ecclesiastical, and it will be explored extensively in Part II of the present work.

In actual fact, bishops seldom appear in the records of the *enquêteurs*. Strayer cites two cases that are, in fact, the two with the most documentation. The Bishop of Béziers petitioned the *enquêteurs*, including Gui Foucois, for the return of a list of rights and properties, including a castle, control of the keys to the city gates, various jurisdictional rights, and rights to certain taxes for specific forms of economic activity.[58] After a thorough investigation into the bishop's claims, the Parlement of November 1265 ruled in his favor regarding some petitions and against him in others and compromised in still others.[59] In the second case, the Bishop of Lodève brought extensive claims against the king and his men. He claimed to have full jurisdiction over all cases, civil and criminal, the sole right to call the men of the diocese to muster. The king's claims and the bishops were in direct conflict. Unfortunately, we do not have the findings of the *enquêteurs*. All we know is what is written in the margins of the *enquêteurs'* record of the bishop's petition—statements like *"non invenitur episcopus aliquas induxisse probationes de hoc."*[60] Furthermore, the case is not substantively different from any number of others dealing with conflicts over jurisdiction between both ecclesiastical and secular persons, cases which dominated the proceedings of Parlement. What these cases demonstrate is not some sort of anti-episcopal prejudice, but rather that as temporal lords the bishops were

---

[57] Matthaei Parisiensis, *Historia Anglorum*, ed. Frederic Madden (London: Longmans, Green, and Co.: 1869), 3:16; in English: *Matthew Paris's English History*, trans. J. A. Giles, vol. 2 (London: Enry G. Bohn, 1853), 199–203.

[58] RHGF, 24:692–95.

[59] *Actes*, 1:995.

[60] RHGF, 24:539–41.

treated by Louis as temporal lords. Their claims to rights or properties were judged according to the same criteria. In fact, what prejudice can be found is clearly, explicitly in favor of ecclesiastical institutions.

If we view Louis not as a proto-absolutist engaged in the business of building a "State," but instead as a "Davidic" monarch engaged in the *business of the peace and the faith*, we can easily see how all the various types of cases handled by the *enquêteurs* fit together. Indeed, while some of the cases encountered by the *enquêteurs* focused on "feudal" matters and others on matters surrounding heresy, the gap between them was bridged by the most common problem faced by the *enquêteurs*, the *faidits*, a term that has unavoidably come up a few times already. Indeed, the *faidits* bridge the gap not only between the "feudal" and the "heresy" sides of the *enquêteurs'* work but also between that work and the work of the ecclesiastical inquisitors into heresy. But, what was a *faidit*? By the 1250s a *faiditus* was someone *extra pacem*—someone outside the peace. Within the *business of the peace and the faith*, this was synonymous with rebellion against either the king or the Church. In 1264 Louis himself defined *faiditi* as those who "make war against the universal Church or us or our successors."[61] But this was not what *faiditus* had always meant, and a brief look at the evolution of the word's meaning affords us an opportunity to see the development of the *business of the peace and the faith* and the shared legal tradition of the *enquêteurs* and the inquisitors.

To the Carolingians the word *faida* and its variations had multiple uses, all of which revolved around violence, in particular personal violence pursued on account of some grievance, and so *faida* has often been translated as "feud."[62] A distinguishing feature of a *faida* was that it occurred beyond the control of the king—it was, we might say, "private."[63] Such violence

---

[61] *Gal. Christ.*, 1:Instrumenta, 10.

[62] Brown, *Violence in Medieval Europe*, 15, 76.

[63] For example: "De diversis generationibus hominum qui in Italia commanent: volumus ut, ubicumque cupla contigerit unde faida crescere potest,

posed a problem for the Carolingians'"Davidic" conception of kingship, and they attempted to control *faida* by compelling the parties to make peace, normally through payments of compensation for damages and an oath.[64] Within the Carolingian conception, *faida* was lumped in with other violations of the Christian order such as thievery, plundering, homicide, arson, or perjury, and the royal obligation to stop *faida* was presented together with such obligations as protecting widows and orphans.[65] As a result the *faiditi* were subject to the *bannum* and ultimately exile;[66] as the emperors wrote, they were "marked as enemies to us and to our people."[67] This understanding of *faida* continued into the tenth- and eleventh-century peace movements and imperial constitutions of the same period.[68] *Faida* was basically the opposite of *pax*.

It was this understanding of unrestrained violence that we see in the sources leading up to and during the Albigensian

---

pro satisfactione hominis illius contra quem culpavit secundum ipsius legem cui neglegentiam commisit emendet. De vero statu ingenuitatis aut aliis quaerelis unusquique secundum suam legem se ipsum defendat"; see *Pippini capitulare* (ca. 790), in *Karoli Magni Capitularia*, ed. A. Boretius, in MGH *Leges Capit.* II, 1:201.

[64] *Capitulare Haristallense* (779), in MGH *Leges Capit.* II, 1:51.

[65] *Capitulare Saxonicum* (797), in MGH *Leges Capit.* II, 1:71–72; *Capitulare Missorum in Theodonis Villa Datum Secundum, Generale*, in MGH *Leges Capit.* II, 1:122–26; *Capitulare Haristallense* (779), 51; *Capitulare Missorum* (819), in MGH *Leges Capit.* II, 1:289–90.

[66] The often repeated article *De faidis cohercendis* reads: "Si quis aliqua necessitate cogente homicidium commisit, comes in cuius ministerio res perpetrata est, et conpositionem solvere, et faidam per sacramentum pacificari faciat. Quod si una pars ei ad hoc consentire noluerit, id est aut ille qui homicidium conmisit, aut is qui conpositionem suscipere debet, faciat illum qui ei contumax fuerit ad praesentiam nostram venire, ut eum ad tempus quod nobis placuerit in exilium mittamus, donec ibi castigetur, ut comiti suo inoboediens esse ulterius non audeat, et maius damnum inde non adcrescat"; see *Collectio Capitularium Ansegisi*, ed. G. Schmitz, In MGH *Leges Capit.* II, 1:637; see also *Capitulatio de partibus Saxoniae*, in MGH *Leges Capit.* II, 1:70.

[67] *Capitula Italica*, in MGH *Leges Capit.* II, 1:217.

[68] See, for example, *Pax Sigiwini Archiepiscopi Coloniensis* (1083), in MGH *Leges Const.*, 1:603–04.

Crusade. And exile (including the confiscation of all property) remained the appropriate sanction (though in the South of France the sanction was, of course, no longer controlled by the emperor or even the king until 1226).[69] To the Church, the *faiditi* were included as "enemies of the Roman Church" along with heretics and all their supporters in a general way: they, like arsonists and thieves, were breakers of the peace.[70] It was primarily in this sense that the word was used in the documents of 1229 and Raymond VII's statutes of 1233.[71] However, it could also be used in a way that focused on the sanction of exile and so signify anyone who had lost his property or been exiled, justly or not. In this sense it could be translated as "exiled" or "disinherited." In the Peace of Paris,

---

[69] One of the statutes, in 1181, promulgated by the consuls and Count of Toulouse reads: "quod is aliquis homo vel femina de Tholosa faidibat, ut guerram faceret comiti vel alicui homini vel femine habitanti in civitate Tholose vel in suburbio vel in rebus eorum mobilibus et immobilibus, quod post malefactum postea non redeat in civitate Tholose vel in suburbio ullo modo" (HGL, 8:360–61). See also: Philippe Ménard, "Rotiers, soldadiers, mainadiers, faidits, arlots, Réflexions sur les diverses sortes de combattants dans la Chanson de la croisade albigeoise," *Perspectives Médiévales* 22 (1996): 166.

[70] See, for example, HGL, 8:646, 648.

[71] Canon 35 of the 1229 Council of Toulouse reads: "Item statuimus ut aliquis amicitiam, familiaritatem, vel treugas non habeat cum fayditis, vel aliis qui guerram moverunt: de bonis suis expensas faciat contra illos, et damna data restituat, allas ad utilitatem domini puniendus." Canon 34 is directed against those who rebel against their lords and canon 36 against "latrones et ruptarios" (Mansi, 23:202). In the statutes imposed upon Raymond by the legate and the king and promulgated by him in 1233, we read: "Item statuimus, ut tranquillitas pacis in terra nostra plene et inviolabiliter observetur, et quod ruptarii, faiditi, predones, latrunculi et stratores de tota terra nostra expellantur et receptatores eorumdem animadversione debita puniantur. Item statuimus quod quicumque pacem de cetero violaverit, si monitus a nobis vel per certum nuncium nostrum no emendaverit infra terminum sibi assignatum, omnia bona ipsius occupentur" (HGL, 8:967). Justine Firnhaber-Baker is wrong to treat the word *faiditum* as narrowly synonymous with the word "heresy" as it is used in the 1229 Council of Toulouse ("From God's Peace to the King's Order: Late Medieval Limitations on Non-Royal Warfare," *Essays in Medieval Studies* 23 [2006]: 21).

Raymond VII swore to make restitution to all those whom he or his allies had "made *faiditi* [exiled] on account of the Church and the lord king of France and the count of Montfort."[72] As late as 1241, Raymond pledged to the Bishop of Albi that he would not receive any people "made *faiditi* or banned" by the bishop's court.[73]

As the sanctions of confiscation and excommunication grew together and the enemies of the peace and the faith became synonymous with the "enemies of the king and the Church" over the course of the *business*, however, this morally neutral meaning (simply "exiled" or "banned") disappeared. As the monarchy stepped into the place of the *pax*, the violators of the peace, the *faiditi* who in the earlier phase of the crusade were referred to as enemies of the Church, became equally enemies of the king.[74] As we have already seen, all breaking of the peace became rebellion against the king and the Church, as did all heresy, and the sanction was the same confiscation and excommunication. And so, after 1226, in most sources *faiditus* can be translated as "rebel."

In the work of the *enquêteurs* of the 1250s and 1260s, therefore, there is no substantive distinction between those who fought against Simon de Montfort, those who fought against Louis VIII, and those who fought in the wars of 1240–1243; all were *faiditi*—violent men, exiled men, and rebellious men—and all were subject to identical legal sanctions. This was the case even though the war under Simon did not involve the Crown, the war under Louis VIII was a crusade with both papal and monarchical elements, and the wars of the 1240s lacked papal involvement (and so, could be seen as simply "feudal"). By the late 1250s, the unity of the *business* as it developed through the wars of the 1240s, and especially after 1254, was read back through its entire history. By the late

---

[72] HGL, 8:881. See also the submission of the Count of Foix (HGL, 8:904).

[73] "Faiditi fuerint vel banniti" (HGL, 8:1058–09).

[74] HGL, 8:1053–54. See also: Ménard, "Rotiers, soldadiers, mainadiers, faidits, arlots," 166.

1250s the *business* was perceived as a single initiative, and any who opposed it were held to be guilty of the same crime: they were *faiditi*.[75]

To be a *faiditus* was to be one who had done *malum*—evil. A couple *faiditi* brothers, for example, made "all the evil that they were able to make."[76] In fact, one was not properly a *faiditus* unless one had done *malum*. So, the *faiditus* status of a hunchback, for example, who could not do *malum*, was mitigated, as was that of those under eighteen years of age.[77] *Faiditi* are depicted as committing all types of violent crimes, from stealing tithes to plundering to murdering clergy.[78] All such *malum* was an affront to the king and, as he assumed the role of the *pax*, essentially rebellion.[79] Being *extra pacem* was the same as being *extra pacem regis*—outside the peace of the king.[80] Raimund de Auriaco was a *faiditus* because he had been accused of murdering a woman as she lay in bed, and he "was exiled from the land of the lord king, and his possessions occupied on account of this crime and held by the lord king."[81] Those who had taken up arms in direct war against the king were the most obvious and

---

[75] This treatment of the whole series of Albigensian conflicts as phases in a single conflict that was, at essence, the same persists throughout the entirety of the *enquêteurs'* records. In 1259, Louis IX wrote to his *enquêteurs* and explicitly linked together as *faiditi* those who had fought against Simon de Montfort, his father, and himself (HGL, 8:1442–43).

[76] "Totum malum quod facere poterant" (RHGF, 24:573 [395]).

[77] RHGF, 24:569 (343), 573 (391). In one ruling the *enquêteurs* write: "Intelligimus autem de faidimento non esse culpandos juniores decem et octo annis, vel decrepitos vel mente captos, vel gravi infirmitate aut alio justo impedimento detentos, vel invito detentos ab hostibus, vel etiam mulieres quae cum hostibus remanserunt, nisi aliter eorum proditioni facto vel dicto consensisse probentur" (RHGF, 224, 669); Louis himself exempted minors and cripples from the penalties due to *faiditi* (HGL, 8:1442–43).

[78] Ibid., 24:572 (381), 591 (646), 612 (923).

[79] Sometimes this is expressed directly as a *faiditus*: "faciendo ei [the king] malum" (RHGF, 24:588 [602]).

[80] See, for example, RHGF, 24:570 (349) (354), 577 (450), 583 (547), 586 (576), 588 (611), 595 (700) (719), 599 (751), 604 (819).

[81] "Fuit exul de terra domini regis, et possessiones eius occupatae propter illud crimen ad manum domini regis" (RHGF, 24:612 [918]).

the most numerous examples of such *faiditi*. *Faidimentum* was used interchangeably with *subversio*, *rebellio*, or *proditio*,[82] but the word *faiditus* itself was used more widely, demonstrating the conceptual unity between all violence and rebellion.

Those *extra pacem*, the *faiditi*, were necessarily both excommunicated and in rebellion.[83] And one could become a *faiditus* either through an act of violence or through remaining contumaciously in a state of excommunication. Either way, one placed himself *extra pacem* and *extra ecclesiam*. In the records of the *enquêteurs*, it is not always clear whether a particular *faiditus* was first a rebel and then a contumacious excommunicate or became a rebel because he was contumacious[84]—either way he was a *faiditus*. And the fact that we cannot tell suggests that the distinction was not conceptually relevant to the *enquêteurs*. While in the records it is very common for *faiditi* to also be condemned for heresy or to be on the run from the ecclesiastical inquisitors, what we see in the 1250s and 1260s is that a *faiditus* was anyone who, while not necessarily himself a heretic,[85] had in some way fought against the *business of the peace and the faith*. And so, we see that as a matter of course *faiditi*, heretics, and contumacious excommunicates treated together, particularly with regard to the sanctions against them. The king, for example, claimed rights to "the possessions and inheritance of *faidits* and of those condemned for heresy."[86]

---

[82] For example, RHGF, 24:666. In the 1259 records of Alphonse's *enquêteurs*, *faidimentum* is used far less often than the general *guerre*, though in the same way; see CAAP, 1:1912, 1919–22.

[83] Men often are described as "*faiditi* and enemies of the Church;" see, for example, RHGF, 24:684.

[84] For example, a certain man was a *faiditi*; he was finally captured by the friar inquisitors and imprisoned for heresy; he was then hanged by the king's men (the punishment for rebellion) (RHGF, 24:659).

[85] It needs to be emphasized that "heretic" was not used to identify people who held certain beliefs. It was used to identify people who lived a certain lifestyle—that of the "perfecti" or the "good men." When I say that the *faiditi* were not necessarily heretics, I do not mean that they did not "believe" the same doctrine as these heretics.

[86] HGL, 8:1302, 1466.

In the work of the *enquêteurs* the close conceptual identification between *faiditi* and heretics manifests itself most clearly
in their treatment of widows who were seeking their confiscated dowries. Throughout their rulings, a woman would be
denied her request if she had married her husband after he was
a heretic or a *faiditus* or if she was a "believer" of her heretic
or *faiditus* husband.[87] Their treatment of women whose husbands' property had been confiscated for heresy was mirrored
absolutely by their treatment of women whose husbands had
fought against the king—it was, within the *business*, ultimately
the same offense and, as we have seen multiple times, was met
with the same sanction. Brunissenda petitioned the *enquêteurs*
for the return of her dowry that had been confiscated on
account of her husband's "faidimentum" in the war of 1242,
arguing that she and her children had never opposed "the lord
king or the Church." She had married before the war, and so
her petition was granted.[88] However, when Ermenjarda asked
for the return of her dowry and certain other properties that
had been confiscated from her husband after he had been held
as suspect of heresy and then escaped and fled from the inquisition, the *enquêteurs* determined that nothing was to be
returned because her husband had been a *faiditus* at the time
of the Count of Montfort and in the wars of the 1240s and had
fled for heresy—in both cases his wife's crime was the same
and the sanction against her was identical—confiscation.[89]
A certain Austorga sought the return of her dowry and the
augmentation made to it by her husband, which, she attested,

---

[87] What it would mean for a wife to be a "believer" of her heretic husband is
obscure enough, but what it might mean for her to be a "believer" in her rebel
husband is even more so. The sense we get from the sources is that "believer"
was a term that was often used to indicate a significant level of support for
someone who was somehow implicated in heresy or related activities. The
fact that the sources speak casually of wives possibly being believers of both
heretic and faiditus husbands reveals the level to which the investigators
conceptually united heresy and rebellion.

[88] RHGF, 24:646.

[89] Ibid., 24:647, 569 (339), 597 (733). See also Ibid., 24:652, 560 (214).

was confiscated when her husband was captured for heresy, though he was later acquitted. The *enquêteurs* ruled that the dowry was to be restored but that the augmentation required more investigation because many witnesses attested to the *faidimentum* of Austorga's husband in the wars of the 1240s, and it could have been confiscated on account of this.[90] Within the logic of their proceedings, *faidimentum* was treated no differently than heresy; in fact, they were often interchangeable. A certain woman's request for the return of her dowry, which was confiscated because her husband was a *faiditus*, was granted because in their inquisition the *enquêteurs* found that she was "catholic and honest."[91] Another woman sought the dowry that was left to her by her brother because he "was catholic and did the king no harm."[92]

The *faiditi* provide a conceptual bridge to the work of the ecclesiastical inquisitors and allow us to see that while the endeavors of the *enquêteurs* and the inquisitors were distinct, they overlapped and took place within a single legal universe. In one set of ecclesiastical inquisitorial records from 1262–1266, *faiditi* are especially prominent.[93] The inquisitors asked the witnesses about *faiditi* in the same sort of way that they did about heretics: Did someone have them in their house? Did someone feed them or eat with them? Did they know they were *faiditi*?[94] The *faiditi* themselves were not heretics, but they were associated with heresy: they sometimes travel with heretics or stay with them in a certain home and are sometimes described as *faiditi pro heresi* or *fugitivus et faiditus propter haeresim.*[95]

---

[90]   Ibid., 24:679, 551 (93), 559 (210), 570 (353), 593 (668), 603 (800).

[91]   Ibid., 24:651, 552 (107), 555 (154), 567 (325), 570 (358), 573 (393), 577 (461), 587 (598), 603 (806) (809).

[92]   Ibid., 24:657.

[93]   Jean Duvernoy, "Cathares et Faidits en Albigeois vers 1265–1275 (Ms Mb 161 de la Bibliothèque Municipale de Carcassonne Extrait du Fonds Doat t. XXV de la Bibliothèque Nationale de Paris)," *Heresis: Revue d'hérésiologe médiévale* 3 (1984): 5–34.

[94]   Ibid., 10, 25, 26, 27.

[95]   Ibid., 10, 26, 27.

But the *faiditi* remain the breakers of the peace as well. According to one witness, a heretic named Raymundus Gauterii stayed at a certain house for eight days and had with him nine or ten persons, among them certain known "faiditi et fugitivi propter haeresim, et arma portantes, scilicent ballistas et arcus, et enses et cultellos serranos." The owner of the house fed the heretics as well as the *faiditi*,[96] who were armed and, unlike the "heretics," ate good food and drank wine. The *faiditi* were not heretics themselves, though they traveled with the heretics and adored them, and some of the *faiditi* were fugitives after having been summoned by the inquisition on account of heresy. While the inquisitors were clearly focused on the heretics themselves, these *faiditi* were integral to their conception of what was to be rooted out and fell within their purview. This mirrors the work of the *enquêteurs*: the inquisitors were primarily concerned with personal relationships (to eat with a heretic or a *faiditus* was a very bad thing), while the *enquêteurs* were primarily concerned about property and legal rights (a woman lost her inheritance for marrying a heretic as much as by marrying a *faiditus*), but there were no hard lines between these offices within the *business of the peace and the faith*.

We can begin to understand what it meant when Louis IX defined *faiditi* as those who "make war against the universal Church or us or our successors."[97] Conceptually, to make war on the Church was to make war on the king, and vice versa. One could become a *faiditus* through armed rebellion against the king or through fleeing from the inquisition; these were two manifestations of the same essential crime: *faidimentum*. To be a *faiditus* meant to be a breaker of the peace, and as we have seen, "the peace" and "the faith" could not be separated within the *business*, which provided the context for the work both of the *enquêteurs* and the inquisitors. A *faiditus*, like a heretic, found himself on the wrong side of a single body of law that moved between ecclesiastical and secular poles: he had

[96]   Ibid., 25.
[97]   *Gal. Christ.*, 1:Instrumenta, 10.

to beware the (mostly friar) inquisitors as much as the (mostly friar) *enquêteurs*.

A person's "canonical" status bore directly on his "feudal" status, and while it did so in a complex manner, it was not in a manner extrinsic to feudal law itself. Indeed, for the king to determine what was demanded by justice in order to maintain peace, he needed to know all of the circumstances. Factors we might consider "religious," "spiritual," or "canonical" were as pertinent as factors rooted in rights or property when determining the correct course of action because the king's office was not bound within some sort of legal positivism in which the system itself ultimately had self-referential validity. Instead, justice was directed toward an immediate telos—the maintenance of peace—that was itself directed toward an ultimate telos—salvation. All factors were relevant to the extent that they bore on this objective. Spiritual considerations, then, were not interruptions of an external force into the functioning of an otherwise self-sufficient secular conception of order and power. To the contrary, temporal power could be said to be legitimate only to the extent that it was ordered toward a goal that it shared with the spiritual power: salvation through faith and love—orthodoxy.[98] And so, every action of the temporal power had an intrinsic spiritual dimension, and likewise every action of the spiritual power had an intrinsic temporal dimension. The situation in the South of France provides an especially fruitful opportunity to see how such a conception was manifested in institutional reality.

What we see in the South of France was an actual integration of the secular and ecclesiastical offices into each other, both at the institutional level and at the level of personnel. In 1259 Louis wrote to his *enquêteurs* answering certain questions

---

[98] See Yves Congar, "L'Église et l'état sous le regne de Saint Louis," in *Septieme Centenaire de la mort de Saint Louis*, (Paris: Belles Lettres, 1976), 260. Clarence Gallagher has demonstrated that in the thirteenth century all "law" was understood ultimately as an expression of theological truth and the aim of law was to establish justice; see *Canon Law and the Christian Community* (Rome: Università Gregoriana Editrice, 1978), 69, 127.

they had concerning their office. He instructed them to rely on the sentences of the inquisitors into heresy in determining whether or not someone was a heretic. If an ecclesiastical inquisition was pending against someone who had made a petition for restitution to the *enquêteurs*, the *enquêteurs* were to consult with the inquisitors and look at their *acta*. If the inquisitors told them that it was likely the suspect would be condemned, no restitution was to be made.[99] In the same letter, Louis told his *enquêteurs* not to deny a petition simply because the petitioner was suspect of heresy, reserving such a denial for those condemned by the inquisitors into heresy, even though in *Cupientes* (1229) he had said otherwise.[100] Some historians have read into this a later softening of Louis's position toward heresy, a sort of humanitarian turn away from his more rigorous youth when he was under the influence of the cardinal legate and his mother.[101] But this is a misreading. What we are, in fact, seeing is the formation of an institutional apparatus for the *business*, one in which the secular and the ecclesiastical could rely on each other entirely.

In *Cupientes*, Louis had instructed his men to hold inquisitions into heresy so that he could determine against whom he was to move. This was in keeping with the legal and practical situation of 1229, at which time "manifest" heretics abounded and the pope's own instructions called for the secular power to suppress them directly, in addition to those heretics actually condemned by ecclesiastical authorities.[102] Nevertheless, as we saw earlier, from as far back as Lateran III, and definitively at the Council of Toulouse in 1229, in the ideal, ecclesiastical judges would exclusively establish canonical status and then those determinations would have direct secular or feudal im-

---

[99] HGL, 8:1441.

[100] Ibid., 8:1440.

[101] William Chester Jordan, *Louis IX and the Challenge of the Crusade: A Study in Rulership*, 157.

[102] See the 1210 letter of Innocent III to Count Raymond of Toulouse, X 5.40.26.

plications that would be enforced by the secular powers. As we also saw, it was one of the central struggles of the *business of the peace and the faith* to make this ideal a reality.

By around 1260, with the firm establishment of the Parisian Dominicans as inquisitors that could be wholly trusted, and with the reform of the bailiffs and seneschals, this ideal was in many respects realized. Probably the clearest description of the interdependence of the secular and ecclesiastical juridical apparatuses is found in *Li livres de jostice et de plet*, the vernacular compilation of royal law and procedure from around 1260. The work describes the king's involvement with heretics in detail, focusing, of course, on the confiscation of property, but this is not grudgingly inserted as a sort of bow to ecclesiastical pressure. Rather, the law and procedure described is precisely what we saw develop over the course of the *business* and especially through the work of the *enquêteurs* discussed above, including the treatment of widows and the provisions surrounding sustained excommunications. This was most certainly a royal law, dictating the proper rights and responsibilities of the Crown, and worked out through the functioning of royal officials such as Gui Foucois. And, significantly, within *Li livres de jostice*, the Crown's role is wholly dependent upon ecclesiastical inquisitions, which are taken to be totally reliable.[103] In the work's list of situations in which the king can make an inquest, heresy is absent. However, he is charged to investigate all cases having to do with rights and property, to investigate his own officials, to aid the poor who cannot defend their own rights, and to hold inquisitions into those renowned for evil, robbers, sinners, and others who customarily bring injuries upon their fellows.[104] Again, in this list we can see the whole history of the *business of the peace and the faith*.

The ecclesiastical inquisitors were therefore necessary

---

[103] 1.3.7, in *Li livres de jostice et de plet*, ed. P. Chabaille (Paris: Firmin Didot Frères, 1850), 12–13.

[104] 19.44.1–16, *Li livres de jostice et de plet*, 317–18.

for the king to fulfill his office and so, appropriately, he not only requested that they be appointed but also paid their expenses.[105] The inquisitors depended upon a papal mandate for jurisdiction, and they clearly worked toward the realization of the papacy's ideal Church, but they were equally necessary for the king's realization of his ideal, and they depended on him as well.[106] The coherence of the offices of the inquisitors and the *enquêteurs* relied on these ideals being congruent. The reality of this congruency is attested to in the development in the late 1250s and 1260s of permanent institutional bridges between the inquisitors and the secular power, as well as in total financial interdependence.

So, just as one can move conceptually from the work of the "secular" power through to that of the "spiritual" power without encountering any "hard" breaks, one can likewise see that there were no such institutional (or even bureaucratic!) breaks between the two. For example, in 1260 Alphonse appointed Jacobo de Bosco as a permanent, salaried companion to the inquisitors into heresy.[107] Wherever the inquisitors traveled, Jacobo was to make contact with the local secular officials and arrange for their needs to be met. He also took diligent notes concerning the proceedings of the inquisitors and served as their council concerning the rights of the count.[108] When a seneschal or one of Alphonse's *enquêteurs* was investigating the propriety of a confiscation predicated upon heresy, they would sometimes deal directly with the inquisitors,[109] but normally they worked through Jacobo, who took counsel with the inquisitors and reported back to the secular court.[110]

---

[105] LTC, 3:4489; HGL, 8:1435–56; *Urban IV, Reg.* 2965.

[106] Louis's support of the ecclesiastical inquisition was therefore not, as Elizabeth Hallam would have it, a peculiar consequence of his personal, exceptional orthodoxy (Elizabeth M. Hallam and Judith Everard, *Capetian France, 987–1328*, 2nd ed. [New York: Longman, 2001], 297).

[107] LTC, 4:4810, 5601, 5631.

[108] CAAP, 2:1947–49; HGL, 8:1453–54.

[109] Ibid., 1:300, 303, 325, 388.

[110] Ibid., 1:428, 493, 779.

When Alphonse heard that the inquisitors into heresy were making great expenses in the city of Toulouse, he wrote to Jacobo to see if they might consider moving to a less expensive location.[111] When the inquisitors asked Alphonse to pay for a notary and a servant to help in their task, he wrote to Jacobo telling him to make it happen.[112] Jacobo filled this position for nearly ten years, over the course of which a number of friar inquisitors not only came and went, but Jacobo himself also became an expert in the law that surrounded the *business*. Indeed, Alphonse relied on Jacobo for expertise not only in the law of heresy but also in that surrounding his rights to certain forests, concerning the insertion of certain clauses into the instruments of restitution in order to ensure the preservation of his rights, and the like.[113]

The inquisitors into heresy were commissioned by the pope[114] and sent under mandate from their superiors. But they came as much at the behest of Alphonse and Louis, who wanted them to prosecute the *business of the faith* in such a manner that their "lands might be purged of heretical filth and the divine name of majesty in the same land perpetually honored,"[115] as they did at the behest of the Church, and by 1260 they were integrated into a legal and institutional apparatus that was as much "secular" as it was "ecclesiastical."[116] By the 1260s the *enquêteurs* were more often than not also Mendi-

---

[111] Ibid., 1:948.

[112] Ibid., 1:412–3.

[113] Ibid., 1:948.

[114] See, for example, LTC, 4:4727, 4955; *Corpus Documentorum Inquisitionis Haereticae Pravitatis Neerlandicae*, ed. Paul Fredericq (Ghent, BE: J. Vuylsteke, 1889), 1:134.

[115] CAAP, 1:932, 949.

[116] As in Alphonse's lands, through the 1260s the Parisian Dominicans acted as inquisitors throughout the rest of the kingdom, and they did so both with a papal commission and at the request of Louis; see, for example, *Urban IV, Reg.*:2965. In these papal commissions, the friars were told explicitly to work within the statutes both of the councils and of the forms of peace that had been made between the Roman Church, the king of France, and Raymond of Toulouse.

cant friars working to ensure "justice, especially with regards to miserable people,"[117] and to "emend all conflicts and fractures in lands and anything else that is right according to God,"[118] and they too came with a papal commission[119] and under the mandate of their superiors.[120]

We are also in a position to understand the coherence of the lives of groups such as the Mendicants or men such as Gui Foucois. When trying to make sense of the Mendicants as *enquêteurs*, William Chester Jordan suggests that they perceived something religiously important in what they were doing. In light of the preceding chapters, his suspicion is confirmed and certainly loses its air of improbability. Likewise, Yves Dossat's exploration of whether Humbert of Romans meant inquisitions into heresy or *enquêtes* when he mentioned friars conducting "inquisitiones, visitationes et correctiones violentie," becomes moot, or at least it loses much of its significance. Humbert could simply have meant both, or either—they just were not that different.[121] Indeed, the Mendicants were sometimes called on to act as "*enquêteurs*" for the pope, investigating violations of papal rights.[122] Also, we can see in many bishops' resistance to the Mendicants' hearing confessions and preaching in their jurisdictions more than just jealousy over, say, the offerings that came along with such activities.[123] Rather, these sacramental functions were wrapped up directly with their offices as *enquêteurs* and inquisitors. The inquisi-

---

[117] CAAP, 1:1043.

[118] Ibid., 2:1886.

[119] LTC, 4:4957.

[120] CAAP, 1:1010–14, 2:1886.

[121] Yves Dossat, "Inquisiteurs ou Enquêteurs? À propos d'un texte d'Humbert de Romans," *Bulletin Philologique et historique* (1957): 105–13.

[122] *Bullarium Ordinis FF. Prædicatorum*, ed. Thomas Ripoll and Antonin Brémond (Rome: Ex Typographia Hieronymi Mainardi, 1729–1740), 1:435.

[123] For example, see Pope Alexander IV's stern reprimand of the Archbishop of Arles in 1257 for promulgating sentences of excommunication against the Mendicants for hearing confessions and preaching (*Gal. Christ.*, 3:450).

tors were more confessors than judges delegate, assigning penances, not sentences, and the *enquêteurs* were often called on to preach—for example, in favor of the king and Count Alphonse's crusade.[124]

There was not a legal, an institutional, a personal, or a conceptual hard break between the inquisitors and the *enquêteurs*—far from it. In fact, legal concepts such as *faidimentum* and institutional offices such as that of Jacobo de Bosco provided bridges between the two offices and united the secular and the spiritual powers within a single initiative that was the *business of the peace and the faith*, not an institution or even a legal "system," but rather an initiative that manifested itself in all aspects of society, in a certain social order or architecture. It is hard to find here two parallel legal systems or institutional structures, one ecclesiastical and one secular. Rather, the one "system" that did exist was both ecclesiastical and secular. This is the difficulty for modern scholars. Within the logic of the "State," within the assumptions that underpin modern political theory, there is no room for such multi-polar arrangements. Who was in charge? Who made the laws? Who decided when to go to war? We must be looking at two rival States! But, as I hope is now clear, we are not looking at "States" at all. What we are looking at is a sacramental society that did not assume that difference necessarily meant conflict. Christ's human nature and his divine nature were in perfect agreement within his single personhood. The three persons of the Trinity formed one God. The Old Testament was fulfilled, not abolished, in the New. Different powers could coexist—in fact, they simply did coexist. That was the nature of the world. Everything had a temporal and a spiritual component. Nothing that *was* existed outside the realm of "religion," and "religion" was not understood as something *beyond* the material—water, oil, bread and wine, the death of a certain man were necessary for salvation.

Peace was found not in the unity forged by the overwhelm-

---

[124] CAAP, 1:1044.

ing violence of the "State" but in the partnership, really the friendship, of these powers engaged in a *business*, in the pursuit of a goal—the sanctification of the world and, ultimately, salvation. Gui Foucois was at the very center of this *business*.

CHAPTER SIX

Gird Thy Sword upon Thy Thigh, O Thou Most Powerful (Ps 44)

> But, true justice is not to be found save in that com-
> monwealth, if we may so call it, whose Founder and
> Ruler is Jesus Christ—for, no one can deny that this
> is the weal of the people. This name, with its varied
> meanings, is perhaps not quite in tune with our lan-
> guage, but this at least is certain: True justice reigns
> in that state of which Holy Scripture says: "Glorious
> things are said of thee, O City of God."
>
> —St. Augustine, *City of God* 2.21

IN THE PRECEDING CHAPTERS I have described thirteenth-century France as sacramental and incarnational. What
I hope has been made clear is that the secular power and the
spiritual power were not operating in different realms. Rather,
the spiritual power was a power precisely insomuch as it operated in the secular world, and the secular power was a power
precisely insomuch as it worked toward a spiritual end. What
made them "powers" and not just violence on the secular side

or ritual functions or preaching on the spiritual side was the combination of their spiritual legitimacy and their efficacy in the temporal society: both were the Church, clerical and lay, in action. The Church in action both constituted the kingdom and pointed beyond it to the unity of Christendom and, ultimately, of humanity itself.

To the modern mind, so used to the idea of the secular as something fundamentally distinct from the spiritual, this can be a difficult concept. But what needs to be accepted is that the Catholicism of the thirteenth century was in no way the "spiritualized" Christianity of the modern period, which seems to be the ultimate basis for the contemporary determination of what is "religious." When Catholics talked about "the world," they did not mean simply the physical realm. They meant the realm of sin, the "city of man." And when they talked about the "kingdom of God," they did not mean heaven only; they meant the realm of grace. The "city of man" and the "city of God" were everywhere and always intermingled.[1] All of creation was permeated with the spiritual, and the spiritual, as far as men were concerned, was encountered in the realm of material things.[2] There was neither a "secular" realm nor a "spiritual" one—in the modern understanding of those words—*everything* was both. This does not mean that the spiritual and the secular (in the medieval understanding of the words) were the same. But it does mean that they existed within a single social space— which the thinkers of the early and High Middle Ages tended to call the Church, the *ecclesia*—and made no sense divorced from each other.

It is perhaps not difficult for us moderns to understand how the spiritual power could have a place in a sacramental order (it was, after all, defined as power over the sacraments themselves), but more difficult is for us to see that the secular power was no less integrated into it. We have already seen this in connection with the persecution of the *business*, especially

---

[1]   See St. Augustine of Hippo, *City of God* 10.32, 15.22, 18.54.

[2]   See, for example, ST I, q. 118, a. 2, ad 3; SCG IV, ch. 74.

with regards to the concept of Davidic kingship, but it deserves some more attention. The images and themes of Davidic kingship are omnipresent in the artifacts of Louis's reign. Rooted in a long tradition that stretched, according to the legends in Louis's time, back to the baptism of Clovis himself (although, in actuality, only back to the unction of Pepin the Short), the Capetians of the thirteenth century understood themselves from within the narrative of Israel.[3] This can be seen clearly in the windows of Sainte-Chapelle, constructed between 1246 and 1248, where the king is depicted as the direct heir to the kings of Israel.[4]

It can be even more profoundly seen in the *Ordo ad consecrandum et coronandum regem*—the *Order to Consecrate and Coronate the King*—commonly known as the *Ordo of 1250*, which was produced sometime in the 1240s, and the very similar *Ordo of Reims*, which was produced shortly before and which served as a major source for the *Ordo of 1250*. Taken together, this coronation rite was the first one that was specifically French in the sense that it included for the first time elements such as the "holy ampulla," the oath to expel heretics, the "knighting" with boots and spurs, and the direct participation of the peers of the kingdom, which would become standard elements in French coronations through the end of the monarchy.[5] The *Ordo* allows us to see the place of the monarchy in the "order" of the kingdom. It was not a rite "constructed" by the Capetians in order to project some "ideo-

---

[3] See "Introduction" in Jacques Le Goff, Éric Palazzo, Jean-Claude Bonne, and Marie-Noël Colette, *Le sacre royal à l'époque de Saint Louis* (Paris: Gallimard, 2001), 10–11. See also Anne D. Hedeman, *The Royal Image: Illustrations of the Grandes Chroniques de France, 1274–1422* (Berkeley: University of California Press, 1991), 2.

[4] For material on the windows, see A. A. Jordan, *Visualizing Kingship in the Windows of the Sainte-Chapelle* (Turnhout, BE: Brepols, 2001).

[5] *Ordines Coronationis Franciae: Texts and Ordines for the Coronation of Frankish and French Kings and Queens in the Middle Ages*, ed. Richard A. Jackson (Philadelphia: University of Pennsylvania Press, 2000), 2:291, 341. Both documents are also edited by Monique Goullet in the appendix to *Le sacre royal à l'époque de Saint Louis*, 257–309.

logical" self-conception over and against the Church or other groups in society. Rather, it presents ritually a cosmology in which all the parties in society find a definitive place and to which they could assent. The microcosm of the *Ordo* made sense as a coherent whole to those who participated in the rite—it was a "complete act."[6] And the cosmos it presents is one in which the temporal and the spiritual are intrinsic to each other, in which the Old Testament must be read through the New, and in which the monarch is indeed the successor to the kings of Israel, but Israel itself, along with all of reality, has been transformed by and has meaning through the Incarnation. Indeed, the entire rite takes place within the context of the definitive Christian microcosm, the Mass.

At the very start of the rite the archbishop prays that God might give the king the ability to rule and then he intones an antiphon from Psalm 19, a prayer that the Lord might come to the aid of King David.[7] The archbishop asks the king to promise to protect the churches' privileges, the law, and justice. After a *Te Deum*, the king promises that by his will (*arbitrio*) the Christian people will serve "true peace," that he will forbid all "rapacities and iniquities," that he will order "equity and mercy" in all judgments, and that he will extirpate from his kingdom all heretics.[8] After stating that he will hold and observe the holy faith passed to him from Catholic men and defend the churches and justice, the archbishop asks the clergy and people whether they want to be subject to the king and they respond, "fiat, fiat. Amen."[9] The

---

6   For the necessity of symbolic, ritual action for societal order (or rather, the need that society itself be constituted by ritual action), see Mary Douglas, *Natural Symbols: Explorations in Cosmology* (London: Routledge, 2003). See also Robert Wuthnow, James Davison Hunter, Albert Bergesen, and Edith Kurzweil, *Cultural Analysis* (Boston: Routledge, 1984), 77–133.

7   *Ordines Coronationis Franciae*, 2:344–45. See also *Le sacre royal à l'époque de Saint Louis*, 259: "Exaudiat te Dominus in die tribulationis; protegat te nomen Dei Iacob."

8   *Ordines Coronationis Franciae*, 2:299–300, 346. *Le sacre royal à l'époque de Saint Louis*, 261, 303.

9   *Ordines Coronationis Franciae*, 2:351.

chamberlain of the kingdom and the duke of Burgundy proceed
to place on the king the boots and spurs of knighthood,[10] and
the archbishop prays that God might glorify the king so that he
might be in possession of the grandeur of the scepter of David,
that God might "Give to you inspiration to rule the people with
gentleness, just as Solomon was made king to obtain peace."[11]
As the archbishop anoints the king, an antiphon from 1 Kings
is sung, recounting the anointing of Solomon and so placing the
king as the direct heir of David.[12] When the archbishop anoints
his hands, he declares himself to be emulating Samuel's anointing of David, and then the archbishop prays that he be the most
perfect king, that peace reign in his kingdom, that the churches
and the monasteries be protected, and that the kingdom be the
most powerful of kingdoms, triumphing over its enemies and
"crushing rebels and pagan nations."[13] The archbishop prays
that God might grant the king the firm faith of Abraham, the
gentle trust of Moses, the courage of Joshua, the humility of
David, and the wisdom of Solomon.[14]

This Davidic kingship, however, was given its content
through a Christological reading of the Old Testament. The
Law had been fulfilled, not abolished, and the David whom
the king succeeded was the David read through the New Testament and so the figure of Christ himself. After anointing
the king, the archbishop prays: "God, the Son of God, our
Lord Jesus Christ, who by the Father with the oil of exultation
was anointed through His participation, likewise through the

---

[10] Ibid., 2:300, 353.

[11] "Da ei tuo inspiramine cum mansuetudine ita regere populum, sicut Salomonem fecisti regnum obtinere pacificum" (*Ordines Coronationis Franciae*,
2:351–52). See also *Le sacre royal à l'époque de Saint Louis*, 267.

[12] "Unxerunt Salomonem Sadoch sacerdos et Nathan propheta regem in
Gyon, et accedentes leti dixerunt, vivat rex in eternum" (*Ordines Coronationis Franciae*, 2:301, 353). See also *Le sacre royal à l'époque de Saint Louis*,
273.

[13] *Ordines Coronationis Franciae*, 2:354–55. See also *Le sacre royal à l'époque de
Saint Louis*, 275.

[14] Ibid., 2:356. *Le sacre royal à l'époque de Saint Louis*, 279.

present infusion of sacred oil let the Spirit of the Paraclete pour over your head the blessing and let him make it penetrate to the interior of your heart, since through this visible and manageable gift the invisible is perceived, and the just management of this temporal kingdom having been executed, let you merit to rule eternally with Him."[15] The bishops, acting as the "vicars" of the saints and the apostles, hand the king his sword while the archbishop evokes Psalm 44: "Gird thy sword upon thy thigh, O thou most mighty." Psalm 44 was universally understood as referring to Christ himself, especially to his humanity, to his role as king.[16]

The identification of the king with Christ only strengthens as the archbishop's prayer develops, as the archbishop articulates the content of Christian lordship:

That you might perform this through the force of equity, let you potently demolish the mass of iniquity and let you fight for and protect the holy Church of God and her faithful ones, and no less let you destroy the enemies who are under a false faith, other than the name of Christian, let you clemently help and defend widows and orphans, restoring the desolate, avenging injustice, let you confirm the well-established, that by doing this with triumph, a glorious and just worshipper, with the savior of the world, whose type in name you bear, who is with the Father, you might merit to rule without end.[17]

---

[15]   Ibid., 2:354.

[16]   See, for example, Hebrews 1:7–10; Irenaeus of Lyons, *Against heresies* 4.33.1; Augustine of Hippo, "In Answer to the Jews," in *Treatises on Marriage and Other Subjects*, ed. Roy Joseph Deferrari, trans. Marie Liguori, *The Fathers of the Church* 27 (Washington, DC: Catholic University of America Press, 1955), 4.5, 395; St. Thomas Aquinas, *Super Ps* 44 (Parma ed. no. 2).

[17]   This is nearly the same as that found in the Roman rite for the coronation of emperors; see *Ordines Coronationis Franciae*, 2:357–58. See also *Le sacre royal à l'époque de Saint Louis*, 281; PL, 78:1241.

The bishops then hand the king the scepter with which he is to pity the pious and terrify the evil, and the archbishop places the king directly in the place of Christ by again evoking Psalm 44 and its citation in Hebrews 1:7–9, where the Father says to the Son, "Thy throne, O God, is for ever and ever: a sceptre of justice is the sceptre of thy kingdom. Thou hast loved justice and hated iniquity: therefore God, thy God, hath anointed thee with the oil of gladness above thy fellows." The archbishop is praying that the king might imitate Christ's anointed kingship in this pursuit of justice and hatred of iniquity.[18] The king was more than the historical David; he was exercising the Davidic kingship of Christ himself; this is the allegorical and the tropological leading to the anagogical David, who was nothing short of Christ himself, whose kingship was as much a part of his salvific work as were his prophetic and priestly roles.[19]

In the world, in the realm of sin, the king wields the sword as did the historical kings of the Old Testament, but he does so not simply to achieve an earthly peace that consists only of submission, even submission to the Law. Rather, he wields the sword to prepare the sinner for Christ and ultimately to convert the kingdom of the Law into that of grace and so into the kingdom of true peace that was ruled by Christ himself. The Old and the New find unity in the person of the king. He is David and he is Christ. He is he who wields the sword and he who abolishes the sword, the Law and its fulfillment.

Jacques Le Goff has written of an "équilibre entre le pouvoir royal et le pouvoir ecclesiastique" in the *Ordo*, and Jean-Claude Bonne likewise of "un remarquable équilibre entre les pouvoirs du roi, du haut clergé et des grands du royaume, comme entre

---

[18] *Ordines Coronationis Franciae*, 2:358–59. *Le sacre royal à l'époque de Saint Louis*, 283.

[19] See Thomas Aquinas, *Commentary on the Gospel of John: Chapters 1–21*, trans. Fabian Larcher and James A. Weisheipl (Washington, DC: Catholic University of America Press, 2010), 19, 2420–21; Thomas Aquinas, *Catena Aurea: Commentary on the Four Gospels, Collected Out of the Works of the Fathers*, ed. John Henry Newman, vol. 1, *St. Matthew* (Oxford: John Henry Parker, 1841), 1, 9.

conception nationale du sacre et conception partageé par la chrétienté, mais aussi entre rituel sacré et cérémonie plus spectaculaire."[20] But such interpretation fails to understand the *Ordo* from within the hermeneutical categories that it itself provides, those of the Old and New Testaments, the senses of Scripture, the sacraments, and the Incarnation, choosing instead those of modern statecraft and the narrative of the triumph of the secular. It would be possible to say that the power of the king and the power of the clergy are in "equilibrium" only if the same could be said of the kingship and priesthood of Christ, of his human and divine natures, or of the veracity of the two Testaments, and this is to misunderstand Christianity fundamentally. Davidic kingship after Christ continues to rule the people of God, but the Old Testament has been fulfilled in the Gospel, and so Davidic kingship becomes transformed by and yet intrinsic to the Gospel; it becomes the kingship of Christ himself. And the Gospel cannot stand without the temporality of the people of God—Christ's very human identity is as the heir to David, as a member of a people in history.

In this allegorical and sacramental universe, the temporal and the spiritual cannot have independent existences or distinct, coherent meanings. The historical could never be left simply as the historical. The historical's meaning came through its allegorical reading, its tropological interiorization, and finally the believer's anagogical participation.[21] The king's succession directly from David could not, therefore, be understood as anything other than his bearing the *vices* of Christ, being the vicar of Christ, and yet this vicarage is not a threat to that of the bishops, any more than the Old Testament is a threat to the New—quite the contrary: they require each other intrinsically, having no identity separate from each other.

---

[20] Jacques Le Goff, "La structure et le contenu idéologique de la cérémonie du sacre," in *Le sacre royal à l'époque de Saint Louis*, 34; Jean-Claude Bonne, "Images du sacre," in *Le sacre royal à l'époque de Saint Louis*, 226.

[21] Henri de Lubac, S. J., *Medieval Exegesis: The Four Senses of Scripture*, vol. 2, esp. 85, 98–99, 101, 132, 140, 177, 183–216.

When the archbishop places the crown on the king's head, he states that he is now participating in the apostolic ministry, that the prelates are the pastors and rectors of the interior of souls, while the king cares for the exterior. God had given the king the office of defending the Church of God and the kingdom from all enemies, and he has done so through the office of the archbishop who bears the *vices* of the apostles and all the saints. If the king performs his office, the archbishop reminds him, he might merit to be "crowned eternally with happiness with the redeemer and savior Jesus Christ, whose name and vicarage you bear, glory without end."[22] The Lord, the archbishop states, anoints priests, kings, and prophets that his grace might be poured out upon them, that they might love justice and lead the people to justice, and that all might merit eternal joy.[23] This is one sacramental society within which the material, the historical, the Old, is not abolished, but rather perfected in a dynamic of ascent which culminated in unity with Christ. Kingship and priesthood together ascend toward Christ as they together convert the kingdom of the world into the kingdom of God.

This understanding flows out of the same tradition as did the *business of the peace and the faith.* For example, the letter that Innocent III wrote to Philip II in 1208 begins, "Notice that through Moses and Peter, the fathers of both Testaments, is signified a unity between kingship and priesthood, since one is called a priestly king, and the other is called a royal priest; by this is signified that Jesus Christ the king of kings and the Lord of lords according to the order of Melchizedek wanted the races of the priests and the kings to be born from each, namely the priestly and the royal."[24] Indeed, much of the French *Ordo* was derived from a long tradition of coronation rites stretching back through Charlemagne, a tradition that

---

[22] *Ordines Coronationis Franciae,* 2:359; *Le sacre royal à l'époque de Saint Louis,* 283–84.

[23] Ibid., 2:353–54; *Le sacre royal à l'époque de Saint Louis,* 277.

[24] PL, 215:1359.

was shared by Rome. In fact, the rite used in Rome for the coronation of emperors and that for the creation of knights shared many elements with the French *Ordo*.[25]

Within the French rite, the king constitutes a point of contact between the temporal and the spiritual, the lay and the clerical: his coronation includes both the *ordines* of "knighting" by laymen and anointing by the archbishop. When the king has been called by name by the peers of the kingdom and others present, the archbishop takes the crown from the altar, the place where heaven touches earth, and places it upon his head. Then all the peers of the kingdom, as much the clerics as the laymen, surround the king and place their hands on the crown, holding it firmly on his head. The archbishop, with the peers still holding the crown, leads the king to be seated on his throne, where he can be seen by all.[26] The archbishop then tells the king to stand and to hold from now on this place, which he had held only through paternal succession up to that point but which now was delegated to him through the authority of God and the bishops' "tradition." And so now, while the clergy are the nearest to the holy altar, being the mediators between God and man, the king is the next closest, as the mediator between the clergy and the people.[27] As David, the king reaches down into history, into the Law, and up into grace, to the sacraments. The gaps have all been bridged, and all the rungs of the ladder of ascent from the Fall of the first Adam to the restoration of the new Adam are in place. The liturgy then progresses to the consecration of the Eucharist. The king and queen receive the sacrament and then process from the church, being led by the seneschal of France, who carries the king's naked sword.[28]

---

[25] PL, 78:1241. See also Léon Gautier, *Chivalry*, trans. Henry Frith (London: George Routledge and Sons, 1891), 73.

[26] *Ordines Coronationis Franciae*, 2:302.

[27] Ibid., 2:360.

[28] Ibid., 2:301, 305, 363.

The cosmos of the *Ordo* is a sacramental cosmos. There are temporal elements and there are spiritual elements, but at no point is one without the other. One might profitably understand it as a continuum in which the sword occupies one extreme and the grace of God the other, but the realm of men is always in the middle, an admixture of the material and the spiritual, the temporal and the eternal, the law and grace, the Old and the New. The monks, the contemplatives who are the closest to the anagogical, bring in the "holy ampulla," and the barons, the warriors who are the closest to the historical, bring in the sword, but both are placed on the altar and given to the king by the archbishop.[29] The king and the archbishop have a special relationship in occupying the center of this continuum.

It is ultimately the Sacrament, the Mass, that bridges whatever divide remains between the extremes. It is the Mass, therefore, that provides the interpretive key to the whole cosmology, since the cosmos is entirely contained within its bounds. The Eucharist is, of course, the ecclesial Sacrament, the Sacrament of unity both horizontally between man and man and vertically between men and God—it is the true Body of Christ and constitutes the *ecclesia* as the mystical Body of Christ.[30] The Mass, then, is the setting for the complete yet mysterious unity of the material and the spiritual. It is the point where the principal "sacrament" of the Old Testament, the paschal sacrifice, is fulfilled without subtraction in the principal Sacrament of the New Testament—this is the mystery of the Incarnation, of Christ, king and priest.[31] While the priest is necessary for the confection of the Eucharist, so too is the laity; for, the matter of the Sacrament, the bread and the wine, are no less essential, and this matter is a product of the social life of mankind in the material and

---

[29] Ibid., 2:298–9, 345–6, 352–3.

[30] ST III, q. 73, a. 3, a. 4. Henri de Lubac, S.J., *Corpus Mysticum: The Eucharist and the Church in the Middle Ages*, trans. Gemma Simmonds, C.J. (South Bend, IN: University of Notre Dame Press, 2007).

[31] ST III, q. 73, a. 4, 75, a. 1.

temporal world.[32] In the Mass, the totality of human reality, indeed all of creation, is sanctified, is brought into union with the Divine.[33] The work of the laity in the material world is completed through the spiritual work of the clergy and so Christ is made present and unity is achieved.

The priest certainly does not "control" this event and, of course, neither does the king. The civil or feudal is not being subjected to the canonical. The king and the archbishop do not have the same powers, for they occupy different *ordines*. But they are not subordinated one to the other, and one's power is not a threat to the other's power, to be dealt with through law or social convention. The peace possible through such social conventions is necessarily a compromise, an "équilibre" peace, a peace achieved through mutual self-interest or when force counters force, but that is not the peace that is to reign between the clergy and the king—their peace is of faith, justice, and charity, the peace of heaven.[34]

The king reigns in the present age as the successor to David in a manner similar to that in which the pope reigns as the successor not to the previous pope but to St. Peter himself, and to that in which the bishops succeed the apostles. (Charlemagne is present neither in the windows of Sainte-Chapelle nor in the *Ordo*.) And so, he is participating in the reign of Christ, a reign that carries over into eternity.[35] The king's *officium* was to produce peace temporally in emulation of the eternal peace of the saints in heaven and, in so doing, to bring heaven and earth together, to reduce the distinction between the *ecclesia* and the world, creating a space for grace to work, for the conversion of the world into the *ecclesia*, and for the elevation and perfection of the world into the *ecclesia*.[36] The king was to build the city

---

[32] ST III, q. 74, a. 4–5.

[33] John Milbank and Catherine Pickstock, *Truth in Aquinas*, (London: Routledge, 2001), 105–07.

[34] *Ordines Coronationis Franciae*, 2:345, 352, 358, 362.

[35] Ibid., 2:360–61.

[36] The *Benedictio* in the coronation Mass reads: "Omnipotens Deus, qui te populi sui voluit esse rectorem, ipse te celesti benedictione sanctificans eterni

of God, the city of peace, the city of faith and charity.[37] As he did this, the proscriptive law would fade away because it had reign only over the realm of sin. In the realm of grace, the law was interiorized in charity. This movement was the pursuit of salvation, of true peace,[38] an objective dependent upon sacramental grace, and so on the priesthood.[39] It was only because the souls of the baptized were no longer subject to the power of sin that true peace could be achieved and the exterior law, the force necessary to compel men to justice, could fade away. In peace the law was fulfilled, for peace was nothing less than the universalization of the love of God and love of neighbor.[40]

This was the very dynamic of salvation history, of the senses of Scripture, of the movement of the interior life—it was, simply, orthodox Christianity. To the extent that peace was achieved, the gap between heaven and earth was closed and Christ's mission was advanced. Both swords were wielded toward this end of peace and so salvation.

A comparison to late-modern capitalist democracy might help us understand this medieval *ecclesia*. We divide our world

---

regni faciat esse consortem. Amen. Concedatque tibi contra omnes christiane fidei hostes visibiles atque invisibiles victoriam triumphalem, et pacis et quietis ecclestice felicissimum te fieri longe lateque fundatorem. Amen. Quatinus te gubernacula regni tenente, populus tibi subiectus christiane religionis iura custodiens undique totus pace tranquilla perfruatur, et te in concilio regum beatorum collocato, eterna felicitate ibidem tecum pariter gaudere mereatur. Amen. Quod ipse prestare dignetur. Et pax eius sit semper vobiscum" (*Ordines Coronationis Franciae*, 2:361).

[37] Cf. Augustine, *City of God* 19.11, 19.20.

[38] See, for example, ST II-II, q. 29, a. 2, ad 3, 4.

[39] The *Secreta* in the coronation Mass reads: "Concede, quesumus omnipotens Deus, his salutaribus sacrificiis placatus, ut famulus tuus ad peragendum regalis dignitatis officium inveniatur semper ydoneus et celesti patrie reddatur acceptus." And the post-communion prayer: "Hec, Domine, salutaris sacrificii perceptio famuli tui N. peccatorum maculus diluat et ad regendum secundum tuam voluntatem populum ydoneum illum reddat, ut hoc salutari mysterio contra visibiles atque invisibiles hostes reddatur invictus, per quod mundus est divina dispensatione redemptus" (*Ordines Coronationis Franciae*, 2:361–62).

[40] Cf. ST II-II, q. 29, a. 3, resp.

into public and private sectors. They are different, but they only make sense together and within a certain régime of political and property rights—they have no independent existence. Indeed, the emergence of capitalism and the emergence of the State are two aspects of the same historical development— the public and the private are intrinsic to this development. If you remove the public sector, the private sector goes with it because there is no entity to enforce contract and property rights and the definition of the private sector is that realm of society in which social interaction is managed through those rights. Conversely, if you remove the private sector, the public sector goes with it because the public sphere is precisely understood as that sphere that uses violence to enforce contract and property rights and to fulfill those functions that the private sector cannot seem to manage through contract. Public property and private property, of course, exist in the same régime of property rights—public property being the private property of the State.

Nevertheless, the public sector and the private sector seem constantly to be fighting with each other. Indeed, political parties make aligning with one or the other the center of their rhetoric. But, it would be a terrible mistake to view the private and the public as incompatible forces in society or as parallel systems or to try and frame our experience as one shaped by the conflict between them. The clear truth is that the real conflicts in our society are waged between conglomerations of interests that are intrinsically both private and public. It is only criminals, but more fundamentally revolutionaries, anarchists, and terrorists—those who attack the whole system—who are outside of it, and their activities are outlawed, condemned by both public and private sectors, and suppressed. We live in a world of private property and public violence. Might we go so far as to assert that this is the juridical structure of our *ecclesia* and those who deny its validity are heretics against whom war is justified?

Similarly to the private and the public in our society, the secular and the spiritual in thirteenth-century France were incorporated into a single *ecclesia*. The secular parts of this *ecclesia* subsisted in the realm of time and things, as do the "secular" parts of our world, but in the thirteenth century the realm of time and things was precisely the realm of the Church Militant—of the incarnate Christ and his Body, the Church and the Eucharist—and it was also the realm of the Church's enemies: infidels, heretics, and malefactors. The realm of time and things was the realm of "religion" itself, and both the spiritual and the temporal swords were wielded within it, by definition. And so, it would make as much sense to say that everything in the thirteenth century was "secular" as it would to say that everything was "religious." The modern distinction simply did not exist.

Perhaps a direct example is in order. As we have seen, the Dominicans of Paris had a close relationship with Louis IX. Between 1254 and 1257 they faced major opposition to their way of life and to their very existence by elements of the kingdom's secular clergy, led by William of Saint-Amour and the secular masters at the University of Paris. William attacked the Dominicans, the power of the king, and that of the pope together, believing them to be different dimensions of the same corruption. He believed the Mendicants, and by extension the pope, to be heretical and the king to be unjust, violent, and undignified, a failure in his office.[41] His support came from among those elements of the kingdom most inclined to resist the king and pope: certain baronial families and the bishops who emerged from them.[42] This group was

---

[41] William's attack against the Mendicants and the power of the pope are the theme of all his writings, but see especially *Tractatus brevis de periculis novissimorum temporum ex scripturis sumptus*, ed. and trans. G. Geltner (Louvain/Paris: Peeters, 2007). For William's most direct attacks on the king, see his sermons in Andrew G. Traver, *The Opuscula of William of Saint-Amour: The Minor Works of 1255–1256* (Münster: Aschendorff Verlag, 2003); Lester K. Little, "Saint Louis' Involvement with the Friars," *Church History* 33, no. 2 (June 1964): 141.

[42] See, for example, HUP, 3:309; *Gal. Christ.*, 7:104, 8:1467, 9:370, 10:1185. For the local nobility's control of many episcopal sees and the manner in

supported by many religious (monks) who viewed the friars as a perversion of the religious vocation. To the Mendicants and their supporters, including the pope and the king, William and his followers were wrong to the point of being heretical and rebellious.[43] His attack on the Mendicants was understood as an attack on the monarchy *and* an attack on the papacy. In conjunction with the papacy, Louis suppressed this attack and sent William into exile.[44]

Thus the "Mendicant Conflict" cannot be seen as simply an "ecclesiastical" issue or as a "political" issue. Rather, it must be understood within the context of baronial and episcopal resistance to royal and papal power and to the worldview that underwrote it—what we have been calling the *business of the peace and the faith*. Writing in the vernacular, the troubadour Rutebeuf railed against the Mendicants and against the king for supporting them, defending William and questioning Louis's commitment to justice.[45] The *Roman de la Rose* (a "breviary of the aristocracy," in the words of Johann Huizinga[46]) reproduced many of William's arguments against the Mendicants and attacked them especially through the character Faux Semblant, the hypocrite.[47] In these writings, as well as

---

which their interests and those of the king or pope came into conflict, see Fernando Alberto Pico, "The Bishops of France in the Reign of Louis IX (1226–70)," (PhD diss., The Johns Hopkins University, 1970), especially 75–104. The Council of Arles (1260) railed against religious usurping the rights of the secular clergy and echoes, even paraphrases, many of the arguments proffered by William of Saint-Amour (*Gal. Christ.*, 3:477).

[43] See, for example, LTC, 3:4262, 4264. See also St. Thomas Aquinas's refutation of William of Saint-Amour in *Contra impugnantes Dei cultum et religionem* (especially 4.11, 3.3, 3.7); in *Opera Omnia*, vol. 41, A (Rome: Ex Typographia Polyglotta S. C. de Propaganda Fide, 1970).

[44] See the documents in HUP, 3:255–84, and LTC, 3:4262.

[45] See Edward Billings Ham, *Rutebeuf and Louis IX* (Chapel Hill: University of North Carolina Press, 1962); Jean Dufournet, "Rutebeuf et les moines mendiants," *Neuphilologische Mitteilungen* 85 (1984): 152–68.

[46] Johan Huizinga, *The Waning of the Middle Ages* (New York: Anchor Books, 1989), 334.

[47] For the immediate connection between Willaim of Saint-Amour and the

in those of William himself, the Mendicants were not understood simply as competition for power or wealth, but rather as
the personification of disorder, hypocrisy, and immorality—
even as the Antichrist[48]—and the king's support of the friars
was viewed as a failure in his obligation to defend justice and
uphold the customs of the land, even a failure in chivalry.[49]
William of Saint-Amour's outrage at the disorder of the Mendicants should be seen as a parallel to the outrage that was
often expressed by members of the nobility when Louis violated their sense of propriety in his informal and "excessively"
pious manners.[50]

The point of this example is that within the sacramental
cosmos, every social faction had, intrinsic to its very self-iden-
tity, elements that we might be inclined to label "secular" and
elements we might be inclined to label "religious." This is not
to say that the monarchy or its opponents justified itself with
a Christian ideology—such a conception preserves the division between the religious and the secular by simply laying
one on top of the other. Within such a conception, this religious ideology could change while the monarchy, for example,
retains categorical integrity as itself secular: the Christianity
of the monarchy is seen as accidental to its essence as the
State.[51] This is the conceptual framework maintained by the

---

    Roman de la Rose, see D. L. Douie, *The Conflict Between the Seculars and
the Mendicants at the University of Paris in the Thirteenth Century* (London:
Blackfriars, 1954), 12.

[48] See Penn R. Szittya, *The Antifraternal Tradition in Medieval Literature*
(Princeton: Princeton University Press, 1986), 25–55.

[49] Ham, *Rutebeuf and Louis IX*, 12–16.

[50] William Chester Jordan, "The Case of Saint Louis," *Viator* 19 (1988):
209–17.

[51] Discussing the increasing role of Louis IX in organizing crusades vis-à-vis
the papacy, James Powell has written: "But the decline in the role of the
papacy did not mean a decline in the role of religious rhetoric in the crusade.
Even though traditional interpretations have continued to link the papacy to
the crusade, it seems clear to me that there was a very substantial change in
the way in which religion was employed. It was moving toward a more exclusively propaganda role. Religion was more and more serving the interests

proponents of the secularization thesis discussed in the introduction.[52] Rather, we must recognize that within a sacramental worldview there is no fundamental conflict between the temporal and the spiritual that needs to be dealt with through an "alliance" of Crown and altar.[53] To the contrary, the spiritual and the temporal are united fundamentally—this is the very definition of a sacrament.

In the same way, to recognize the sacramental nature of thirteenth-century social reality is not to posit some sort of idyllic harmony between different groups of society or to argue that popes and kings always got along or always worked together. Looking for universal agreement between popes and kings, or any attempt to explain away all conflict, is to fall back into the statist error because it is to assume that the only alternative to the State is either some sort of sinless paradise or a war of all against all. Rather, conflicts were waged within the sacramental context, within a conceptual universe where the temporal and the spiritual were intrinsically bound up together.

The Mendicants shared an orthodoxy with Louis that encompassed entirely both the spiritual and the secular, both the friars' roles as brothers or priests and the king's role as Davidic monarch.[54] Those outside this orthodoxy were po-

---

of secular rulers" ("Church and Crusade: Frederick II and Louis IX," *The Catholic Historical Review* 93, no. 2 [April 2007]: 264).

[52] See, for example, Gabrielle M. Spiegel, "The Cult of Saint Denis and Capetian Kingship," *Journal of Medieval History* 1 (1975): 43–69; Jacques Le Goff, "Aspect Religieux et Sacre de la Monarchie Française de X^e au XIIIe Siecle," in *Pouvoirs et libertés au temps des premiers Capétiens* (Maulévrier, FR: Hérault, 1992): 309–22; Jacques Chiffoleau, "Saint Louis, Frédéric II et les constructions institutionnelles du XIII siècle," *Médiévales* 17 (1998): 13–23.

[53] The "alliance" concept dominates the limited work that has been done explicitly on the relationship between Louis and Pope Clement IV; See Ulrich Bünger, "Das Verhältnis Ludwings Des Heiligen Zu Papst Clemens IV (1265–1268)" (PhD diss., Verheinigten Friedrichs-Universität, 1897).

[54] See Jacques Krynen, "Saint Louis Législateur au Miroir des Mendiants," *Melanges de l'Ecole Française de Rome* 113 (2001): 945–61; William Chester Jordan, "Isabelle of France and Religious Devotion at the Court of Louis

tential converts, certainly, but also potential enemies of both Church and Crown. The enemies of this orthodoxy viewed the world in an incommensurable, but not widely divergent, manner. Whether they were heretics and *faiditi* of the South or barons and secular clergy of the North, a challenge to the king or a challenge to the Church (as understood by the papacy and groups such as the Mendicants) was necessarily understood as a challenge to a whole orthodox social architecture—both institutional and ideological. And what these challengers sought to defend was likewise as much religious as it was secular—their own version of "orthodoxy"—because, in a sacramental universe, all legitimacy is rooted in the union of the immanent and the transcendent. In such a structure, the boundaries of orthodoxy were under constant negotiation, with most conflicts remaining within the bounds of the broadly orthodox *ecclesia*. However, through persistent conflict factions might grow into truly rival *ecclesiae*, drifting away from each other in material interests, in doctrine and in praxis until each side ultimately indentified the other as heretical and violent. Such a reading, it seems to me, is capable of offering an account of factions within Christendom with truly distinct understandings of proper social order. It would certainly be capable, for example, of an account of both the material and ideological components of the conflicts between the papacy and the German emperors, an account that goes well beyond the scope of the current study.

We see, therefore, that any attempt to discern Louis IX's "ecclesiastical policy," to determine his "relationship" to "the Church," is predicated on a misconception of the thirteenth century's politico-ecclesial landscape. The Crown did not have an "ecclesiastical policy" because the Church was not a self-contained power distinct from the Crown with whom it could be in "alliance" or "conflict." Rather, the spiritual and the secular powers interpenetrated each other at every level and,

---

IX," in *Capetian Women*, ed. Kathleen Nolan (New York: Palgrave, 2003), 209–23; Little, "Saint Louis' Involvement with the Friars," 125–48.

indeed, relied on each other for their very self-conception. The whole history of the *business of the peace and the faith* and the construction of institutions such as the *enquêteurs* and the inquisitors demonstrate this point. This was not some theory of Parisian intellectuals; it was a social order that actually existed and in which people actually lived.

To the orthodox engaged in the *business of the peace and the faith* heretics and violent men were both enemies of the peace. They refused both the love of God and the love of neighbor that held the city of God together and they could not be suffered.[55] As we have seen, it became part of the very definition of the monarchy to suppress them. But more than this, as the sacramental orthodoxy described above became more deeply embedded, all conflict had to be somehow placed within its matrix. And so, in practice all sustained conflict, by definition, was ultimately seen to be caused by rebellion and heresy on someone's part. Within this logic the legitimate use of force becomes identical to holy war and crime or rebellion becomes identical to heresy. We might be tempted to think that this is a recipe for theocracy, for an intolerant authoritarianism. Within this understanding, are not all conflicts in society ultimately conflicts between rival, totalizing theocracies? The answer is no, and the reason is that the overriding logic of this understanding is the logic of peace, not that of violence. What this means is that the legitimate wielding of both swords was dramatically limited by the laws of justice. As the Dominican Vincent of Beauvais wrote to St. Louis, "Any prince or prelate legally rules those under him, not in so far as they are human, but in so far as they have become brutish."[56] To the extent that people lived in peace, neither the king nor the priests had the power of their swords over them because both swords were ordered toward this same peace and were necessarily wielded against those who had placed themselves outside of it. The

---

[55] Cf. Augustine, *City of God* 19.16.

[56] Vincent of Beauvais, *The Moral Instruction of a Prince*, trans. Priscilla Throop (Charlotte, VT: MedievalMS, 2011), 43.

king could not use the sword except against the violent and the priest could not refuse the sacraments except to the mortal sinner. The objective of both swords was to render themselves obsolete. There was no sovereignty here. But there was authority, and government happened through associations of friends, networks of "counsel and aid." This is the subject of Part II of this book.

PART II

Counsel and Aid

Meanwhile, God teaches him two chief commandments, the love of God and the love of neighbor. In
these precepts man finds three beings to love, namely,
God, himself, and his fellow man, and knows that he is
not wrong in loving himself so long as he loves God. As
a result, he must help his neighbor (whom he is obliged
to love as himself) to love God. Thus, he must help
his wife, children, servants, and all others whom he
can influence. He must wish, moreover, to be similarly
helped by his fellow man, in case he himself needs such
assistance. Out of all this love he will arrive at peace, as
much as in him lies, with every man—at that human
peace which is regulated fellowship.

—St. Augustine, *City of God* 19.14

In the Introduction to this book, I articulated two planks that underwrite the conventional narrative of the medieval "problem of Church and State." The first was the conflict between the religious and the secular. It was the objective of Part I to undermine this first plank. The second is the idea of sovereignty. Sovereignty is that thing over which Church and State were supposedly fighting. But, what is sovereignty? The sovereign is conceived of as the source of organized and legitimate force. The sovereign is not simply he who wields the most power in society, but rather he who wields a power that is categorically different from any other power in that it somehow stands outside of society and provides it order. The referee on the soccer pitch would be sovereign only if he made up the rules and could make exceptions at his will—otherwise, he is just a policeman.

I contend that it is an assumption of modern politics that sovereignty exists someplace, even if it is obscured by constitutional arrangements, opaque structures of power, or certain rhetorical constructions. I further contend that this notion of sovereignty carries with it certain assumptions about society and certain approaches to social reality that were absent in the Middle Ages. Indeed, the monopoly of violence that sovereignty demands is actually organizationally possible only through the technology of the modern State, and the ideological component of sovereignty—the belief that monopolized violence is "legitimate"—is constructed and sustained only as a response to the conviction of the ubiquity of violence or scarcity, the conviction that all "difference" is ultimately conflict and that reality is fundamentally a sequence of "differences" (a foundational belief of modern social theory).[1] Sovereignty as understood by modern

---

[1] For example, Pierre Bourdieu clearly, and I think correctly, stated that it is a basic assumption of sociology that a "gratuitous" act is impossible (*Practical Reason: On the Theory of Action* [Stanford, CA: Stanford University Press, 1998]), 76. Leo Strauss wrote of Max Weber, "Nothing is more revealing than the fact that, in a related context when speaking of conflict and peace, Weber put 'peace' in quotation marks, whereas he did not take this precautionary measure when speaking of conflict. Conflict was for Weber

theory is essentially the monopolization of legitimate violence within a society that is understood as conflict. Such a society is necessarily ordered by force or the threat of force—either legitimate (the sovereign) or criminal. This is why sovereignty is ultimately absolutist. If all interactions are ultimately founded upon scarcity and so end either in contract or in violence, then legitimate force operates at every level in society: violence must be suppressed and contracts enforced.[2] Thus legitimate force

---

an unambiguous thing, but peace was not: peace is phony, but war is real. Weber's thesis that there is no solution to the conflict between values was then a part, or a consequence, of the comprehensive view according to which human life is essentially an inescapable conflict" (*Natural Right and History* [Chicago: University of Chicago Press, 1953], 64–65).

2   This is, it seems to me, the great irony of liberal thought. Ludwig von Mises, for example, stated: "There are two different kinds of social cooperation: cooperation by virtue of contract and coordination, and cooperation by virtue of command and subordination or hegemony. Where and as far as cooperation is based on contract, the logical relation between the cooperating individuals is symmetrical. They are all parties to interpersonal exchange contracts. John has the same relation to Tom as Tom has to John. Where and as far as cooperation is based on command and subordination, there is the man who commands and there are those who obey his orders. The logical relation between these two classes of men is asymmetrical" (*Human Action: A Treatise on Economics*, 4th rev. ed. [San Francisco: Fox and Wilkes, 1996], 195). However, to Mises cooperation based on contract is possible only because of the hegemonic power of government. In a state of nature, according to Mises, all individuals seek hegemonic relations with their fellows in a state of perpetual warfare. He writes: "In order to establish and to preserve social cooperation and civilization, measures are needed to prevent asocial individuals from committing acts that are bound to undo all that man has accomplished in his progress from the Neanderthal level. In order to preserve the state of affairs in which there is protection of the individual against the unlimited tyranny of stronger and smarter fellows, an institution is needed that curbs all antisocial elements. Peace—the absence of perpetual fighting by everyone against everyone—can be attained only by the establishment of a system in which the power to resort to violent action is monopolized by a social apparatus of compulsion and coercion and the application of this power in any individual case is regulated by a set of rules" (ibid., 208). For Mises, then, the fundamental scarcity of resources on which the war of all against all was predicated is not somehow removed by the institution of government and so by the advent of contractual relations. Rather, because the State enforces contract, the State simply changes the calculus made by indi-

deployed as a juridical order becomes the source of all order. In every encounter, both parties have particular legal standing with particular rights and every material thing is necessarily a piece of property. When the "legal" order is order itself, when they are coterminous, the entity that has the ability to determine when that order is violated (that is to say, the entity that has the ability to use violence to keep the inherent conflict of society within the bounds of the managed conflict that is the juridical order) necessarily has no legal limit to its field of action, since it could, of course, suspend such a limit in the name of peace and order (the reasons for the juridical). In other words, it can make war. Constitutions spell out the functioning of the norm, but they do not ultimately limit the actions of the sovereign: war, including civil war, is always a sovereign option.

Some might protest that postmodern readings of power have undermined this notion of sovereignty. I think this is true in only a very limited sense. Postmodern readings of society have served only to radicalize the assumption of universal violence. Following Nietzsche, some sort of transcendental violence is the one universal truth, the one ahistorical constant, through which all reality must be read.[3] Since fundamental

---

vidual actors who are seeking to maximize their advantage over and against their fellows: open war is no longer the most profitable course of action. Ultimately, all relations remain hegemonic in their motivations. Since all human action is, to Mises, a form of exchange (ibid., 97), it seems to me necessary by the logic of his system that the hegemonic power of the State be somehow involved always and everywhere, even if just as a threat of force, in order for the contractual, which is to say the peaceful, form of cooperation to exist. In a nutshell, the essential function of the government is protecting "the smooth operation of the market economy against aggression, whether on the part of domestic or foreign disturbers" (ibid., 282), and all human action takes place within the "operation of the market economy." Therefore, the sovereign State judges all human action and must reserve always and everywhere the ability to act. What is more, why exactly those who control the State would refrain from using its power in the pursuit of their own hegemonic interests remains, in my opinion, rather unclear. Are they an exception to the laws of human action?

[3] Friedrich Nietzsche, *Beyond Good and Evil*, trans. Walter Kaufmann (New York: Vintage Books, 1966), 203: "Here we must beware of superficiality

warfare is the very fabric of social reality, all social power is necessarily the exercise of a will over and against the will of others, and therefore "sovereignty" is retained as the ultimate prize of the conflict. The postmodern approach does not set aside the functional value of sovereignty, therefore, but rather strips it of its legitimacy,[4] of its "divine" or "natural" mythology, which it replaces with an equally arbitrary (and metaphysical) radicalized myth of violence and power.[5]

The idea of sovereignty, therefore, rests both on the institution of the State and on the notion of the ubiquity of violence, both of which were lacking in thirteenth-century France. Rather, society was organized around the notion of peace, a peace that was real, and not simply another name for submission. This peace was constantly being shattered by outbursts of violence, and legitimate power fought this violence, kept it at bay, and protected the peace. Legitimate power, however, was not monopolized, and there was no notion that it should be. As I have asserted, the desirability of a monopoly on the use of force is a consequence of the belief in the ubiquity of violence; when that belief falls, this desirability falls with it. There was no State because there was no juridical order that even theoretically encompassed all social activity. The construction of such a juridical order is, again, founded on the notion of the ubiquity of violence or scarcity, a notion which the society of St. Louis's France lacked. It is the objective of the second part of this book to bring this social order, rooted in peace, into view, even if it will remain, inevitably, blurred and distorted by modern political concepts.

In this society, difference did not equal violence. In fact,

---

and get to the bottom of the matter, resisting all sentimental weakness: life itself is essentially appropriation, injury, overpowering of what is alien and weaker; suppression, hardness, imposition of one's own forms, incorporation and at least, at its mildest, exploitation. . . . Life simply is will to power."

[4] Raymond Geuss, *History and Illusion in Politics* (Cambridge: Cambridge University Press, 2001), 47–68.

[5] John Milbank, *Theology and Social Theory: Beyond Secular Reason*, 2nd ed. (Malden, MA: Blackwell Publishing, 2006), 21.

in an inversion of the modern understanding, peace was the product of difference, of inequality. When people were somehow "the same," violence erupted. Interactions operated not according to abstract laws and batteries of universal rights, but according to the relationships between the interacting persons within the immediate context of time, space, and issue at hand. Social interactions occurred within a differentiated space.

We will have the opportunity to explore this in greater detail in the following chapters, but it is valuable here to point out how drastically different this society was from our own. In our system, it is the order of universal and predictable coercion that allows for the mobility of equals within the social space. Citizens have rights always and everywhere that are identical, and these rights are protected within a disinterested juridical order that in theory has nothing outside of it. This provides for the free movement of goods and people through society without outbreaks of private violence. Strangers can meet each other, exchange goods, make contracts, and depart from each other without knowing anything particular about each other. All the knowledge that is needed is, in fact, written down in clear abstract language that everyone understands. This is a thoroughly undifferentiated society, which, I contend, is congruent with a metaphysics of violence or scarcity.[6]

The Christian society of thirteenth-century France, however, was congruent with a metaphysics of peace and abundance, of which the Trinity is the ultimate manifestation.

---

[6] Liberal society is so thoroughly "undifferentiated" that even one's "rights" to be oneself, to one's own ideas and own body, are often envisioned within the totalized system, and so we get the idea of self-ownership, within which, in order to make sense of why a human being can do as he pleases, we have to posit him to be an owned thing whose owner happens to be himself. Thus "ownership" and so "property" come conceptually before "humanity" or "personhood." Undifferentiation is so complete that it flattens any distinction between people and property: people and things are ultimately the same within the juridical order, and property rights become the only rights on which all others are based.

The Persons of the Trinity are completely differentiated, each defined by his relationship with the other persons: the Father is only the Father because he is the Father of the Son; the Son is the Son and not the Father because he is the Son of the Father; and the Holy Spirit is in similar relations to both the Father and the Son.[7] Their peace, however, is complete—so complete that the three Persons are one Divinity. Similarly, a father and a son in a human family live together in differentiation.[8] This differentiation is the foundation of their peace, and it is only when one party fails to be as "different" as he ought to be in relation to the other that conflict erupts. This familial differentiation remains recognizable even in modern society as a little island in a vast sea of sameness: in the family we experience the breakdown of the contractual/rights-based mode of interaction based on constant, if mitigated, conflict—we think peace should really be possible. Most of the time, we recognize that a father has a relationship with his son that is not a part of the same scarcity-based juridical social order as is his relationship with his employer.[9] Rather than based on contracts, the father-son relationship is based on things like duties, self-sacrifice, obedience, gifts, and ultimately love—all things that rely upon a fundamental inequality between persons. The father, because he is the father, acts a certain way, and the son, because he is the son, acts in a different way—and it is in this

---

[7] See ST I, q. 28.

[8] See Ibid., q.96, a.3, ad 2.

[9] There are exceptions that demonstrate the norm. For example, in order to maintain the ruthless consistency of his property-based understanding of politics, the libertarian Murray Rothbard had to maintain that parents own their children and that they can sell them or starve them to death (*The Ethics of Liberty*, with intro. by Hans-Hermann Hoppe [New York: New York University Press, 1998; first published 1982], 102–04). This is, of course, a solution to the problem of the family within a liberal system that reduces all rights ultimately to individual property rights. That fact that any normal person understands Rothbard's solution as monstrous, even though it is nothing more than the consistent application of the widespread belief that rights are based on self-ownership, demonstrates how different our concept of the family is from our concept of society at large.

difference that they form a family at peace, a truly "common good," a good that can only be had when it is had together. In fact, they are fully father or son only within this peace. To the extent that their relationship requires rules, laws, contracts or compromises, their relationship is not essentially that of father and son.

We should not have too much trouble imagining this type of relationship extending beyond the immediate family in ever bigger circles, involving more and more of the people with whom an individual interacts—even to the point of encompassing an entire society. Imagining such a thing is not the same as imagining a society without conflict: fathers and sons argue all the time. Rather, it is imagining a society in which their conflict does not fit, in which it is a tear in the social fabric rather than the threads that make it up. I have already had the occasion to cite Hostiensis concerning the Trinitarian nature of society, but I will do so again here: "These three types, namely, the laity, the secular clergy, and the religious, are a trinity: but in the holy union of the Church and in the Catholic faith they are a unity. Likewise, the Persons of the Father and the Son and the Spirit are a Trinity, but in essence and divinity a unity."[10]

In the following chapters, I attempt to show what such a society looked like and how it was ordered and governed at the ground level, at the level of everyday life and justice, and at the level of the actual actions of kings, bishops, cardinals, and popes. Among other things, we will see that the spiritual and temporal powers fit into this society peacefully. We will see that there was no conflict over sovereignty because there was no State over which to be sovereign. Rather, there was an almost infinitely complex world of individuals and corporations interacting with each other in a radically differentiated manner. This world was understood to be at peace at its core. But, it was rent with crime and sin, human actions that brought violence. Force was legitimate only as a reaction

[10] Henry of Susa, *Summa aurea* (Venice, 1574), 8.

to violence, only when directed at restoring the peace—but it was necessary and widely used. Society-wide initiatives were possible through networks of friends, of people who used their differentiated power toward a common goal—networks of *consilium et auxilium*, "counsel and aid."

In the chapters to come, I will continue to follow the life of Gui Foucois. As we saw in Part I, he came into the service of the king in 1254. In the mid-1250s Louis established Parlement as a permanent institution. Parlement was the king's curia, his court, and it met several times a year to hear cases and make rulings. When Gui's wife died in 1257, he took Holy Orders and was elevated to the see of Le Puy. He also became one of Louis's counselors in Parlement.

Parlement dealt with an incredibly wide range of cases, from questions about the pasturing of pigs in a certain field to questions concerning the waging of war. Because of this, its records afford us a wonderful window into the society. We can see not only how things worked, but also how they failed. We can see what people believed to be just, what actions they demanded of the king, and what arguments they believed would sway him to such action. What is more, the records are ample. From 1254 to 1270, we have records for about five thousand cases. The first two chapters of Part II focus on these records and attempt to explicate an order without sovereignty. We will then shift gears and discuss the networks of friends, of *consilium et auxilium* (counsel and aid), through which "government" actually happened.

Gui's elevation to the see of Le Puy and his subsequent 1259 transfer to the archbishopric of Narbonne allow us to see these networks in action. With his elevation to the cardinalate in 1261, the papal curia and the king's curia became united within a single network. By exploring Gui's 1264 papal legation to France (directed at helping Louis bring peace to the troubled kingdom of England), we will be able to see not only this network in action but also the extent to which, far from the fullness of royal power being a threat to the papacy's functioning, that power was, in fact, defended fiercely by the pope and his legate, Gui. Part II will end with Gui's 1268 election to the papacy as Clement IV and so the ultimate "merger" of the apostolic and the royal within the differentiated friendship of king and pope.

CHAPTER SEVEN

The Lord King Orders That the Plain Truth Be Found

Finally, there is justice. Its task is to see that to each is given what belongs to each.

—St. Augustine, *City of God* 19.4

THE STORY OF THE "problem of Church and State" in the Middle Ages is typically the story of the rise of the national monarchies and the decline of the papacy. It begins with the question "how did the secular, sovereign State come to be?" The analysis is conducted with categories that are constructed within modern politics: State, Church, secular, religious, sovereignty, law, bureaucracy, rationality, and so on. Unsurprisingly, what such analysis finds in the historical record is the decline of the political power of the Church and the rise of the secular State, the privatization of religion, the rationalization of government, the bureaucratization of offices and laicization of the social order, and the rise of national sovereignty and the decline of ecclesiastical universalism. Thirteenth-century

France and England are at the very center of this narrative. It was here, as the narrative would have it, that the State was built, both in practice and in theory. It was in St. Louis's France that the power of the monarchy approached the realization of sovereignty and that the State necessary to wield that power was built. St. Louis's grandson, Philip IV, when he defeated Boniface VIII, when he nationalized the Templars, and when he invaded Flanders, acted in a way that may very well have horrified St. Louis's pious sensibilities but was the natural consequence of his saintly grandfather's statecraft. Philip, we are told, realized the "absolutism" for which Louis had laid the foundations.[1]

But, does the actual evidence support this narrative of Church and State? Was St. Louis attempting to build a sovereign State focused on himself? What we find in the records of Parlement is that its charge was not to enforce the State's monopoly on violence. Rather, Parlement's functioned primarily to adjudicate rival "peaces," to determine which party in a conflict was the peaceful one, to determine what constituted the peace, and to make sure it was respected. The notion that violence was somehow properly restricted to a certain man or institution throughout the kingdom was foreign to the logic of the institution. According to this logic, peace existed in society through its nature as radically differentiated. Society existed ordered in justice. Injustice ripped this fabric of order here or there, but it was the exception rather than the rule. Human nature was wounded, not totally depraved. Coercion was therefore deployed justly only in response to violence and never proactively—otherwise, it was more violence.

The right to deploy this exceptional use of physical force was itself dispersed throughout society, and it was profoundly context-bound: here, in this place, in this situation, between these particular men, a certain person could wield the sword—

---

[1] For a summary of the standard reading of monarchical state-building, including that of Louis IX see Kaeuper, *Chivalry and Violence in Medieval Europe*, 96–106.

change one piece of context, and it could be someone else. Legitimacy arose out of differentiation and not out of the sameness of contract, administration, or modern rights, even if posited in a hierarchical feudal model. Holding lands did not mean holding justice, and the legitimate use of force in the kingdom was not divided up into little "sovereign" kingdoms.[2] Rather, force could be used by those who peacefully used it—those who used it not proactively but within the context-bound social order that was known as the peace.

The king's concerns with the use of force were, to put it simply, whether the peaceful order was being respected and whether, through that respect, justice was being done. The king, however, was not the master of this peace; he was its servant. Throughout this chapter, I will make assertions and give examples, but the examples and the cases cited in the notes are almost always only representative of the many more cases on which I base my conclusions. There are so many individual cases that citing them all would be both tedious and unnecessary.

In modern thought, the punishment of criminals is the undisputed realm of the sovereign State. In fact, the State could be defined precisely as that entity that performs this function. In the records of Parlement the coercion of criminals—their trial, judgment, and punishment—is called simply "justice." Possession of justice was not a monopoly of the Crown or a delegation from it. Rather, different entities in different locations held different shares of justice. For example, early in 1257 two men had been captured around the village of Sanctus Georgius, on the outskirts of Paris, by knights of a local abbot. Their crime was passing counterfeit money at the market, and the men of the abbot tried them and hanged them. The abbot did this because he believed himself to hold justice over the crime of false money in the village. The king's provost in Paris claimed that justice over this crime, in fact, pertained to the king because he held "high justice." This

---

[2] Olim, 1:237 (II); 1:530 (XI).

was the term that was normally used for jurisdiction over capital crimes—murder, rape, treason, sometimes thievery, and so on—sometimes called "justice of blood."[3] Because of the provost's claim, the king ordered that the hanged men be taken down from the abbot's gallows and re-hanged on his. The abbot protested, and so the king ordered an inquest. The investigation determined that indeed the abbot did have the possession of justice over false money in the village, but not because he held all high justice. Rather, the question of who held high justice remained open, except in the case of robbery, which the inquest had found that the king held. Because of this ruling the king ordered that the criminals be taken down from his own gallows and hanged yet again on the abbot's gallows. This, the records of Parlement state, was to "show that the way of justice had been liberated."[4]

There is no notion here of some sort of special claim of the king over legitimate violence. What made violence legitimate was that the enforcer held the right to wield it in a tangible and not abstract way. The king had no special claim as king. In fact, in all the cases that Parlement heard regarding whether the king or someone else held justice in a certain circumstance, more often than not, the court ruled against the king. What is more, the king was not always one of the parties. Sometimes he just happened to be, but at other times, Parlement adjudicated between two other parties.[5] The records of Parlement are full of cases concerning justice but devoid of any notion that justice was the prerogative of the king or was organized in some sort of meta-organization.

---

[3] Olim, 1:38 (X); 1:209 (X).

[4] Olim, 1:19 (XV).

[5] Olim, 1:14 (XXIV); 1:21 (XX); 1:28 (III); 1:34 (IV); 1:34 (V); 1:35 (X); 1:50 (XXX); 1:51 (XXXI); 1:53 (XL); 1:57 (XI); 1:66 (X); 1:78 (IV); 1:88 (IV); 1:92 (IV); 1:101 (I); 1:120 (VII); 1:158 (X); 1:162 (VIII); 1:186 (III); 1:187 (V); 1:190 (III); 1:207 (VI); 1:212 (III); 1:219 (V); 1:227 (XVIII); 1:228 (XIX); 1:232 (V); 1:234 (IX); 1:519 (XI); 1:522 (X); 1:527 (II); 1:544 (II); 1:545 (III); 1:554 (X); 1:560 (II); 1:572 (XIV); 1:573 (XVIII); 1:580 (XIII); 1:676 (XXIV); 1:701 (XII).

The second thing we should see in the example is the "empty space." There was a problem with false money, and Parlement determined that the abbot held the right to justice in this case, just as it also determined that the king had the right to thieves. But, who held the right to justice over other crimes? This remained an open question because it had not come up as a dispute. Parlement did not assign or delegate the legitimate use of violence; it "discovered" who had it. This discovery occurred in reaction to conflict, to a shattering of the peace. For example, when a thief was captured in a certain location in Soissons, a conflict arose. The count claimed that his ancestors had held justice in that place for as long as anyone could remember. The canons of the cathedral chapter, however, claimed that they had made use of justice there multiple times. Parlement's inquest determined that neither party had possession of justice in that particular place, but the king thought that the canons had the stronger claim, and so justice went to them and a little gap was filled—but only after a conflict had arisen.[6] Similarly, when a conflict arose between the king's men and the Abbot of Saint-Luc in Beauvais concerning who possessed justice over murders in a certain village (because a murder had been committed), Parlement's inquest determined that neither had "use" of justice in that particular place, meaning there was no memory of either of them possessing it. The king, however, determined that the abbot should have possession of justice, with the reservation that if at some point evidence might be found in the Crown's favor the question could be reopened.[7] This is open space, an idea impossible within the bounds of sovereignty.

In a colorful example, a certain squire brought a case against the deacon and chapter of Sens, arguing that he had the right to try and punish thieves captured in the lands of the chapter. When its men captured them, the chapter was indeed handing such thieves over to the squire, but the squire claimed that the problem was that they were handing them over nude

---

[6]   Olim, 1:184 (XVII).

[7]   Olim, 1:690 (XXIX).

(or else in the "vilest" clothes)—taking a rather literal understanding of what it meant to hand "the man" over. This, the
squire contended, was a violation of his right. The chapter
countered that there was, in fact, a charter that touched on this
right and that it said nothing about a thief's clothes. What is
more, they had the right, through long use, of handing thieves
over nude if they wanted. The squire responded that while
it may have been the case that they had long handed thieves
over naked, they had not the right to do so because they had
not had the use of the right peacefully. Rather, he had always
opposed them. Parlement commissioned an inquest to determine whether the chapter had a use of this kind and whether
the squire had indeed always opposed it. The inquest ruled in
favor of the chapter: they could hand thieves over in whatever
clothes or lack of clothes they wanted.[8]

We can see here the sub-divisible nature of justice. There
were no set categories or abstract principles that were to be followed, although there were some ideas that seem to have had
general purchase. In the first example, the crime of false money
was normally listed among the claims to high justice,[9] but as we
saw, that did not mean that having the right to justice over false
money necessarily meant one held high justice, or vice-versa.
There was no reason why legitimate use of force was some sort
of package deal. In the case of the nude thieves, what we see
are wholly new categories of rights emerging simply through
people behaving in certain ways. The chapter had the right to
the clothes of the thief simply because they had consistently
actually taken them. This sub-divisible nature of the right to
use force is important because it emphasizes the complete lack
of some sort of hierarchical understanding. Various people held
various pieces of justice over various territories or over various
men, and these rights were not continuous: there was no need
for them all to be organized in one system. Indeed, if we added
them all up, they would not cover the whole social space.

---

[8]   Olim, 1:221 (VI); 1:222 (VII); 1:695 (IV–V).
[9]   Olim, 1:563 (XVII).

The fact that justice was capable of being partitioned down to the smallest unit is demonstrated in the case of a certain hospice in Paris. A murder was committed in the house, and the king's men captured the culprit. The owner of the hospice immediately petitioned for custody because he held high justice in the house, a right he could prove through an ancient charter, if not through frequent use, a fact that everyone conceded was due to the rarity of crime in his home. Parlement ruled in favor of the hospice.[10] Here, the owner of a single house in the crowded city held the right to wield justice in capital cases, the power over life and death, in the building. In another example, the Abbot of Saint Medardus held justice over the men who lived in the village of Cusiaco unless a case had something to do with their houses, which pertained to the bishop.[11]

The sub-divisible nature of the right to legitimate force was really without limit. Justice could be divided along lines of different offenses: high justice, low justice, thieves, bandits, counterfeiters, heretics, and so on.[12] Justice could be divided along lines of different places: villages, roads, fields, or even individual buildings.[13] Justice could be divided along the lines of different people: residents of a certain town, serfs of a particular person, servants of a certain church, or merchants during a specific market.[14] Justice could be divided along lines of procedure: one person holds what we might think of as police power, and another the power to judge, and yet another the power to administer punishment.[15] Justice could even be divided along

---

[10] Olim, 1:519 (II).

[11] Olim, 1:8 (XIV).

[12] Olim, 1:9 (XVII); 1:9 (XIX); 1:18 (XI); 1:66 (VIII); 1:126 (I); 1:128 (VII); 1:195 (II); 1:537 (VI).

[13] Olim, 1:11 (VIII); 1:19 (XV); 1:79 (VI); 1:81 (XII); 1:121 (IX); 1:170 (XI); 1:576 (V).

[14] Olim, 1:18 (XII); 1:83 (XVIII); 1:159 (XII); 1:160 (IV); 1:185 (XIX); 1:193 (XIV); 1:502 (XXVII); 1:545 (V); 1:550 (XVII); 1:558 (XVII); 1:564 (XIX).

[15] Olim, 1:5 (XIV); 1:64 (V); 1:158 (VIII); 1:180 (IX); 1:190 (VI); 1:212 (V); 1:542 (XVIII).

the lines of different seasons or times of day: summer, after sunset, during the "time of acorns," and so on.[16] Sometimes justice was just divided mathematically: one person had two thirds and another one third.[17]

Legitimacy was context-bound. For example, Denis Farinelle operated a tavern in the town of Ambazie. When his servants were leaving the establishment carrying pots full of wine, some men of the local lord stopped them and smashed the pots. Denis complained to Parlement that an injury had been done to him. His reasoning, though, went straight to the particular relationship between himself and the lord of Ambazie: he was not a burgher of the lord, he contended, nor was he subject to him in anything, and so the local lord had no jurisdiction over him. In fact, Denis maintained, he was a burgher of the lord king. The lord countered with contextual particulars that changed the situation: he accepted that Denis was a free man and that he held no right to justice over him, but during the time of a certain type of ban, the custom was that while men could drink wine in taverns, it was not to be brought outside. He enforced this custom by breaking the pots and vases of people in his lands who violated it, and he had long done so, and such a ban, the lord explained, was in place at the time of the incident in question. Parlement heard the arguments, looked into the situation, and ruled in favor of the lord.[18] In such a manner, street violence was distinguished from police action.

When the Abbot of Vallis-Sarnaius charged Thesauraria, a noble lady, of injustice and violence when her men burst into one of his taverns and seized the measures with which the monks measured wine, she countered that she did this not through violence but through her right, for she had been in possession of all such measures since before anyone could remember. Parlement agreed, and so thievery was revealed as

---

enforcement.[19] Persons, actions, custom, time, place, duration—the entire context of a particular incident underwrote the legitimate use of force. Arguments in Parlement turned on establishing context, on establishing the relevant particular, differentiated relationships in a given situation. The line between justice and violence was traced within the actual reality of the peace that existed between two particular people and the circumstances that led to its destruction.

Throughout the hundreds of recorded investigations and rulings of Parlement concerning this web of rights to justice, there is never some notion that all of it is derived from one "meta-right" to justice that is somehow delegated by the king to subordinates. Reading this into the documents is a great temptation for modern historians who want so badly to find top-down sovereignty somewhere. However, I do not believe it to be there. It was quite possible for it to be an act of criminal violence for the king to capture, try, and punish a particular criminal because he did not possess justice in that particular circumstance.[20] Nor was the king trying to aggregate all justice to himself (even when he had possession of justice, he would often give it away!).[21] For example, when the king freed a group of his serfs in the domains of a certain prior, at the petition of the prior, Parlement acknowledged the transfer of justice over them from the king to the prior.[22]

Rather, the idea that underwrites the king's actions is that justice is something that is good and necessary in society, that it is right that wherever there is crime, some force should capture, try, and punish the criminals. The Crown clearly believed this, and where it was the case, all was well—there was peace. Justice was being done. The Crown intervened only when this peace was broken, when two or more parties disagreed on who had possession of justice. Parlement's task was to then investi-

---

[19] Olim, 1:206 (III).
[20] Olim, 1:519 (I).
[21] Olim, 1:166 (XVII); 1:512 (XIV).
[22] Olim, 1:567 (IV).

gate, not into who held some abstract right or some delegated authority, but rather into who in fact had wielded or had the "use" of the rights in question peacefully and for how long: one particular party held this particular bit of justice over these particular people because they had peacefully done so.

In a typical example, there arose a conflict in 1259 between the commune of Beauvais and a local monastery. The commune had seized the goods of men who had sworn oaths to it but had failed to fulfill them and who lived in lands over which the monastery claimed all justice. The abbot complained that the commune had therefore done violence against the monks and had despoiled them and caused them great injury, and so he summoned them before an ecclesiastical court. The commune admitted the seizures but asserted that they had not thereby done violence to the monks because they had possession of such actions over men in the monastery's lands if those men had sworn oaths to the commune concerning matters over which the commune had the right to judge. Parlement ordered an inquest to look into whether the monastery had possession of justice in those lands and for how long, whether the commune had possession of the particular actions that they had committed and for how long, and finally, whether these possessions had been held peacefully. What was the peace that had been shattered by this conflict? Who had committed violence? Which version of the peace was true? Parlement ruled against the monks.[23]

The king was not asserting that he had a right to justice everywhere or that those who held it did so as his delegate[24]—far from it. If Parlement determined that the king or his men had acted against the peaceful order of a time and place, it was very fast to declare their actions to be violent (upsetting to the

---

[23] Olim, 1:94 (IX). For other typical examples, see Olim, 1:584 (V); 1:676 (XXIV).

[24] Olim, 1:79 (VII). On the rare occasions where he did argue that someone's possession of justice was or ought to be a delegation from himself, it is clear: e.g., Olim, 1:606 (XIII).

peace) and to rectify the situation.[25] The king defended the peace, but he was not its source. Parlement approached the peace with a profound respect. It bowed to the peace. It sought to discover the peace. Parlement worked under the assumption that if it could just find out the truth of the particulars of what a certain place had been like before there had been conflict, the answer to the way things should be would be clear.[26] There are very few abstract rights involved—this is concrete.

What is more, rights to the wielding of force were not somehow privileged. This is an important point. In modern political theory, we single out physical coercion as being categorically distinct from any other activity in society. The reason we do this, though, is that the order of our society is based on the monopolization of coercion by the State. Our society tends to abhor any act of so-called private violence because such use of force necessarily challenges the basis of our society's peace—which rests on the exclusive violence of the State. Non-State violence is taboo. This was not the case in thirteenth-century France. Peace did not rest on violence. Rather, peace was understood as the way things were. A criminal fractured this peace through violence, and when he did so, he needed to be stopped and peace restored. In order for this exceptional but necessary action to take place without more conflict, in any given situation only one person should act. But this one person worked for the peace, right order, and justice itself, not for the State. He derived his legitimate use of force from the very nature of society. He derived his legal right to wield that force from the simple fact that he was the one in those parts that did so when those parts were at peace.

When the Templars of Tours built new gallows and hanged a criminal from them, Parlement ruled that they had violated the king's possession of justice in those parts. There

---

is no notion that they had somehow committed homicide because they killed someone outside the bounds of a monopoly on justice. It is right that criminals be hanged; the Templars simply were not the ones there that normally hanged them.[27] The deacon and chapter of Saint-Peter's in Soissons accused Lord Radulph of Soissons of violence for usurping their possession of justice—violence against them, not against the criminals that he executed.[28] When the friends of a certain knight who had been banned by the king because of a conflict he had had with the Abbot of Saint-Richard in Ponthieu delivered the knight (against his will) to the same abbot, the abbot kept him in his prison "for healing in mind and body." The king protested because the abbot had acted against his ban without license. The abbot claimed that the king's mother, Blanche, had told him to try to apprehend the knight and to bring him "punishment and love." The king accepted this and asked that when the knight decided that he wanted to make peace the abbot should inform the king.[29] Conflict emerged when two parties tried to possess the same bit of justice, not when someone acted outside some juridical order.

This was not a free-for-all, however. A suspect in a crime might protest his innocence and claim that he was treated unjustly when someone used force against him or that the person who used force against him did not have the right to do so, and the king might look into it. If the suspect was right, then violence had indeed been done against someone, either himself or the rightful holder of justice. In one case, the Bishop of Claremont had captured some burghers of the city who were accused of murder. Before he could try them, the townspeople "violently" seized them and took them to their own court. The bishop complained to the king that his possession of justice had been violated. The suspects themselves agreed and asked to be sent to the court of the bishop for judgment, "according

---

[27] Olim, 1:67 (XII).

[28] Olim, 1:117 (III).

[29] Olim, 1:435 (VIII).

to the use and custom of the city," and the king agreed.[30]

In another, there had been an armed conflict in the village of Saint-Pourçain, and the local prior who held all justice in the place confiscated some men's property in order to compel them to make amends. These men complained to the king, claiming that the prior was acting outside his rights. The king heard their case and determined that the prior was well within his possession of justice and they were returned to his court for judgment.[31] In yet another case, the monks of Verzelaius were wrong to have a servant of the king's whipped because they did not have justice over him, and so they needed to make amends to him.[32] In a final example here, Johannes Tanpiere had been banned from the village of Peronne for murder. He argued that the deceased had actually attacked him with a club and that he had managed to take the club and defend himself, leading to the death of the aggressor. Parlement ordered the village to lift the ban, but instructed Johannes to go and make peace with the family of the deceased.[33]

In all of this, there was no notion whatsoever that the private use of force was in and of itself somehow violent. What is relevant is the justice of the use of force.[34] What is more, the just use of force was not contained within the "network" of those people who were recognized in court as possessing a right to justice. Rather, such official recognition was an exception in the sense that it emerged only when there was some conflict. When there was a conflict between the king's men and Arnulphus Bailledart concerning justice over thieves and murderers, Parlement ordered an inquest into who had actually made use of justice over murders in the land, "because this was an uncertain thing."[35] Once the inquest was over, this

---

[30] Olim, 1:417 (II).

[31] Olim, 1:608 (XVI).

[32] Olim, 1:437 (XV).

[33] Olim, 1:66 (IX).

[34] Olim, 1:67 (XIII).

[35] Olim, 1:656 (XV).

uncertainty was gone and Parlement knew who used force against murders in those parts. But this knowledge did not somehow legitimize an action that had been previously illegitimate or violent: it had always been legitimate, that is to say, peaceful, even before there was a recognized "right." Violence was violence because it was unjust or because it was opposed to the peace, not because it happened outside a closed juridical order.[36]

Up to this point, I have been discussing the use and possession of "justice," the use of force in society. But, this is really to do violence to the sources in order to cater to modern prejudices. As I stated above, rights to the wielding of force were not somehow privileged and Parlement was not especially interested in possession and use of justice. Indeed, "justice" was not categorically different from rights that had nothing to do with the wielding of force. The arguments heard and the procedures followed by Parlement concerning who had the right to justice were substantively identical to those over who had a right to the trees that fell in a certain wood, or who had the right to pasture their pigs in a certain field in June and who in August, or who had the right to charge a toll for crossing a certain bridge, or who had the right to build a mill in a certain village. An inquest (or inquisition) into rights and a criminal trial were the same procedure.[37]

Whenever there was a situation in which differentiation had broken down, where scarcity led to conflict, issues concerning "possession" and "use" arose and Parlement sought to determine and maintain the peace. In this process, rights made an appearance: rights to justice, rights to resources, rights to certain taxes, rights to certain offices, even rights to certain interpersonal interactions. But these rights only emerged once a scarcity-induced conflict had, in fact, occurred, and such a conflict could occur in any "sector" of society. There was no universal code of law and rights within which conflict and co-

---

[36] Olim, 1:94 (VIII).
[37] Olim, 1:111 (XXI); 1:111 (XXII); 1:161 (V).

operation could function. Rather, all conflict was eligible for a "rights" solution.

For example, the peasants of a certain village went every spring to a nearby wood to cut down the dead trees for firewood. One year the local knight stopped them on the way and took their laden carts. They protested, saying, "We have always taken firewood from this forest." Indeed, responded the knight, "but you have always taken only one cartload; this year you have two." Parlement held an inquest and ruled that in the previous forty years sometimes the peasants had loaded one cart sometimes two. The knight was wrong and violated the peace through his actions and he was to pay amends. But, what is really important is that now the peasants have a "right" to that dead wood in the forest, two cart loads. Before the conflict, it was just something they did within the peace. Conflict changed the situation, and the conflict was not solved by appeal to abstract and universal rights and laws but to the particulars of time and place before the conflict had erupted—that is to say, to the peace.

Nearly all of the activities of society operated in such a way. There were hundreds of thousands of people engaged in countless activities and interacting with each other in countless ways. Some of these activities and interactions we now associate with the State or with government, others we would now associate with economics, family, entertainment, or religion. But our categories are largely irrelevant. All of these activities, the way the population went about all its business, constituted the society's order, known as "the peace." Conflicts were discrete events that occurred when differentiation broke down, when scarcity and so conflict emerged. Scarcity exists socially in actuality only when two parties are in fact attempting to possess something that cannot be possessed by both. The modern notion that scarcity is ubiquitous is based on the hypothetical situation of everyone wanting more of everything at the expense of everyone else in every possible situation. It is assumed that in every interaction scarcity will be the defining condition. Scarcity is therefore made an economic law, an axiom; it is turned into a totalized concept or theory. The people of the thirteenth century, however, dealt with actual scarcity, not such hypothetical, absolutized scarcity. The peace was the field on which individual instances of scarcity emerged and were played out to resolution. Instances of scarcity (and so, conflict) were exceptions: peace was a condition of abundance.

To put it in terms of modern economics, peace was the sum total of uncontested (in thought as much as practice) monopolies. When there was a conflict, what needed to be determined was what the peace had been, and in making this determination, rights were born. On account of conflict, monopolies that had once been only a matter of differentiated practice within the peace became a right. A certain knight of Chartres claimed that the merchants who stayed in his lands had to use his ovens. Parlement agreed and the knight gained a right, a recognized monopoly.[38] Rights, therefore sprung up here and there, not in some abstract or systematic manner that led to a hierarchical or juridical ordering of society. Rather, rights were little patches that were sewn onto the tapestry of society where an unfortunate tear had developed. The king was the tailor. Rights to justice, rights to the wielding of physical coercion, were not distinct from other rights in this society, and the idea of sovereignty was completely absent: the king's rights were not different than those of anyone else, even if there were more of them. It is sometimes said that the medieval understanding of rights and the modern understanding are radically distinct. I do not believe this to be the case. In both, rights emerge only where there is conflict: rights are something held by one person over and against another. The difference is found not in rights themselves, but in the extent of the conflict that they assuage. Modernity has posited universal conflict and so has universal, human rights, whereas the Middle Ages of St. Louis posited conflict as an exception and so had limited, disconnected and particular rights.

---

[38] Olim, 1:64 (III).

Let us look at some more examples. The Templars of a certain house claimed to have the right to pasture their pigs in a local lord's wood, and Parlement agreed.[39] When the Archbishop of Bourges built a new oven, the abbot of a local monastery complained, and Parlement ruled that the archbishop's oven must be removed and that the abbot was to remain in possession of his.[40] Parlement investigated whether the men of Goniex had been "conquered" by the men of Asnières, specifically whether they had been despoiled of a pasture, and found that they had not been.[41] Parlement commissioned an inquest to determine whether injury had been done to the knight Philip when the provost of Bray had let his pigs into his game preserve and ruled that the provost owed him twenty pounds for damages.[42] An inquest was commissioned to determine whether the chapter of Bayeux had the use of holding the church of St. Peter de Darnetel when their see was vacant and so during the time of the king's "regalia" rights. Nothing could be proved for either party, and so the case was suspended.[43] The abbess of Doeseto-Juriori claimed to be in possession of fishing in a certain river, and Parlement agreed.[44] When a conflict arose over the possession of a bridge, Parlement determined which family had built the bridge and granted them possession.[45] A house of Templars had confiscated the cart full of wood from a leper house, claiming that the house had the right to send only one servant with a one four-wheeled cart pulled by one horse into their forest and that the house had sent two servants. Parlement ruled against the Templars, saying that the leper house could send two or three servants.[46] A servant of the king named Bartholomew claimed that he had

---

[39] Olim, 1:119 (V).
[40] Olim, 1:120 (VI).
[41] Olim, 1:161 (VII).
[42] Olim, 1:163 (X).
[43] Olim, 1:165 (XV).
[44] Olim, 1:178 (V).
[45] Olim, 1:218 (IV).
[46] Olim, 1:493 (XI).

a right to all the fines that were paid to the king on account of people fraudulently measuring wine. This claim was based on the possession and use of his predecessors to his office. Parlement ruled in his favor, revealing that the king's own administration and household could assert rights against the king from *within* the king's rights.[47]

Parlement, therefore, approached a conflict looking for the peace, and the parties to the conflict inevitably presented rival versions of what constituted this peace: they presented rival "peaces."[48] Parlement's investigations were, therefore, appropriately and profoundly unconcerned with law in any sense that modern people would recognize. Rather, they were above all interested in what they called "use" or "possession." When the Abbot of Saint-Exparchius complained of having been dispossessed of a certain castle, an inquest was commissioned to find out "whether he had been in possession, for how long, how he was ejected, and by whom."[49] One had possession of a certain function, piece of property, or right if it could be demonstrated that he had somehow disposed of it or if he was generally reputed to have done so. To have "possession" was to have legitimacy.[50] This legitimacy could be recognized explicitly after the advent of some conflict, as in the case of the peasants and the carts of wood discussed above, a recognition that carried with it the implicit retroactive "possession" of this right before it became a right. Or possession could be granted outright, given by one who had possession to one who did not.[51] To hold something without having "possession" of it, either implied or explicit, was an act of injustice or violence.

"Use" was different but very closely related. To have use was to have actually made use of something that one possessed.

---

[47] Olim, 1:571 (XIII).

[48] Olim, 1:168 (V); 1:214 (VII).

[49] Olim, 1:193 (XII).

[50] Olim, 1:15 (I); 1:19 (XIV); 1:67 (XI); 1:170 (X); 1:234 (IX); 1:521 (VII).

[51] *Actes*, 423.

Discussions concerning use were discussions about what was the actual status of the peace in practice. Demonstrating "use" was the way one demonstrated the reality of "possession."[52] And so, use was the ultimate criteria of the investigations of Parlement. When Lord Amalcircus de Meulan claimed that his father had had possession of selling wood from a certain forest "for the past three kings," he was quick to add that his father had actually made use of this possession.[53] When the men of Credulius sought recognition of their right to dry wood in the boundary lands of their village, they presented evidence that they had used this wood since the time of King Philip.[54]

Use and possession, however, were not private property. When the lepers of Bayeux began selling firewood, the king's bailiff objected: the lepers were in possession of collecting as much firewood as an ass could carry in a day for their own use, but selling it was an innovation beyond this possession and usage. Parlement agreed: the lepers had possession only of what the wood could actually do, for example, "burn or be assembled into a building."[55] The Abbot of Beaulieu, on the other hand, successfully demonstrated that he could use his possession of wood rights to fuel his ovens to make bread to sell.[56] Like possession of justice, possession of any function, right, resource, or property was capable of infinite subdivision and contextualization. One had possession not in the absolute sense of property, but within the context of the differentiated peace. When the mayor of Amiens claimed that a certain woman owed a particular tax because her husband was a merchant, she protested that, in fact, her husband was a leper and so now exempt. That may be, the court decided, but the woman still lived with her husband and still held his property, and so she owed the tax: the context, the actual relationship

---

52 Olim, 1:4 (V); 1:185 (I); 1:205 (I).
53 Olim, 1:179 (VI).
54 Olim, 1:192 (X); See also: Olim, 1:77 (II).
55 Olim, 1:566 (II); 1:233 (VII).
56 *Actes*, 411.

between the woman and the town, had not changed enough to change her obligations, and so the town retained possession of the tax.[57]

Use was more important than anything else. Use was the thing that Parlement was ultimately after. Who had it and for how long?[58] The answer to these questions was the key to answering the question "what was the peace?" because the peace was concretely the summation of all peaceful activity, of all the "uses" of society. Therefore, use was not properly use if it was contested—indeed, "use of this kind had no strength."[59] The mere fact that someone had managed to do a certain thing did not give that person the "use" of doing so, properly speaking.[60] The men of Noion were denied use of a certain forest because whatever use they may have previously made was demonstrably forced.[61] A certain noble family claimed that they had held a piece of land for their own use for twenty-five years. The local inhabitants, however, asserted this was done only through force and that they, in fact, had use of pasturing their animals on the land. Parlement ruled in favor of the inhabitants.[62]

Use and so possession had to be peaceful.[63] Each party in a case was therefore presenting a rival version of the peace, and they had to go back far enough to find uncontested practice. In a conflict over possession of high justice between the Hospitallers and the Count of Blois, Parlement found that the count had had possession "peacefully and without complaint until four years ago," and so his right was recognized.[64] The men of the village of Saint-Richard claimed that until ten years prior, they had "peacefully and without contradiction" held certain

---

57   Olim, 1:578 (VIII)
58   Olim, 1:156 (V); 1:190 (VII); 1:192 (VIII); 1:212 (I); 1:217 (I); 1:224 (XII); 1:571 (XIII).
59   Olim, 1:547 (XII).
60   Olim, 1:83 (XVI); 1:535 (III).
61   Olim, 1:7 (VII).
62   Olim, 1:74 (XXVII).
63   Olim, 1:228 (XX); 1:237 (II); Olim 1:77 (II).
64   Olim, 1:5 (XIV).

types of justice, but the abbot of the local monastery denied this, saying that the justice was his.[65]

The demonstration that a certain "use" had been contested from the beginning was demonstration that it was not a "use" at all because it was a demonstration that the use was not peaceful, and what Parlement was after was the peace. Even if there had been a period of uncontested use, the challenging party could argue that the period was very short and that the actual peace was to be found before it began.[66] But, this was not always successful. The monks of Royaumont argued that they had the use until recently of bringing their goods through the lands of the commune of Mantes without paying any tolls. The commune argued that they had been collecting these tolls for at least sixteen years. The monks lost.[67] Duration of peaceful use, therefore, became the primary criterion by which Parlement ruled: how long had a party behaved in a certain way without opposition from rivals? In 1264 Parlement commissioned an inquest to determine "whether Arnuphus, called Bailledart, and his ancestors had use of a tax in Montchaton, and which tax, and for how long, and over which people, and how, and if peacefully, and if with the knowledge and not the contradiction of the king's men, and if there was *fama* concerning this, and if the village recognized it."[68] If one could demonstrate that he had acted in peaceful possession for a significant period of time (ten years was normally enough, forty years was much better, and living memory trumped all else), he was determined by Parlement to have possession through his use and so to hold a right to that possession, and the king upheld his right.[69] Otherwise, one could lose his property or "uses" to the last person who could demonstrate peaceful possession.

---

[65] Olim, 1:128 (VII).

[66] Olim, 1:554 (XI); Olim 1:488 (I).

[67] Olim, 1:190 (IV).

[68] Olim, 1:186 (II); 1:181 (XII).

[69] Olim, 1:11 (V); 1:78 (III); 1:78 (V); 1:126 (IV); 1:168 (IV); 1:170 (XIII); 1:193 (XIII); 1:502 (XXVIII–XXIX); 1:508 (IX); 1:542 (XVI); 1:553 (VI); 1:585 (VIII).

A certain knight petitioned Parlement to return a castle that his father had lost during the Albigensian wars and which was currently in the possession of another knight named Jordanus. Jordanus defended his possession, claiming that he had held the castle peacefully for the past thirty years. Parlement found that Jordanus had misrepresented his possession, and so it was accounted as no possession at all: the castle was transferred to the challenging knight.[70] When a knight in a local court ruled that it was acceptable that two squires appropriated a pasture from the men of Bobiez, notwithstanding the "long duration and peaceful use" of the men, the king quickly corrected the knight's error because "through his force many poor men in many locations would be hurt."[71]

Notions of time and memory were, therefore, intrinsic to order. It was truly the temporal order over which the king ruled. In the modern liberal system, time is irrelevant to law in principle. The definition of law itself is not concerned with time; law operates outside of time. The few exceptions demonstrate the point. We feel that there is something "medieval" and out of place, perhaps even unjust, but at least exceptional, about such things as common-law marriage, squatters' rights, or statutes of limitation, and so it is not surprising that the tendency in recent law has been toward the suppression of these "old-fashioned" temporal laws. In the society under investigation, however, temporality was intrinsic to the peace and so to justice and law.

This appears a paradox. Society is viewed as fundamentally at peace. This peace is what Parlement's inquests were trying to find and what the king was trying to maintain. However, this peace was conceived of within an understanding of time, of change. Time was not the enemy of peace; it was the "situation" of peace, its setting. The peace subsisted in time and was defined by time. It was understood that things change. Change was not the problem; conflict was the problem. When

---

[70] Olim, 1:549 (XVI).
[71] Olim, 1:595 (VIII).

something changed without conflict, it was understood to have happened within the duration and flux that was the temporal peace. If conflict arose in response to something new happening, that new thing was by definition not within the peace.[72] When the noble who was in charge of the defense of Sancerre attempted to extend his control over the selling of grain, an abbot protested that he had the use and liberty to sell grain freely, and so the noble's men who had confiscated his goods had done so "through violence." Parlement agreed with the abbot.[73] Had no one opposed the noble for a considerable time, his control of the grain would have been, by definition, within the bounds of the peace.

If conflict arose after a long period of peaceful use, it was the instigator of the conflict that was, in fact, doing something new and the person defending his long use was resisting this new thing from within the peace.[74] It was as much a violation of the peace to attempt to constitute a new use over the objections of others as it was to object to a possession that had long been peacefully in use. A serf who fled his lord violated the peace; a lord who captured his serf who had been living in a city for a year and a day, however, was the violator of the peace.[75] There was little notion of timeless, absolute rights or possessions. For example, the men of the village presented a long list of complaints against two local knights: The knights and their ancestors had "through violence" imposed a new warenna (land reserved for hunting); the knights had "violently" appropriated the village's common loom; the knights had "violently" seized mattresses from the homes of the men who opposed them; and the knights and their ancestors had "usurped" the villager's rights to fish in the local brook. The villagers asked the king to compel the knights to restore everything to the village. The knights countered, zeroing in on the role of their "ancestors,"

---

[72] Olim, 1:13 (XIX); 1:74 (XXVIII); 1:490 (VI); 1:530 (IX).

[73] Olim, 1:63 (I).

[74] Olim, 1:178 (I); 1:600 (I).

[75] Olim, 1:85 (I); 1:86 (II); 1:116 (II); 1:181 (XIII); 1:627 (XXII).

that all of these possessions had been held peacefully for a long time and so even the seizing of mattresses from the men's homes was not "violent." Parlement's inquest found that indeed the knights had legitimate possession and that the possession was to be maintained.[76] The villagers, it seems, were the ones upsetting the peace—too much time had passed without conflict and so the center of the peace had shifted. When a conflict erupted between a knight and an abbot over possession of a wood, Parlement ruled that neither party had been in peaceful possession for sixty years—the king actually had—and so it would remain.[77]

It was not always clear, however, which party was the breaker of the peace. Sometimes, Parlement changed its mind. In 1260 it agreed to hear the complaint of the Abbot of Saint-Vincent against Enguerran de Couci. The abbot claimed that Enguerran's father had despoiled him of a forest. Enguerran responded that his father, his brother, and he had possessed the forest for more than ten years uncontested, and so Parlement dismissed the abbot, determining him to be attempting to upset the peace. The abbot pressed his case, arguing that Enguerran's father had possessed the forest through continual violence. When he died, Enguerran's older brother was away on crusade and Enguerran himself was a minor. The abbot, therefore, had no choice but to wait to contest the possession. The ten years of possession were only seemingly peaceful because of special circumstances. The king himself reviewed the case and determined that Parlement should indeed hear the abbot's case: Enguerran's possession was dubiously peaceful.[78]

It is clearly wrong to think of this order as static. Rather, change was at its very heart. Change, the passage of time, and the flux of human relationships with each other, with material things, and with institutions were the conditions within which the king's justice operated: "How long?" was a necessary ques-

---

[76] Olim, 1:105 (V).

[77] Olim, 1:232 (IV).

[78] Olim, 1:492 (X).

tion. It is, in fact, modern law that should be seen as static in the sense that time does not affect it. In a modern conflict we consult books of abstract and immutable, timeless statutes. In St. Louis's France they investigated change, time—the living experience of people in a temporal order that was at its core one of continuous transition.

Sometimes historians will refer to this society as one based on custom, but this is not accurate, at least not according to the terminology used in the thirteenth century. Custom was not the principle of order. Rather, custom was mostly procedural law used to adjudicate disputes within the social order just described.[79] For the most part, custom determined how one dealt with a conflict. Custom could, however, be what we might call quasi-statutory. When certain problems arose over and over again—for example, problems concerning inheritance or marriage—customs could develop as assumed rights, as solutions to persistent points of conflict.[80] (A "new" custom, therefore, was by definition an act of violence.)[81] Such custom, however, was considered the "peaceful" course of action only by default. This custom approached a modern conception of law in the sense that it could grant rights to an individual in an undifferentiated manner: everyone had this set of rights or obligations, but only by default.[82]

The differentiated practice, if it could be identified and, if it was in conflict with custom, displaced custom through a certain type of right often known as a "liberty." One had possession of a liberty and made use of it just like any other right. Custom did not constitute the peaceful status in any particular situation. Actual, demonstrable use trumped custom, and so the context of particular conflicts had to be investigated.[83] For

---

[79] Olim, 1:59 (I); 1:99 (I); 1:539 (IX); 1:557 (XVI); 1:567 (V); *Actes*, 427.

[80] Olim, 1:4 (II); 1:53 (IV); 1:72 (XXII); 1:84 (XXI); 1:195 (III); 1:495 (XV); 1:527 (VIII); 1:569 (VIII); *Actes*, 597, 670.

[81] Olim, 1:123 (XVI).

[82] Olim, 1:216 (XI); 1:548 (XIV).

[83] Olim, 1:119 (IV); 1:570 (IX); 1:570 (XI); 1:583 (IV); 1:606 (XII).

example, a certain knight claimed that his predecessors had peacefully sold the dead wood from one of the king's forests without license from the king, which was necessary according to custom. Parlement investigated and determined that he did not hold this liberty.[84] The men of Berville won their case against the knight Gui, who insisted that they pay him the dues that he was customarily paid because "through the time of four or five lords, for forty years or more," they peacefully paid a lesser amount.[85] Custom was, therefore, decidedly not law in the modern understanding. It was more of what we might think of as a social habit: the same type of conflict arises over and over again, and so rights are discovered repeatedly and these rights are eventually given the provisionally universal status of a custom.[86] But actual use—which, in the context of a conflict, would manifest itself as a real, differentiated right— necessarily rendered such custom null.[87]

Charters and privileges were similar to custom. In the records of Parlement, charters are surprisingly rare, given the common image of the period as particularly litigious and legalistic. When they did appear, charters were treated as evidence of a resolution of a particular conflict or as evidence of a particular situation in a certain time and place, such as the transfer of possession of some right. Charters helped establish what had constituted the peace, but they had little legally binding authority in the sense of a modern statute or a modern contract. They were a testament to a public act.[88]

But, when they were in conflict, custom almost always displaced charters and peaceful use displaced both. When the Abbot of Saint-Riquier evoked a royal charter in support

---

[84]	Olim, 1:41 (XXIX); 1:53 (II); 1:63 (I); 1:77 (II); 1:186 (IV); 1:189 (II); 1:207 (V); 1:211 (XIV); 1:212 (II); 1:212 (VI); 1:216 (X); 1:226 (XV–XVI); 1:514 (I); 1:533 (XIX); 1:543 (XX).

[85]	Olim, 1:601 (IV).

[86]	Olim, 1:160 (III).

[87]	Olim, 1:70(XIX). There were very few exceptions, and they prove the norm: e.g., Olim, 1:43 (XXXIII).

[88]	Olim, 1:77 (I).

of his right to remove the mayor of the town at his will, the townspeople responded by arguing that it had never been used this way before. The abbot claimed that this was because the monks had liked the mayors, and so their lack of use should not be held against the charter. The abbot lost.[89] The bakers of a certain town argued that they had a charter that clearly stated that only bakers can make and sell bread. Therefore, the widows of bakers should be forbidden from doing so. The widows, however, argued that while their husbands lived they had long made bread and sold it, and what is more, as widows they had continued to do so for a long time. The bakers lost.[90]

Time and again, a party to a conflict would present a charter attesting to their rights and Parlement would rule either that these rights were never consistently exercised or "used" and so were defunct or that they had been "used" and so were still valid. When the Abbot of Colombes presented a charter attesting to his right to justice over a certain thief and the local bailiff was not able to demonstrate his own possession of such justice, the thief was handed over to the abbot.[91] Charters were conditioned by use.[92] They could help determine what the peace had been and for how long, but they did not create order or abstractly delegate legal rights as we would understand them. They were a type of witness and their testimony was judged along with all the evidence of the peace.[93]

The fact that use and so possession arose out of the duration of the peace and gained their legitimacy from it, does not mean that one could do as one pleased within his possession. One possessed the right to administer justice, for example, through the peace, but one still had to administer justice, and justice was not something that one was empowered to make

---

[89] Olim, 1:523 (XIV).

[90] Olim, 1:559 (I); 1:575 (III).

[91] Olim, 1:497 (XVIII).

[92] Olim, 1:209 (IX); 1:435 (IX); 1:488 (I); 1:495 (XIV); 1:538 (VII); 1:573 (XVII).

[93] Olim, 1:198 (VIII); 1:552 (V); 1:655 (XIII); 1:687 (XXIV).

up or manipulate. Those who possessed justice were not a law unto themselves: justice, like any possession or use, was not private property. Its possessors had an obligation to uphold the peace, and it was the king's responsibility to make sure that they did so.[94] When the Count of Sancerre complained that he was being unjustly judged in Bourges because the court was made up of townspeople, Parlement investigated. The townspeople and clergy of Bourges argued against the count, saying that he had always been judged in the town and that the count's own court was made up of knights related to him and suspect of partiality. Parlement determined that it was true that the count had always been tried in the town, and what is more, the court of Bourges was just, being made up not only of townspeople but also of clerics and knights, and so Parlement ruled against the count.[95] In another example, Parlement ruled that the burghers of Compiègne did have possession, through long use, of the right to capture and hold in their prison debtors in the town but that such men were to be treated humanely, not placed in stocks or shackles, and with provision for their necessities.[96] Parlement took possession of justice in a certain village from a canon of the church of Orleans and returned it to his chapter because of the canon's "misrule" in a case involving a local convent.[97] The mayor of Senlis was fined forty pounds and forbidden from holding office for five years because of a bad judgment that he made against a certain Jean, called Neret.[98] Justice, what was right, stood outside and above the particulars of any given situation or constellation of rights and uses.

The king was responsible for insuring that justice was done. However, it would be a grave mistake to read this as proof that the possession of justice was a delegation from the

---

[94] Olim, 1:73 (XXVI); 1:45 (VIII).

[95] Olim, 1:510 (XI); 1:544 (I).

[96] Olim, 1:539 (VIII).

[97] Olim, 1:541 (XIV).

[98] Olim, 1:587 (X). See also 1:655–66 (II–III).

king. Indeed, there was nothing particularly distinct about the king's behavior with regards to the possession of justice. He was similarly concerned with the possession of any right. If one had possession of a certain bridge and so the tolls that came with it, that person was obliged to maintain the bridge.[99] If one had possession of a certain tax that was levied in order to defend the safety of travelers, he had the obligation to do so.[100] Possession was often as much a responsibility as it was a right.

To put it another way, control of resources or rights carried with it obligations, and vice-versa. When the Templars presented their case that a certain man who joined them was not, in fact, a serf, all they had to prove was that he had been obliged to pay the census of Issoudun because the men who paid this census were known to be free. They won.[101] Rights and obligations were together a part of what constituted the peace, and the king was charged with defending the peace.[102] But neither the rights nor the obligations emanated from the king as their source. This means, however, that the king was making judgments according to principles that lay outside the matrix of rights, use, and possession. He judged according to what was right, just. He determined where right was, who in any given situation was superior and who inferior: he entered into the differentiated social matrix and saw who was right and who was wrong, who was peaceful and who violent.

This was the role of the king and his men. They judged, personally. They did this according to principles outside themselves and outside the quasi-legal system of possessions and uses. Ultimately, they judged according to divine law and with wisdom: this was the authority they bore. Their judgment, however, was totally dependent on the reality of use and possession because divine law did not stipulate whether it was lawful

---

[99] Olim, 1:496 (XVI).
[100] Olim, 1:212 (IV); 1:622 (XIV).
[101] Olim, 1:531 (XIII); 1:537 (II).
[102] Olim, 1:208 (VIII).

for Fulk to cut down a tree in a certain wood at a certain time
of year. Rather, divine law stipulated that he ought not to cut
the tree if he was using violence or if he was using his superior
power to hurt another. This is what the king had to determine.
This was the authority of the judge. In one circumstance the
king might determine that cutting down the tree was lawful,
but in another that it was unlawful. Thus the king can be seen
as a source of explicit law (that is, the mechanism by which
practice was identified and cataloged juridically). But, unlike
Louis XIV, he most certainly was not the State.

Because the whole order rested on peace and so on fundamental justice, the king as judge could rule in uncertain cases
and so innovate to the degree compatible with justice.[103] He
could temper the strict rule of use and possession if he believed it to cause harm or to somehow work against the peace
that it was supposed to constitute.[104] The simple fact that one
stayed within the letter of his "rights" did not mean that his
"uses" and his "possessions" allowed him to hurt another. Conflict demonstrated that the understanding of such rights was
in need of amendment, and the king could make such determinations. When a conflict arose concerning the extent of the
Abbot of Ferraria's use of leading his pigs into the wood called
Bellechaume during the time of acorns, the result of Parlement's investigation, while affirming the abbot's possession, had
reservations about its extent. Parlement, therefore, ruled that
while the abbot could retain possession, he was not to be understood to have a right and that if anyone complained, he was
to be heard and justice done.[105] A certain man of Bourges and
his heirs were forgiven their obligation to pay a certain amount
to the king every year. The man had had to pay the amount
for the right to mint money in the city, but he claimed that no
money had been so minted in living memory. The king commissioned an inquest. There were no charters and there was

---

[103] Olim, 1:622 (XV); 1:665 (II); 1:561 (IX); 1:589 (XII).
[104] Olim, 1:604 (IX); 1:541 (XV).
[105] Olim, 1:215 (VIII).

no use to be found, and so the investigating bailiff asked the people of the city what they knew of the situation. He reported back to Parlement that the *fama* in the city supported the man's story: he paid his fee every year for an office that was defunct and so he was not actually in possession of anything of value. The king therefore nullified his own right to the payment and freed the men's children from the obligation.[106]

It was worthwhile to argue that some new action would hurt the peace. Even if one did not have a "legal" case, the king had to consider what course of action would damage the peace more. The men of Crépy, for example, tried to have the king stop a certain Master Thibaut from building a mill near the village because they had possession of the king's mill there and the new mill would hurt them. The king ruled in favor of Thibaut because he had the clear right to construct a mill, but with the reservation that if he could find some more significant royal right against the construction, the mill would be destroyed.[107] However, when the Abbot of Cluny and all the surrounding nobles complained to the king that a squire named Stephan was building a castle on the top of a hill, the king ruled that even though the squire and his ancestors had held the hill throughout living memory, a new castle would do "much damage to all the patria" because all the local nobles were opposed to it, and so the castle must be torn down.[108] Use and possession were defended to the extent that they constituted the peace. They were most certainly not absolute rights.

Beyond this, though, the king could suppress what were called "bad customs." If customs can be seen as social habits, good customs were virtues and bad customs were vices. Bad customs lacked the force of custom because they were not constitutive of the peace, but rather sowed conflict and disorder. The king could judge and suppress such customs,[109] but this

---

[106] Olim, 1:615 (VI).
[107] Olim, 1:555 (XII).
[108] Olim, 1:576 (VI).
[109] Olim, 1:497 (XIX); 1:562 (XII–XIV); *Actes*, 651.

was something that had to be done with great care and it was very rare. Other changes could also be made. Actions could be taken for the common good of the "patria" or they could be taken because some need had arisen that had not been previously dealt with. But such situations had to be approached very carefully and action taken only after full consideration of whether it might somehow endanger the peace. When the chapter of Amiens sought to build a new cloister, the king, seeing that "many opposed" the construction and that it would "be to the detriment of many," ruled that the chapter would not be allowed this new thing.[110] Allowing a manifestly new thing or making a significant change to the way things were done that would affect people's explicit rights normally meant acting only after having taken counsel with and having received the consent of a large number of highly respected men who determined that the action was in furtherance of the peace.[111] There was no "constitution" here: the king's power was bound by judgment.

Indeed, this was not a closed legal order. It was an order that looked outside itself for its principle and so it was an order that was full of exceptions and considerations and judgments. I was once giving a lecture on Parlement to a group of academics and I overheard one of them whisper to his colleague, "It was all so arbitrary." But nothing could be further from the truth: the arbitrary was precisely that which this order could not abide. Nothing was arbitrary. Practices were defended and maintained because they were just and peaceful and not, as in our system, because they fit properly into a certain constellation of written laws that somehow manage to justify their own authority without reference to what is in fact right. (It would certainly seem to the jurists of Parlement profoundly arbitrary that the people of the state of Washington are regulated not with regard to how they, in fact, relate to each other, but with regard to how they fit into categories devised in Washington, DC.) When, in 1259, Philip, the new chaplain in the royal

---

[110] Olim, 1:18 (X).

[111] Olim, 1:553 (VII); 1:608 (XVII).

church of Beate-Marie de Clarmonte, asked for new clothes from the king because his predecessors were accustomed to receive such a gift, he was asserting a right. Parlement commissioned an inquest and ruled against him.[112] Peter, a squire, claimed that whenever the king had a tree cut down in a particular forest, he and his ancestors had the use of the branches but not the trunk. Parlement agreed.[113] "Particular" and "arbitrary" are opposites, and this world was rather particular.

Even the so-called "ordinances" of the king were not laws in the modern sense. Rather, the king's ordinances were overwhelmingly procedural rules that he made concerning his own rights in certain places or concerning his men's functions as arbitrators in conflicts. They were not "laws of the land."[114] For example, in 1261 the king issued an ordinance that stipulated that in the royal domains the lands of debtors in default were to be sold before their pledges. He was regulating his own enforcement of his rights to justice, as was the case with most royal ordinances.[115] The most obvious example of this type is the *Grande Ordonnance* that I considered in Part I of this work. There could also be emergency ordinances for the good of the *patria*, but these were truly extraordinary and were justified only because they clearly served the peace.[116] When they did somehow infringe on someone's possession, it was the ordinance that normally gave way.[117]

This is a terribly important point, and to demonstrate it let us go back to this idea of the monopolization of legitimate violence. Probably no supposed ordinances of the king have received more attention in the historiography than his famous "bans" on private warfare and duels. Given what I have said already, the reasons for this should be fairly obvious. If the

---

[112] Olim, 1:84 (XIX).
[113] Olim, 1:209 (IX).
[114] Olim, 1:420 (XI).
[115] Olim, 1:520 (V); *Actes*, 429, 463.
[116] Olim. 1:522 (XI–XII).
[117] Olim, 1:8 (XV).

king was really attempting to build absolutism, slowly but surely enforcing his sovereignty, it was perfectly fitting that he would move to monopolize warfare—the *sine qua non* of the State. In a State, of course, there are no private armies, and it was precisely the chaos caused by such private armies that supposedly preceded the rise of the monarchies. What was so unique about the anti-war ordinance of 1258, we are told, was that Louis IX "promulgated this text as a simple royal act on the basis of his authority as king."[118] The king was aggregating all power to himself, it seems. However, when the ordinance concerning private war is read within the context of the *negotium pacis et fidei* and of actions of Parlement, this absolutist reading falls apart.

The ordinance actually comes to us in the form of a letter that Louis wrote to the faithful of the diocese of Le Puy in the South of France. Before we turn to the letter itself, though, we need to consider its recipient: he was none other than our protagonist Gui Foucois. Gui, as we saw in Part I, was the king's faithful servant. He had worked tirelessly in Louis's service conducting precisely the types of inquests that underwrote all of Parlement's actions. As an *enquêteur* he was one of the men on the ground working for the peace. However, when his wife died in 1257, Gui took Holy Orders and within a year was elected to the see of Le Puy. The particulars of his election will be addressed in the next chapter, but what is important here is that when he became a bishop, he also became a part of the king's *consilium*. Gui was one of the judges of Parlement[119] and continued to work for the king conducting inquests and enforcing Parlement's rulings in the South.[120] Louis's letter, then, was written to a member of his own apparatus of justice and, as we will explore in the next chapter, a member of his

---

[118] Justine Firnhaber-Baker, "From God's Peace to the King's Order: Late Medieval Limitations on Non-Royal Warfare," *Essays in Medieval Studies* 23 (2006): 20.

[119] *Olim*, 1:75 (XXIX).

[120] *Olim*, 1:495 (XIV); 1:512 (XIV).

network of *consilium et auxilium*. What is more, Gui, as Bishop of Le Puy, held all justice in the diocese, high and low, and so he was responsible for the maintenance of the peace. The text of the letter reads:

> Louis . . . etc., greetings to all the faithful of the kingdom in the diocese of Le Puy and the fiefs of the church of Le Puy. You should know that having had deliberations with our counsel we have inhibited all wars [*guerras*] in our kingdom, and arson, and the per-turbing of traveling wagons. Hence we mandate to you with strict warning, lest you might act against our said prohibition of wars, or might make fires, or disturb the peasants who drive wagons or the plow. If you presume to do otherwise, we give to our Seneschal the order to help faithfully and attentively our faithful and beloved G. [Gui Foucois] the elect of Le Puy to make peace in the land, and to punish the breakers of the peace on account of their guilt.[121]

Louis was here committing himself to the preservation of the peace in support of the local bishop, who held all justice in the territory. Anyone breaking that peace, an action that was necessarily crime, would be acted against. Louis was not doing anything bold or innovative. The letter is perfectly consistent with the entire program of Parlement as sketched above and with the *negotium pacis et fidei*, neither of which involved the monopolization of the use of force. What Louis was doing was making sure that everyone knew that he supported the bishop in his possession of justice and in his efforts to defend the peace, actions that as we have seen did not mean an appropriation of all coercion to some sovereign center. The word *guerra* itself was often used in reference to aggressive feuding or sedition, rather than what we might call open war, and Louis associates these *guerras* directly with the outright violent crimes of arson

---

[121] *Ordonnances*, 1:84.

and attacking peasants on the road.[122] Indeed, it is an anachronistic misreading to see Louis attempting to monopolize force, even force of a military nature, in this letter.

Examples from Parlement illustrate the point. In 1260 Parlement heard a complaint brought by a certain Louis, a knight. Louis accused another knight, Thomas, of wounding him treacherously. Thomas stated in his defense that he had been attacked and wounded by the nephew of Louis previously and that he had waited over forty days before attacking Louis in retribution. What Thomas was referencing was a custom of the land that had been accepted by the Crown in 1245 and that mandated that whenever some violent offense was committed against someone, he had to wait forty days before responding, and that during this time the relatives of the culprit had to be made aware of the crime and given a chance to restore peace.[123] If they failed to do this and, rather, helped the criminal, they could be acted against. Parlement looked into the case and decided in favor of Thomas, stating to Louis (the "victim") that given the circumstances, he should have been on his guard.[124] This case directly refutes the notion that St. Louis had somehow outlawed "private war," because the custom that decided the case was explicitly about open war between subjects. This is one example, of which there are many, where we can see clearly that the Crown was not attempting to monopolize what we might think of as military-type activity. Feuding, waging war of a sort, was allowed as long as it was conducted peacefully, so to speak—not through burning down barns or attacking peasants on the road.

Let us look at another example that reveals a different aspect of this private warfare issue. In 1260 Parlement ruled that the inhabitants of Tours were bound to come in arms to the defense of the chapter of Saint Martin de Tours when

---

[122] See J. F. Niemeyer, *Mediae Latinitatis Lexicon Minus* (Leiden: E. J. Brill, 2002), 1133.

[123] *Ordonnances*, 1:56.

[124] *Actes*, 436.

summoned by the chapter. The townspeople had protested that they were not bound to provide such armed service because the chapter did not have the right to high justice in the town. This is an interesting case because the townspeople were equating the right to try capital cases with the right to call up the militia. This makes sense to us as moderns because both actions reflect a monopolization of legitimate violence. In the modern State the distinction between the police and the army is blurry. But, the king's court ruled against this understanding. The townspeople were bound to come to arms because that was the way things had been done for as long as anyone could remember. The chapter had a right to call them up, and this right had nothing to do with any other rights that the chapter may or may not have held, such as the right to high justice.[125]

There are numerous cases in Parlement in which armed forces were condemned as acting criminally, where, say, the townspeople marched against their bishop and seized the castle, and Parlement ruled against them, saying that they acted violently. But it would be a huge mistake to read into these cases a categorical position of the Crown against private armed action. Rather, these cases must be read alongside the numerous cases similar to that in Tours, wherein people had an obligation to bear arms and fight.[126] It is hard to argue that the king was here working under some notion of sovereignty. Rather, rights to military-type behavior and the obligations to provide it were simply integrated into the web of reciprocal rights and duties, uses and possessions that held the whole society together. We see in Parlement just a glimpse of this activity: when the peace was somehow torn, either through unjust use of force or through the lack of the use of force when it was called for, we see the creation and maintenance of rights.

But, as was asserted above, rights were a result of exceptions to the rule. For every Tours, where the townspeople stopped raising a military force in the defense of the chapter,

---

[125] Olim, 1:116 (I); *Actes*, 496.
[126] Olim, 1:681 (XIII); 1:712 (XXXVII).

there are thousands of locations in the kingdom where we are forced to assume that local armed groups responded as they had always done, where there was no tear in the peaceful order and so no records in Parlement and, indeed, no rights at all. Acts of large-scale use of force that we would have to consider military in nature were treated within the same paradigm of justice as small uses of force: sometimes they were peaceful, sometimes violent.[127] Parlement had to look into the particulars: How many men came? Were they armed or unarmed? How many were armed? Did they have the use of carrying weapons? What acts of violence did they commit? Why did they do so? And on whose command were they acting?[128]

Closely related to Louis's supposed ban on private warfare is his supposed ban on duels. In 1260 Louis issued an ordinance in Parlement stipulating that in his domains the judicial battle was to be replaced with testimony of witnesses and with proofs. This is normally presented as yet another step in the march toward the State, a step toward monopolizing violence, a step toward rationality, bureaucracy, and the other Weberian planks of modern organization. This reading fits perfectly into the narrative of the inevitable and desirable appearance of the secular State, but, as with the common reading concerning the prohibition of private war, it is mistaken.

It is clearly true that Louis was concerned with innocence and guilt. In his courts, Louis wanted the innocent to prevail and the guilty to suffer the consequences for their actions, and we are right to see this imperative in his ordinance concerning duels. What is a grave mistake is to read into this ordinance a movement of the Crown to eradicate non-State violence from the kingdom. Rather, the ordinance was a procedural regulation that pertained exclusively to the king's men who were working in territories where the king held rights to high

---

[127] Olim, 1:14 (XXI); 1:67 (XIII); 1:93 (V); 1:110 (XIX); 1:170 (IX); 1:180 (VIII); 1:197 (VII); 1:436 (X); 1:556 (XIV); 1:584 (V); 1:608 (XVI); 1:637 (X); 1:693 (XXXV); *Actes*, 688.

[128] Olim, 1:131 (XII); 1:190 (V); 1:211 (XVI).

justice.[129] Duels themselves were not directly relevant to the
rights of the two parties. They were rather a question of judicial procedure in cases that had to do with those party's rights.
Duels were not a solution to a point of conflict; they were a
form of trial, of procedure to determine a solution, to determine guilt and innocence. Procedure, unlike rights, was subject
to reform and modification. The entire establishment of Parlement and the various regional courts that the Crown set up are
a demonstration of this point. The king did not want his men
to make use of the duel as a procedure because he believed it
to be questionable both logically and morally. However, as we
have seen, the king held rights to justice in a way no different
from how countless others in the kingdom held similar rights.
The king could not eradicate the duel from other people's jurisdictions. Nor did he try.

For example, the king's bailiff in the village of Saint-Pierre
acted on the king's ban of duels. The problem was that the
king shared the right to high justice in the village with the
local prior. The prior protested the bailiff's actions, saying
the king should not do such a thing without his consent. The
king agreed. He responded that the prior could indeed oversee
duels, but that the king's men were to have no part in them.
What is more, the king wanted his portion of any revenue that
might be generated by duels returned to the parties because he
did not want to be associated with duels in any way.[130] In numerous cases involving high justice, Parlement affirmed third
party rights that included the right to hold duels.[131] The point
here is that like in the case of private war, the king did not
make a kingdom-wide statute that abrogated legitimate violence under the umbrella of the Crown. Rather, with duels we
can easily see that the king operated at two levels with regards
to justice. He was himself the holder of rights to justice in
certain territories or over certain men, just like any number of

---

[129] Olim, 1:491 (VII).
[130] Olim, 1:494 (XII); 1:667 (VIII); *Actes*, 818.
[131] Olim, 1:24 (V); 1:128 (VII); 1:185 (XIX).

other people in the kingdom, and in this capacity he banned duels as a procedure of trial. But, he was also the upholder of rights in the face of violence against the peace of the realm. In this capacity he was king, and here he defended duels. The key thing to realize, though, is that it was precisely as king that his actions against third party violence were most limited. As king, he had extremely limited control over who used force when and under what circumstances. And if the behavior of Parlement is any indication of his motives, Louis had very little desire to change this.

So, let us return to the question: Was St. Louis attempting to build a sovereign State focused on himself? My conclusion is that he was clearly not doing so, not even in a "medieval" or "feudal" sense, through fiefs or oaths. For example, the Bishop of Vézelay complained bitterly to the king that the royal sene-schal had received the oaths on the king's behalf of every man in a certain village. This was in grave prejudice to his rights, the bishop contended, and had never been done before. The king was deeply concerned and asked the seneschal why this happened. The latter responded that the villagers themselves had asked to swear the oath and had claimed that they were accustomed to do so. The king was not satisfied and asked the two previous seneschals what the situation in the village had been during their time in office. They confirmed the bishop's story. The king declared the oath to be new and so completely void.[132]

The truth is that sovereignty can be found in St. Louis's reign only through the practice of sorting the historical data into modern categories. These categories are those that under-pin the State and its corollary, the market. We see the world as a sea of more or less interchangeable individuals, citizens and workers, engaged in a univocal social order underwritten by scarcity (or conflict) that is regularized through precise lan-guage and bureaucracy. There is no empty space in this order: every bit of power is accounted for, as is every bit of property.

---

[132] Olim, 1:617 (VIII).

Sovereignty is the one thing that stands over and against this homogeny: the sovereign wields ubiquitous violence in perfect keeping with the rationality of the social order. Our mistake is to suppose this order of things is the way human beings are in their nature. Thirteenth-century France was not so ordered. There was a great deal of empty space and thousands upon thousands of unique actors with masses of disconnected rights and liberties. It was this way, I contend, not because they had not yet figured out how to build the State. It was this way because they understood the world as temporal, differentiated, and ultimately peaceful, rather than as somehow eternal, entirely undifferentiated, and ultimately in perpetual conflict.

CHAPTER EIGHT

The Spiritual and the Temporal

The words, "And they went up over the breadth of the earth and encompassed the camp of the saints, and the beloved city," obviously do not mean that they gathered or will gather in some one place where, we must suppose, the camp of the saints and the beloved city is to be, for, of course this City is Christ's Church which is spread over the whole world. Wherever His Church will be (and it will be among all nations, "over the breadth of the earth"), there is to be the camp of the saints and the beloved City of God. There will she be, surrounded by all her enemies, intermingled with her as they are and will be in every people, girt with the appalling magnitude of that besetting, hemmed in, straitened, and encompassed by the pressures of that mighty affliction; but never will she give up her fighting spirit, her "camp," as St. John says.

—St. Augustine, *City of God* 20.11

IN THE PREVIOUS CHAPTER I focused on temporal concerns at the expense of ecclesiastical or spiritual. I did so in order to establish a vision of a social order very different from the liberal without introducing the problem of Church and State. As we have seen, this was an order that was not closed in on itself through a self-referential juridical system that rested ultimately on some sort of sovereignty. The realm of practice was in many ways an open field, ordered not by ubiquitous law but by a notion of justice that found its foundation in "the peace." In the previous chapter, one could not help but notice, I would think, the extent to which the prelates of the kingdom were integrated players on this field of temporal justice, use, possession, and rights. What we will see in this chapter is that spiritual power operated on the same field. In the introduction to this book, I quoted the popular theorist of secularization Philip Gorski. Referring to the medieval temporal and spiritual swords, he writes: "There was no question that the two should be, and were, distinct. The popes were to rule over the Church, and the princes were to rule over the state, and each had its own property, personnel, and politico-legal apparatus."[1] It would be hard for me to disagree more profoundly. In fact, the "property, personnel, and politico-legal apparatus" of each, not to mention the metaphysics that underwrote them, interpenetrated each other at every level: there was one field of action upon which both the spiritual and temporal functioned.

Historians often fail to recognize this, and reading modern notions of the secular and religious (of Church and State) back into the period, they identify Louis's behavior toward certain churchmen in certain circumstances as his position toward "the Church" as a whole. The most obvious example of this is the oft-cited account in Jean de Joinville's memoir of Louis's life in which the king is seen refusing to enforce

---

[1]   Philip S. Gorski, "Historicizing the Secularization Debate: Church, State, and Society in Late Medieval and Early Modern Europe, ca. 1300 to 1700," *American Sociological Review* 65, no. 1 (2000): 157.

certain excommunications promulgated by some of the kingdom's bishops. This account has often been used as evidence
for Louis's resistance to ecclesiastical power and his insistence
on the independence of royal power.[2] But, a careful reading of
Joinville's account in light of the context discussed at length
in the current book reveals the opposite to be the case. The
Bishop of Auxerre, representing a group of bishops, approached Louis and complained that Christendom was falling
to pieces because no one had any fear of excommunication.
The bishops, therefore, petitioned Louis to order his officers
to force those who had been in a state of excommunication
for a year and a day to give satisfaction to the Church. Louis
responded to the petition by stating that he would gladly
order his bailiffs to enforce such excommunications, but not
without first determining whether or not the sentences were
just. The bishops refused to accept this, claiming that it would
give the king cognizance of what pertained to them. The king,
however, replied that if he did otherwise he would be giving
them cognizance of what pertained to him and that for this
reason he would never order his men to force excommunicates
to seek absolution regardless of the justice of the censure. "For
if I did so," the king said, "I should be flying in the face of
God and justice," and he gave the bishops the example of the
Count of Brittany, who remained excommunicated for seven
years only to be absolved from all wrongdoing by the court of

---

2   Jean Richard, *Saint Louis: Crusader King of France*, ed. Simon Lloyd and
    trans. Jean Birrell (New York: Cambridge University Press, 1992), 219;
    Robert E. Lerner, "The Uses of Heterodoxy, the French Monarchy and Un-
    belief in the XIIIth century," *French Historical Studies* 4 (1965): 196; Gerard
    J. Campbell, S.J., "The Attitude of the Monarchy toward the Use of Ecclesi-
    astical Censures in the Reign of Saint Louis," *Speculum* 35, no. 4 (October
    1960): 535–55, at 547; Within the context of Joinville's account, Jacques Le
    Goff shows how the concept of an "alliance" between Church and Crown
    is predicated upon the same assumptions as that of conflict: "Although he
    sometimes rejected some of the excesses of the Church and the papacy—
    notably in matters of excommunication and finances—through his piety and
    conduct Saint Louis brought the alliance between the Church and the mon-
    archy to its highest point" (*Saint Louis*, trans. Gareth Evan Gollrad, 552).

Rome. If the king had forced him to seek absolution after a year, he would have sinned.[3]

Of course, as we saw in Part I of this book, Louis had no problem whatsoever in using force against contumacious excommunicates. Indeed, from the beginning, the practice was as much royal as ecclesiastical, and the use of secular power against heretics and excommunicates was a fundamental component of the *negotium pacis et fidei—the business of the peace and the faith.* This fact goes to the very heart of the common misinterpretation of Joinville's account. Those historians who would see Louis defending the independence of the royal power from that of the Church can do so only because they have set up a false dichotomy between the ecclesiastical and the secular wherein, if the king enforces an excommunication, he is acting as a servant to the ecclesiastical power. According to this reading, when the king demands that he first investigate ecclesiastical censures, he is essentially denying ecclesiastical power and establishing the self-sufficiency of royal power. There is here posited a zero-sum game, a contest over sovereignty. But this interpretation assumes that excommunication was not directly the business of the Crown: it assumes that excommunication was something that the king could ignore without the Crown itself being undermined fundamentally. It assumes that excommunication operated outside the field of Louis's justice, that those who wielded the censure did so as a part of a different "order," even of a different "State," from that defended by Louis in his own right as the temporal power. According to my reading, these assumptions are not supported in the sources.

In point of fact, the rights, powers, liberties, and obligations of ecclesiastical persons subsisted within the same differentiated peace that Louis was charged to defend. They formed a part of the context of an encounter between actors in the same manner as did "secular" rights and obligations. Persons approached

---

[3] *The Memoirs of the Lord of Joinville: A New English Version*, trans. Ethel Wedgwood, 348–49.

each other within the peace bearing batteries of rights, uses, possessions, and experiences of practice. Some people bore ecclesiastical or spiritual rights, uses, or possessions, and others did not. But all people operated in the same space, according to the same notion of justice, and the peace could be destroyed through the abuse of any practice or right.

From within the typical paradigm of Church and State, it might appear that there is a discontinuity between the king's actions against heretics or contumacious excommunicates in some circumstances and his refusal to act against excommunicates in other circumstances. In fact, however, both actions derive from the same royal imperative: to defend the peace. A heretic shattered the peace. An unjust excommunication shattered the peace. An act of banditry on the road shattered the peace. An unjust ruling in a local court shattered the peace. When the king enforced an excommunication, he was at no point doing the Church's bidding (to the extent that "the Church" even existed as an actor). Rather, the king was fulfilling his office of defending justice within the reality of a thoroughly differentiated society that was as much spiritual as it was temporal.

For example, in 1265 a certain burgher died. He had entrusted his will to the Abbot of Saint-Richard. In it, he had stipulated that two hundred pounds should go to a certain chapel for his soul. The abbot, though, was faced with a problem. The two hundred pounds was in the form of letters of debt that had been deposited with the officials of the town of Bray. These officials would not hand the letters over to the abbot because, as they claimed, the bishop had threatened them with excommunication if they did so. The officials claimed that they would be happy to give the abbot the letters if they could also maintain peace with the bishop. The abbot, for his part, argued that the bishop had not approached him with any problems concerning the two hundred pounds and that if such a problem did exist and if the bishop made it known to him, he would do what he needed to solve it. Parlement considered the case in great detail and determined that the officials of the

town had to hand the letters over to the abbot regardless of the
opposition of the bishop.[4] Which category, secular or ecclesiastical, Church or State, should we sort this case into? Was
Louis resisting the power of the Church here or buttressing it?

The bishops had the right—the power—to excommunicate
in a way similar to how one might have the right to justice over,
say, thieves. These rights, as we have seen, did not derive from
the king. But, when there was conflict, when there was some
debate over the justice of how these rights were exercised, the
role of the king was to investigate and discern who was at fault,
who had shattered the peace, and then to correct the problem
to the best of his ability. In the case of an excommunication
that persisted for over a year, either the excommunicate was
at fault, in which case the king would act against him, or the
bishop was at fault, in which case the king would not so act. In
the episode recorded by Joinville, this was what he meant when
he responded that if he enforced the bishops' censures without
regard for their justice he would be granting them the royal
power—that is, the power to judge what was the peaceful use
of rights and to enforce them with the sword. Louis did not
claim the right to lift an excommunication himself or to force
an absolution or, of course, to actually strike someone with the
censure. This would have been for him to usurp the spiritual
power: the flow of grace was not his prerogative; the blade of
the sword, however, was.

Examples from Parlement allow us to see in what way the
spiritual power operated on the same field as the temporal
power. In 1266 the city officials of Beauvais complained to the
king that the bishop was dragging them into his court under
threat of excommunication concerning matters that pertained
to the court of the king—that is to say, temporal or secular
matters. The bishop said, to the contrary, that the issues at
hand related directly to his spiritual jurisdiction. Parlement
ruled in favor of the bishop.[5] Again in Beauvais, the townspeo-

---

[4]   Olim, 1:629 (XXIV).

[5]   Olim, 1:648 (XIII).

ple complained to the king that the bishop's knights and men rode through the town destroying property and asserted that the king's court should determine appropriate damages. The bishop, however, claimed that he had jurisdiction. The king looked into the case and determined that since the damage was to the property of individuals and not to that of the commune itself, the bishop had jurisdiction over both the clerics and the laymen and that both were to appear in the bishop's court.[6] Spiritual jurisdiction was not somehow "outside" the system or some sort of exception to it. Rather, it was another jurisdiction within it.

Holding spiritual jurisdiction was a right that was held along with any number of other rights, and it was not understood as something fundamentally different. Prelates held temporal jurisdiction without the slightest suggestion that it was somehow inappropriate to their offices.[7] Likewise, they held fiefs from the king and offices in the royal administration. They were powerful men with great liberties and rights like any other. They also held spiritual power which was exercised through rights and jurisdictions. But all these rights were centered on them as differentiated individual actors, not as placeholders within parallel hierarchies or, even more remotely, officers within undifferentiated administrations. When a prelate held temporal jurisdiction, his exercise of it was practiced in the same court as his exercise of his spiritual jurisdiction.[8]

In 1264 the town officials of Laon brought a case in Parlement against the deacon and chapter. Apparently, the townspeople had built an oven and pastured their animals in prejudice to the liberties of the chapter. After the townspeople refused to desist, the chapter summoned the officials to appear in their court. The officials refused to appear, and so the chapter excommunicated them. The officials, therefore, approached the king, asking that he force the chapter to absolve

---

6   Olim, 1:637 (X).
7   Olim, 1:651 (V); 1:185 (XIX).
8   Olim, 1:94 (IX); 1:18 (IX); 1:590 (XIV).

them. The king summoned the parties before his court and
heard their cases and inspected their privileges. He responded
to the officials that he did not believe himself competent in
this case because it was clear that the chapter held the privilege
of excommunicating and absolving. Therefore, if they believed
themselves excommunicated, the king continued, they should
seek absolution in an ecclesiastical court. However, through
the pressure of the king, the chapter conceded that absolution would be given without corporal or monetary penalties
imposed.[9] Spiritual rights and powers and secular rights and
powers were part of a single battery of rights that an ecclesiastical person held. In a conflict between the townspeople of
Mantes and the chapter over a barrel of wine, the king ruled
that the ecclesiastical court was competent because the case
involved mobile goods and the defendants were clerics.[10] The
"rights of the church" were particular to a time and place and
were as much secular as spiritual.[11]

Clerics were different from laymen, however. Clerics, especially bishops, were capable of holding types of jurisdiction
that laymen could not. This was a part of their differentiated
practice, and there were other types of people who had similar
restrictions or capabilities. For example, Parlement ruled that
a knight did not have to swear homage to a "rustic" even if he
held a fief from him.[12] Nobles, peasants, serfs, priests, and
bishops all had particular abilities or limitations.[13] That a man
was a cleric was a part of the "who, what, where, when, and how
long" context that underwrote all rights and obligations.

However, it is a mistake to think that the affairs of the
Church somehow operated outside the king's justice. Parlement records are simply full of cases where both parties in

---

9   Olim, 1:578 (IX).

10 Olim, 1:489 (IV).

11 Olim, 1:523 (XIV).

12 Olim, 1:497 (XVII).

13 Olim, 1:85 (I); 1:86 (II); 1:116 (II); 1:164 (XIII); 1:181 (XIII); 1:205 (I);
    1:517 (IX); 1:529 (VII); 1:564 (XIX).

a conflict were clerics. Sometimes, the conflict was little less than small-scale war, as when the chapter of Noyon sent men into the land of the monastery of Saint-Nicholas de Arrouaise, burning their barns and walls, breaking their fences, stealing their pigs, destroying their mill, and generally laying waste.[14] The king heard the case and no one supposed that it was somehow inappropriate. There were other cases that were completely internal to a particular church's governance. When a question arose about whether it was the use and custom of the church of Saint-Quentin in Aisne that its guards had to repay any stolen treasure out of their own pockets, the king's court commissioned an investigation.[15]

The use, possession, and custom of ecclesiastical entities were integrated into the same field as those of non-ecclesiastical entities. Parlement ruled that the men of Rouen did not have to appear before the Master of the Templars of Normandy when summoned (for spiritual or temporal matters, we do not know), accepting the laymen's argument that the Master could only summon them if he had the permission of his religious superior. The Master disagreed, saying that it was his use to summon people without his superior's involvement.[16] The use internal to a religious order was a part of the field. Within this field, there were certain situations in which clerical status was relevant and others in which it was not. This is simply the way all personal characteristics were handled within this context-heavy order. A layman could not hold the right to administer the sacraments or to level ecclesiastical censure. He was not the right type of person for that. But, he could hold rights to administer prebends, even rights to tithes, or rights to other "ecclesiastical" things, as when the king held all ecclesiastical properties during an episcopal vacancy. Such things were sorted out through custom, use, and possession.[17] The things

---

[14]　Olim, 1:170 (IX).

[15]　Olim, 1:208 (VIII).

[16]　Olim, 1:528 (IV).

[17]　Olim, 1:198 (VIII); 1:165 (XV); 1:689 (XXVIII); *Actes*, 580.

that we would consider properly ecclesiastical operated within the same peace as did all things.

In the narrative of the "problem of Church and State," the idea of the "liberty of the Church" figures large. It was the rallying cry, after all, of the Gregorian reformers and other papal ideologues against the imperial power. In St. Louis's kingdom, however, the idea had much more modest connotations. The liberty of the Church was, in practice, the liberties of certain ecclesiastical persons, and like all liberties they existed within a framework of use and possession that did not clearly section off the spiritual from the secular. The king violated the "liberty of his Church," claimed the Bishop of Amiens, when he granted certain tax privileges to the townspeople.[18]

Clerical "immunity," or the liberty of a cleric to be tried in an ecclesiastical court, is often considered the ultimate example of the "liberty of the Church," but even it was subject to contextual readings. When a man was murdered in the prison of the Bishop of Chalons-sur-Marne, the king summoned the bishop on account of his negligence. The bishop resisted, saying that since he was a priest and a bishop and since this case touched his person (meaning it was not just about property), he was not held to respond in the king's court. The king responded that he had to appear not as a bishop but as a baron and a peer of France and that the king was acting against him because of a defect in his administration of lay justice. The judges of Parlement considered the bishop's arguments for immunity but ultimately ruled against him.[19] The Abbot of Compiègne claimed jurisdiction over a certain townsman who had been arrested by the king's men. The abbot argued that he had tonsured the man, and so he was a cleric. The king inspected the privilege of the abbot through which he claimed the right to tonsure men, and he considered that the man in question had continued to pay taxes to the king as if a layman and ruled that

---

[18] Olim, 1:644 (V); 1:490 (V).
[19] Olim, 1:665 (II)–1:666 (III).

the man was not to be handed over to the abbot.[20]

The immunities of clerics were real, but they, like all rights and liberties, were applicable in certain contexts; in others, they were not.[21] A certain pauper complained to the king concerning Theobald, a cleric. Theobald claimed that he did not have to respond to the complaint because he was a cleric and the issues touched his body; therefore, he should be judged by his ordinary. The pauper responded that the issues at hand pertained to Theobald's service to the king and so should be judged by the king. Louis agreed, stating that he would judge every issue that pertained to Theobald's royal service but that all other issues must be dealt with by his ordinary.[22] In this differentiated society, context was almost never irrelevant.

The relationship between spiritual jurisdictions and secular jurisdictions was managed and conflicts adjudicated from within the overall paradigm of the peace—of use, possession, custom. For example, in 1258 the bishops of Normandy approached the king with a series of complaints. These complaints overwhelmingly concerned procedural matters in situations where spiritual and temporal jurisdictions overlapped or when bishops had to appear before secular courts, and they covered a great many topics. It was the custom of Normandy for as long as anyone could remember, the bishops argued, that whenever a bishop was summoned to the king's court, the king's messenger should be accompanied by four knights. They asked that the custom be restored. Likewise, when a servant of a bishop was cited to the king's court, it was the immemorial custom that the citation be brought by another servant of the bishop, or at least that he accompany the king's man. Custom dictated, the bishops informed the king, that investigations concerning patronage should be conducted by four knights and four priests. It was the old custom, the bishops asserted, that when a cleric came before an ecclesiastical court and claimed that a layman

---

[20] Olim, 1:529 (VI).

[21] Olim, 1:501 (XXVI); 1:698 (VIII); *Actes*, 409.

[22] Olim, 1:541 (XIII).

had despoiled him of his alms and if the layman denied this, saying that the property was not alms at all but a fief and so the case should be heard in a secular court, the following procedure be followed: the king's bailiff should conduct an inquisition; if he found that the property was held by the cleric as alms in peace for thirty years, the case was to be remitted to the ecclesiastical court, but otherwise it was to be handled by the secular court. Similarly, if a layman approached the king's courts and claimed a piece of property from a cleric that the cleric claimed to be alms and so rightfully handled by an ecclesiastical court, the bailiff should conduct an inquisition and send the case to the ecclesiastical court if he found the cleric to speak the truth. Likewise, if a cleric brought a layman before an ecclesiastical court asserting a right to something that he claimed to be alms but that the layman claimed to be his fief, the bailiff ought to conduct an inquisition. If he determined that the cleric did have rightful possession, the case should be heard by the ecclesiastical court, but if he determined that the layman was right, he should remain in peaceful possession of the property. The bishops of Normandy listed several other procedural customs and asked the king to ensure that his men were following them, and the king ordered his men to look into these and to obey all of them that they found to be true.[23]

In 1265 the king's men entered a church of the Friars Minor in Tours and captured a thief there. The Archbishop of Tours asserted that the church was devoted to the Divine Cult and so exempt from secular power, and that therefore, according to both written law and use, the church should be given possession of the thief. The king's men argued that through written law and use in that diocese the king had possession of justice over such malefactors caught in the act, even in churches. The archbishop denied this and said that even if the king could prove use, it would be unlawful use. Having heard these arguments, Parlement ruled that the thief was to be returned to the church. However, the secular officials

---

[23] Olim, 1:59 (I).

were to wait outside until he left. He was then to be subject to secular justice.[24] Custom, possession, use, time and memory—these things bridged the gaps between all jurisdictions, and sometimes the gap was between ecclesiastical and secular jurisdictions, but these cases were not categorically distinct from others. The prelates' jurisdiction existed within and not beyond the boundaries of this field of action, and Parlement was competent across the field, even if only to determine the boundaries of its own prerogatives.[25]

We ought not to be looking for some sort of "constitutional" arrangement between "Church" and "State." The society operated overwhelmingly in the open, complex space of differentiated practice, and the interaction between the spiritual and temporal happened in this space. Conflicts concerning spiritual rights took place within this space and it was not always clear how temporal rights and powers ought to or were able to respond. When the monks of Saint-Symphorien were continuously dragging laymen into their court for secular issues and excommunicating them, the king ordered that they stop doing so and commanded them to absolve the excommunicated men, unless, of course, their excommunication was on account of a sin against God.[26] How Louis would have enforced such an order is not clear. In another situation where a bishop extorted oaths through his power of excommunication, the king declared the oaths themselves null and void.[27] When the Abbot of Saint-Vedastus in Arras claimed that the liberty of his convent had been infringed by the count, he evoked both papal and royal charters. The king was concerned that these charters be respected and so he went through them carefully, having the important sections marked and interpreting sections that were unclear.[28]

---

[24] Olim, 1:631 (III).

[25] Olim, 1:590 (XIV)–1:591 (XV).

[26] Olim, 1:94 (IX); 1:22 (II).

[27] Olim, 1:564 (X).

[28] Olim, 1:687 (XXIV).

In 1260, Louis heard a case brought by a certain Guillaume against the chapter of Orleans. Guillaume claimed that the chapter was selling candles even though he had a royal charter granting him the exclusive right to do so. The chapter did not deny Guillaume's claim, but they countered that his charges touched the "liberty and immunities" of their church, which had been granted them through papal letters.[29] What power would such papal documents have in a royal court? Such questions did not stop Louis from the conviction that they mattered in his decision, that they were a part of the peace that was to be respected and protected. There seems to be ambiguity or confusion here, but such "problems" stem from our modern inability to accept that justice was above the law and was the foundation for the law rather than something defined by the law, an inability that St. Louis did not share.

The line between secular and ecclesiastical justice was sometimes so fluid that we find Louis imposing what appear to be penances. In 1266 the sub-bailiff of Arras and his men committed violence against the "liberty and immunity" of the church of Arras: they hit a servant of the church; they pushed Robert, the chaplain, after he refused them entry to the choir, calling him a "*sacerdotem ribaldum*" and threatening to disembowel him; they poked another priest, Peter, in the eye after he accused the sub-bailiff of evil; and finally, they beat a servant (the man they were chasing) in the choir. Such violence against clerics was a severe offense that in canon law was reserved to the papacy. Nevertheless, the king ordered his sub-bailiff to make amends through multiple processions to the church.[30] For a particularly bad crime, Louis compelled Enguerran de Couci to take the Cross and swear to go to the Holy Land on crusade, an oath that could be annulled only through papal power.[31]

---

[29] Olim, 1:490 (V); 1:513 (XVII).

[30] Olim, 1:238 (III). Violence against clerics seemed to be particularly troubling to Louis: Olim. 1:45 (VIII); 1:46 (IX).

[31] LTC, 4:4697.

We looked in some detail at the *enquêteurs* in Part I, but we are now in an even better position to understand them. They conducted inquests or inquisitions into the uses, possessions, customs, and status of the land and sought to rectify past acts of royal violence. The logic behind their activity was identical to that of Parlement itself, though narrower in focus. We saw in our discussion of the *enquêteurs* that the people who filled this office overlapped directly with those who served as ecclesiastical inquisitors. This overlap between the ecclesiastical and the secular was even more dramatic in the case of Parlement. Indeed, Gorski's claim that Church and State had their own "personnel" is mistaken if, as it seems, he means that the people who served one did not serve the other. Rather, both the judges and the investigators that facilitated the functioning of Parlement were as often clerics as laymen. And they were not just "clerics of the king," or nominally clerical administrators, or some other proxy for the modern bureaucrat. Rather, the *consilium*—the council—of Louis included important and powerful ecclesiastics: bishops, archbishops, abbots, canons, and masters.[32]

These men often simultaneously held not only major ecclesiastical office but also special commissions from the pope to act as apostolic judges.[33] After his election to the see of Le Puy, Gui Foucois was just such a person, and we will look at this phase in his life in great detail in the next chapter. These churchmen were as concerned as Louis with the maintenance of the peace and conservation of justice. After all, they were as integral to the social order as was any knight or burgher.

In addition to Louis's *consilium*, Parlement relied on an untold number of investigators. Parlement's normal *modus operandi* was to commission an investigation into all aspects of a conflict's time and place, and then to use the findings of that investigation to determine the status quo against which

---

[32] Olim, 1:75 (XXIX); 1:127 (VI); 1:503 (XXX)

[33] Olim, 1:579 (XII); LTC, 4:4697. This subject will be covered in much more detail in subsequent chapters.

it could evaluate the statements of witnesses and charters and so determine what was just in context. These investigations, sometimes called inquests, sometimes inquisitions, were commonly carried out by the local royal officials: bailiffs, seneschals, or provosts. Very often, however, special investigators were commissioned, and these investigators could be either laymen or clerics. Often investigations were carried out by a team that included both. The clerics were sometimes "clerics of the king,"[34] but most of the time they held ecclesiastical positions: abbots, priors, masters, deacons, or canons.[35] Sometimes they were Mendicants.[36] It seems to be the case that Parlement was particularly careful to have ecclesiastics involved in investigations of conflicts that included other ecclesiastics.[37] In cases where one party was ecclesiastic and the other lay, the investigations were very often conducted by a lay-ecclesiastic team. Parlement sought to maintain peace in the temporal realm and the clerics most certainly lived and dispensed the sacraments in the temporal realm. Indeed, the whole field of action was as much "the Church" as it was "the kingdom."

While the above examples probably suffice to demonstrate the mistake of extracting some sort of royal "ecclesiastical policy" out of Joinville's account of St. Louis's encounter with a certain group of bishops, an examination of the spectacular case of the inquisition into the Bishop of Toulouse will further demonstrate how the temporal and the spiritual were bound up together in a single "field." Sometime in 1262 or 1263 Pope Urban IV commissioned Archbishop Maurinus of Narbonne, the Bishop of Maguelone, and the prior of Nérac to inquire

---

[34] Olim, 1:105 (V); 1:122 (XI); 1:126 (I); 1:157 (VII); 1:158 (VIII); 1:159 (XII); 1:166 (XVII); 1:175 (V); 1:181 (XIV); 1:186 (II); 1:189 (I); 1:195 (IV); 1:209 (IX); 1:223 (VIII).

[35] Olim, 1:99 (I); 1:111 (XXIII); 1:121 (IX); 1:158 (X); 1:168 (VIII); 1:187 (VI); 1:192 (VIII); 1:193 (XII); 1:201 (XIII); 1:215 (IX).

[36] Olim, 1:68 (XIV); 1:161 (VI).

[37] Olim, 1:43 (XXXIII); 1:127 (V); 1:160 (II); 1:185 (I); 1:197 (VI); 1:198 (VIII); 1:210 (XIII).

into the veracity of charges of simony, fratricide, and general destitution that had been leveled against Raymond, the Bishop of Toulouse.[38] Raymond was a Dominican and, as a worker in the *business of the peace and the faith*, had a long career as a friend of both the Crown and the papacy, and so the charges are surprising.[39] Urban, however, had obviously heard tales that disturbed him, and the case almost immediately spun out of control.

The pope had given Bertrand, the provost of the church of Toulouse, who was visiting the pope in person, a very limited commission to order Raymond to appear before the inquisitors if he happened to meet him upon the road as he traveled from the papal curia back to Toulouse.[40] He also gave Bertrand a mandate to seize the goods of the church of Toulouse, using ecclesiastical censures with apostolic authority against resisters, in order to preserve them for the church of Toulouse from any disruptions that might occur on account of the inquisition.[41] Bertrand returned to Toulouse without coming across Raymond on the road. After a legally suspect summons of Raymond to appear before the inquisitors, and

---

[38] The charges of fratricide and simony are listed by the monks who compiled the *Gal. Christ.*, vol. 13, *Ecclesia Tolosana*, ch. 28. Urban, in a letter to Alphonse, Count of Poitiers and Toulouse, states that the smoke of Raymond's wickedness had ascended all the way to him; HGL, 8:509 (III), col. 1532. The Archbishop of Narbonne writes that the pope had heard the *fama* of Raymond's dissolute life (HGL, 8:509 [I]), col. 1528. Pope Clement IV states that the inquisition was commissioned for Raymond's "many crimes" and "certain excesses"; *Clément IV, Reg.*, 757, 389.

[39] Marie-Humbert Vicaire, O.P., *Saint Dominic and His Times* (New York: McGraw-Hill, 1964), 215n163; Bernardus Guidonis, *De Foundatione et Prioribus Conventuum Provinciarum Tolosanae et Provinciae Ordinis Praedicatorum*, ed. P. A. Amargier, O.P., Monumenta Ordinis Fratrum Praedicatorum Historica 25 (Rome: Institutum Historicum Fratrum Praedicatorum, 1961), 15, 20, 23, 32–33, 48, 78, 122, 180, 248; *The Chronicle of William of Puylaurens*, trans. W. A. Sibly and M. D. Sibly (Woolbridge, UK: Boydell Press, 2003), 88–89; Guillaume Pelhisson, *Chronique*, ed. Jean Duvernoy (Paris: CNRS Editions, 1994), 40, 44, 78.

[40] *Clément IV, Reg.*, 757.

[41] *Urban IV, Reg.*, C419; C437.

knowing that Raymond planned to travel north, Bertrand read his papal mandates before a local council (with Raymond in attendance).

This public display disturbed Raymond and he promptly left the council, intending to travel to France (meaning, north).[42] He was convinced that Bertrand's commissions were far too narrow to allow for this display of apostolic power.[43] Bertrand was apparently enraged at Raymond's disregard for his supposed apostolic authority and so, under the pretext of the authority granted him by Urban to confiscate the goods of the bishopric, took a multitude of armed men, some of whom were of the Archbishop of Narbonne's household, and attacked Raymond and his entourage in the streets of Béziers as he prepared to leave. Bertrand stole the bishop's horses and all the money, vases of silver, and everything else he carried, with which he had intended to pay for his trip and as gifts for St. Louis.

In response, the king's seneschal in the region and many other officials of the municipal government (who, as Urban would later put it, "seeing such rapine in the streets, and not wanting the security of the royal roads so weakened") restored the goods by force to Raymond, who started his journey north. Using the faculties conceded him in his mandate, Bertrand excommunicated the seneschal and all the officials in question and placed the city of Béziers under interdict.[44] He then wrote letters to Urban, telling him that he had been attacked in the course of fulfilling his mandate, informing him of the resultant censures and asking for apostolic letters concerning the enforcement of the sentences.[45] Urban therefore sent letters to the Bishop of Elne and the archdeacon of Narbonne ordering them to announce and enforce the sentences,[46] and

---

[42] *Clément IV, Reg.*, 757.

[43] Ibid.

[44] Ibid., C415, C429, C437; HGL, 8:502, cols. 1505–06.

[45] Ibid., C415.

[46] Ibid., C415, C437.

they promptly started promulgating further censures against citizens of Béziers.[47] Bertrand, no doubt feeling empowered by the papal letters, expanded his operation to include the confiscation of the goods and demolition of the fixed property of not only the bishop but also the clerics and laity who supported him.[48]

While Raymond was in France he sent two procurators to explain himself to the three inquisitors. The procurators presented several "exceptions" against the procedures that had been followed thus far as explanation for Raymond's absence. The inquisitors were not interested in the procurators' arguments and would not even provide them with copies of their apostolic mandates, as was clearly required in canon law.[49] The procurators, therefore, submitted an appeal to the Holy See.[50] The inquisitors, claiming themselves justified on account of their mandates, disregarded the appeal as illegitimate, declared Raymond contumaciously absent, informed Urban of the excommunication but not the appeal, and began the investigation late in 1263.

Meanwhile, Raymond met with St. Louis's brother Alphonse, the Count of Poitiers and Toulouse. He told Alphonse of the abuse he had suffered at the hands of Bertrand and the men of the Archbishop of Narbonne and asked for help. Alphonse wrote to his brother, St. Louis, expressing outrage at the assault on such a friend to the Crown and asking him for permission to do something about the situation.[51] St. Louis wrote to Pope Urban.[52] Raymond traveled back to Toulouse and became aware that the inquisitors had ignored the argu-

---

[47] Ibid., C437.
[48] Ibid., C419; HGL, 8:509 (IV), col. 1534.
[49] *Clément IV, Reg.*, 757; HGL, 8:509 (V), col. 1535. The procurators were here following the procedure laid out in canon 48 of Lateran IV (Tanner, 1:256).
[50] Ibid., 757.
[51] HGL, 8:502, cols. 1505–06.
[52] While the king's letter does not survive, Urban notes that St. Louis had complained about the situation (*Urban IV, Reg.*, C419).

ments and appeal of his procurators. Raymond, therefore, set out personally for the papal curia.[53]

The inquisitors' investigation, meanwhile, ran into serious problems. Many clerics of the church of Toulouse, including the chancellor, as well as notable men of the city, refused to testify. They argued that with the papal appeal of Raymond pending, the inquisitors had no jurisdiction and could not compel their appearances. The inquisitors attempted to compel them to testify by promulgating sentences of excommunication, suspension, and interdict, but to no effect. They then wrote to Urban explaining that these officials of the church of Toulouse were both refusing to testify themselves and, through threats, flattery, money, or other means, coercing others into not testifying. The pope, therefore, sent the inquisitors letters extending their faculties of censure to include any of these witnesses, mandating that if the officials and witnesses remained contumaciously in their state of excommunication, the inquisitors might deprive them of their offices, dignities, and benefices, finally adding that if they still refused, these offices, dignities, and benefices might be given to other candidates. The inquisitors made use of these faculties and promulgated censures and privations and assigned the offices to new clerics.[54]

These same officials of the church of Toulouse refused to provide the inquisitors with goods and necessities from the bishopric, on the basis of the same appeal. When informed, Urban, in January of 1264, wrote to the seneschal of Alphonse, to the consuls of Toulouse, and to Alphonse himself, mandating that they become involved.[55] He also wrote to the inquisitors, praising them for the industry and solicitude they had displayed in the inquisition, giving them copies of the letters he had sent to the secular powers, and extending them

---

[53] *Clément IV, Reg.*, 757. When this occurred is not clear, but it must have been sometime in the spring of 1264.

[54] *Urban IV, Reg.*, C445.

[55] LTC, 4:4901, 4902, 4903; HGL, 8:509 (III), col. 1532.

the faculty of compelling the secular powers to comply.[56] The Archbishop of Narbonne promptly had the letters copied and circulated to make the apostolic mandate generally known.[57] He also wrote to Alphonse, insisting that he order his men to comply with the apostolic mandate.[58]

At the time of Urban's letters to the secular powers in January 1264, he had clearly heard nothing of the appeal of Raymond, he had not received the letters from St. Louis or Alphonse, and he had apparently not heard from any of the many people who had been censured by the inquisition. Indeed, his sole source of information seems to have been the inquisitors and Bertrand. In his letter to Alphonse, he wrote that Raymond was absent from Toulouse against apostolic mandate and "as if conscious of his guilt," and that because of his contumacy and the obstructionism of his officials the inquisition had promulgated excommunications against them. They remained, he added, in this state, "a danger to their souls," and he mandated that Alphonse, in virtue of the obedience he had always shown the Holy See, order his seneschal and bailiffs to support the inquisition and force Raymond's men to relinquish the bishopric's goods.[59] Urban's focus on the contumacy of Raymond and his men is echoed in a letter by Maurinus (Archbishop of Narbonne and chief inquisitor) to Alphonse. The archbishop argued that "for the salvation of their souls" Alphonse must act against Raymond's men, who remained in their state of excommunication "in contempt for God."[60]

It is at this point that we find ourselves observing a similar situation to that related by Joinville: certain ecclesiastical persons, in this case including the pope himself, demanded

---

[56] Ibid., 4904, 4905; HGL, 8:509 (I), col. 1528.

[57] Ibid., 4914.

[58] HGL, 8:509 (I), col. 1528.

[59] Ibid., 8:509 (III), col. 1532. Urban confirms later that he wrote these letters based on what the archbishop had told him regarding Raymond's contumacious absence and his officials' disregard for their own excommunications (*Urban IV, Reg.* C446).

[60] HGL, 8:509 (I), col. 1528.

that the secular power act against excommunicates. And Alphonse's response sheds light on St. Louis's response to the bishops in Joinville's chronicle because it demonstrates the complexities with which the secular power had to contend and its method of exercising its power. By the time Alphonse had received the letters of Urban and of the Archbishop of Narbonne sometime in March 1264,[61] he had already met with Raymond and had heard his side of the story. He was aware of Raymond's appeal and that he was at that very moment in route to the papal curia. He knew that the king had written to the pope and that the letter had likely not yet arrived. Alphonse knew that the inquisitors were likely acting outside their mandate and he knew of the violence of Bertrand. He was, therefore, fully aware of how much more he knew about the situation than did the pope himself. Alphonse instructed his seneschal, Peter de Landreville, to seek the counsel of wise men and to proceed cautiously in fulfilling the papal mandate, giving Raymond's men an opportunity to demonstrate that they were in the right.[62] In short, he ordered Peter to hold an inquest into the justice of the excommunications that he was being called on to enforce. There was an obvious conflict going on—the peace was in tatters: there had been outright violence in the streets and there had been excommunications thrown left and right. Alphonse had to act—this much was clear—but against whom?

Peter, Alphonse's seneschal, brought Raymond's men before him so that he might hear their side. They argued that the pope's letters clearly displayed a lack of knowledge of what was going on. It was apparent, they asserted, that the pope did not know about the appeal or Raymond's trip to the papal curia. Given this situation, Raymond's men contended, Peter ought to wait and allow the pope himself to determine if the censures were valid and just. The chancellor of the church of

---

[61] Based on the dates of Maurinus's follow-up letters: LTC, 4914, 4915; HGL, 8:509 (I), col. 1528.

[62] HGL, 8:509 (V), col. 1535; LTC, 4918.

Toulouse added to these arguments a threat: if Peter moved against Raymond's properties or those of his church, he would be promptly excommunicated. This left Peter in a tricky spot. Since the inquisitors had already promised to excommunicate him if he failed to enforce the papal mandate, he faced ecclesiastical censure regardless of his ruling. Nevertheless, he looked at the merits of the arguments laid before him and considered the fact that Raymond was currently at the papal curia. This convinced him that any action of the secular arm was premature: the context was simply not yet clear. It was not clear that Raymond was contumacious in his excommunication, and the secular power had no interest whatsoever in becoming a pawn in someone else's power struggle. Realizing that he and his men were about to be excommunicated, Peter wrote to Alphonse and submitted a preemptive appeal to the pope.[63] After being informed of Peter's inquest and his decision, the inquisitors promptly promulgated sentences of excommunication against him and the officials of the city of Toulouse.[64]

Things in Toulouse went from bad to worse. After Raymond's flight north Bertrand had terrorized his supporters, confiscating their goods and occupying their lands and castles. After Raymond left for the papal curia, Bertrand became even more violent. As the pope would later recount, Bertrand attacked a certain castle and church of the bishop's with many armed men, burning down the buildings, killing the people inside, and putting "untold" men to the sword.[65] After the inquisitors excommunicated Alphonse's seneschal and the officials of the city of Toulouse, they ran into problems themselves. According to Maurinus, the inquisitors were patiently conducting the business of the inquisition in the cloister of Saint-Étienne in Toulouse when the chancellor of Toulouse, whom they had previously excommunicated and who called himself a relative of the count, arrived with a multitude of armed men. In the

---

[63] Ibid., 8:509 (V), col. 1535; LTC, 4978.
[64] *Urban IV, Reg.*, C446.
[65] Ibid., C419, C429.

entranceway of the cloister they made a great clamor, shouting,
"To death, to death, to blood, let them not escape!" The archbishop's household fought them off, but the band came across
the archbishop's shield-bearer, who was returning from water-
ing the horses. In the public street, they demanded the horses,
and when he refused, they mortally wounded him. They then
held the inquisitors in a sort of siege in which scarcely anyone
could leave the building, even to procure provisions. Finally,
the inquisitors managed to flee Toulouse. The archbishop
wrote to Alphonse demanding that something be done about
this outrage perpetuated against them, or rather, against the
"Supreme Pontiff and the Roman Church."[66]

Alphonse waited. By mid-March, Urban had begun to
hear news of what was happening in Toulouse and to try to
get control of the situation. His first bit of reliable information seems to have come from St. Louis's letter regarding the
assault on Raymond in Béziers, which had finally arrived, and
he responded by revoking Bertrand's mandate to confiscate the
goods of the bishopric.[67] By May, however, Urban had been
made aware of the severity of the situation: Raymond had
arrived at the curia, the pope had received Peter de Landrevil-
la's letters and appeal, and he had heard "innumerable shouts"
concerning the cruelty and disorder of Bertrand.[68] Urban
quickly moved to correct the situation.

He absolved Raymond, *ad cautelam*,[69] of all the sentences

---

[66] HGL, 8:509 (II), col. 1530; LTC, 4926.

[67] *Urban IV, Reg.*, C419. This letter, dated March 2, 1264, reveals Urban's still
very limited knowledge of the situation. This is explained in that he had received a letter from St. Louis, who had received a letter from Alphonse, who
had met with Raymond before he had returned to Toulouse. Urban was not
even apparently aware of the excommunications Bertrand had promulgated
in Béziers.

[68] Ibid., C415, C429, C446.

[69] Absolutions *ad cautelam* maintained the theoretical force of an excommunication while granting the litigant full legal rights and postponing any other
consequences of the censure; see Richard H. Helmholz, "Excommunication
as a Legal Sanction," *Zeitschrift der Savigny-Stiftung für Rechtsgeschichte. Kanonistische Abteilung* 68, no. 99 (1982): 202–18, at 206; F. Donald Logan,

that had been promulgated against him because it was unseemly that someone so censured might come before the pope. He received an oath from Raymond that should his appeal fail he would obey all the rulings of the inquisition and provide it material support, and so wrote to the inquisitors telling them to stop the public denunciation of Raymond.[70] In order to make sure that word got out that Raymond was absolved, Urban wrote to the Bishop of Béziers and the archdeacon of Carcassonne mandating that they announce the absolutions, another common practice.[71]

Urban wrote to Bertrand, revealing that he had become aware of the full extent of his actions, including the incident in Béziers and the context for the many censures Bertrand had promulgated. Urban expressed dismay at the great scandal Bertrand had caused, which had reached all the way to the king and to the papal curia, and the pope reprimanded him for misleading him into issuing letters to the Bishop of Elne and archdeacon of Narbonne mandating that they enforce the sentences. He had made it clear to Bertrand that the commission was to be pursued without hatred and rancor, but rather with the zeal of charity, but it was apparent that he had done the opposite.[72] Urban, therefore, ordered Bertrand to desist from all confiscations, to make full restitution of all property, and to absolve everyone he had censured within eight days.[73] In order to make sure this happened, Urban wrote to Alphonse, his seneschal in Toulouse, and the seneschal of St. Louis in Béziers mandating that they protect the property of Raymond and his allies.[74] He also wrote to the Bishop of

---

Excommunication and the Secular Arm: A Study in Legal Procedure from the Thirteenth to the Sixteenth Century (Toronto: Pontifical Institute of Medieval Studies, 1968), 118.

[70] *Urban IV, Reg.,* C417.

[71] Ibid., C418.

[72] Urban is here echoing canon 8 of Lateran IV, which calls for inquests into prelates to be pursued in love and not hatred (Tanner, 1:238).

[73] *Urban IV, Reg.,* C415, C429.

[74] Ibid., C420, C421, C422; HGL, 8:349 (IV), col. 1534; LTC, 4937.

Béziers and the archdeacon of Carcassonne mandating that they compel Bertrand with ecclesiastical censure if he failed to obey the apostolic mandate.[75] They were also to investigate all the censures that had been promulgated and revoke the unjust.[76] While the appeal of Raymond against his excommunication for contumacy was being pressed at the curia on October 2, 1264, Urban died. One year later his successor Clement IV (Gui Foucois) promulgated his decision in favor of the appeal.[77]

In this conflict, the pope had called out the secular power first for one side and then for the opposite side. We can see here again a parallel with the Joinville account in which Louis offered the example of the Count of Brittany, who had endured an unjust excommunication for years before finally being absolved by the papacy. The secular power's resistance to enforce certain excommunications, therefore, had nothing whatsoever to do with resisting ecclesiastical power or of asserting the royal agenda in the face of a rival hierarchy. Rather, contumacious excommunicates, far from being something the Crown could ignore, were a direct threat to right order as Louis understood it.[78] Rather than resisting ecclesiastical power in the abstract, when the secular power refused to act against certain excommunicates, it was resisting injustice in a particular context. The papacy itself railed against unjust excommunications and made eliminating them a centerpiece of its seemingly perpetual attempts at clerical reform.

Lateran IV had taken great care to legislate against such excommunications, especially those promulgated on account of avarice, and to put procedures in place for appeal against such censures and for the punishment of ecclesiastical persons who

---

[75] Ibid., C430, C437.

[76] Ibid., C445, C446.

[77] *Clément IV, Reg.,* 757.

[78] Campbell, "The Attitude of the Monarchy," 537; EAAP, 64, 71; *The Établissements de Saint Louis: Thirteenth-century Law Texts from Tours, Orléans, and Paris,* trans. F. R. P. Akehurst, 1:127, 84–5.

promulgated them.[79] These concerns were reiterated at Lyons I and through an untold number of papal letters.[80] When St. Louis and Alphonse looked into the excommunications of Raymond and his men, they were, in fact, making sure that the pope's own interests as well as their own were being pursued and that his authority was not being usurped in a local power struggle. They were looking into the context of a particular deployment of rights—in this case, ecclesiastical rights of the highest kind. They were determining the who, what, where, and when of the violence that had shattered the peace. This was simply necessary, both practically and from within their understanding of social order.

The fact that ecclesiastical rights and spiritual power did not descend from Louis, the fact that they found their source through the clerical side of society, was not a threat to Louis's self-understanding: as we have seen, nearly all rights found their source and so legitimacy outside of royal power. Indeed, the spiritual power and ecclesiastical rights were integral to a society that lacked sovereignty, within which they held their place, defended by the king and intermixed with secular rights and powers. While the particulars of the politics in Toulouse are unclear, it *is* clearly the case that this conflict was between two conglomerations of lay and ecclesiastical persons. Excommunications flowed into armed conflict without seam and it was violence in the street that had first involved the secular power. In this conflict, who was "the Church" that the narrative of "Church and State" would see the secular power as "obeying," "resisting," or "in alliance with"? There were certainly a large number of ecclesiastical rights being exploited and a large quantity of spiritual power being wielded, or at least claimed, but "the Church" as an actor is extremely difficult to locate. Indeed, if we were to grant that St. Louis had some sort of an "ecclesiastical policy," are we to see it as aimed at the Bishop of Toulouse, the Archbishop of Narbonne, or the

---

[79] Tanner, 1:255, 256.

[80] Ibid., 1:291.

papacy itself? Joinville's account does not show us the limits of St. Louis's support of the Church any more than the king's refusal to support the violence of some ambitious lord shows us the limit of his support of the secular power. The whole paradigm is flawed because it rests on a notion of sovereignty.

St. Louis was concerned with peace and justice in a social space that was characterized by an assumption in favor of these and so devoid of sovereignty. These concerns cut across clerical-lay lines. When the Dominican Vincent of Beauvais, writing to Louis on kingship, asserted that all the king's actions must be rooted in divine law and based on the Sacred Writings,[81] he was looking to the exact same source of legitimacy as Gratian did for canon law in his *Decretum*. Indeed, the *Decretum* and the glosses that grew up around it treated ecclesiastical and secular enactments as fundamentally of the same kind: human law rooted in divine law. They were rooted in the peace and subject to the same use, custom, and statute considerations discussed at length above. According to the Ordinary Gloss to the *Decretum*, the use of the people could abrogate even papal pronouncements without the pope even being aware that his "law" was being abolished through peaceful practice. This was so because when it came to law, the pope was just like a prince.[82] Indeed, the world was governed by two swords, but both of these swords came from God and both of them were wielded in defending and building his most peaceful "city." The peace, rooted in divine law, simply included the spiritual and the temporal. In this life, the spiritual subsisted within the temporal and the temporal was elevated by the spiritual. It was the spiritual that made the kingdom Christian and it was the temporal that made it a kingdom. It is not that they cooperated in some sort of "Gelasian" division of spheres—you

---

[81] Vincent of Beauvais, *The Moral Instruction of a Prince*, trans. Priscilla Throop (Charlotte, VT: MedievalMS, 2011), 61.

[82] *Decretum Gratiani*, dist. 4, can. 3, in Gratian, *The Treatise on Laws*, trans. Augustine Thompson, O.P. (Washington, DC: Catholic University of America Press, 1993), 13.

have your space and I have mine. Rather, they formed a unity that was, simply, the Church.

As Vincent of Beauvais wrote, "The whole Church is made up of two orders, clergy and laity, as if two sides of one body."[83] The baptized laity and the sword they wielded was as much the Church as the ordained clergy and the sword they wielded. Both were rooted in a sacramental world: it was only through baptism that one could wield the Church's material sword and it was only through ordination that one could wield her spiritual sword.[84] There was no conflict here. Conflicts, rather, could arise anywhere in the field of action, anywhere in the "city." The fabric of the peace could be torn anywhere, by clerics as easily as by laymen, by the misappropriation of temporal power as easily as that of spiritual power. Louis sought to maintain the peace, and in this, he was engaged in the same project, the same business, as the faithful clergy, especially the papacy. As we will see in the next chapter, the pursuit of this same business led, over time, to the growth of a network of friends, a network of men who deployed their differentiated power in pursuit of the same ends, a network of *consilium et auxilium*, "counsel and aid," that included both secular and spiritual power and, ultimately, united the royal and apostolic courts.

---

[83] *The Moral Instruction of a Prince*, 3.

[84] Ibid., 16.

🌿 CHAPTER NINE

COUNSEL AND AID

Even granted the ordinary miseries and mistakes, of which all human relationship is full, there is no greater consolation than the unfeigned loyalty and mutual love of good men who are true friends.

—St. Augustine, *City of God* 19.8

THE PREVIOUS CHAPTERS described a society that lacked centralized organization and control, not just technologically, but conceptually. It was a differentiated space in which every actor and every interaction had its own "legitimacy" that emerged from the bottom up and that participated in an overarching legitimacy that was nothing less than the justice of God himself, a justice that was manifested in peace. It would seem that large-scale initiatives would be, therefore, impossible without disrupting this order—that is to say, without violence. The king judged and maintained this order, but he was not able to manipulate it, bend it, redirect it, or appropriate its resources in the manner of the modern State. Rights,

as we have seen, were defused throughout society. The king
could not "control" them. However, it does not follow from
this that large-scale action was impossible. Large-scale action
had to be achieved not through the appropriation of resources and power to the center, in the fashion of the State, but
through the coordination of the differentiated resources and
power of various actors. The king could not himself control
the resources of the kingdom, but what if he could get the
men who did control them, within their differentiated spaces,
to join him in an initiative? What if he could bind them to
him in a pact of loyalty, even friendship? Indeed, what if he
could build a network of friends aimed at a certain initiative
or a certain vision of right order? Such friendships could not
be forced or administered or organized through a bureaucracy,
but they could certainly be managed through a code of right
behavior, a code that had its own enforcement mechanisms
that lay outside what we would consider the realm of the State,
but that rather participated in that same divine justice that
was the source of the society's very cohesion, its peace. Such
a network of friends would have no place for our concepts of
Church and State, for there is no reason why a bishop should
not be friends with a local knight or with the king himself.
Such a network would operate within the differentiated space
of uses, possessions, rights, and obligations discussed above,
within which both spiritual and temporal power functioned,
rather than over and against it.

When we approach the sources without the categories
of Church and State obscuring our view, such networks
become visible. We can see that social power was wielded not
through controlling "proto-absolutist" institutions such as
"the Church" or "the State," but through building networks of
cooperation, of loyalty, of debt, of favor, and of friendship.
In short, such networks of relationships would be based on
the ubiquitous *consilium et auxilium*—"counsel and aid"—of
the sources, networks that cut across any lines we might be
tempted to draw in order to construct "Church" and "State." It
is these networks—made up as much of bishops as of lords,

of friars as of burghers, and of canons as of knights—that we ought to recognize as being in conflict or in cooperation with each other. They interacted with each other within a shared sacramental social reality within which they upheld "orthodoxies" presenting a coherent understanding of social order and deployed what power they controlled in a manner congruent with this order.

In the historiography, one most often comes across *consilium et auxilium* within a narrowly feudal context. As a part of historians' construction of feudalism, *consilium et auxilium* has taken on a legal and contractual character describing what a vassal owed his lord.[1] In the transition from feudalism to the State, historians often see *consilium* transitioning from a duty owed by the vassal to a right demanded by the vassal, resulting in the emergence of representative government. *Auxilium*, as it is said, became synonymous with military aid, which, with the growth of centralized administration and the commercialization of wealth, was substituted for monetary payments, and so taxation emerged.[2] This feudal-State understanding of *consilium et auxilium*, however, fails to comprehend the importance of the concept because it forces it into the contractual and absolutist constructs that underwrite modern political theory.

Because of this prejudice in favor of the State, *consilium et auxilium* is treated almost exclusively as a component of the feudal oath. The sin here, though, is one of omission. For, it is certainly the case that the concept was included in oaths sworn by *fideles*, vassals, from the ninth century on. In the beginning of the eleventh century it was most famously mentioned in Bishop Fulbert of Chartres's description of the relationship between a *fidelis* and his lord and the oaths sworn.[3] *Consilium*

---

[1] See Susan Reynolds, *Fiefs and Vassals: the Medieval Evidence Reinterpreted* (Oxford: Oxford University Press, 1994).

[2] See Thomas N. Bisson, "The Military Origins of Medieval Representation," *The American Historical Review* 71, no. 4 (1966): 1199–218.

[3] Charles E. Odegaard, "Carolingian Oaths of Fidelity," *Speculum* 16.3 (1941): 284–96; Bisson, "The Military Origins," 1203. Fulbert's letter was included in the *Decretum* and in the *Liber Feudorum* and so received a great deal of

et auxilium is clearly important for understanding such feudal oaths, but a near exclusive concern for them has obscured the facts that *consilium et auxilium* was not a creation of feudal law and that it did not primarily exist within feudal, oath-bound, and unequal relationships. The swearer of the oath was pledging to behave faithfully toward his lord, to make his lord's problems his own, and to expend his resources in the service of his lord's initiatives. He was swearing to behave toward the lord as if a faithful member of his kin, as a true "friend." But "friendship" was not defined by oaths or by unequal or contractual relationships. Rather, we ought to recognize that the content of the feudal oath was drawn from extralegal norms of proper behavior. *Consilium et auxilium*, as part of the meaning of friendship, had social significance (both temporally and conceptually) prior to the oaths—that is why the oaths included them.

Nevertheless, even within a feudal context, *consilium et auxilium* was not simply something owed by vassals to their lords. In a feudal context it was understood as a concept of reciprocity. In 851 the sons of Louis the Pious, Lothair, Charles, and Louis swore to render each other *consilium et auxilium*, to behave properly toward each other as brothers and with no sense of subordination to one another.[4] Fulbert himself stated that the lord ought to return to his *fidelis* all that that man had sworn to him, otherwise he would be thought a *malefidus*.[5] And the thirteenth-century Ordinary Gloss to the *Decretum* stated that a lord owed *consilium et auxilium* to his vassals, seemingly

---

attention from medieval legal scholars and from modern scholars of the medieval law (Kenneth Pennington, "The Formation of the Jurisprudence of the Feudal Oath of Fealty," *Rivista internazionale del diritto comun* 15 [2004]: 57–76).

4   Odegaard, "Carolingian Oaths of Fidelity," 292.

5   *Decretum*, Causa 22, q. 5, c. 18: "sicut ille, si in eorum prevaricatione vel faciendo, vel consentiendo deprehensus fuerit perfidus et periurus" (*Decretum Gratiani*, ed., Emil Friedberg, in *Corpus Iuris Canonici*, vol. 2 [Leipzig, DE: Bernhard Tauchnitz, 1881]).

reversing the feudal obligations.[6] The point is that rendering *consilium et auxilium* was part of the content of peaceful, benevolent relationships, with father-son and brother-brother relationships as the exemplars.

Such relationships were sometimes sealed with an oath by one or both parties and sometimes with subordination, but neither oaths nor subordination were intrinsic to them. Rather, an oath added a layer to the relationship and was used within certain types of benevolent relationships that we tend to call "feudal." Circa 1170, the canonist Johannes Faventinus pointed out that while a vassal who betrayed his lord committed perjury because he had sworn an oath not to do so, a lord who betrayed his vassal did not. Rather, the unfaithful lord was bad: he was a *malefidus* worthy of moral condemnation. There was a mutual, ethical relationship prior to the vassal's oath, which makes perfect sense when we consider that the vassal-lord relationship was, in the ideal, an extension of kin-type relations to those without blood ties.[7]

But if we back out of the narrowly "feudal" realm, we find that the concept of *consilium et auxilium* is extremely common in the documents of the thirteenth century and was used in far more contexts than those surrounding a feudal relationship. To name a few examples: In 1226, the proctors for the church of Lyon argued against the papacy's plan to reserve a prebend in every church for the use of the pope, stating that "the plan would deprive them of the property, *consilium*, and, *auxilium* in performing divine service that canons, their friends, and their servants provide the churches."[8] A 1234 council in Arles exhorted all the bishops gathered to exhibit mutual *consilium et*

---

6   JC-1582, 1:1696.

7   Pennington, "The Formation of the Jurisprudence," 60.

8   "Et contra, ipsi procuratores allegabant incommoda sua, scilicet dampna rerum consiliorum et auxiliorum divinorum obsequiorum, que in ecclesiis possent fieri per canonicos et suos amicos et suam sequelaim" (*The Council of Bourges, 1225: A Documentary History*, ed. Richard Kay [Aldershot, UK: Ashgate, 2002], 284–86).

auxilium in defense of the peace.[9] A 1267 council in the same
location decreed excommunication for a cleric who gave *consilium, auxilium,* or *favorem* to someone who sought to impede
the will of a testator.[10] When the apostolic see sent legates,
nuncios, or commissioned inquisitors, it routinely exhorted
the prelates of the territory to render them *consilium et auxilium.*[11] The popes would exhort the king himself to extend
consilium et auxilium to papal legates and nuncios sent on a
wide range of missions, from making peace between warring
lords, to raising money for a crusade, to collecting debts owed
to the papacy by merchants.[12] In 1235 a group of northern
French bishops petitioned the king for *consilium et auxilium*
against "the excesses of the citizens of Rheims."[13] Suffragans
swore to grant *consilium et auxilium* to their archbishops.[14] St.
Thomas Aquinas defined divination as the attempt to learn
the future through the *consilium* and *auxilium* of a demon.[15]

The cumulative effect of the sources' use of *consilium et
auxilium* is to reveal its content: one rendered *consilium et
auxilium* when he used the resources at his disposal, his liberties, rights, and usages—economic, political, spiritual—in the
service of another. People in a relationship of mutual *consilium
et auxilium* had united their purposes and their power toward a
common end and shared responsibility for each other's actions,
be they praiseworthy or worthy of condemnation.[16] Christian
consilium et auxilium was a part of the content of faithfulness
and charity, of differentiated friendship, and it was through
networks of people so bound together in *mutuum auxilium*

---

[9] Mansi, 23:338.

[10] *Gal. Christ.,* 3:493.

[11] See, for example *Bullarium Ordinis FF. Prædicatorum,* ed. Thomas Ripoll
and Antonin Bremond 1:435; LTC, 4:4849–51.

[12] See, for example *Urban IV, Reg.,* 586, 1764; LTC, 4:4934.

[13] Mansi, 23:367.

[14] *Gal. Christ.,* 3:490.

[15] ST II-II q.95, a.3, resp.

[16] Ibid., q.14, a.3, ad.4; ST Supplementum, q.71, a.1, ad.3; ST Supplementum
q.23, a.2, resp.

that society was governed, and it was these networks that contended with each other for control.[17]

Networks of *consilium et auxilium* were made up of the differentiated individuals of this context-bound society. Such a network could unite these individuals' disparate rights and obligations, powers and uses, into a single "organism," not one based on undifferentiated administration or abstract "power" flowing from some sovereign source, but rather on their personal relationships as kin and friends. To grant someone *consilium et auxilium* was to bind oneself, to obligate oneself, to seek his interest. This is why kings demanded the *consilium* of their vassals and why vassals were sometimes hesitant to give it, and this is why petitioners to Parlement asked that the king might give his *consilium* and why Parlement often refused to do so.[18]

The *consilium* of the king was a powerful thing. In response to Pope Alexander IV's pleas for *auxilium* for the Holy Land, a council was held in 1260 in Bordeaux. The assembled bishops

---

[17] Cardinal Ottoboni, legate to England in 1267, wrote to St. Louis asking for his help: "Novit et attendit paternitatis vestre consideracio qualiter inclitum regnum Anglorum, magnum tam in temporalibus quam in spiritualibus ecclesie membrum, fide ac devocione fecundum, diebus proximus, quorum adhuc malicia non quiescit, turbatum fuerit et subversum. Et quidem gracia divina prestante multa post ingressum nostrum requies non modo ecclesiasticis verum etiam secularibus personis et rebus adveniens, si ab extrinsecus venientiubs malis sollicite non defendatur, et tanti scitis formidanda esse venena, et tenera cicatrix a malis iuxtapositis et adhuc ferventibus non secura, per extrinseca facila turbari valeat, et in pristinam plage materiam suscitari. Proinde cum regnum prefatum, sicut intra sinum matris ecclesie regnum Francorum iuncta facie respicit, ita fraterno in fide, caritate, cunctisque auxiliis, affectu ipsius respicere debeat et fovere. Maxime autem per eos quos ipsa mater ecclesia pro se et pace fidelium nostrum misit, voluimus vestram providenciam invitare ut omnia hiis adversancia per sapiencie vestre sollicitudinem reprimatis, ut, quasi extenso usque ad nos brachio vestro, gaudeat mater que nos misit quod per mutuum auxilium commissa fidelia feliciter gubernentur" ("Letters of Cardinal Ottoboni," ed. Rose Graham, *The English Historical Review* 15 [January 1900]: 112).

[18] Olim, 1:70 (XXI); 1:73 (XXVI); *Actes*, 409.

condemned as heretics anyone who entered into a confederation with the Muslims and asserted that *auxilium* ought to be given to those kingdoms in danger. They continued that since any subsidy ought to be collected from secular persons as well as ecclesiastical persons, they would approve such a collection only through "common consent, and having had the *consilium* of the lord king," since they believed "for certain that barons, knights, and other laity cannot be induced to such a subsidy" through their power alone.[19]

Consilium et auxilium created a partnership that went both ways. In 1257 the Archbishop of Narbonne argued that he wanted to be a "faithful friend" of the king, and so the king should seek his *consilium*. In fact, the Archbishop asserted, custom required that his *consilium* be sought before the king's seneschal acted against a breaker of the peace, granting him an equal place as judge.[20] A person's *consilium et auxilium* was the social power he could bring to bear, his rights and obligations, and so we can understand why the king sought the "*consilium* of many prelates and of other good men" before ruling in especially problematic cases.[21] When Parlement brokered a peace between the vicecountess of Limoges and a certain Peter, one of her vassals, after he had joined a rebellion against her, Peter had to swear before the king's "full court and over the Holy Gospels and with the king present, that he will not adhere to the vicecountess's enemies, nor present to them *consilium* nor *auxilium*, and the same vicecountess he will serve faithfully as his lord."[22]

The many "confederations" and "pacts" that are mentioned in the sources are often directly associated with *consilium, auxilium*, or, similarly, *favorem*. When, in 1258, Parlement looked into whether such a confederation had been newly made in Orleans, it also wanted to know whether the local abbot had

---

[19] Mansi, 23:1045.
[20] HGL, 8:1424.
[21] Olim, 1:608 (XVII).
[22] Ibid., 1:693 (XXXV).

given it *consilium vel auxilium*. He had, and in so doing he had demonstrated his support.[23] Such confederations were networks of *consilium et auxilium* that had been formalized through some sort of oath. Since they wielded real social power, they were a concern for rival power, a concern that we can see expressed over and over again in the sources. The repeated prohibition of such sworn societies points to both how common they were and potentially problematic.[24]

Networks of *consilium et auxilium* included relationships of subordination—both "feudal" (based on oaths and fiefs) and "sacramental" or "jurisdictional" (based on ordination and appointments to benefices)—but they also cut across these hierarchies and encompassed them. These networks were capable of organizing and deploying immense material and social resources, but they most certainly were not States wielding some sort of overwhelming violence. Rather, they operated within the peace, through it, through the rights and obligations that sustained it. Indeed, counsel and aid tapped into the divine justice that was the foundation for the peace, and because of this, networks of counsel and aid had "ideological" or "theological" content.

To give counsel and aid to one's neighbor was a universal precept of Christianity, something that was owed by all to all. To give service to another Christian was simply the right thing to do. As the canonist Huguccio pointed out, this would seem to render an oath of fidelity redundant. It did not, however, because the power of the oath, he argued, lay in its specific nature: to break a specific promise is more sinful than a general one.[25] So, the feudal oath was a specifically codified example of the general promise demanded of all Christians. Nevertheless, the general promise, the universal relationship among Christians, was morally binding. The common end toward which this universal network of *consilium et auxil-*

---

[23] Ibid., 1:74 (XXVIII).

[24] CAAP, 2:1946; Mansi, 23:1264; Olim, 1:13 (XIX); 1:74 (XXVIII).

[25] Pennington, "The Formation of the Jurisprudence," 63–65.

ium was directed was salvation itself, and so Christians were bound to provide it to each other only in the service of this objective. Specific relationships within the universal were, therefore, subject to the same qualification. Huguccio, for example, explained that a vassal was not bound by his oath if fulfilling it forced him to sin, and he was not required to fight for his lord in an unjust war.[26]

Fundamentally, the rendering of counsel and aid was not a matter of relative rights but was a matter of moral obligation. What this means is that networks of *consilium et auxilium* had intrinsic to them "orthodoxies," common moral understandings in the service of which they functioned; if they lacked this they would break up, with members refusing to deploy their resources in the service of an "immoral" or "unjust" objective. It was divine justice, after all, that underwrote whatever legitimacy one could claim in this society. To knowingly act with injustice was to surrender one's legitimacy. And so, rendering *consilium et auxilium* to the right people in the right circumstances was a part of what it meant to be orthodox, and doing so to the wrong people in the wrong circumstances was a part of what it meant to be heretical, or at least sinful. For example, to go on crusade was to give Christ *auxilium* worthy of the full indulgence.[27] In the 1260s, if one rendered *consilium et auxilium* to crusade preachers one could share in this indulgence, but, if one gave *consilium, auxilium*, or *favorem* to the Saracens, he suffered excommunication.[28] The whole city of Genoa was excommunicated for giving "consilium, auxilium, vel favorem" to Michael Palaeologus, the schismatic emperor of the Greeks.[29] To refuse *consilium et auxilium* to the orthodox or to give it to the heretical or excommunicated

---

[26] Ibid., 65–66.

[27] See. for example, *Urban IV, Reg.*, 344.

[28] *Ludwigs des Heiligen Kreuzzug nach Tunis 1270, und die Politik Karls I. von Sizilien*, ed. Richard Sternfeld (Berlin: E. Ebering, 1896), 318; LTC, 5:5104; TNA, 2:196; *Clément IV, Reg.*, 1477.

[29] *Urban IV, Reg.*, 182.

was to place oneself outside the society of the faithful: it was grounds for excommunication.[30] And excommunication, as we saw in Part I, was conceptually and legally united with felony and rebellion.

The Church herself, the society of the baptized, was in the ideal a single network of *consilium et auxilium* within which smaller networks functioned. These networks often jostled for position, pushing and pulling each other. They bled into each other; they merged, reformed, or broke up. They could be concentric, overlapping, or completely separated from each other. They entered into conflict and made peace. As they did so, there was always a moral and spiritual component: it was one's duty to give counsel and aid to the just and the orthodox, and so it was hard to see how a rival, to whom one did not give counsel and aid, was not sinful and violent, perhaps heretical. A good Christian was forbidden to align with such people. Other networks that one was not in conflict with were perhaps legitimate, but they were oriented toward a different objective, or perhaps two networks simply lacked the personal relationships that would bring them together as one. The fact that two persons were not friends did not mean that they could not become friends, and it certainly did not mean that they were enemies. Where were the lines to be drawn between networks that fell within the larger network that was the Church and those that spilled over her borders? People argued and maneuvered about this, and through this dynamism the boundaries of practical justice, of moral action, of peace, of sin, of orthodoxy, and of the Church itself were negotiated and staked out.

With this dynamic in mind, we can understand even more fully Joinville's account of St. Louis's encounter with the Bishop of Auxerre that was treated in the previous chapter. The bishop approached Louis with the complaint that no one feared excommunication and that because of this Christendom itself was falling to pieces. He therefore asked Louis

---

[30] ST Supplementum, q. 23, a.2.

to use force against contumacious excommunicates. Louis responded that he would not do so without first investigating the justice of the censures, stating: "For if I did so, I should be flying in the face of God and justice."[31] We already saw how the false dichotomy between Church and State has led many historians to incorrectly perceive here some clash between parallel State-like institutions over some form of sovereignty. Within this reading, difference, in this case different institutional hierarchies, necessitates a conflict that can be ultimately overcome only when the difference itself is eliminated and undifferentiated relationships based on abstract categories are established. As long as real difference persists, peace is achievable only through some sort of subordination. This is a reading that emerges from a deist conception of the universe and is profoundly modern. In a Trinitarian cosmos, however, difference does not necessitate such conflict. Rather, differences can coexist and cooperate through friendship, through mutual giving and trust, and through a shared vision of divine justice.[32] This is what *consilium et auxilium* is all about.

It is the lack of this friendship that is apparent in Joinville's account. From the beginning he presents the bishops as up to no good, as trying to pull one over on the king, and the monarch as too wise to fall for their ploy: Louis answers the bishops well, arguing that justice is the ultimate law, a law that, the king is quick to point out, the papacy also enforces. The conflict that we see in Joinville, therefore, is not about whether the bishops or the king calls the shots; the conflict is about rival conceptions of justice. Each believed that the other was acting unjustly, and each argued that to go along with the other would be a violation of the cognizance of their offices, which were ultimately to do right "in the face of God and justice." This was a negotiation between networks of *consilium et auxilium*.

---

[31] *The Memoirs of the Lord of Joinville: A New English Version*, trans. Ethel Wedgwood, 348–49.

[32] David Bentley Hart, *The Beauty of the Infinite* (Grand Rapids, MI: Eerdmans, 2003), 178.

If, however, bishops and king could agree on the content of justice and treat each other as friends, if they gave each other *consilium et auxilium*, the conflict could fade away without any subordination, without any declaration of independence or self-sufficiency of one power in the face of the other, and without the elimination of their differentiation: they could become one circle of friends. In the Christian ideal, there would be only one network of *consilium et auxilium* and so universal but differentiated peace: as the cardinal legate Ottoboni wrote, "in His eternal *consilio* God dissipates the *concilia* of men."[33]

What we see in the Joinville account is a reality that is visible throughout the sources: elements of the episcopate, along with the noble families from which they came, were often outside the king's more intimate network of *consilium et auxilium*. Barons and bishops often opposed the king and his episcopal friends. We have already seen this in connection with the Mendicant Conflict and spectacularly in the case of the inquisition against Raymond, Bishop of Toulouse, and the account of Joinville should be read within this broader context. Louis's conflict with these bishops concerning the enforcement of their excommunications was not a Church-State issue. It was more an issue of conceptions of order coming into conflict with one another, conceptions of order organized in certain networks of *consilium et auxilium* that were made up as much by churchmen as by laymen.

The Joinville account, furthermore, is an example of such a conflict that remained within the bounds of orthodoxy as each side understood it. They were accusing each other of sin, no doubt, but heresy did not come up. The participants in such conflicts, though, if they were escalated, would find themselves before too long compelled to see heresy in their opponents, to interpret the boundaries of the Church and so of legitimacy as excluding their rival. This was what happened in the Mendicant Conflict. Representing the secular masters, William of Saint-Amour accused the friars of being false apostles and

---

[33] "Letters of Cardinal Ottoboni," 119.

heretics, and St. Thomas, for his part, returned the charge.[34]
When this happened, violence, even war, was called for—it
became the right thing to do.

The ultimate example is the Albigensian Crusade.
Through the *negotium pacis et fidei*, the *business of the peace
and the faith*, the Roman Church and the Crown sought to
dismantle an entire heretical world of *consilium et auxilium*
and replace it with their network and their orthodox understanding of right order. Pope Innocent III had demanded that
all the barons and consuls and other Christians of the region
give *consilium et auxilium* to Simon de Montfort, the leader
of the first expedition, in his *business of the peace and the faith*
against "those who attack the Catholic faith and disturb the
peace."[35] The oaths that were sworn in 1214 by the capitulating
southern nobles focus on *consilium, auxilium,* and *favorem.* The
lords would stop giving them to marauders and heretics and
start giving them to the Roman Church and her allies.[36] When
Raymond VII of Toulouse was excommunicated in 1226, so
too were all those who gave him *auxilium et consilium.*[37] When
Louis VIII finally entered the fight in 1226, it was only after
having "taken *consilium*" with the great barons, and so directing
the collective resources of a large network to the war.[38] At the
end of the war in 1229, the Peace of Paris sought not only to
dissolve the network that had opposed the crusade, but to integrate Raymond VII into the victorious network of Louis IX

---

[34] William of Saint-Amour, *Tractatus brevis de periculis novissimorum temporum*, 59, published in *Magistri Guillielmi de Sancto Amore Opera omnia*
(Constantiae: Apud Alithophilos, 1632). For Aquinas's response, see *Contra
impugnantes Dei cultum et religionem* 3.7 in *Opera Omnia* (Leonine ed.), vol.
41 lns. 448–71, (p. 68) (note: the corpusthomisticum.org online holding of
this work, while stating the Leonine edition as its text, locates this passage in
pars II, cap. , 2, ad 8).

[35] Mansi, 23:936.

[36] LTC, 1:1068.

[37] Mansi, 23:9–10.

[38] LTC, 2:1742.

and the Roman Church.[39] Likewise, the canons of the Council of Toulouse display the dismantling of one network and the extension of another, focused on the practices of orthodoxy: anyone who gave *consilium* or *auxilium* to heretics or breakers of the peace would be considered as such themselves; everyone was expected to give *consilium et auxilium* to those opposed to such enemies of the peace and the faith; new sworn associations were forbidden.[40]

Even after the war, the *negotium*, the *business*, continued: the destruction of such a network and the extension of another of this scale was a long-term project. In 1246 a council at Béziers excommunicated those who gave *consilium* or *favorem* to heretics.[41] The *business of the peace and the faith* was the business of orthodoxy in both its secular and spiritual manifestations. The extension of this orthodox network was an ongoing project. For example, a synod at Marseilles in 1263 decreed that since the sin of heresy had been extirpated from the diocese, it was time to turn to the sin of not paying the tithe. Therefore, anyone who failed to pay the tithe, along with anyone who gave them *consilium*, *auxilium*, or *favorem*, was excommunicated. If they still refused to pay, they and their supporters were to be condemned as heretics.[42]

Within this reading of the social dynamic, the power of the "Church" was not a threat to the power of the "State." Rather, certain conglomerations of spiritual and secular powers were threats to certain other conglomerations of spiritual and secular powers. Peace, then, came not from the destruction or usurpation of the power of a rival institution, but in the spread of one network of *consilium et auxilium* to encompass more and more of the social field. Once we understand this, we are in a position to see how unhelpful it is to talk about things like an "alliance between Crown and altar,"

---

[39] HGL, 8:883–92.
[40] Mansi, 23:194–204.
[41] Ibid., 23:694.
[42] Ibid., 23:1113.

or the "problem of Church and State." Rather, we ought to talk about things like the *business of the peace and the faith* and its opponents. As we shall see later, this dynamic is found explicitly and repeatedly in the fight against Manfred in Italy, in the baronial rebellion in England, and in many other conflicts, large and small. Feudal and canonical hierarchies were subsumed into this larger dynamic, and the historical data of conflicts that have traditionally been read as battles between Church and State fit better into these categories than those of modern politics.

The mission of Gui Foucois and his fellow *enquêteurs* in the late 1250s, which was discussed in Part I, was essentially to bring peace to the lands of the South through extending the king's network of *consilium et auxilium* to include more and more people, to integrate the peace of the South with the peace of the Crown. This meant not only doing justice (righting wrongs) but also negotiating the settlements of long-standing disputes between the Crown and local powers, especially among the episcopate. For example, Gui negotiated a settlement between the king and the Bishop of Maguelonne concerning royal jurisdiction in the city of Montpellier and accepted the bishop's oath to the king in 1257.[43] But it is in Gui's promotion to the episcopal see of Le Puy in 1257 that we can see most clearly how the royal peace was extended. This peace was extended not so much through the construction of jurisdictional or institutional mechanisms of top-down control as through the extension of the king's network of friends and the propagation of the orthodoxy and the *negotium* within which this network of friends understood itself. Legal instruments and claims to rights were important, but they were not the primary manner in which the kingdom was constructed. The law came into play only when the peace failed; where peace succeeded, positive law faded away. They were not building a State.

There had been a long-running conflict between Louis and the bishops and chapter of Le Puy regarding the king's

---

[43] LTC, 3:4156, 4312.

regalia rights during a vacancy. This conflict had become especially acute because the see had been vacant between 1251 and 1255.[44] The chapter of Le Puy clearly wanted to reach a settlement with the king, and so when their bishop died in May of 1257, they unanimously elected Gui Foucois, who had only just taken Holy Orders after the death of his wife. This was a bold move on the chapter's part, for Gui was a "cleric of the king."[45] This election should be seen as a bid on the part of the chapter to enter into Louis's network, to switch from opposition to cooperation with royal power.[46] The manner in which the church of Le Puy was integrated into this network shows the negotiations between the various actors that constituted it and through whom it was directed.

Gui did not accept the chapter's election at first. Rather, he put the matter into the hands of the famous Hugh of Saint-Cher, cardinal priest of Saint Sabina.[47] Hugh was the first Dominican cardinal and had been granted direct control over the entire Dominican order by the papacy. He was also French and had been a master at the University of Paris.[48] Hugh was solidly in the papal-royal network at the highest level. He was not only institutionally powerful; he was also someone whom Gui could trust to understand the power dynamics in play and to work toward an outcome beneficial to the various interests involved. Also, the church of Le Puy pertained directly to the Roman See, so any election had to be confirmed by the pope.

---

[44] Fernando Alberto Pico, "The Bishops of France in the Reign of Louis IX (1226–70)," 285; Yves Dossat, "Gui Foucois, enquêteur-réformateur, archevêque et pape," *Cahiers de Fanjeaux* 7 (1972): 37.

[45] LTC, 3:4388. In January of 1257, Gui began to be called *clericus domini regis Francie* (LTC, 3:4317).

[46] Such attempts were not always successful. When the people of a certain village took it upon themselves to swear an oath of loyalty to the king, their bishop objected. Such an oath was a novelty and threatened his rights. Parlement agreed and suppressed the oath; see Olim, 1:617 (VIII).

[47] LTC, 3:4388.

[48] Salvador Miranda, "The Cardinals of the Holy Roman Church" (1998), last updated August 18, 2015, http://www2.fiu.edu/~mirandas/bios1244.htm#Saintcher.

Hugh had the position in Rome to ensure that this happened if the election was deemed beneficial.

The nuncios of the chapter and Hugh brought the matter before Pope Alexander IV, who agreed to confirm the election but left the ultimate decision in the hands of Gui, which in effect left the matter in the hands of the king.[49] With the papal side squared away, the chapter turned to Louis, asking him to direct Gui to accept the election and to invest him with the regalia.[50] This the king did, and Gui, too sick to travel to Rome, was consecrated by the Bishop of Nîmes sometime in the winter of 1257–1258, but only after swearing an oath of fidelity to the pope and the Roman Church.[51] Gui's election to the See of Le Puy was therefore not decided upon or dictated by the papacy, by the king, by the chapter, or by Gui himself. Rather, the whole "network" was consulted, and through a sequence of petition, agreement, and then deference, Gui was put in place and Le Puy was integrated into the "peace" of the network. Gui became the Bishop of Le Puy, and with its interests now his own, he swore an oath of fidelity to the Roman Church and remained a cleric of the king.

As the Bishop of Le Puy, Gui split his time between his see and the king's Parlement, where he acted as one of his most important counselors.[52] The pre-existing legal conflict concerning the rights of the see of Le Puy and those of the king were, through Gui's elevation, brought into the personal relationship between the king and his *enquêteur* and legal advisor. In the Parlement of Pentecost 1258, two cases involving Le Puy were presented. The first had to do with the bishop's jurisdiction in the city. Gui claimed it was complete, *merum imperium*, but a faction within the city disputed this. The Parlement ordered an inquiry into the case, the outcome

---

[49] *Les Registres d'Alexandre IV*, eds. Charles de La Roncière et al. (Paris: A. Fontemoing, 1902), 2261; LTC, 3:4388.

[50] LTC, 3:4388.

[51] *Les Registres d'Alexandre IV*, 2360.

[52] See, for example, Olim, 1:75.

of which is unknown.[53] The second case concerned the king's rights to regalia in the bishopric. The Parlement determined his rights to be very limited: during a vacancy he had the rights to the bishop's revenues and justice in the city itself. He controlled nothing outside the city, nor did he control the prebends of the chapter, and the chapter did not have to announce the death of their bishop to him, nor did they have to seek his permission to elect a successor.[54] The king issued a public instrument announcing this ruling, and Gui himself delivered it to the chapter of Le Puy, who responded with a letter to the king accepting the ruling entirely and declaring peace between the Church and the king.[55]

Legal conflict between Le Puy and the Crown came to a quick conclusion with its integration, through Gui, into the Crown's network of *consilium et auxilium*. The Crown was willing to relinquish claims to legal rights to friends, and we can see how mistaken Gerard Campbell is when he writes of this case that an attempt of the monarchy "to penetrate the province of Bourges was rebuffed."[56] Legal or jurisdictional rights to regalia are hardly the whole story and are certainly not the sole measure of the extent of royal "government." The king may have had fewer "rights" in Le Puy, but this did not mean that he had less control. And so, we can understand why, shortly after the conclusion of the Le Puy case, the provost of Brivadois offered to Gui and his successors a prebend in the chapter with *plenitudine juris canonici*, thus pulling Le Puy and Brivadois together.[57] This is the way peace was made and the way real "government" happened.

What is more, this extension of the network was the immediate context for Louis's "ordinance" directed to the faithful

---

[53] Olim, 1:32.

[54] Ibid., 1:35.

[55] *Gal. Christ.*, 2:Instrumenta, 234; LTC, 3:4505.

[56] Gerard J. Campbell, S.J. "Temporal and Spiritual Regalia during the Reigns of St. Louis and Philip III," *Traditio* 20 (1964): 375.

[57] *Gal. Christ.*, 2:Instrumenta, 233.

of Le Puy concerning the supposed outlawing of private war that was discussed above.[58] Rather than some sort of universal statute extending the sovereignty of the Crown, what we are seeing is that with the integration of the diocese of Le Puy into the network of the king, the bishop's rights to justice were now backed by the power of the king. The king's resources and the bishop's resources were now united in a single initiative: the *business of the peace and the faith*. The king's officer was committed to work with Gui to act against *factores pacis*—enemies as much to the Church as the Crown, enemies to the *negotium* and to the social order it sought to build. This ordinance—a letter, really—ought to be read as a part of the process through which the church of Le Puy was integrated into the king's network of *consilium et auxilium*. The episcopal power, the necessary ecclesiastical side of the *negotium pacis et fidei* was, in the person of Gui, held by a man already a part of the network that pushed the *negotium* forward. The king was ordering that his officer participate fully with Gui in the *negotium*. The concept of modern sovereignty has no place in this story.

As Bishop of Le Puy and after 1259 as Archbishop of Narbonne, Gui was an important player in the negotiations directing the power of the network of relations that included the king and the papacy.[59] In September of 1259 Pope Alexander IV wrote to Gui, then still Bishop of Le Puy. The Archbishop of Narbonne (the archbishop previous to Gui), the pope

---

[58] "Louis ... etc., greetings to all the faithful of the kingdom in the diocese of Le Puy and the fiefs of the church of Le Puy. You should know that having had deliberations with our counsel we have inhibited all wars in our kingdom, and arson, and the perturbing of traveling wagons. Hence we mandate to you with strict warning, lest you might act against our said prohibition of wars, or might make fires, or disturb the peasants who drive wagons or the plow. If you presume to do otherwise, we give to our Seneschal the order to help faithfully and attentively our faithful and beloved G. [Gui Foucois] the elect of Le Puy to make peace in the land, and to punish the breakers of the peace on account of their guilt" (*Ordonnances*, 1:84).

[59] Very little survives concerning Gui's translation to Narbonne. Pope Urban IV mentions it in a letter to Gui's successor (*Urban IV, Reg.*,147).

related, had complained to the papal curia about the king's men offending the rights and liberties of his church. The pope therefore asked Gui to discuss the issue with the king and encourage him to hear kindly the archbishop's complaints.[60] Also in 1259 a conflict arose between the king and the Archbishop of Arles concerning Beaucaire and the territories of the diocese located in the kingdom as opposed to the empire, territory once held in fief from the church of Arles by the counts of Toulouse. These territories had passed to the king through Simon de Montfort in 1229, and Louis had neither rendered homage to the archbishop nor paid the census the archbishop claimed to be owed. The archbishop demanded recompense for this loss[61] and complained to the pope, who commissioned Gui with a special mandate to settle the dispute. The procurator of the archbishop came to Parlement to plead his case, and as both a regular member of Parlement (as the counselor of the king) and a bearer of a papal commission, Gui mediated a compromise settlement acceptable to both parties.[62]

As a bishop, Gui continued to work as an *enquêteur* for the king, continued to bear royal commissions and to accept royal mandates. He remained a cleric of the king. A Narbonnaise Hebrew account described Gui as "beloved of the king and appointed in his stead for all affairs of the land, needing to flatter no one nor to fear anyone's power."[63] In 1260 Louis wrote to Gui, then Archbishop of Narbonne, asking that he finish his investigation into the inheritance of a certain Ramunda de Ventajou, which had been confiscated on account of her father-in-law's *faidimentum*. Gui did so and then, with the authority of the king, ordered the seneschal of Carcassonne to enforce the sentence.[64] In 1261 Gui was commissioned by the king to hold

---

[60] *Regesta pontificum romanorum*, ed. August Potthast, vol. 2, no. 17674.

[61] Dossat, "Gui Foucois," 38.

[62] *Gal. Christ.*, 2:Instrumenta, 235.

[63] Robert Chazan, "Archbishop Guy Fulcodi of Narbonne and his Jews," *Revue des estudes juives*, 132 (1973): 589.

[64] RHGF, 24:692.

an inquest into the holdings of Berenger de Puisserguier. He investigated Berenger's family's possession of the properties and whether they had lived "in peace with the Church and the lord king" and determined that Berenger held his fiefs illegally, that his father had come to them through violence, through warring against the king in the last rebellion of the Count of Toulouse.[65] These cases were right in line with the types of cases Gui had dealt with as an *enquêteur* and as a member of Louis's Parlement. As a bishop, however, he was in a position to be entrusted with even more important business for the king, such as negotiating an agreement between King James of Aragon and the Bishop of Maguelonne concerning homage and rights to justice.[66] In 1260 Gui was recommended by Louis to serve as an arbitrator in the negotiations surrounding the peace between Louis and Henry III of England. Henry agreed, believing Gui to be "good and trustworthy."[67]

Simultaneously with his royal commissions, Gui was commissioned ecclesiastical cases by the papacy. For example, he was sent by Urban IV to hold an inquisition into the Bishop of Cahors, concerning whom the pope had heard the most heinous of charges. The bishop resisted the inquisition, and it dragged on for years to be concluded only by Gui as Pope Clement IV.[68] But it would be a mistake to place Gui's work for the Crown and work of the papacy in sealed off compartments. Rather, they find a unity within the context of the *negotium pacis et fidei*, and most of the time Gui worked with both papal and royal interests in mind and, more often than not, bearing legal mandates and commissions from both authorities simultaneously.

---

[65] Olim, 1:148–49.

[66] *Gal. Christ.*, 6:372; LTC, 4:4681.

[67] *Documents of the Baronial Movement of Reform and Rebellion, 1258–1267*, selected by Reginald Francis Treharne and ed. Ivor John Sanders (Oxford: Clarendon Press, 1973), 166–67 (doc. 14), 170–73 (doc. 15).

[68] *Urban IV, Reg.*, 2970; *Bullarium Franciscanum Romanorum Pontificum* (Rome: Typis Sacæ Congregationis de Propaganda Fide, 1759–1804), 3:54, 102.

For example, in 1262, right before he elevated Gui to the cardinalate, Pope Urban IV wrote to Louis IX. He recounted that his predecessor, Alexander IV, had, at the behest of Louis, given a papal commission to Gui some years earlier to arbitrate a peace between the queen and Charles of Anjou, the king's brother (Charles was at constant odds with the wife and daughters of Ramon Berenguer IV, Count of Provence, concerning their respective claims to the county).[69] Gui had long been involved in this conflict, having acted as an arbitrator between Charles and his mother-in-law several years earlier while still a layman.[70] But what are of real interest are the reasons Urban gave for Alexander's commission of Gui. The Roman Church prayed and worked with great zeal that the king's "most Christian kingdom" might be free from the discord over which the Church wept and might live in the tranquility of peace over which the Church rejoiced. This was especially true because the kings of France had worked so hard to protect the Church and to prosecute those who would attack her. It was in this *negotium pacis*, Urban recalled, that Gui had been commissioned by Pope Alexander to arbitrate between Charles and his mother-in-law. Urban regretfully informed the king that Gui would no longer be able to work in this endeavor because the pope had called him to the cardinalate, where his efforts could bring the same benefits to the universal Church.[71] Peace was as much the Church's business as was the faith, and the faith as much the Crown's as the peace—this is the central point of the *negotium pacis et fidei*—and Gui was a central player in this "business" and in the network that advanced it.

Indeed, the *negotium pacis et fidei* was the context for Gui's entire career and this continued seamlessly into his term as a bishop. Before he had been made a cardinal, upon his 1259 translation to Narbonne, Gui had issued a series of statutes for his new jurisdiction. There was nothing profoundly origi-

---

[69] AE, 22:91.
[70] LTC, 3:4300.
[71] AE, 22:91–2.

nal in the statutes—they read like any number of similar lists
promulgated by French bishops of the period. But that is really
their interest: he legislated against those who molested religious women; he threatened with suspension any cleric who
held a secular office; he threatened with excommunication
clerics who violated other priests' parishes; he ordered priests
to warn those who missed Mass for three consecutive Sundays
and, if they continued in their negligence, to excommunicate
them and to invoke the help of the secular arm; he forbade
merchants from doing business on Sundays with threat of
censure; and finally, he decreed that if a bailiff failed to enforce
this last statute against the Jews, he was to be struck with the
sentence of excommunication, *quam nunc ferimus in rebelles.*[72]
Gui, the *enquêteur*, who had spent the vast majority of his
career as a married layman lawyer in the direct service of the
secular power, promulgated ecclesiastical canons that could
have just as easily been promulgated by a career ecclesiastic.

The same Hebrew account mentioned above recounts
how the Jews of Narbonne had come to Gui and petitioned
him for protection against the extortions of the Crown's officers—as was his duty, the Jews reminded him. And, the Jewish
writer concluded, "Thanks be to the Lord," he accepted our
words and did as we requested."[73] There was no fundamental tension between Gui as churchman and Gui as servant of
the Crown—there was no fundamental tension between "the
lay" and "the clerical" as such. He was a part of a network of
consilium et auxilium that was engaged in the *negotium pacis et
fidei.* This network was made up of churchmen and laymen,
and he could move from layman to cleric without any sort of
fundamental change in his understanding of right order. As
bishop, Gui could demand that bailiffs enforce ecclesiastical
censures and not extort money because he had demanded the
same when he was a layman. In fact, as a layman, he had been
intimately involved in the crafting of this image of right secular

---

72 Mansi, 23:1029–32.
73 Chazan, "Archbishop Guy Fulcodi of Narbonne," 589–90.

and ecclesiastical order. The role that Gui assumed as a bishop was that of the reform-minded ecclesiastic demanded by the *negotium pacis et fidei*. He therefore bore royal commissions against corrupt secular officials or nobles, and he acted under his own authority or bore papal commissions against corrupt prelates or against heresy—there was no incoherence or even tension here.

In the consultation to the inquisitors that he wrote as an *enquêteur*, Gui had taken pains to demonstrate that the inquisitors did not answer to the ordinaries. He had, however, stated that the prelates had an obligation to give the inquisitors *consilium et auxilium*.[74] The pope, likewise, mandated that the bishops give the inquisitors *consilium et auxilium*.[75] The ideal, then, was one of cooperation rather than subordination. He fulfilled this ideal himself when in 1261 he wrote a lengthy *consilium* to the friar inquisitor in Narbonne. It covered much of the same ground as his early *Consilium*, concerning degrees of guilt and of procedure. He also counseled, indeed petitioned, the inquisitor to proceed according to God and justice without regard for nobility or power and to force the lords who received the goods of heretics to use them for the good of the poor.[76] Ideally there would be no conflict between the papal inquisitors and the bishops: they would be members of the same network of *consilium et auxilium* and the legal claims to rights and prerogatives would become moot. The same can be said for the relationship between the bishops and the king or the pope himself, and Gui attempted to fill this role.

One of the things we see happening in the 1250s and especially in the 1260s is the tightening of the bonds between

---

[74] *Consilium*, 324.

[75] LTC, 4:4000, 4001.

[76] Celestin Douais, *Documents pour servir à l'histoire de L'Inquisition dans la Languedoc* (Paris, 1890), 66–68. For attribution to Gui, see Antoine Dondaine, O.P., "Le manuel de L'Inquisiteur (1230–1330)," *Archivum Fratrum Praedicatorum* 17 (1947), 151. For dating, see Dossat, "Gui Foucois, enquêteur-réformateur," 41n80.

the Crown and the papacy—the incorporation of each into the same network. Since Louis VIII and the crusade in the South, the papacy and the monarchy had found far more opportunity for cooperation than for conflict. But in the 1260s the papacy and the Crown were brought together within a much tighter network of *consilium et auxilium*; they became not just allies, but friends. The social order that the Crown was trying to build and that which the papacy was trying to build were basically the same—they were two aspects of the same organization of thought and power—and both believed the role of the other to be essential. As we will see, when Gui was elevated to the cardinalate in 1261, his membership in the king's network did not cease. But at the same time he most certainly was not the king's stooge, as some historians have asserted.[77] There is no need to posit such inherent conflict. Rather, the monarchy and the papacy "shared" Gui—and Gui worked with great devotion in a *negotium* that he believed placed him, without incoherence, solidly in the service of both Crown and papacy. Indeed, when we take a look at Gui's time as a cardinal, as we will in the next chapter, and especially his legation to France in which he and Louis worked together to try to bring the troubles in England to an end, we can see clearly that Gui believed that the power of monarchy and the power of the papacy rose or fell together—they were two columns of the same structure that he had spent his whole life building.

---

[77] Geoffrey Barraclough, *The Medieval Papacy*, 118.

CHAPTER TEN

IN THE FULLNESS OF ROYAL POWER

From this earthly city issue the enemies against whom
the City of God must be defended.

—St. Augustine, *City of God* 1.1

ON JANUARY 23, 1264 Louis IX issued his famous *Mise of
Amiens*. The *Mise* was Louis's decision as arbitrator between
Henry III of England and his rebellious barons and prelates, led
by Simon de Montfort (the son of the leader of the crusade in
the South of France), and is often seen as Louis's clearest explication of his understanding of royal power. In it, he condemned
the Provisions of Oxford, the attempt by Simon's faction to
assert some level of direct control over the governance of the
kingdom at the expense of the king, which are often seen as a

precursor to England's parliamentary government.[1] By 1264, Popes Alexander IV and Urban IV had already condemned the Provisions, a fact cited by Louis as contributing to his decision. Charles Wood, the author of the most cited work on the *Mise of Amiens*, explains this coincidence of papal and royal opinion as purely opportunistic: "the whole tendency of monarchical policy, at least since the reign of Philip Augustus, had been so contrary to any acceptance of papal sovereignty over matters of state that it becomes difficult to take at face value Louis's seeming acceptance of it here." Rather, Wood contends, when Louis happened to find his views to be in agreement with those of the popes, he made opportunistic use of this support: "Papal sovereignty might from time to time be acknowledged, but for all practical purposes the king of France claimed freedom from its jurisdiction."[2] However, when the *Mise* is read within the context of the actual relationship between Louis and the papacy, and more particularly between Louis and his old *enquêteur*, Gui Foucois, who was papal legate to England at the time, what is found is not an opportunistic, realpolitik alliance, but a profound agreement. Louis and the papacy agreed about kingship. They agreed that it was necessary to defend the fullness of royal power and they agreed concerning the content of that power. What is more, "sovereignty" simply has nothing to do with it. The fullness of royal power was not the power of an absolutist monarch, it was not "sovereignty," and it was not the monopolization of violence. It was the power to maintain peace through the construction of a society ultimately based upon friendship.

We cannot go into great detail here concerning the intricate and complex political situation of the 1250s and 1260s,

---

[1] Indeed, in 1965 a plaque was placed at Simon de Monfort's grave which reads:

> Here were buried the remains of
> SIMON DE MONTFORT, EARL OF LEICESTER
> pioneer of representative government who was
> killed in the Battle of Evesham on 4 August 1265.

[2] Charles Wood, "The Mise of Amiens and Saint-Louis' Theory of Kingship," *French Historical Studies* 6. no. 3 (Spring 1970): 304.

but what needs to be understood is that the whole period was overshadowed by the problem of Sicily and Manfred, the heir of Emperor Frederick II. The papacy felt that it could not allow Manfred to hold Sicily, and Manfred, for his part, seemed determined to rebuild his father's power in southern Italy at the expense of the Roman Church. The papacy was convinced that it was only through a resolution to this Sicilian problem that other large-scale initiatives such as a crusade to the Holy Land might become possible. While Louis IX was hesitant to become directly involved, it seems clear that he believed the papacy was correct that a successful crusade, something to which he was committed, required peace in Italy.[3] Since 1252 the papacy had looked to Henry III of England as a potential champion against Manfred, and Innocent IV invested Henry's second son, Edmund, with the kingdom in 1253, with the expectation of an invasion.

The English expedition to expel Manfred, however, was repeatedly delayed, leading Pope Alexander IV in 1258 to threaten Henry with excommunication if he failed to live up to his obligations.[4] From 1257, Henry argued that his continued hostilities with Louis IX were the primary obstacle to his prosecution of the Sicilian business and that the first step was to make a formal peace with the French king.[5] Alexander IV recognized the truth of this claim and saw a peace with Louis as an opportunity for French resources to be directed toward the service of Henry's expedition. In particular, the pope suggested that a part of any peace treaty be that Louis provide Henry with five hundred knights with whom he might unseat Manfred.[6]

---

[3] Norman Housley, *The Italian Crusades: The Papal-Angevin Alliance and the Crusades against Christian Lay Powers, 1254–1343* (Oxford: Clarendon Press, 1982), 67–82.

[4] *Documents of the Baronial Movement of Reform and Rebellion*, 2–3.

[5] *Foedera*, 1:630; *Royal and Other Historical Letters Illustrative of the Reign of Henry III*, ed. Walter Waddington (London: Longmans, Green, Reader, and Dyer, 1866), 2:DXXXI (p. 147).

[6] Ibid., 1:666.

Henry's position within his own kingdom was, furthermore, insecure. In the summer of 1258 a group of barons, led
by Simon de Montfort, had compelled the king and his first
son, Edward, to agree to the "Provisions of Oxford," which basically forced the king to rule in "consultation" with a council
of barons that he did not himself choose.[7] The barons' relative
power was in part a consequence of the massive debt that Henry
had incurred to the papacy in his pursuit of Sicily.[8] The barons
wanted this problem resolved as much as did the king, and so
they were in agreement in their desire for peace with Louis.[9]
Louis, for his part, was inclined toward peace both because
he found war between Christians abhorrent and because he
understood that ultimately a successful crusade would depend
upon these problems being resolved.[10] As the papacy repeatedly reminded everyone, only with Italy secure could the Holy
Land be definitively succored.[11] Louis and Henry were, furthermore, brothers-in-law, each having married a daughter of
Ramon Berenguer IV, Count of Provence.

This was the context for the 1259 Peace of Paris between
Henry and Louis. Sicily remained at the forefront of the
peace process, and so, as Henry reminded the pope and the
cardinals, it was very much in the papacy's interest to help
make peace a reality.[12] When peace was finally agreed to,
both Henry and Louis requested that the pope send a legate
to confirm it,[13] which Alexander promised to do as soon as
he could.[14] While a peace was agreed to in 1259, discussions
concerning its implementation continued throughout 1260,
especially with regard to Louis's provision of five hundred
knights for Henry—the crux of the peace's impact on the

---

[7] *Documents of the Baronial Movement of Reform and Rebellion*, 97 (doc. 5).
[8] Ibid., 3.
[9] Ibid., 195 (doc. 29).
[10] Housley, *The Italian Crusades*, 67–82.
[11] *Urban IV, Reg.* , 804, 809; LTC, 4:4853.
[12] *Foedera*, 1:667, 672.
[13] Ibid., 1:679–80.
[14] Ibid., 1:666.

Sicilian business. In these talks, Henry was represented by Simon de Montfort (as he had been in all the peace talks with Louis),[15] and Louis by Gui Foucois, then Bishop of Le Puy.[16] Throughout 1260, Henry became increasingly anxious for this issue to be settled because, as he wrote to the pope, to Louis, and to Louis's wife Marguerite, the whole Sicilian affair turned on it.[17]

Over the course of 1260, however, Henry's relationship with Simon de Montfort and his allies among the English prelates and barons continued to sour, to the point where clearly Simon was no longer interested in helping the king procure five hundred knights from France, and he began to work against Henry's interests at home and abroad.[18] This compounded Henry's problems, further delaying any action in the Sicilian business and taking from the king "his power and royal dignity."[19] Nevertheless, Henry continued to work toward a resolution of the Sicilian business, with papal support.[20] Henry begged the pope to send a legate[21] and asked Louis for help against his enemies.[22]

Alexander did not send a legate, no doubt because the college of cardinals consisted of only eight men and he himself was sick (a papal election was imminent). But, in the spring of 1261 the pope did absolve Henry of his oath to uphold the Provisions of Oxford, upon which the barons justified their

---

[15] *Royal and Other Historical Letters*, 2:DXI (p. 121).

[16] *Documents of the Baronial Movement of Reform and Rebellion*, 166–67 (doc. 14), 170–73 (doc. 15), 195 (doc. 29); *Royal and Other Historical Letters*, 2:DXXV (p. 138), DXXXII (p. 148).

[17] *Foedera*, 1:681, 683, 705; *Royal and Other Historical Letters*, 2:DXXXV (p. 153).

[18] *Documents of the Baronial Movement of Reform and Rebellion*, 189 and 205–09 (doc. 25), 210–19 (doc. 30), 220–39 (doc. 31).

[19] Ibid., doc. 30: "alii subtraxerunt regi posse suum et dignitatem regalem quod nullus perficit preceptum suum sed minus obedient mandato suo quam minori de consilio" (pp. 212–15).

[20] *Royal and Other Historical Letters*, 2:DXXXIV (p. 152).

[21] *Foedera*, 1:687.

[22] *Documents of the Baronial Movement of Reform and Rebellion*, 189 (doc. 25).

actions by stating that it was cause "for justified wonder that the axe should turn against him who wields it or the saw against him who uses it, or that those, forsooth, whom a lawful order of subordination have subjected to the more powerful should be raised against the authority of the rulers, and that princes, who are the lords of laws, whom celestial ordinance has inscribed at the head of their partners, should be curbed by the will of their subjects."[23] Alexander charged the Archbishop of Canterbury to compel the barons, through excommunication if necessary, "to cleave faithfully to their king as to their chief, and to obey him, showing him the debts of prompt fidelity and the obedience of peaceful subjection, and not, on pretext of these constitutions, ordinances, and undertakings in any way hindering him from using freely in all things the untrammeled fullness of the royal power."[24] One seldom comes across a more forceful statement of royal power. But what did it mean?

It is perhaps possible to read Alexander's letters as simply cynical: the pope wanted Henry to defeat Manfred, and the barons in England were keeping him from doing so; he, therefore, supported the power of the king against the barons and concocted whatever theoretical justification he needed in order to do so. This reading plays directly into the standard narrative to the extent that it sees the papacy as unwittingly constructing the power of the English and French monarchies in an attempt to win those monarchies' support against the Hohenstaufen. Ultimately, according to this narrative, the sovereign power of these monarchies would be turned against the incommensurable claims of the papacy, especially in the Philip IV–Boniface VIII conflict, and lead to royal absolutism. However, this reading is not borne out in the events that followed Alexander's bulls. As we will see, its elements fall one by one.

Rather, what happened was a concerted effort on the part of the network of the *negotium pacis et fidei*—Louis and the papacy represented by Gui—to enforce in England an under-

---

[23] Ibid., 242–45 (doc. 34).
[24] Ibid.

standing of right order that did not include any conception of "sovereignty" in the modern sense and that certainly did not see any conflict between the fullness of papal and the fullness of royal power, an order in which, indeed, princes and popes together stood in for Christ and ruled over societies predicated not on continual violence but on a primordial peace. The enforcement of this understanding of order was understood as integral to success in the Holy Land and Sicily, but it was not simply a means toward that end. Apostolic and royal power worked in concert toward the achievement of shared ends, with neither side bending the other to its will.

Alexander died a few weeks after issuing his bulls and a three-month papal vacancy ensued. During this time both Henry and the English barons, led by Simon de Montfort, asked Louis to intervene.[25] Simon had negotiated with Louis throughout the previous year and trusted him: in his 1261 defense against Henry's charges of unfaithfulness, Simon repeatedly appealed to the memory of Louis, stating that he would accept whatever Louis recalled as having happened.[26] Because of Louis's new peace with Henry and their family bonds, and through his obvious friendship with Simon de Montfort, whose father had led the first wave of crusaders in the South of France and who had himself fought there with Louis VIII, St. Louis was an obvious candidate for arbitrator. And he had a genuine interest in concord being restored to England—his crusading plans depended on it. Henry and Simon therefore agreed that Louis should arbitrate their dispute.[27] Louis took up the challenge and he met with representatives of the king and the barons throughout the summer and fall of 1261, trying to find a way for Simon to return to the "peace and graces" of

---

[25] *Foedera*, 1:724; *Documents of the Baronial Movement of Reform and Rebellion*, 38–40.

[26] *Documents of the Baronial Movement of Reform and Rebellion*, 194–95 and 202–03 (doc. 29).

[27] *Royal and Other Historical Letters*, 2: DXLV (pp. 168–69), DXLVI (p. 170), DXLVII (p. 171).

Henry. He was unsuccessful, and the conflict between Henry and Simon deepened.[28]

The papal vacancy was a problem. Alexander had promulgated his absolution of Henry's oaths only weeks before his death, and with the uncertainty of the vacancy, this promulgation had not been enforced by the Archbishop of Canterbury and the other prelates whom the pope had so charged.[29] The vacancy ended in August with the election of Jacques Pantaleon, the patriarch of Jerusalem (who had been at the papal curia to press for the support of the Holy Land), as Urban IV.[30] Urban was from Troyes and had served as the archdeacon of Laon and then Bishop of Verdun.[31] He had also attended the schools of Paris, and Henry's procurator at the papal curia was quick to point out to the king Jacques's relationship as a Frenchman with Louis.[32] Urban himself, in his letter announcing his election to Louis, mentioned that he was from France and that the election of a man from the kingdom was a long time in coming, and that he intended to show the utmost love for Louis and for his most devoted kingdom.[33]

But, Jacques had a long and close relationship to the papacy as well. Indeed, he had been elevated to the see of Verdun through a papal provision and had served as a papal legate to Eastern Europe.[34] As the patriarch of Jerusalem, he was the standing papal legate in the Holy Land. Jacques was an excel-

---

[28] Foedera, 1:742.

[29] *Urban IV, Reg.*, 797.

[30] Ibid., *Reg.*, 1.

[31] Horace K. Mann, *The Lives of the Popes in the Middle Ages* (London: Kegan Paul, Trench, Trubner and Co., 1929), 15:134–42; Maxime Souplet, *Jacques de Troyes le "pacificateur"* (Verdun, FR: S. I., 1954).

[32] Due to a very unfortunate lacuna in the manuscript, we do not know exactly how Henry's representative at the papal curia represented Jacques's relationship to Louis, but he certainly expressed a clear one. The manuscript reads, "quod dicto die patriarcham Jerusalem oriundum ... domini regis Franciae in Romanum pontificem elegerunt" (*Royal and Other Historical Letters*, 2:DLVI [p. 188]).

[33] *Urban IV, Reg.*, 2.

[34] Mann, *The Lives of the Popes*, 15:134–42.

lent candidate for bringing the French Crown and the papacy even closer together, and that was most likely the reason for his election. With the Sicilian business obviously front and center in their deliberations, the cardinals seem to have at first turned to Hugh of Saint-Cher, the French Dominican, and then to the English Cistercian John Tolet, both of whom refused the papal throne.[35] This would seem to suggest that the cardinals continued to believe that a solution to the English problems was an important component to success against Manfred, and that because of the close involvement of Louis in the affair, this solution could be expedited as much through a French pope as through an English one. Urban IV quickly set about binding the papal curia closely to the curia of Louis.

Around Christmas of 1261 Urban IV named seven cardinals. Among them were three "clerics of the king"—counselors to Louis: Gui Foucois as cardinal of St. Sabino, Simon de Brie as cardinal of St. Cecilia, and Radulph Grosparmi as cardinal of St. Albano. Simon and Radulph had very similar careers to Gui. Master Radulph was a lawyer who had served the king in Parlement, along with Gui, while holding various ecclesiastical offices.[36] He was the holder of the Royal Seal—no small sign of the king's confidence.[37] When Radulph was elected Bishop of Évreux in 1259, Louis and his two eldest sons attended the consecration, which was performed by Louis's close friend, the Franciscan Eudes, Archbishop of Rouen.[38] Like Gui, as Bishop of Évreux, Radulph held both royal and papal commissions, sometimes simultaneously in the same case, and worked as a point of contact between apostolic and royal powers.[39]

Simon de Brie was the treasurer of St. Martin de Tours

---

[35] *Royal and Other Historical Letters*, 2:DLVI (p. 188).

[36] For a summary of his early life, see Andreas Fischer, *Kardinale im Konklave: Die lange Sedisvakanz der Jahre 1268 bis 1271* (Tubingen: Niemeyer, 2008), 133–36.

[37] *Olim*, 1:75; Jean Richard, *Saint Louis: Crusader King of France*, 219.

[38] *Chronicon Monasterii Sancti Taurini Ebroicensis* (RHGF, 23:476); *Eudes, Reg.*, 393.

[39] *Gal. Christ.* 8:1358; LTC, 4:4697.

and the chancellor of the king of France at the time of his elevation, and he too had at one time held the seal of the king.[40]
Like Gui and Radulph, Simon served the king as a counsel-
or in Parlement. His position vis-à-vis the king was similar
enough to that of Gui that when Gui was translated from Le
Puy to Narbonne in 1259, the chapter of Le Puy offered the
see to Simon, clearly hoping for continuity with regard to their
relationship with the king (Simon turned them down). He was
also a papal chaplain.[41]

It is not only in hindsight that these men are grouped together. Louis IX himself wrote that "the Lord Pope has ordained
and elevated seven cardinals to the Holy Roman Church, and
that amongst these, three members of our *consilium* have been
so elevated, to wit, the Archbishop of Narbonne, the Bishop
of Évreux, and the treasurer of St. Martin de Tours."[42] French
chroniclers took similar notice of the significant event, listing
the three by name or office and describing them as counselors
of the king,[43] as did Henry III's procurator at the papal curia
in his letters to the English monarch.[44] With the elevation of
these men, the council of the pope, the college of cardinals,
and the council of the king found real integration: these men
remained in the king's network—this was the reason for their
elevation—but were not thereby less in the council of the pope,
far from it.[45] As we will see, all three were sent into France
as papal legates. Gui was ultimately elected as Pope Clement

---

[40] *Eudes, Reg.*, 479; Richard, *Saint Louis*, 219.

[41] *Urban IV, Reg.*, 475.

[42] *Eudes, Reg.*, 479.

[43] *Chronicon Girardi de Fracheto* (RHGF, 21:4); *E Chronico Normanniae* (RHGF, 23:216).

[44] *Foedera*, 1:740; *Royal and Other Historical Letters*, 2:DLXIX (p. 204).

[45] Simon received a papal dispensation to retain his offices in the French church. He was a cardinal, and he was the treasurer of St. Martin de Tours, a position solidly in the royal network of *consilium et auxilium* and within which he continued to actively work (*Urban IV, Reg.*, 1584, 2193, 2196; *Clément IV, Reg.*, 1440). Alphonse of Potiers, Louis's brother, asked Radulph to take the part of the royal candidate before the pope concerning a disputed episcopal election to the see of Reims CAAP, 2:2039).

IV, and Simon was elected pope as Martin IV. Radulph died young, in 1270, as legate on crusade with Louis. With the election of Urban IV and the consequent elevation of these men to the cardinalate, the Crown's network of *consilium et auxilium* and that of the papacy merged into each other, and within the kingdom of France both apostolic power and royal power were wielded by this network in the pursuit of a single *negotium*. With his elevation, Gui moved to the papal curia, where he worked as Urban IV's legal advisor just as the Dominican theologian Thomas Aquinas served as his theological advisor.

It has been suggested that these three Frenchmen were elevated to the cardinalate as a part of the papacy's attempt to get Louis's brother, Charles of Anjou, to accept the Crown of Sicily and to convince Louis to support his brother's bid.[46] This reading fails initially simply because the chronology is wrong. In 1261 and through most of 1262 the papacy continued to place its hopes in the English monarchy, and Henry continued to aim at a Sicilian crusade.[47] Not until late 1262, after the situation in England had deteriorated to low-level civil war, did the papacy begin serious discussions with Charles,[48] and it was not until August of 1263 that a tentative agreement was arrived at and Prince Edmund of England was formally divested of the kingdom in favor of Charles.[49] What is more, by the time of the *Mise of Amiens* and Gui's subsequent arrival in France as papal legate with a mandate to deal with the English rebellion in the spring of 1264, the arrangement with Charles was in the final stages of negotiation. If expediency in solving the Manfred problem were the overriding imperative, then the papacy's and Louis's increasing concern with the English situation would seem misplaced.

Sicily was clearly on everyone's mind and bore on the

---

[46] Jean Dunbabin, *Charles I of Anjou: Power, Kingship and State-Making in Thirteenth-Century Europe* (New York: Longman, 1998),130.

[47] *Royal and Other Historical Letters*, 2:DLXX (p. 206), DLXXI (p. 207).

[48] *Urban IV, Reg.*, 146.

[49] *Foedera*, 1:769–71.

decisions made by all the major players, but we must look beyond immediate political expediency to understand the integration of the papal and Capetian curias that occurred in the 1260s. It had a long history and had far-ranging implications. Indeed, what we see is that while the Sicilian affair was a major problem that the network of king and pope was attempting to solve, the English civil war emerged as a distinct, though not unrelated, problem: the agreement between Charles, Louis, and Urban IV stated explicitly that it was a precondition of Louis's full support that the business of the English king be settled and peace made.[50] Louis and the pope were not going to "move on" and leave Henry to his fate now that he was no use in Sicily.

The situation in England deteriorated in 1262 and 1263, and both sides looked to Louis as a possible mediator. But, while Henry's relationship with Louis improved, Louis's with Simon de Montfort became strained.[51] This made sense. Henry III and Louis were not only both kings but also at peace, and they were brothers-in-law who were in frequent communication with each other's wives.[52] It is not surprising that they found it increasingly appropriate to give each other *consilium et auxilium*, to see the other's interests as their own.[53] Indeed, in August 1263 Henry traveled to France to meet with Louis so that the French king could give him *consilium et auxilium* and thus improve his situation. As Henry's interests became Louis's, it became harder for Louis to act as a friend to Simon de Montfort. Nevertheless, he continued to struggle to find some compromise, some way of peace, between Henry and the barons.[54] Henry, Louis, and their wives repeatedly petitioned

---

[50] *Urban IV, Reg.*:798.

[51] *Royal and Other Historical Letters*, 2:DXCIX (p. 242), DCV (p. 248).

[52] See, for example, *Royal and Other Historical Letters*, 2:DXLIX (p. 173).

[53] In 1262, there was an explicit effort to unite the network of Louis with that of Henry, an effort to ensure that all those who had received privileges or gifts from Louis were loyal to Henry (*Royal and Other Historical Letters*, 2:DLXXXIV [p. 223], DXCVI [p. 239]).

[54] *Foedera*, 1:773, 775; *Royal and Other Historical Letters*, 2:DXCI (p. 234).

the pope for a legate to help in this task.[55] Finally, in November Gui was commissioned with a full legation to England, Wales, and Scotland.[56]

In the documents surrounding Gui's commission, "peace" is the central concept through which reality is read. Urban writes that peace was the most precious gift of Christ, announced by the angels at his birth, purchased with his Precious Blood, and left to his disciples as their inheritance. Peace, the pope writes, is God's place on earth, and we find our union with him through an indissoluble covenant—both union with God and union with each other are found in peace. This is salvation. Within this theology, peace, as a gift, is the fundamental principle of the cosmos, the principle that unites the transcendent with the immanent, the vertical with the horizontal. As such, the pope states, it is a most useful gift, leading to the conservation of human society, the flight of hatred, the calming of discord, the increase in power, the relieving of poverty, and the furnishing of prosperity. Peace is the right order of the world in which it finds harmony with its Creator. And, the pope continues, the Creator, the King of kings and the Lord of lords, in order to lead the world to this order, dispersed his rule through the distinction of kingdoms.[57]

However, he constituted the primacy of the Church Militant over all nations and kingdoms. In a lofty watchtower the vicar of the peaceful King is placed, bearing in the home of the Lord the office of lookout. The pope is the always watchful shepherd who must look everywhere and at everything, leading the flock to those things that lead to peace, and restraining those scandals through which the salvation of souls is impeded. "And thus," the pope says of Gui, "like a dove, carrying an olive

---

[55] *Urban IV, Reg.*, 586, 587; *Foedera*, 1:757–79.

[56] *Urban IV, Reg.*, 588. Gui's legatine register survives as *Processus legationis in Angliam Guidonis episcopi Sabinensis postmodum Clementis papae IV* [hereafter, *Processus legationis*], published as an appendix in Joseph Heidemann, *Papst Clemens IV* (Münster: Heinrich Schöningh, 1903), 194–248. For Henry's involvement in Gui's commission, see *Processus legationis*, 16.

[57] *Urban IV, Reg.*, 581.

branch in his mouth, as the Holy Spirit is figured in the dove, let him be strong with spiritual works, and preserving in the sign of peace in the olive branch, let him preach peace, warn to peace, and in the bindings of peace let him serve unity." Peace is the pope's one consideration, and he continues with an extended discussion of Christ calming the tempest: the tempest is the discord of the world, and the pope states that this especially applies to England. This storm, this fight between the king with his secular and ecclesiastical followers and the barons with theirs was growing so fierce that there was danger that all would perish. Like Christ sleeping in the boat, his vicar, the pope, was roused to action. It is this grave and oppressive burden that the pope shifted onto Gui's shoulders: he was charged to go and make peace, to restore the proper order.[58]

The monarchies were integral to this order, to peace, not at odds with it. It was through them that the peaceful kingdom of Christ was dispersed through the world. Their rule was ordered toward peace. Kingship and the papacy were different offices animated by the same imperative: both the popes and the monarchs stood in the place of Christ, though differently. When peace had been made between Henry and Louis in 1259, Alexander IV had written to Henry, stating: "With happy soul and jubilant heart we are able to say that you, who holds the place of God in the land, bring peace and illuminate the patria, and to the people, to your subjects, procure quiet; that through you the Most High is glorified in heaven, and peace ministered on earth to men of good will."[59] This is a profoundly Christological understanding of kingship. Kings, as we saw in the Capetian coronation *ordo*, were called to work for peace and justice—an office that itself could in no way be understood as incompatible with the vicarage of Christ in the papacy. Rather, they found unity within the unity that constituted the gift of Christ's peace, which is his very presence in the world and manifest to the extent that his body, the Church, is realized in

---

[58] Ibid., 581.
[59] *Foedera*, 1:666.

actual human practice.

This was not just abstract thought or a dissembling rhetoric of power on the part of the papacy and the kings. It was manifested in the form their governance took, as we saw in previous chapters, and in the lives of particular men. In his letter to Louis announcing Gui's commission, Urban IV began by stating that he knew that Louis, as the imitator of the King of Peace, held in his heart and mind the desire for tranquility in all the kingdoms of the world and especially in England. Since the pope had been unable to calm the situation, he was sending Gui as a *de latere* legate to bear his office in those lands. The pope stated that he chose Gui because both he and the king were fully aware of his abilities. Urban exhorted Louis to extend the right arm of royal power and show honor to the legate and through him to the apostolic see, giving him royal *favorem, consilium,* and *auxilium* so that the king of England might regain his status, that the liberty of the Church be repaired, and that peace and tranquility return.[60]

Of course, Louis's conception and practice of his own office was deeply compatible with the pope's language. Louis was devoted to the peace both in his own kingdom and in England. He was invested in bringing peace to England as an aspect of his own understanding of himself, his office, and his obligations to those to whom he gave *consilium et auxilium*. And it was Louis, along with Henry, who requested a legate to help—who foresaw no potential problems between apostolic and royal power. What is more, the legate himself, Gui, was not torn between king and pope. There are no grounds for supposing that this "cleric of the king" found anything in what Alexander or Urban had written about the very structure of the universe and the role of popes and kings within it as problematic. With the commission of Gui as legate, apostolic power and royal power became united within a network of personal relationships of friendship, of *consilium et auxilium*, and this power was brought to bear on the English situation. With

---

[60] *Urban IV, Reg.,* 586.

the commission of Gui, it is simply untenable to maintain that either the papacy or the monarchy was manipulating or dominating the other. The realpolitik reading fails in the face of the lives of actual people: Gui and Louis were old friends who shared, profoundly, an orthodoxy and a worldview.

Within this view, violence was nothing less than the "tares" sown by the devil, his direct attack on peace.[61] Indeed, as Urban wrote, "Satan, having left the face of the Lord, and sending a strong wind from the region of the desert strikes the kingdom of England [Job 1:19], setting it ablaze with the fire of indignation."[62] Gui's charge was to root him out. As a *de latere* legate, he was given almost unlimited power. Apostolic power, of course, was to be found everywhere in thirteenth-century society through dispensations, privileges, offices, and rights. It was a tapestry of rights and obligations that had grown up over the centuries and into which was interwoven local differentiated relationships based on possession, use, custom, "feudal" relationships, and networks of *consilium et auxilium*. Gui, like all *de latere* legates, was given a massive dossier of papal documents, empowering him to manipulate all aspects of this tapestry—no manifestation of apostolic power could compromise his mission because he bore that power fully in his person as a very part of the pope's body.[63]

Of course, in the order of peace, this power would be at harmony with all local ecclesiastical power, with all secular powers, and with the practices of the people, and the pope announced Gui's legation to all the parties involved in the conflict—the ecclesiastics and prelates of England (both those on the side of Simon and those on the side of the king), the king of England and his sons, Simon de Montfort and his allies, and Louis himself—in the form of petitions that they might give him *consilium et auxilium* and graciously receive his in return—an invitation to a single network of friends, to the

---

[61] Ibid., 595.
[62] LTC, 4:4864.
[63] *Urban IV, Reg.*, 588–630.

ideal that was the Church.[64] Those who did not do so, those who persisted in the way of violence, were rebels against peace itself. The pope was defining the boundaries of the Church, and networks that lay outside those boundaries were to be opposed. He gave Gui the power to deploy all available means against such networks of rebels. He could use ecclesiastical censure against all "archbishops and other prelates of the church, counts and barons and any others,"[65] who were rebels or who showed rebels *favorem, consilium,* or *auxilium,*[66] and he was to move against them spiritually and temporally as was expedient, "dissolving their conspiracies, sworn associations, and confederations," suspending ecclesiastics and depriving nobles of their fiefs.[67] Acting outside the universal network of *consilium et auxilium* and so beyond the legitimacy provided by that network's participation in divine justice, such men could be understood only as holding their possessions and offices through violence.

But if these actions failed, Gui was given the power to preach crusade against them and all those who gave them *auxilium* and to grant the full indulgence not only to all those who took up arms but also to those who gave the crusaders *auxilium et consilium*. Such a conflict, if necessary, could be accounted as equal to that overseas and Gui could commute crusader vows in favor of the campaign.[68] The society of peace and orthodoxy, that of Christ himself, was to use all of its resources in the battle against the society of violence and rebellion, that of the devil. This was a crusade in principle if not yet on the battlefield.

Much has been made of so-called "political crusades." As the narrative goes, in such wars the papacy cynically used its spiritual powers in the attempt to construct and maintain its

---

[64] Ibid., 582, 583, 584, 585, 586, 587.
[65] Ibid., 596.
[66] Ibid., 596, 598, 599.
[67] Ibid., 595, 597.
[68] Ibid., 596.

political power. In doing so, it lost credibility and ultimately lost its contest with the monarchies over sovereignty.[69] But such distinctions between the spiritual and the political seem misplaced. Within the context of the thirteenth century itself, within the *business of the peace and the faith* of the papacy and the French monarchy especially, what we actually see is the convergence of the secular and the ecclesiastical within a single social order: both were political; both were spiritual. An orthodoxy of explicit beliefs and an orthopraxy of social order encompassed both the papacy and the monarchies, and this order was built and maintained by a network of people, secular as much as ecclesiastical, who understood themselves from within it. As we have seen, from within this order, excommunication and rebellion became basically interchangeable, as did heresy and violence—ultimately, any distinction between just war and holy war collapsed. Obstinate and contumacious resistance to the rule of Davidic kingship and to the rule of the papacy as the vicarage of Christ could ultimately be understood only as resistance to the rule of Christ himself, in which both kings and popes participated.

Leaving England for a moment and turning our attention again to Sicily, in the papal letters of 1264 condemning Manfred and praising Louis and his brother Charles, we see clearly how monarchy and papacy were bound up together in a single conception of right belief and right order. The pope explained that Frederick II, Manfred's father, had been a terrible tyrant whose violence rent the Church. This malice was passed on to the viper's brood, drawn into his children with his blood, for just as children succeed their parents in the flesh, so they do in their works. The pope presented Manfred as the anti-king, the opposite of the Davidic king. He comes from a violent and unjust line, and his rule is built upon injustice and

---

[69] Joseph Strayer, "The Political Crusades of the Thirteenth Century," in *Medieval Statecraft and the Perspectives of History*, ed. John F. Benton and Thomas N. Bisson (Princeton: Princeton University Press, 1971), 123–58, at 153–55.

unbelief. His crimes are all-encompassing: he is friends with the Saracens, receiving their *auxilium*, giving them *consilium et favorem*, and allowing them to practice their rites; he oppresses churches, mutilates and kills clerics and religious, and despoils holy places and the holy vessels of the Mass; he has utter contempt for the keys and the power of ecclesiastical censure; he attacks travelers and prefers schismatics; he defends heretics and oppresses those who would proceed against them; and the list goes on and on. Because of this profound misrule, "heresies pollute almost everywhere in Italy, the divine cult is minimized, faithful Catholics are oppressed, rather the status of the faithful are suppressed and oppressed, the liberties of the church are made to be subservient and ecclesiastical rights are trampled." Manfred offended the divine eyes and was a danger to the universal Church, to both bodies and souls.[70]

Manfred, the anti-king, is contrasted with Louis and his brother, Charles. They are catholic, orthodox, industrious, and faithful: born of a truly royal lineage, they are sons of benediction and rejoicing who exert powerful *fama*, and they are the upright sons of proper *auxilium et favorem* from the most famous and "most Christian kingdom." Louis was an angel of peace, an eradicator of the tares of discord, who planted the seeds of peace. It was from the very height of heavenly *consilium* that the yoke of the liberation of the Church had fallen on the shoulders of this most Christian house, that through their royal power, with the *favorem* of God, Manfred was to be overcome, for in liberating the Church, Charles would be re-creating what his ancestor of the same name, Charlemagne, the son of Pepin, had done when the Roman Empire was transferred from the Greeks to the Germans. This would result in "not only the relief of the Roman and universal Church, but also the exaltation and promotion of the faith, the salvation of souls, the strengthening of the standing of the faithful, the weakening of that of the unfaithful, and the expansion of

---

[70] *Urban IV, Reg.*, 804, 809.

divine worship."[71]

It might be tempting to dismiss this language as so much rhetoric and to look for the underlining "political" motives in the papacy's actions. But to do so would be to miss the obvious fact that rhetoric and propaganda are used because they tap into a shared conception of what is right and that what the pope wrote was profoundly congruent with the whole structure of orthodox society. The pope's description of Manfred as anti-king is parallel to what we saw in Part I concerning mercenaries as anti-knights. The papacy was taking part in a discourse concerning right power and order that it shared with the French monarchy.

Indeed, Manfred was not just a sinner, an individually bad man; he came from an evil house, a polluted lineage—Frederick II was directly contrasted with Charlemagne, from whom Louis, the most Catholic king, was descended. Louis's house was the opposite of the Hohenstaufen, the "dukes of wickedness,"[72] and like Manfred, Charles followed his parents, both in the flesh and in the imitation of their works, albeit pious rather than wicked.[73] In these letters, the papacy was incorporating fully into the discourse on Christian kingship in the service of the Church the idea of royal lineage that historians normally associate with the growing self-sufficient "consciousness" of the monarchies. Clearly, however, from the pope's point of view, such "royalist" lines of thought were not just compatible with the discourse on Christian lordship but were an intrinsic component of that discourse.

Historians have typically asked, where did such discourse originate and who controlled it? Did the Church invent it in order to control the kings, in order to turn them into little more than police officers for the pope, or did the nobility and especially the monarchs invent it in order to give legitimacy to their

---

[71] Ibid., 804, 809.

[72] Ibid., 802.

[73] LTC, 4:4934; The same language is used concerning Louis' other brother Alphonse here (*Urban IV, Reg.*, 2175).

power, in order to incorporate themselves into orthodoxy and justify their wielding of the sword? But this question between an imperializing Church and a Christianizing nobility presupposes an underlying incompatibility between the secular and the spiritual that it has been the purpose of the current work to undo. The reality is not simply that the Church and the monarchy shared interests or got along well. Rather, they were simply the same people engaged in building a social order that rested on temporal as much as spiritual columns. They saw the world in the same way and in this world both swords were necessary.

Gui Foucois was instrumental to the construction of Louis's monarchy, to the conception of his kingship and the institutions that made it a reality. He was elevated to the cardinalate and commissioned with a legation to help Louis defend the power of monarchy in England. Simon de Brie was similarly involved in the construction of the French monarchy: he had been made a cardinal along with Gui, and he was also sent to France as papal legate in 1264 in order to help organize Charles's campaign against the anti-king, Manfred (events we will explore in a later chapter). There is no incoherence in these men's missions. In fact, we see nothing but consistency. The fullness of papal power and the fullness of royal power were not in conflict—they were participations in the power of Christ himself within a sacramental cosmos in which the temporal and the spiritual were united. The point is that the concept of a "political crusade" is an oxymoron—just "feudal" war and holy war against the enemies of Christ had become the same thing. That Gui was granted the power to call a crusade against those who would overthrow the fullness of royal power in England is an indication of how profoundly integral royal power was to orthodoxy.

It is with these considerations in mind that we can turn back to Louis IX's famous *Mise of Amiens*. In December of 1263 Simon de Montfort and Henry III appeared before Louis and made their cases, having sworn to abide by the king's decision.[74] In the following January, before Gui had left the papal curia for his legation to England, Louis promulgated his ruling. He ruled in favor of Henry, writing: "We concluded that through the provisions, ordinances, statutes, and obligations of Oxford and through those issues which had arisen from them or had followed in consequence of them, the rights and honour of the king had been greatly harmed, the realm disturbed, churches oppressed and plundered, and that very heavy losses had befallen other persons of the realm, both ecclesiastical and secular, native and alien, and that there was good reason to fear that still worse would follow in the future."[75]

The Provisions of Oxford had caused violence—they were, in fact, themselves an act of violence—and so Louis quashed and invalidated them, "especially since it is apparent that the pope, by his letters, has already declared them quashed and invalid."[76] The *Mise of Amiens* offers no abstract considerations of kingship. Rather, it is concerned with undoing the Provisions of Oxford, with returning the kingdom of England to the status quo ante, to the peace. As we saw in the work of Louis's *enquêteurs* and again in that of his Parlement, violence was seen as something that forces itself upon the peaceful order and peace was restored by the removal of its intrusions. So, the *Mise* calls for the return in all things to the conditions before the Provisions of Oxford. It is within this context that Louis wrote, "We decree and ordain that the said king shall have full power and free rule in his kingdom and in all that pertains to it, and shall be in that same state and fullness of power, in and for all things, that he enjoyed before this time."[77]

Of what did this "fullness of power" consist? We must refrain from thinking in the terms of modern political theory:

---

[74] *Documents of the Baronial Movement of Reform and Rebellion*, 280–87 (doc. 38); *Royal and Other Historical Letters*, 2:DCIX (p. 251).

[75] Ibid., 286–87 (doc. 38).

[76] Ibid.

[77] Ibid.

this was no claim to absolutism. In fact, the next clause in the *Mise* reads, "But we do not wish or intend, by the present ordinance, to derogate in any way from the royal privileges, charters, liberties, statutes and laudable customs of the realm of England which were in force before the time of the provisions."[78] This way of understanding justice should be deeply familiar from our explication of actions of Parlement in a previous chapter. The power of the king is confined by that which is peaceful. As Alexander IV and Urban IV had stated so forcefully, kings were the agents of peace, the maintainers of peace. Again, as we saw with the *enquêteurs* and Parlement, any attempt to change "laudable customs" was an act of violence— and the king had no power to commit violence. There is no sovereignty, in the modern sense, here. The king is the custodian of peace, and to this end he has fullness of power. Louis's commitment to the peace of the status quo ante is clearly expressed in the last clause of the *Mise*, in which he decrees that Henry shall fully pardon all the barons and renounce all rancor toward them and that they shall do the same in return. Louis was not making any claims to the constitutional content of monarchical power. He did not attack Magna Carta or the peculiar institutions and customs of England. Rather, he was acting as a peacemaker, and the way one made peace was to remove the source of discord, the initial act of violence—here, the Provisions of Oxford. This is precisely the pattern Louis followed in his own kingdom.

While the *Mise* is most certainly not a treatise on monarchical power, Louis does single out particularly Henry's power to choose his own council and appoint his own officers (which, the *Mise* notes, he had before the Provisions) as especially important. He has the power, Louis states, to call to his council anyone he believes to be useful and faithful to him.[79] Henry had complained bitterly that on account of the

---

[78] *Documents of the Baronial Movement of Reform and Rebellion*, 288–89 (doc. 38).

[79] Ibid.

Provisions, the king's council was not made up of his friends, that it did not share his mind, and that it had appointed ministers throughout the kingdom who worked against the king's interests; that they had failed to give him *consilium et auxilium*, but rather had given it to his enemies;[80] and basically that its members had attempted to supplant his network of faithful men with theirs. As we saw above, it was through the extension of the king's network of *consilium et auxilium* that Louis sought to bring peace to his kingdom, dismantling and supplanting other networks. The ideal, of course, was an entire society of friends. If we are to give the "fullness of power" specific content, this would be it: the king has the power to choose his friends and it is the king's friends who are to maintain peace throughout the kingdom. The king is at the head of the network of *consilium et auxilium* that is focused on maintaining the peace. This was an understanding shared by the papacy and by Gui Foucois as legate.

Pope Urban IV praised Louis for his arbitration. Louis was the most Christian prince, with pure zeal and devotion to God, who hated hatred and detested injuries, who loved peace and embraced justice.[81] The pope quickly confirmed the *Mise*, listing all its provisions and stating that it was through orthodox kings and princes that the peaceful status of the kingdoms was maintained and that he gladly reinforced them through apostolic fortification.[82] The pope commissioned the Archbishop of Canterbury and the Abbot of Saint-Denis with the *Mise*'s enforcement.[83] Louis and the papacy were in agreement, not because Louis was willing to bend to the will of the pope when it suited his own purposes, as has been suggested,[84] but simply because they agreed. There is coherence to the whole event, in ideas and practices, in institutions and in the behav-

---

[80] Ibid., 210–19 (doc. 30).

[81] *Urban IV, Reg.*, 766.

[82] *Foedera*, 1:781–82.

[83] Ibid., 1:782.

[84] Wood, "The Mise of Amiens," 304.

ior of particular men. This coherence needs only to be simply recognized, and it becomes obvious beyond all doubt through an examination of Gui Foucois's legation to England.

Gui Foucois had stayed at the papal curia for some weeks after the *Mise of Amiens*, hoping that peace would be established and that his legation would become unnecessary.[85] This proved not to be the case, for the rebellious faction of barons and prelates refused to accept the *Mise* and civil war broke out in England. In the first round of open conflict, Henry III and his son Edward were captured by Simon de Montfort. Spurred on by this troubling news, Gui quickly set out for England through France[86] and arrived in Paris in May of 1264 and met with Louis.[87] From that point on, Gui and the king, his longtime master and friend, worked together on the English problem. In fact, they became for all intents and purposes a unit. Letters were addressed to the "king and legate," messengers were sent to one or the other with the simple expectation that they were being sent to both, each enforced the others decisions, and each acted with the other's *consilium*.[88] This uniting of monarchical and apostolic power within a single network of *consilium et auxilium* had, of course, been the reason for Gui's elevation to the cardinalate to begin with, and it was most certainly the reason for his commission with the legation to England, the problems of which were Louis's special concern. It should be reiterated that when Gui was elevated to the cardinalate, he did not thereby cease to be a part of Louis's council. In fact, when Gui arrived in France as legate, he once again heard cases in Parlement.[89] When we look at Gui's actions and writings as legate in some detail, the conception of monarchy that was integral to the order that this network sought to build and maintain gains further clarity.

---

[85] *Processus legationis*, 20.

[86] Ibid.

[87] Ibid.,18.

[88] See, for example, Ibid., 10, 18, 20

[89] *Olim*, 1:579 (XII).

In June of 1264, having consulted with Louis and having been warned of danger to his person if he arrived in England,[90] Gui sent messengers to the island to announce to all parties his imminent arrival and make his mandate known.[91] Upon their landing at Dover, the messengers were beaten up, robbed, and detained by Simon de Montfort's men. Their letters, and so any authority they might be able to claim, were taken from them and destroyed.[92] Simon sent messengers to Gui and to Louis,[93] telling them that neither legates nor their messengers were allowed to enter the kingdom unless specifically invited. He also complained of the behavior of Louis IX, claiming that Louis was violating the Treaty of Paris. Simon argued that according to the Treaty, Louis owed Henry stipends for five hundred knights. But, these knights had a specific purpose: to fight in Sicily. And they were to be deployed with the approval of the important men of England. The clause in the treaty reads: "The king of England ought not to use them [the five hundred knights], except in the service of God or the Church, or in a way beneficial to the kingdom of England, and this with the advice of honest men [*proborum hominum*], who shall be elected by the king, and through other men of the land."[94] Louis, however, was using the money to raise an army to send against Simon and his allies.[95] Obviously, Louis and Simon disagreed on whether the conditions of the clause in the Treaty were satisfied. Simon suggested they hold a meeting in Boulogne.[96] Gui responded that the Roman Church could visit anywhere, including England, at her own discretion, but he did show a certain sympathy for Simon's complaint about the five hundred

---

[90] *Processus legationis*, 15.

[91] Ibid., 1–10.

[92] Ibid., 18.

[93] Ibid., 13.

[94] *Foedera*, 1:690.

[95] *Royal and Other Historical Letters*, 2:DCXIV (p. 257).

[96] *Processus legationis*, 13, 14; Henry, Simon's captive, wrote to Louis likewise asking for a meeting at Boulogne (*Royal and Other Historical Letters*, 2:DCXV [p. 258]).

knights. Indeed, Gui informed Simon that he had been able to restrain Louis from raising an army directly. However, he had not and would not be able to keep stipends from being paid because these had been already agreed to and many had been already paid out.[97]

It appears that Gui and Louis were playing a classic diplomatic game—Louis played the aggressor while Gui played his more restrained friend. Gui was less restrained in his own records of this sequence of events. His register indicates that he was outraged by the mistreatment of his nuncios. He called the barons "those who usurp the rule of the kingdom, assuming the spirit of dangerous rebellion, who damnably turn their faces away from devotion to the Holy Roman Church, their mother, which they prove by disdaining with contempt her legate."[98] Gui, therefore, did call for a meeting at Boulogne, but not on Simon's terms. Rather, the legate called all the prelates and barons of England to meet him in September for a council to discuss the English situation. He knew this would be perceived as an aggressive act and be resisted by the barons, as well as by the prelates themselves, and so he fortified his summons with a threat of papal excommunication and interdict against both those who would not heed or who might impede the summons and those who might give them *favorem, iuvamen,* or *consilium.*[99] Indicating that this was a move of Louis and Gui together, Gui assured the prelates that Louis had given them clear safe passage in his kingdom, so any excuses along the lines of fear for safety would not be accepted.[100]

Simon sent messengers to Louis and Gui. These messengers carried letters from Simon and Henry III, who was still Simon's captive, claiming that peace had been made between the king and the barons and seeking to arrange a meeting to

---

[97] Ibid., 16.
[98] Ibid., 18.
[99] Ibid.
[100] Ibid., 15, 18.

discuss it.[101] This so-called "peace," Gui asserted, was a mockery of the imprisoned Henry, Louis, and of the apostolic see. On August 12, with the explicit agreement of Louis,[102] Gui called together the people and clergy of Boulogne and read aloud a lengthy statement against Simon and his allies.[103] Gui started by recounting the events up to that point: the kingdom was once peaceful, celebrated, and devout, but it had been rocked by a severe tempest when a group of crafty barons and prelates made the Provisions of Oxford, which was an act of violence against the liberty of the head of the kingdom, the king, usurping his power and transferring it to miserable people. Pope Alexander had mercy on England and absolved all oaths connected with these iniquitous laws. But the barons' and prelates' rebellion against God and all justice only intensified. The pope, saddened by this and fearful that, God forbid, these new errors might take hold in the West, declared the Provisions null and void. This had little effect in England and so he decided to send a legate from his most holy side to reform peace in the kingdom. In the meantime, however, Louis, the most serene king of France, issued his *Mise*. In order to protect the king of England in his *plenitudo potestatis*, which was, Gui stated, just as the king of France had expressed it, Pope Urban IV confirmed the *Mise* and fortified it with apostolic power.[104]

This narrative was, of course, explicitly consistent with the ideas that underpinned the *Mise of Amiens*. And Gui developed them further. He announced that he had written letters of warning to the barons telling them that their actions against the pope and the king of France were a sacrilege, as was their indecent treatment of the king of England. What is more, he had heard that they were trampling on the liberties of the Church and abusing clerics. They were, therefore, to cease all these activities and reinstate the king of England in "all things

[101] *Royal and Other Historical Letters*, 2:DCXVII (p. 261), DCXX (p. 264).

[102] *Processus legationis*, 26.

[103] Ibid., 19, 20.

[104] Ibid., 20.

customary" and in "all old liberties" and "with the free plentitude of royal power as much in justice as is exercised outside of
justice." Having done these things, the barons were to appear
before the legate at the council he had called for September.
If they remained contumacious and if they failed to fulfill
these things, he would strike them with excommunication and
their lands with interdict. Furthermore, all those who gave the
rebels any *auxilium, consilium,* or *favorem* would be likewise
struck, including all those who traded with them or conversed
with them. Pointing to Gui's understanding of the content of
such associations, he stated that Henry and his clerics could
converse with the rebels without incurring excommunication
because they were known not to "adhere to the same mind."[105]

Gui then turned his attention to the so-called "peace"
treaty that Simon claimed had been made between Henry and
the rebels and in favor of which he had received letters from
both the English king and many prelates of England.[106] This
forma pacis stated that "three prudent and faithful men of the
realm shall be chosen and nominated, who shall have authority
and power from the lord king of choosing and nominating, in
the place of the lord king, nine counselors" and that with the
counsel of these nine, the king would dispose of all the affairs
of the kingdom.[107] Gui wrote to Henry that he was unable to
accept a "peace" of this kind because it was against God and
all justice. It was not acceptable to God because through it the
authority of the royal majesty was purged in all things and
the censure of the apostolic see was destroyed. England would
be exposed to many divisions, the legate argued, because ef-

---

[105] Ibid.

[106] Ibid., 21.

[107] *Documents of the Baronial Movement of Reform and Rebellion,* doc. 40: "Ad
reformationem status regni Anglie eligantur et nominentur tres discreti
et fideles de regno, qui habeant auctoritatem et potestatem a domino rege
eligendi seu nominandi, vice domini regis, consiliarios novem; de quibus
novem, tres ad minus alternatim, seu vicissim semper sint in curia presentes.
Et dominus rex, per consilium eorundem novem, ordinet et disponat de cus-
todia castrorum et omnibus aliis regni negotiis" (pp. 294–97).

fectively three kings were created and true peace could only be based on the immobile foundation of free monarchy. This proposed "peace," Gui contended, was no peace at all, but material schism, the root of bitterness and the origin of dissensions, and they must rather direct all their efforts toward true peace.[108] Writing to the prelates of England, Gui stated that he simply doubted their commitment to peace because they clearly destroyed the liberty of the king and, having done so, elevated three new kings to the throne. With multiple heads the kingdom would be exposed to dangers and schisms and the customary order would be confused. What is more, the authority of the pope was destroyed. Rather, they must follow the *Mise* of the most serene king of France, which was confirmed by the pope, and which was both correct and beneficial, and stop giving *consilium, auxilium,* and *favorem* to the rebels.[109] To the rebellious barons he wrote that he could not accept their proposal for peace, and that if they wanted true peace, they should open the borders of the kingdom to him, because its reformation was his sole mission.[110]

The prelates of England responded that the legate ought not to call the three principal ministers and counselors of the king, as described in the peace treaty, kings themselves—they were more servants than lords, more knights than princes. There were plenty of examples of such things, the prelates asserted, from the highest to the lowest: God, the ruler of all the heavens, gives movements to inferior powers that are the causes of natural movements, and the pope rules the Church through the cardinals. And yet, the prelates concluded, we do not say that there are many gods or many popes.[111] Gui's rebuttal to this line of argument allows us to see the essence of his and Louis's conception of royal power. It is true that God rules the heavens through his angels, Gui stated, but God is

---

[108] *Processus legationis,* 22.
[109] Ibid., 23.
[110] Ibid., 26.
[111] Ibid., 28.

not constrained by his own law. Though it would never happen because God does not err, if he found a privation in one of his angels, he could most certainly replace him with another. Gui continued that because kings are men, they are uncertain of the future, and as times and circumstances change, without any inconsistency, they can vary the men that they call to be their council. If, on the other hand, they are bound by necessity to rule with the "consilium" of certain persons, the liberty of their power is greatly diminished.

The same holds true for the papacy. For, while the pope rules with the *consilium* of the cardinals, he certainly is not bound by it, and he is likewise not bound by the Church's own law—this is the essence of the pope's liberty. Without the liberty to choose his own council, the king is no king at all and real dominion would rest with three little kings and nine sub-kings. As stated in the *Mise of Amiens* and in the complaints of Henry against his barons, the essence of royal power is found in the liberty to choose one's council and ministers, to rule through one's friends. Indeed, Gui and Louis explicitly discussed this issue: Gui recounted to the prelates that the French monarch had remarked that he would rather be a plowman, crushing dirt, than be such a prince. Gui finished his rebuttal by reiterating that the pope had confirmed the *Mise of Amiens*, that that was the path to peace, and that in refusing it they undermined apostolic power directly.[112]

We can see here not only Gui's and Louis's agreement about the fullness of royal power (given their relationship, this is to be expected) but also the actual content of this power. God had the fullness of power over the heavens because he was not bound by a law. Likewise, the king had fullness of power because he was not bound by positive law, but was the source of this law. This is not to say that the king wielded arbitrary power to do as he pleased. As we saw in previous chapters, positive law, prescribed force, was not understood as the principle of order, as it is in modern political theory. Rather, the

---

[112] *Processus legationis*, 29.

assumption was that a peace existed primordially and that human law rightly intervened only when some violence had upset that peace—otherwise, it itself was violence.

And law was only one form legitimate force could take. As we have seen, in his own rule, Louis claimed no monopoly over the use of force against violence. Rather, the king was the guarantor of peace. This conception makes "constitutions" impossible because government was not a State but a network of friends, each of whom wielded his differentiated power on the field that was the peace, and with bits of law inserted here and there. It was not a negotiation of forces in contractual relationships that rested ultimately on violence manifested in a closed juridical order or a State whose scope was, at least potentially, all-encompassing. There was no State for a constitution to structure. The fullness of royal power was the power to preserve peace, which amounted to being able to choose one's own friends, to build the network of *consilium et auxilium* that was the network of peace, and to attempt to incorporate all others into it. Force existed justly where this was as yet imperfect, where peace failed and violence had to be suppressed, and law was one regularized form of this force.

The "peace" proposed by the rebels, however, introduced law, introduced force, a "constitution" we might say, at a level prior to the functioning of royal power; they made royal power exist within a juridical construction, subject to and circumscribed by positive law—which is to say, by violence. This was antithetical to Gui's and Louis's understanding, within which the king as the custodian of peace could not be subject to such law. Rather, he had to decide when law, when force, was legitimate, when it was called for, when the peace that existed prior to his power had been shattered. But this power did not make him sovereign. There was no sovereignty. True peace would exist only when a single network of friends encompassed the social world, forming a body with a single head. As Gui and Louis saw it, within the *forma pacis* advanced by Simon de Montfort, the king was removed as the head of the governing network of friends. He and his counselors and ministers would not be of one mind; their relationship would be based on force (law), and so violence would be at the core of the arrangement and any hope for peace would be lost.

Louis and the legate formed a united front against this *forma pacis*, even though Henry III himself (still in captivity) repeatedly attempted to get them to accept it and to convince them to refrain from invading England.[113] Gui and Louis shared a vision of right order and an understanding of how it should be brought about, and they worked together to construct the social order that they believed to be orthodox and useful and to extend this construction into more and more of society. Henry III and Louis were at peace—they were in the same network of *consilium et auxilium*—and it is clear that Louis took this seriously. England was to be incorporated into the orthodox and peaceful order, and the Provisions of Oxford and the *forma pacis* proposed by the barons were incompatible with this order—they were an attempt at the construction of a different order by a different network of *consilium et auxilium*, one that fell beyond the boundaries of the orthodox network.

Henry and the rebellious barons and prelates understood that the papal legate and the king of France were basically interchangeable and they treated them as such throughout the fall of 1264.[114] Through September and the beginning of October, Simon de Montfort attempted to find some sort of compromise with Gui and Louis (Henry III was always involved in these letters and exchanges of nuncios and proctors, but it is simply impossible to say to what extent he was free to act according to his own interests, remaining a captive of Simon).[115] But these attempts were ultimately unsuccessful, and the deadline for the rebellious faction to appear before Gui and to open the borders of England to his legation having

---

[113] *Guillelmus de Nangiaco* (RHGF, 20:559); *Processus legationis*, 40, 41; *Foedera*, 1:796–97; *Royal and Other Historical Letters*, 2:DCXXII (p. 267), DCXIII (p. 268).

[114] *Processus legationis*, 30–39.

[115] *Foedera*, 1:796, 797, 798, 800; *Processus legationis*, 36–37, 39–41.

come and gone, on October 20, 1264 Gui issued a formal proc-
lamation of excommunication against the barons and prelates
and interdicted their lands. He also threatened with excommunication anyone, on either side of the channel, who gave
them *auxilium, consilium,* or *favorem.*[116] This was a declaration
that they were outside the Church.

By this time, however, Pope Urban IV had died. When the
news reached the legate, Gui hurried to Italy but was elected
pope before his arrival.[117] During Urban's reign, the college of
cardinals had been expanded in the direction of those with
French sympathies and with connections to the royal family.
The election of Gui as Clement IV solidified the integration
of the papal court with the French court, for Gui was most
certainly a member of Louis's network of *consilium et auxilium,*
and this did not change with his election to the papacy. There
was no reason why it had to and no reason why it should have.
Networks of friendship, which was how "government" most
often happened, could cross between the monarchy and the
papacy without any incoherence whatsoever.

Among Clement IV's first acts were to confirm the excommunication of Simon de Montfort and his allies[118] and
to reiterate that a crusade would be called against them if it
proved necessary.[119] He sent Cardinal Ottoboni as legate to
England, "to bring peace to England, restore the authority of
the Crown there, preach the Cross, and drive the pestilent man
Earl Simon from the country."[120] Simon would die excommunicate in August of 1265 at the hands of Edward, Henry's son,
and a resurgent royalist force supported by Louis at the battle
of Evesham. Henry III reclaimed his throne with his fullness

---

[116] *Processus legationis,* 50–52; *Foedera,* 1:798; Mansi, 23:1221.

[117] *Clément IV, Reg.,* 1.

[118] *Ex Annalibus Clerici, ut videtur, Parisiensis* (MGH SS, 26:583).

[119] *Clément IV, Reg.,* 56, 58.

[120] Bruce Beebe, "The English Baronage and the Crusade of 1270," *Bulletin of the Institute of Historical Research* 48 (1975): 129; TNA, 2:200–01.

of royal power restored,[121] supported by Pope Clement IV and King Louis IX. Gui Foucois had spent his whole life building and defending the power of the monarchy. As a legate of the Holy See he had continued to do so, articulating some of the strongest theoretical support for monarchy of the period. There is no indication during his papacy that this understanding of royal power was in any way challenged by his understanding of the fullness of papal power.

In fact, Clement IV himself drafted one of the strongest statements of papal power of the period in a 1267 letter to the Greek emperor Michael Palaeologus, a letter that would become the basis of the definition of papal primacy agreed to by the Greeks at Lyons II and from there would be repeated over and over through to the First Vatican Council's declaration of papal infallibility in 1870. Within the context of a summation of the Catholic faith that included everything from the procession of the Holy Spirit to the seven sacraments, Clement wrote:

> Also this same holy Roman Church holds the highest and complete primacy and spiritual power over the universal Catholic Church which she truly and humbly recognizes herself to have received with fullness of power from the Lord Himself in Blessed Peter, the chief or head of the Apostles whose successor is the Roman Pontiff. And just as to defend the truth of Faith she is held before all other things, so if any questions shall arise regarding faith they ought to be defined by her judgment. And to her anyone burdened with affairs pertaining to the ecclesiastical world can appeal; and in all cases looking forward to an ecclesiastical examination, recourse can be had to her judgment, and all churches are subject to her; their prelates give obedience and reverence to her. In her, moreover, such

---

[121] *Documents of the Baronial Movement of Reform and Rebellion*, 316–37 (doc. 44).

a plentitude of power rests that she receives the other churches to a share of her solicitude, of which many patriarchal churches the same Roman Church has honored in a special way by different privileges—its own prerogative always being observed and preserved both in general Councils and in other places.[122]

Gui defended the power of monarchy and the power of the papacy with equal vigor. Within the "complete act" of his life there was no essential conflict between the temporal and the spiritual, no fundamental struggle between the fullness of royal power and the fullness of apostolic power, no issue of who was sovereign. Sovereignty, when read back into the period, forces us to find this conflict. But, it is present, in fact, in neither the sources nor the coherence of Gui's and Louis's lives. The opposite is the case. Gui asserts repeatedly that the challenge to royal power in England was equally a challenge to the power of the papacy. Both the spiritual and the temporal were rooted in a single conception of legitimacy and order. This was a single sacramental and incarnational world within which the material and the spiritual were always and everywhere intertwined: Church and State did not exist.

---

[122] LTC, 4:5254; AE, 22:215–216; *The Sources of Catholic Dogma*, ed. Henry Denzinger and Karl Rahner, trans. Roy J. Deferrari (St. Louis, MO: B. Herder, 1954), 185; see also John A. Watt, *Theory of Papal Monarchy in the Thirteenth Century* (New York: Fordham University Press, 1965), 75.

PART III

THE FULLNESS OF PAPAL POWER

What is far more a matter of wonder is that some, who share with us the belief that there is but one principle of all things and that nothing (except the divine nature) can exist apart from creation by God, still refuse to believe, with a good and simple faith, in this good and simple explanation of the creation of the world, namely, that it is the nature of a good God to create good things, and that good things exist—other than God and inferior to Him—which only a God who was good would have created.

—St. Augustine, *City of God* 11.23

IN THE FOURTEENTH CENTURY, if you wanted to know what happened to a papal legation when the pope died, you would turn to title 15 of the first book of the *Liber Sextus*, the 1294 supplement to the 1234 canon law, *Liber Extra*. There you would find an excerpt from a letter written by Gui Foucois as Pope Clement IV in 1265 to the cardinal legate in France, Simon of Brie, which stated that his legation had not expired with the death of Clement's predecessor Urban IV. You would also find a gloss to that letter written around 1304. The gloss's explanation for why such legations survive the death of a pope is straightforward. First, it states that some legates are called *de latere*—from the side—because they are cardinals, who constitute the body of the pope and so are literally sent out from his side.[1] Such legates, the gloss continues, have ordinary jurisdiction and are a normal part of the hierarchy in the provinces committed to them. Indeed, they have *imperium*. This is so because they equal proconsuls. Like proconsuls, who shared the secret *consilium* of the emperor, the cardinals, the gloss asserts, share the *consilium* of the pope who sends them: they are of one mind, and therefore, when the pope dies, the office of legate remains. Indeed, the gloss states, we do not suspect the jurisdiction of other ordinaries when the pope dies and neither should we that of legates. It does not matter, the gloss continues, whether the legate has not yet entered his province when the pope dies, for *de latere* legates pertain to the Holy See, which never dies. Accordingly, during a papal vacancy, these legates fall under the control of the cardinals, to be sent or recalled by them.[2]

Why this seemingly obscure discursion into fourteenth-century canon law? In the historiography of the medieval papacy, we are often presented with the image of a centralizing papacy that was attempting to bring all things under the cognizance of its sovereignty—Gregory VII, Inno-

---

[1] Throughout the thirteenth century, *de latere*, *ex latere*, and *a latere* were used interchangeably. Here, *de latere* will be used.

[2] *Liber Sextus*, liber I, De officio legati, tit. XV, cap. II, in JC-1582, 3:249–50.

cent III, *Unam Sanctam*, and so on. Canon law is often seen as the mechanism for this construction of a universal theocracy, and the office of cardinal legate is normally treated as a relatively predictable manifestation of the papal structure, and so it gets little attention. The law of the fourteenth century that I just summarized does not seem very problematic for the dominant narrative; if anything, it supports the notion of an imperial papacy. The office of cardinal legate is, therefore, emblematic of the papal monarchy, and by exploring it in detail we get at the heart of the papacy. In Part III, therefore, in order to get at the particular type of spiritual power held by the pope—apostolic power—we are going to explain the development of each part of the fourteenth-century law of legations, if sometimes in a roundabout manner.

What we find is that it was during the second half of the thirteenth century that the fully formed office of cardinal *de latere* legate, as it appears in the *Liber Sextus*, was constructed in both law and practice.[3] What emerged was what amounts to a new office in the Church hierarchy, a gubernatorial office ruling over the vast domain of apostolic power in a province with ordinary, and so permanent, authority. Gui Foucois, as Pope Clement IV, developed this office, legally and practically, during his short reign. But, he did not create it *ex nihilo*. Rather, his understanding was rooted in his experiences in France, in his vast experience in the service of the Crown and the papacy. Clement IV developed the office of *de latere* legate because it was an office that had a natural place within the social order he had spent his life building. Within this order, apostolic power was integral, not all-encompassing, to be sure, but always present—the necessary spiritual complement to the secular power of the king. The *de latere* legate, under Urban

---

[3] A great many legations before this time period were, of course, referred to as *de latere*. The argument here is simply that it is during the period under consideration that *de latere* legates become in theory and practice what later canon law would define, not that the use of the term *de latere* itself was novel.

IV and then even more so under Clement IV, emerged as the king's counterpart: no longer a messenger or a judge delegate, the legate was the spiritual governor of a province. Together, legate and king ruled over the spiritual and temporal society that was the kingdom. The legates were not a part of a de-velopment of a papal theocracy that somehow stood over and against the monarchy. Rather, the construction of the legates and the construction of the monarchy were two aspects of the same *negotium*, the construction of France as the "Most Chris-tian Kingdom."

By looking at the development of the office of legate from the beginning of Urban IV's reign through the death of Louis in 1270, we can see how theory and practice interacted in this *negotium*. Things were done because they were believed to be proper and what was believed to be proper developed as things were done. Legal definitions and formal institutional offices were occasional codifications of this dynamic, and the dynamic involved temporal and spiritual powers because it was rooted in a sacramental universe. Indeed, what we will see in the fol-lowing chapters is that both Clement and Louis had a direct hand in the construction of the legatine office not only in the field of practice but also in the field of theory and codification.

This occurred within the context of a power dynamic that was rooted in networks of *consilium et auxilium* and not in proto-States. It was a network that included both the papacy and the French monarchy that built the new legatine office, in theory and practice, in the pursuit of the construction of the social order its members believed to be proper—the order that Parts I and II of this work attempted to explicate.

CHAPTER ELEVEN

IN THE IMAGE OF A PROCONSUL

From this care arises that peace of the home which lies in the harmonious interplay of authority and obedience among those who live there. For, those who have the care of the others give the orders—a man to his wife, parents to their children, masters to their servants. And those who are cared for must obey—wives their husband, children their parents, servants their masters. In the home of a religious man, however, of a man living by faith and as yet a wayfarer from the heavenly City, those who command serve those whom they appear to rule—because, of course, they do not command out of lust to domineer, but out of a sense of duty—not out of pride like princes but out of solicitude like parents.

—St. Augustine, *City of God* 19.14

THE DECRETISTS AND EARLY Decretalists of the twelfth-
and early-thirteenth centuries paid very little attention to the
question of what happened to a legate when the pope died. In
fact, the office of legate itself was not well-defined in either
practice or theory.[1] Nevertheless, the basically unexamined
assumption was that legations expired with the death of the
pope. This assumption was pervasive enough that simply no
papal decretals or council canons directly touched the matter.[2]

However, in the mid-thirteenth century, canonists began
to consider the question, largely because of the intersection
of the increasing use and importance of legations with the
increasing frequency and duration of papal vacancies. In the
twelfth- and early-thirteenth centuries, when the papal throne
had been vacant normally just a few days or even hours at a
time, it was customary for a new pope to confirm legates in
their commissions.[3] This changed, however, with the death
of Gregory IX in 1241. The apostolic see was vacant for ten
months between Gregory and Celestine IV, for nineteen
months between Celestine and Innocent IV, for three months
between Alexander IV and Urban IV, four months between
Urban IV and Clement IV, and an impressive thirty-four
months between Clement IV and Gregory X, and this trend
continued into the fourteenth century. Between 1241 and
1316 the apostolic see was vacant for thirteen years.[4] Over
the same period, the transition of legates from messengers or
judges to a type of ambassador or governor was occurring.
Under such circumstances, we can understand why the legal

---

[1] See Robert C. Figueira, "The Canon Law of Medieval Papal Legations"
(PhD diss., Cornell University, 1980), 10–114.

[2] Christopher Robert Cheney, "The Death of Popes and the Expiry of Legations in Twelfth-Century England," *Revue de droit canonique* 28 (1978):
84–96.

[3] See I. S. Robinson, *The Papacy, 1073–1198: Continuity and Innovation*
(Cambridge: Cambridge University Press, 1990), 58.

[4] Pascal Montaubin, "Le gouvernement de l'Église Romaine *sede vacante* aux
XIIIe et XIVe siecles," in *Sede vacante: la vacance de pouvoir dans l'Église du
moyen age* (Brussels, BE: Facultés universitaires Saint-Louis, 2001), 118.

status of legates during a vacancy became increasingly worrisome for the canonists.

It was within the context of these developments that both the theory and the practice of the office of *de latere* legate as described in the *Liber Sextus* were constructed. The understanding of the legatine office expressed in Clement's 1265 letter, which formed the basis for the *Liber Sextus*'s treatment, was his reconciliation of the legal tradition with his experience of apostolic legations in practice in France, an experience that was dominated by the *negotium* of the temporal and spiritual powers that we have discussed at length.

In 1265, after a four-month papal vacancy, the cardinal legate in France, Simon of Brie, who was one of the Frenchmen elevated to the cardinalate along with Gui, wrote to Gui, now Pope Clement IV, asking him to put to rest the assertions made by some in the kingdom that his legation had expired with the death of Urban IV. Clement responded that legates such as Simon, to whom the legatine office was committed in certain provinces that they might "root up and scatter, build and plant"[5] in the image of "proconsuls and of other governors of provinces," were ordinaries in their provinces and therefore, he declared, Simon's legation had not expired at the death of Urban IV.[6]

---

[5] Jer 1:10: "Lo, I have set you this day over the nations, and over kingdoms, to root up, and to pull down, and to waste, and to destroy, and to build, and to plant."

[6] "Clemens episcopus servus sevorum Dei dilecto S. tituli S. Caeciliae presbytero cardinali apostolicae sedis legato salutem et apostolicam benedictionem. Et parte tua fuit propositum coram nobis, quod quum felicis recordationis Urbanus papa praedecessor noster tibi tam in regno Franciae, quam in quibusdam aliis partibus plenae legationis officium duxerit committendum, nonnulli dubitationem sollicitam excitantes, dubitare se asserunt, an commissum tibi huiusmodi legationis officium post eiusdem praedecessoris obitum duraverit, vel illius fuerit potius morte finitum. Quare humiliter petebatur a nobis, ut dubitationem huiusmodi nostrae declarationis oraculo sopiremus. Nos igitur legatos quibus in provinciis certis, ut inibi evellant et dissipent, aedificent et plantent, committitur, legationis officium, ad instar proconsulum ceterorumque provinciarum praesidum, quocunque speciali

Neither Clement's use of Jeremiah 1:10 nor his use of the proconsul were themselves novel. However, this makes the letter all the more interesting because, in it, Clement presented a clearly novel legal conclusion as being a simple implication of what a legation was in practice and used two concepts as his rationale—one biblical and the other legal, one spiritual and the other temporal—both of which had long been associated, albeit separately, with legations, but without Clement's conclusion being drawn from them. What Clement did differently was bring these two concepts together fundamentally, along with all the traditional understanding that underpinned them, into one definition. He brought the spiritual and the temporal together into one definition. What Clement defined for the first time was the office of apostolic governor. In what follows, I will treat the two planks of this definition and then show the implications of their unification in Clement's thought.

We turn first to Jeremiah. The eighth-century *Vita Gregorii* stated of Gregory the Great that the Lord constituted him over the nations and kingdoms as Supreme Pontiff "ut iuxta illud propheticum vitiorum radices evelleret, destrueret atque disperderet, sicque demum aedificaret, plantaretque virtutes."[7] An early medieval Gallic lectionary had Jeremiah 1:10 read at the ordination of bishops,[8] and the *glossa ordinaria* had seen in

---

nomine censeatur, quibus certae sunt decretae provinciae, quarum illis moderatio demandatur, ordinariam gerere dignitatem, et provinciarum sibi commissarum ordinarios reputantes, praesenti declaramus edicto, praefatum legationis officium a dicto tibi praedecessore commissum, nequaquam per ipsius obitum expirasse." A version of this final portion of the letter was incorporated into the *Liber Sextus*, liber I, De officio legati, tit. 15, cap. II, in JC-1582. The full letter is printed in a note to this canon in Aemilius Friedberg, *Corpus Iuris Canonici* (Leipzing, 1879; repr. Graz: Akademische Druck- u. Verlagsanstalt, 1959), 2:col. 984. A slightly different version of the letter is printed in TNA, 2:121.

[7] *Vita S. Gregorii* (PL, 75:90), quoted in Yves M.J. Congar O.P., "Ecce constitui te super gentes et regna (Jer. 1.10)," in *Theologie in Geschichte und Gegenwart*, ed. Johann Auer and Hermann Volk (Munich: K. Zink, 1957), 677.

[8] Congar, "Ecce constitui te," 676.

Jeremiah's commission an image of the Father's commission to Christ of the power to overthrow the kingdom of the devil and to establish the Church, and it tied the passage, through its agricultural metaphor, to the parable of the sower, as well as to the preaching of the Word of God as the means to this victory.[9] Traditionally, then, the passage tied together the mission of Christ and the pastoral office in the Church, especially its preaching component, and it was in this sense that it was consistently deployed throughout the Middle Ages.[10]

Preaching, it should be remembered, was not understood as simple instruction or exhortation, as it would come to be in the modern period, but as prophetic—the preacher was the mouthpiece of the Holy Spirit.[11] Jeremiah 1:10 was often applied by the reformers of the eleventh century and by St. Bernard and many others in the twelfth to the office of the papacy, the universal pastor: in the Vicar of Christ the identification of the pastoral office with the mission of Christ himself was complete.[12] This trend culminated in Pope Innocent III's

---

[9] *Biblia Sacra cum Glossa Ordinaria et Postilla Nicolai Lyrani* (Venice,: Magnam Societatem, 1603), 4:583–85.

[10] See, for example, the Archbishop of Haute-Pierre, Guillaume I de Arguel, writing of the episcopal office in the second decade of the twelfth century: "Pastoralis officii est ut evellat et destruat, ut disperdat et dissipet, ut aedificet et plantet. Quia ergo ad hoc nos praefecit populo suo omnipotens Deus, ut vineam Domini Sabbaoth disciplinis regularibus excolamus, ut vitia evellere, superflua destruere, virtutumque plantaria inserere studeamus" (PL, 166:847).

[11] See, for example, Humbert of Romans, "Treatise on the Formation of Preachers," in *Early Dominicans: Selected Writings*, ed. Simon Tugwell, O.P. (New York: Paulist Press, 1982), 204: "There are plenty of people to teach other arts, and they are easy to get hold of; but there is only one who can teach this art [preaching], and there are few who have access to him: and that is the Holy Spirit. That is why the Lord did not want those pre-eminent preachers to start preaching until the Holy Spirit had come to teach them everything. After he had come and entered into them, then they began to speak 'as the Holy Spirit gave it to them to speak' (Acts 2:4)." For a treatment of the sacramental and sacrodotal nature of preaching, see Andrew W. Jones, "The Preacher of the Fourth Lateran Council," *Logos* 18, no. 2 (Spring 2015): 121–149.

[12] See, for example, Pope Victor II (†1057) (PL, 143:835); Bernard of Clairvaux (†1153) (PL, 182:356); Pope Alexander III (†1181) (PL, 200:1184).

explicit identification of the commission of Jeremiah as a figure of the Petrine commission.[13] By the thirteenth century, the papal chancery was making regular use of the passage when describing papal primacy.[14]

However, it never lost its pastoral, and indeed Christological, emphasis and so remained distinct from concepts with a more legal emphasis such as *plenitudo potestatis*, or more narrowly construed scriptural passages such as those surrounding the Petrine commission itself.[15] Indeed, the commission to Jeremiah was understood as the commission to the priesthood in general, a commission that reached a type of perfection in the papal office but was not limited to it.[16] Hostiensis, for example,

---

[13] *Between God and Man: Six Sermons on the Priestly Office*, trans. Corinne J. Vause and Frank C. Gardiner (Washington, DC: Catholic University of America Press, 2004), xxv.

[14] In Innocent III's famous bull *Novit Ille*, the passage is a crucial part of the *ratione peccati* argument: "Apostolus quoque nos monet corripere inquietos, et alibi dicit idem: 'Argue, obsecra, increpa in omni patientia et doctrina.' Quod autem possimus et debeamus etiam coercere, patet ex eo, quod inquit Dominus ad prophetam, qui fuit de sacerdotibus Anathot: 'Ecce constitui te super gentes et regna, ut evellas et destruas, et dissipes, et aedifices, et plantes.' Constat vero, quod evellendum, destruendum et dissipandum est omne mortale peccatum. Praeterea quum Dominus claves regni coelorum B. Petro tradidit, dixit ei: 'Quodcunque ligaveris super terram, erit ligatum et in coelis, et quodcunque solveris super terram, erit solutum et in coelis.' Verum nullus dubitat, quin omnis mortaliter peccans apud Deum sit ligatus. Ut ergo Petrus divinum iudicium imitetur, ligare debet in terris quos ligatos esse constat in coelis" (X 2.1.13).

[15] Innocent III, for example, continued to use the passage when discussing the pastoral duties of prelates generally (*Between God and Man*, 46). Likewise, Peter the Chanter used it to describe the pastoral office in its totality (PL, 205:172, 198, 348). Peter of Blois, at the turn of the thirteenth century, gave a particularly rich Christological exegesis of the passage that allows us to see the full theological force behind its use by the papacy (PL, 280:791–94). Henry of Susa uses the passage repeatedly in his treatment of the office of bishop (Clarence Gallagher, *Canon Law and the Christian Community* [Rome: Università Gregoriana Editrice, 1978], 141, 143, 147).

[16] In his letter of summons, Innocent III set forth the purpose of the Fourth Lateran Council thus: "To eradicate vices and plant virtues, to correct faults and reform morals, to remove heresies and strengthen faith, to settle discords and establish peace, to get rid of oppression and foster liberty, to induce

in listing the twelve "offices" of the prelate, includes the office of "agricultoris, ut evellat, et dissipet, aedificet, et plantet. Ergo corrigat, dissipet, et informet."[17] In support, he cites a particularly strongly worded letter of Innocent III to the emperor of Constantinople in which the pope deployed Jeremiah, along with all the other standard texts, in defense of the primacy of the spiritual, pontifical power over the imperial.[18] St. Thomas Aquinas takes the first chapter of Jeremiah as an opportunity to discuss the sacramental economy, and when he writes that Jeremiah was placed over the nations "quasi mediator inter ipsas et Deum," we can see how the most abstract theological exegesis could be bound up with how the papacy, which described itself as the mediator between God and man, made use of the passage.[19] When the popes wanted to describe their

---

princes and Christian people to succor the Holy Land" (Norman Tanner, "Pastoral Care: The Fourth Lateran Council of 1215," in *A History of Pastoral Care*, ed. G. R. Evans [London: Cassell, 1999], 113). The Latin text reads: "ad exstirpanda vitia et plantandas virtutes, corrigendos excessus, et reformandos mores, eliminandas haereses, et roborandam fidem, sopiendas discordias, et stabiliendam pacem, comprimendas oppressiones, et libertatem fovendam, inducendos principes et populos Christianos ad succursum et subsidium terrae sanctae tam a clericis quam a laicis impendendum" (PL, 216:823).

17 Henry of Susa, *Summa aurea* (Venice, 1574), ad liber I, De Electione et electi potestate, Praelati quae official habeant, col. 138; Gallagher, *Canon Law and the Christian Community*, 141–47.

18 X 1.33.6: "Potuisses autem praerogativam sacerdotii ex eo potius intelligere, quod dictum est: non a quolibet, sed a Deo; non regi, sed sacerdoti; non de regia stirpe, sed de sacerdotali prosapia descendenti, de sacerdotibus videlicet, qui erant in Anathot: *Ecce constitui te super gentes et regna, ut evellas et dissipes, aedifices et plantes.* Dictum est etiam in divina lege: *Diis non detrahes, et principem populi tui non maledices* quae sacerdotes regibus anteponens istos Deos et alios principes appellavit." For a thorough treatment of Innocent III's use of Jeremiah in his discussions with kings and emperors, see Andrew Willard Jones, "The Two Swords and the Two Testaments: Pope Innocent III, the Senses of Scripture, and the Meaning of Kingship" (forthcoming).

19 *Super Jer* 1, lec. 3: "Ecce constitui te super gentes, diversas, quibus praedicavit, quasi mediator inter ipsas et Deum. Exod. 7: ecce constitui te Deum Pharaonis. Psalm. 17: constitues me in caput gentium. Tertio exponit officium: ut evellas, mala quantum ad radicem, destruas, quantum ad malae ordinationis

office in its totality—not just its powers, but its duties, not just its jurisdiction, but its prophetic and sacerdotal aspects—it was often to Jeremiah that they turned. The popes' identification of themselves with Jeremiah was an identification with the Church herself.

It was as such an expression of the papal office that it was used in the description of some legates. Well before formal distinctions between judges, nuncios, delegates, and legates, not to mention specific powers and characteristics of certain types of legates had been introduced into canon law, the papacy had described the commission of certain legates with Jeremiah 1:10, often describing them as *de latere*—from their side.[20] By the thirteenth century the passage was being used only with regard to cardinal legates, often (but not always) described as *de latere*, and its purpose was to illustrate the extent not only of the power but also of the discretion of those commissioned with the full legatine office, to illustrate that the cardinal truly

---

machinationem, disperdas, malorum adunationem, dissipes, mali defensionem, aedifices bona quantum ad ordinem, plantes, quantum ad radicem. Non enim indigent exteriori munimine quasi sepe. Eccl. 49: consecratus est propheta, evertere, eruere et perdere, et iterum aedificare et renovare."

[20] For example, John VIII wrote to Basil I in 878: "Portamus quippe omnium onera qui gravantur, imo portat haec in nobis amator vester beatus Petrus apostolus qui nos in omnibus sollicitudinis suae protegit ac tuetur haeredes: sed quia et professionis nostrae officio cum Jeremia nihilominus dicitur: Ecce constitui te hodie super gentes et super regna, ut evellas et destruas, et disperdas, et dissipes, et plantes, etiam vestra pietas ab apostolatu nostro pro hoc ipso personas postulat. Ecce strenuos e latere nostro viros dirigimus, qui si qua illic inter haec diligenti studio deprehendant, et his radicitus, secundum Domini mandatum, evulsis, destructis, dispersis et dissipatis, pacem et unitatem et charitatem et congruenter aedificent simul et plantent" (PL, 126:766). For a discussion of the formalization of distinctions between different types of offices bearing apostolic authority of some sort, see Robert C. Figueira, "The Classification of Medieval Papal Legates in the *Liber Extra*," *Archivum historiae pontificiae* 21 (1983): 211–28; Donald Queller, "Thirteenth-century Diplomatic Envoys: *Nuncii* and *Procuratores*," *Speculum* 35 (April 1960): 196–213; Clifford Ian Kyer, "Legatus and Nuntius as Used to Denote Papal Envoys: 1245–1378," *Mediaeval Studies* 40 (1978): 473–77.

bore the *vices* of the pope or even of Christ himself.[21] Such a legate was not only sent to hear a specific case or to deal with a narrow problem but was also granted power that he might "correct the erring, reform the deformed, root up the noxious, and plant the salutary" in such a manner as God indicated to his prudence as appropriate.[22] He was given true authority.

The relationship between such Jeremiahian cardinal legates and *de latere* legates, the type discussed by the *Liber Sextus*, was not clear in 1265 when Clement IV wrote his letter to the legate Simon. There was no codified legal definition. In fact, Jeremiah 1:10 was simply not a text used in legal thinking: it does not appear in the *Liber Extra* in this context, and the major Decretalists did not use it in their commentaries with reference to legates. Up until Clement IV, when the lawyers wrote about cardinal legates, they sometimes discussed *de latere* legations, but they did not include discussions of Jeremiah. Clement was innovating. What did he mean and from what tradition was he drawing?

In his introductions to several canons of the *Liber Extra* (1234) St. Raymond of Peñafort seems to use *de latere* legate and cardinal legate interchangeably, though ambiguously.[23] But, he also suggests that *de latere* legations are not identical to general legations, but are rather a special case among them.[24] Goffredus of Trani, in his *Summa* from around 1240, maintained that a *de latere* legate could be a cardinal or "another

---

21 See, for example, Innocent III, Reg. 31: "per apostolica vobis scripta praecipiendo mandantes quatenus eum vice nostra, imo potius vice Christi" (PL, 216:827).

22 *Les Registres de Grégoire IX*, ed. Lucien Auvray (Paris: Albert Fontemoing, 1955), 1:229: "errata corrigat, et deformata reformet, noxia evellat, plantetque salubria, ipsamque terram diu obsitam sentibus vitiorum, et fructus iniquitatis ac amaritudinis proferentem, auctore Deo, faciat germinare; in regno Francorum plene legationis officium duximus committendum, data sibil libera potestate destruendi et evellendi, dissipandi et disperdendi, edificandi atque plantandi, disponendi, ordinandi, statuendi, diffiniendi et faciendi quecumque, secundum datam sibi a Deo prudentiam, viderit facienda."

23 X 1.30.3, 1.30.4, 1.30.6, 3.38.28, 5.39.20.

24 X 1.30.2, 1.30.3, 1.30.4.

official of the curia."[25] On the other hand, in canon 7 of the First Council of Lyons, Pope Innocent IV divided those holding a *plenam legationem* into two categories: those sent from the pope and those claiming the dignity on account of their churches. He then exempted cardinal legates from the canon's distinctions "because just as they rejoice in a prerogative of honor, so we wish them to exercise wider authority."[26] In his commentary on the Decretals, Innocent IV limits *de latere* legations to cardinal legates who, in virtue of being cardinals, were distinct from, and had wider discretion than, other legates who "do not have more power than is contained in their privilege."[27] So, for Innocent IV, the cardinal legates, as cardinals, have special legatine powers, and it is they who are accordingly called *de latere*.[28]

---

[25] Goffredus of Trani, *Summa super titulis Decretalium* (Lyon, FR, 1519), 52r: "Legati qui ex ipsius latere non mittuntur, ut cum papa non cardinalem vel alium officialem curie sed prelatum aliquem in legationem mittit talis non absoluit nisi provinciales et in provincia constitutos…"

[26] Tanner, 1:285: "Proinde praesenti decreto statuimus ut ecclesiae Romanae legati, quantumcumque plenam legationem obtineant, sive a nobis missi fuerint sive suarum ecclesiarum praetextu legationis sibi vendicent dignitatem, ex ipsius legationis munere conferendi beneficia nullam habeant potestatem, nisi hoc alicui specialiter duxerimus indulgendum. Quod tamen in fratribus nostris legatione fungentibus nolumus observari, quia sicut honoris praerogativa laetantur sic eos auctoritate fungi volumus ampliori." The three types of legates mentioned in the canon, then, are cardinal legates, sent legates, and legates claiming the dignity on account of their churches, which correspond to the traditional tri-partite division of *legatus de latere*, *legatus missus*, and *legatus natus*. See, for example. Goffredus of Trani, *Summa*, 52r.

[27] Innocent IV, *Apparatus in quinque libros Decretalium* (Frankfurt, 1570), ad 1.30.3: "Et hoc intelligo verum in legatio, qui a latere Papae mittitur, scilicet, Cardinali. Inf. de sen. excom. ad eminentiam [5.39.20]. Alii autem legati qui non sunt Cardinales, et qui ex privilegio sunt legati, non plus habent potestatis quam in privilegio continetur."

[28] There is some direct support in papal letters for the position that cardinals, as cardinals, had special powers when commissioned as legates. For example, in 1263, Urban IV wrote to a certain abbot, stating "that no one, delegated or subdelegated with letters from the apostolic see or its legate, unless he be a cardinal, can promulgate a sentence of excommunication, suspension, or interdict against his person" (*Urban IV, Reg.*, C399).

In his *Summa* of 1253, however, Hostiensis asserts that *de latere* legates need not be cardinals; they could theoretically be from the pope's *familia* or even entirely foreign. Nevertheless, Hostiensis states, in practice, the "Roman Curia understands only cardinals, who assist the pope also in *consilium*, as being sent *de latere papae*."[29] To Hostiensis, the papal curia sent only cardinals *de latere*, but these legates were not called *de latere* because they were cardinals. Rather, what distinguished *de latere* legations was the physical, personal, *viva voce* commission.[30] The *glossa ordinaria* to the Decretals, compiled or written by Bernard of Parma before 1263, largely supports Hostiensis. It states that while other legates are bound by their privileges, legates sent *de latere papae* have greater powers intrinsically "because they are to be understood as a part of his body."[31] Such *de latere* legates, the gloss asserts, need not be cardinals by their nature; they could be chaplains or other officials of the curia, so long as they assist at the pope's side and are sent to a province with a general legation, even if only the cardinals participate *in secretis consiliis*.[32] Nevertheless, the gloss states, it is the cardinals who are most properly called *de latere* because they are said to be "part of the body of the Lord Pope" and because more of the pope's power is given to them than to others. It then goes on to cite canon 7 of the First Council of Lyons mentioned above.[33] To the gloss, then, *de latere* legates had, by their nature, more power than other legates. Since cardinal legates had in practice more power than all other legates, it was necessary logically that *de latere* legates be cardinals.

---

[29] Henry of Susa, *Summa aurea*, liber I, De officio legati, *quot species*, cols. 317–18 (ad 1.6.31): "Sed Romana curia solos cardinales, qui assistunt papae etiam in conciliis . . . intelligit de latere papae missos."

[30] Henry of Susa, *Summa aurea*, De officio legati, *quot species*. See Figueira, "The Classification of Medieval Papal Legates," 220.

[31] *Decretales Gregorii Papae IX* (Rome, 1582), ad 1.30.9, 1.30.1, 1.30.4, 1.30.6.

[32] Ibid., ad 1.30.9; The gloss to 1.30.1 states: "Alii vero legati Cardinales vel etiam alii qui mittuntur de lateree domini Papae, habent maiorem iurisdictionem."

[33] Ibid., ad 1.30.9.

Although it is clear that there was not a consensus concerning the theoretical relationship between cardinal legates and *de latere* legations among the canonists of the mid-thirteenth century, they did concur that *de latere* legates and cardinal legates were in practice the same, and that such legates had more power than other legates, not on account of greater privileges in their commissions, but on account of the nature of this type of legation itself. The consensus held that this greater power was a consequence of the legate's personal intimacy with the pope himself, with his body. Cardinals had a greater intimacy with the pope than did anyone else. They shared with him "secret council," and so were said to be members of his body. This intimacy was the reason for the practical, if not theoretical, identification of *de latere* legates with cardinal legates.

It is in relation to the greater intrinsic stature or power of these legates that we can see how the Jeremiah concept, a theological rather than juridical concept at its root, comes into play. Such legates share in the fullness of the Petrine office, a prophetic and Christological office: they bear the *vices* of the pope and so his Jeremiahian commission. In his letter to Simon, Clement takes this idea and restructures it in juridical terms:

> We, therefore, declare with the present edict that legates to whom in certain provinces the legatine office is committed to them, that in that place they might root up and pull down, build and plant, in the likeness of proconsuls and other governors of provinces, by whatever special name they might be reckoned, their decrees are firm in those provinces, that government having been demanded of them, to bear the dignity of an ordinary, and to be reputed an ordinary of the province commissioned to them, the aforementioned office of legate commissioned to you by our predecessor, in no way expires through his death.[34]

---

[34] "Nos igitur legatos quibus in provinciis certis, ut inibi evellant et dissipent, aedificent et plantent, committitur, legationis officium, ad instar procon-

It is in this equation of a theological idea that long had no legal significance with explicitly juridical concepts that the true import of Clement's thought emerges. Due to the cardinal legates' Jeremiahian commission, they are in the likeness of proconsuls. It is hard to imagine a more temporal office than that of proconsul, of Roman governor, and Jeremiah 1:10 described the very essence of the sacerdotal office. Clement effortlessly brings these together in one office. Cardinal legates are governors whose offices are Jeremiahian and so Petrine. In order to understand the significance of this, we must explore the history of the proconsul concept and its traditional use in the explication of papal legations.

In Roman law distinctions were made between delegated, mandated, and ordinary jurisdictions, which were often explained as the distinctions between judges in a specific case, procurators, and governors. Judges commissioned with a specific case had delegated jurisdiction, which was closely bound by the conditions of the commission. Only in relation to that particular case did the delegate have jurisdiction, and his ruling could be appealed to the delegator.[35] In the thirteenth century the Roman law surrounding delegated jurisdiction was, for obvious reasons, most consistently used to explicate the office of papal judge delegate.[36]

Mandated jurisdiction, on the other hand, was closely

---

sulum ceterorumque provinciarum praesidum, quocunque speciali nomine censeatur, quibus certae sunt decretae provinciae, quarum illis moderatio demandatur, ordinariam gerere dignitatem, et provinciarum sibi commissarum ordinarios reputantes, praesenti declaramus edicto, praefatum legationis officium a dicto tibi praedecessore commissum, nequaquam per ipsius obitum expirasse" (*Liber Sextus*, liber I, De officio legati, tit.15, cap. 2). The full letter is printed in a note to this canon in Friedburg's edition. A slightly different version of the letter is printed in TNA, 2:121. Proconsuls were a particular type of *praesides*; see *Digest of Justinian* 1.18.1: "Praesidis nomen generale est eoque et proconsules et legati Caesaris et omnes provincias regentes, licet senatores sint, praesides appellantur: proconsulis appellatio specialis est."

[35] Adolf Berger, *Encyclopedic Dictionary of Roman Law* (Philadelphia: The American Philosophical Society, 1953), 524.

[36] See any commentary to X 1.29.

and personally bound to the mandator: "He to whom jurisdiction has been delegated possesses none peculiar to himself,
but must only exercise that of the magistrate who conferred it
upon him."[37] Since one with mandated jurisdiction possessed
no jurisdiction of his own, even in a delegated sense, appeals
went not to the mandator but to his superior, and mandated
jurisdiction ended when the mandator either revoked it or
died.[38] Mandated jurisdiction fell under the category of mandates generally, which were a form of personal contract rooted
in the duty of friendship.[39] The most commonly discussed
type of mandate in Roman law was that between the *dominus
negotii* and his *procurator* in court or business, and it was in this
context that the concept was most often used in canonical discussions.[40] However, there was often no clear distinction made
between delegated and mandated jurisdiction within papal or
canonist writings.[41]

In contrast to those with delegated or mandated jurisdiction, those officers with *imperium*, who ruled from the inherent
power of their offices—such as consuls, proconsuls, praetors,
and propraetors—were said to have ordinary jurisdiction.[42]
The proconsulate itself was not temporary or unusual, but
rather a permanent aspect of governance. As Ulpian stated,
"There is one proconsulate and the welfare of the province
requires that there should always be someone through whom
the people may transact their business."[43] It was in reference
to the ordinary position of the proconsulate in the imperial

---

[37] *Digest of Justinian* 1.21.1.1.

[38] *Codex* 4.35.15: "Mandatum re integra domini morte finitur." See Berger,
Encyclopedic Dictionary of Roman Law, 524.

[39] *Institutes* 3.26; Digest 17.1.1.4.

[40] See, for example, Innocent IV, *Apparatus*, ad 1.29.30.

[41] One need only read through X 1.29 to see the extent of this.

[42] Figueria, "Canon Law," 136.

[43] *Digest* 1.16.10: "Meminisse oportebit usque ad adventum successoris omnia
debere proconsulem agere, cum sit unus proconsulatus et utilitas provinciae
exigat esse aliquem, per quem negotia sua provinciales explicent: ergo in adventum successoris debebit ius dicere."

hierarchy, right below the emperor himself, that the office was often invoked in the Medieval Church, most often in order to express the precedence of divine mandates over all earthly powers.[44] It was the office's fixed place, its very ordinariness, that made it useful in discussing hierarchy generally,[45] and that made its use by Clement important.

Earlier canonists had sometimes compared legates to proconsuls or other *praesides* and had occasionally even asserted that papal legates were ordinaries to buttress their arguments concerning the relationships between the jurisdictions of various ecclesiastical offices.[46] But these assertions were never consistently made, nor were they central to the arguments being advanced, and it is impossible to read later medieval distinctions between legates with ordinary jurisdiction and judge delegates or procurators back into canonical commentaries written in the

---

[44] See, for example, St. Augustine, *Sermo LXII, De verbis Evangelii Matthaei* 8 (PL, 38:421).

[45] For example, Aquinas writes in defense of the power of bishops: "Sed parochianus quisque magis tenetur obedire episcopo quam presbytero parochiali, ut patet per Glossam ad Rom. XIII, 2: ubi dicitur, quod maiori potestati est magis obediendum quam minori, sicut proconsuli quam curatori, et imperatori quam proconsuli: quod ad potestatis ordinem pertinet, qui multo magis in spiritualibus potestatibus quam in temporalibus invenitur. Ergo episcopi, qui sunt in superiori potestate constituti, magis habent curam de subditis quam etiam ipsi sacerdotes parochiales"; see *Contra impugnantes* 4.7 in *Opera Omnia*, vol. 41, A (Rome: Ex Typographia Polyglotta S. C. de Propaganda Fide,1970), lns. 512–22 (p. 74) (note: the corpusthomisticum.org online holding of this work, while stating the Leonine edition as its text, locates this passage in pars II, cap. 3).

[46] For example, Johannes Teutonicus glossed Causa 7, q. 1, c. 11, of the *Decretum*, which stated that bishops were the legates of God, thus: "ut legatum Dei. Episcopus dicitur legatus Dei, et tamen est iudex ordinarius. Unde patet quod legatus Papae est iudex ordinarius, ut proconsul"; quoted in Figueira, "Canon Law," 13. See also Kenneth Pennington, "Johannes Teutonicus and Papal Legates," *Archivum Historiae Pontificiae* 21 (1983): 183–94. Gui Foucois (Clement IV) himself wrote in ca. 1255: "Nam legatum comparant omnes Doctores proconsuli" (*Consilium domini Guidonis Fulcodi*, printed in an appendix to César Augustin Nicolas, *Un pape Saint-Gillois, Clément IV dans le monde et dans l'église, 1195–1268* [Nîmes, FR: Impr. Générale, 1910], 516).

twelfth and thirteenth centuries.[47] It was only over the course
of the thirteenth century that the Roman law was extensively exploited in canonical jurisprudence, and its categories and
concepts were appropriated in an ad hoc manner in order to
help explicate certain legal problems. It is, therefore, a mistake
to attempt to read neat civil law distinctions back into canonical
discourse. When the canonists of the thirteenth century used
Roman law, they were doing so in order to help explain ecclesiastical offices and procedures that predated the systematic
study of the civil code. These ecclesiastical structures were not
built from the code. Rather, the code was applied to them here
or there. Apparent inconsistencies often arise because we are
looking for uniform application of the civil law when, in fact,
the point of unity is the objective institution being described,
not the legal categories (or "packets" of legal reasoning) being
used to help describe it. What this means is that when canonists used some aspect of the law of delegations to explain legates
in one context and then some aspect of the law of mandates to
describe legates in another, this is not necessarily an indication
of "confusion," as some historians would have it.[48] The object
under consideration is the office itself, not the law as such.

In such a way, the thirteenth-century commentators on
the *Liber Extra* (X) had made wide use of the proconsul in
order to explain the superior jurisdiction of certain legates to
judge delegates, local ordinaries, or other legates in particular
circumstances. Goffredus of Trani, for example, attempted to
explain why *de latere* legates can absolve certain excommunicates outside their provinces while other legates cannot (X
1.30.9) by pointing out that proconsuls could use their insignia and exercise limited jurisdiction outside their provinces.[49]
But the comparison is limited to the instance, and when discussing whether a legate can call a council, Goffredus bases his
treatment on the powers and limitations of mandated jurisdic-

---

[47] Figueira, "Canon Law," 43–46.

[48] See, for example, ibid.

[49] Goffredus of Trani, *Summa*, 52r, citing Digest 1.16.1; 1.16.2.

tion, and to him, as is consistent with mandated jurisdiction, a legation ends when the pope dies.[50]

In his *Summa*, Hostiensis makes relatively little use of the proconsul or *praeses*. Rather, he offers a largely theological, Christological definition of legations. In continuity with the traditional understanding, he states that the death of the pope ends a *de latere* legation because the legate relates to the pope personally.[51] *De latere* legates came from the side of the pope and were to be understood as a part of his body.[52] Hostiensis explains that what distinguishes such legates from others is that the pope commissions them "with living voice, as if they might touch the hem of his garment and be made healed and privileged."[53] Paraphrasing the Gospel, he understood their commissions Christologically: the authority of Christ himself was physically transmitted through the pope to the legate. Such a legate bore the *vices*, the place, of the pope's physical body, and when it died, so did his mandate. And so, the expiration of a legation at the pope's death was a simple consequence of what such a legation was.

If it were otherwise, Hostiensis argues, we would have to

---

[50] Ibid., 53lr.

[51] Henry of Susa, *Summa aurea*, liber I, De officio legati, *et qualiter finiatur*, cols. 328–29: "qaundo personalis est."

[52] Henry of Susa, *Summa aurea*, liber I, De officio legati, *quot species*, cols. 317–18.

[53] Ibid.: "Et intelligi potest de lateree papae missus, etiam si non sit Cardinalis, sed et si sit de familia, vel etiam si sit extraneus, dum tamen ab eo mandatum recipiat, viva voce, ut si tetigerit fimbriam vestimenti eius, quo ad hoc saluus sit, et privilegiatus, et vides, quod quando episcopi de curia veniut in honore summi pontificis, quem tetigerunt et osculati sunt eisdem processionaliter obuiatur." A particular emphasis on the authority that is communicated through an in-person commission of the pope is common in the sources of the period, often making use of the "living voice" formula. For example, in 1264, Urban IV commissioned two cardinals as judges to rule in a particularly difficult and long-drawn-out dispute between an abbot and his monks. They prefaced their ruling thus: "itaque, auctoritate apostolica nobis specialiter in hac parte commissa et de speciali dicti domini pape mandato facto nobis oraculo vive vocis, providemus, statuimus, ordinamus. . . ." *Urban IV, Reg.*, 1062. Similarly, see *Urban IV, Reg.*, 1051, 1544.

conclude that two men, the pope and the legate, separately held the papal authority, that they simultaneously occupied the same dignity, and this is not the case.[54] When he does cite the Roman gubernatorial offices, it is superficially and not to the effect of the legates having ordinary powers. For example, in his explication of the special authority of *de latere* legates, where he asserts that their judgment is to be understood as the judgment of the pope himself, Hostiensis cites the Digest's chapter on *praesides* together with a decretal of Innocent III that states that the legate (in the circumstances of the decretal) was simply the *exsecutor* of the pope's will with no authority of his own.[55] Like Goffredus of Trani, Hostiensis invokes the proconsul when discussing the limited powers of the legate outside his province.[56] And, he again cites the Digest on *praesides* when he asserts that a legation ends when the legate leaves his province.[57] However, when he states that a legation ends with the death of the pope, he cites a letter of Gregory the Great that emphasized the profoundly personal, and limited, nature of the pope's bestowing of his *vices*.[58]

For both Goffredus and Hostiensis, then, Roman law on governors was deployed primarily when they were discussing the territorial and narrowly jurisdictional aspects of legations. The primary similarity upon which they drew was that both governors and legates had provinces committed to them. The

---

[54] Henry of Susa, *Summa aurea*, liber I, De officio legati, *et qualiter finiatur*, cols. 328–29.

[55] Henry of Susa, *Summa aurea*, liber I, *quot species*, col. 317: "Et hi maximae auctoritatis sunt, nec credendum, quod aliter iudicent quam ise papa faceret, (X 2.28.43, Digest 1.18.1) et intelliguntur pars corpotis domini papae."

[56] Henry of Susa, *Summa aurea*, liber I, De officio legati, *quando suam iurisdictionem*, col. 328; liber I, *et in quo loco*, col. 328.

[57] Ibid., liber I, De officio legati *et qualiter finiatur*, col. 328–29.

[58] Ibid. He here cites X 2.23.6, a commission by Gregory the Great of the "vices of the apostolic see" to a bishop, Maximianus, to hear minor cases involving the religious of Sicily. The letter concludes: "Quas videlicet vices non loco tribuimus, sed personae, quia ex transacta in te vita didicimus, quid [etiam] de subsequente conversatione tua praesumamus."

actual content of the legatine office, however, and the nature of the relationship between the legate and the pope were explained with reference to other legal or theological principles that emphasized the profoundly personal nature of the relationship.

Innocent IV was different. In his treatment, he basically adopts the office of proconsul as a mirror of the office of a cardinal, *de latere* legate. He buttresses his assertion that such legates are ordinary judges holding *imperium* with multiple references to Roman law texts, but not a single canonical text. Such legates' similarity to proconsuls, and therefore their ordinary jurisdiction, is not treated as a proposition in need of proof, but rather as a starting point for Innocent's reasoning concerning legatine powers.[59] However, Innocent's treatment is narrowly juridical. He does not assert an understanding of the relationship between the pope and legates, nor does he expound upon the content of the *imperium* that the legates hold. Like the other canonists, Innocent uses the proconsul comparison largely in order to demonstrate the jurisdictional superiority of the *de latere* legate in his province, but one difference between Innocent and the others is that the legate as *judex* is the only aspect of the office that he discusses. He does not even mention what happens to a legation when the pope dies. Nevertheless, he does assert repeatedly that legates are ordinaries, and his comparison of legates to governors is foundational and sustained.[60]

---

[59] Innocent IV, *Apparatus*, ad 1.30.3: "Sed quid dices de indulgentiis, quas dedere, durant ne finita legatione eorum, et quid dices de sententiis, quae feruntur sic, quicunque fecerit furtum sit excommunicatus? Respondo quod sic, legatus enim est iudex ordinarius C. de offi. Rec. quia habet imperium ff. de offi procon. 1. et ideo, legatus enim si est ex cardinalibus, similem dicimus proconsuli. ar. ff. de offi. procon. 1.1. et ult. Alios autem legatos singulos similes dicimus praesidibus. arg. ff. de offi. Praesi. 1.1. praeterea apparet eum ordinarium, qui universae cusae criminales et civiles provinciae ad eum deferuntur. sup. eod. c. 1. cum autem hoc possint alii ordinarii. Inf. de senten. excommu. A nobis. inf. de poeni. Et remis. nostro, multo fortius legati habent enim maius imperium omnibus iudicibus in provincia post Principem. ff. de offic. Procon. Si in aliqua §penult. et l. nec quicquam."

[60] Ibid., ad 1.30.3, 1.30.6.

What Clement IV did in his letter of 1265 was combine Jeremiah 1:10 with the Roman gubernatorial offices. He took Innocent IV's foundational comparison of the legate to the proconsul—the claim that the legate had *imperium*—and then gave that *imperium* content beyond the narrowly juridical. The Jeremiahian legate *ad instar proconsulum*—in the image of a proconsul—held the *imperium* of the papacy, which is not *imperium* at all, but the highest *spiritualem potestatem*—the power to root up and to plant. And it was ordinary: as all power in nature came from the creator and all legal power came through the divine law, Jeremiahian power, the spiritual power, came through the sacramental reality of the Church, personified and even incarnated in the pope,[61] and was not a temporary or exceptional thing—rather, it persisted.[62] The Church was a society through which this spiritual power permeated, which was held together by the spiritual power, most perfectly, of course, through the sacraments, but also through the manifestation of the spiritual power in the canon law, which, as Hostiensis stated, brought together the natural and temporal with the theological and spiritual.[63]

---

[61] Agostino Paravicini-Bagliani, *The Pope's Body*, trans. David S. Peterson (Chicago: University of Chicago Press, 1994), 62–71.

[62] See *Super II sent.* d. 44 q. 2 a. 3, expos.: "Respondeo dicendum, quod potestas superior et inferior dupliciter possunt se habere. Aut ita quod inferior potestas ex toto oriatur a superiori; et tunc tota virtus inferioris fundatur supra virtutem superioris; et tunc simpliciter et in omnibus est magis obediendum potestati superiori quam inferiori; sicut etiam in naturalibus causa prima plus influit supra causatum causae secundae quam etiam ipsa causa secunda, ut in Lib. de causis dicitur: et sic se habet potestas Dei ad omnem potestatem creatam; sic etiam se habet potestas imperatoris ad potestatem proconsulis; sic etiam se habet potestas Papae ad omnem spiritualem potestatem in Ecclesia: quia ab ipso Papa gradus dignitatum diversi in Ecclesia et disponuntur et ordinantur; unde ejus potestas est quoddam Ecclesiae fundamentum, ut patet Matth. 16. Et ideo in omnibus magis tenemur obedire Papae quam episcopis vel archiepiscopis, vel monachus abbati, absque ulla distinctione."

[63] The thesis of his *proemium* to his *Summa* is essentially that the canon law, the law and knowledge of the secular clerics, is where the natural law and its manifestation in the civil law are brought together with the Law of the

To Clement, it was in this society that the legate was *ad instar proconsulum*, a fixed and ordinary aspect of the hierarchy. This bringing together of the theological with the legal informed the meaning of both. The prophetic office was as much taking on gubernatorial meaning as the gubernatorial office was being extended beyond the juridical: the equation of the governor's duty to clear his province of "bad men" with the prelate's duty to "root up the roots of vice" worked both ways.[64] Clement's declaration, then, was consistent with both Hostiensis's theological legates and Innocent IV's juridical legates and must be understood as a manifestation of the movement by which the Church sought to reconcile the sacramental and the governmental (the spiritual and the temporal) aspects of itself, which was the real root of the thirteenth-century construction of canon law.

Rather than a development sequestered within abstract jurisprudence, Clement's letter was predicated on the reality in practice of a type of legation clearly distinct from judge delegates and from limited, mandated commissions such as those of executors or nuncios. Christopher Cheney is, therefore, slightly mistaken when he presents Clement IV's declaration as profoundly innovative and opposed to the then ruling custom concerning legations.[65] Clement was not creating a new type of legate, but instead defining an office that he perceived to already exist. And while Clement's letter defined the continuation of such legations in law, it did so under the assumption that such a definition was simply the rational implication of the office's reality. This is why the central rationale of the letter could be a comparison to the proconsulate of Roman law, Roman law being treated as exemplary legal reason and not

---

Gospel and its manifestation in theology. Within this "trinity," the civil law corresponds to the Father, to the laity and to power; theology corresponds to the Holy Spirit, to the religious and to grace; and the canon law corresponds to the Incarnate Son, to the secular clerics and wisdom. All three are united in the Church.

64 Digest 1.18.13; *Biblia Sacra cum Glossa Ordinaria*, 4:583.
65 Cheney, "The Death of Popes," 96.

as itself statutory.[66] Clement took two concepts that had long been associated separately with reference to legates, Jeremiah and the proconsulate, and applied them to each other and to the legatine reality as he understood it. In doing so, he created something new in law: a spiritual, pastoral, and permanent apostolic governor of a province.

Clement's understanding was obviously rooted in his experiences in France. As has been demonstrated, during the reign of St. Louis, especially after 1254, spiritual power and monarchical power had been progressively integrated into a single apparatus of governance that had centers of authority and legitimacy in both the Crown and the apostolic see. By the 1260s apostolic power permeated the kingdom and was an essential aspect of its governance. Because the papacy and the Crown shared common goals and a common conception of the ideal Christian society, over the years the overlap between ecclesiastical and secular institutions grew in both size and importance. As pointed out above, all three of the *de latere* legates who spent considerable time in France in the 1260s emerged from this overlap: Gui Foucois (the future Clement IV), Simon of Brie (the legate to whom Clement wrote and the future Martin IV), and Radulph Grosparmi. All three had been personal counselors to the king, royal clerics, and held high offices in his administration.[67] These men were actively involved in the construction of the kingdom's governance from the inside, and they crossed from service to the Crown to service to Pope Urban IV, himself a Frenchman, with no apparent anxiety or inconsistencies in behavior. It seems that

---

[66] John A. Watt, *The Theory of Papal Monarchy in the Thirteenth Century* (New York: Fordham University Press, 1965), 6. Gallagher writes, "Medieval Roman lawyers held that the Roman law, based as it was on the natural law, should be taken as an expression of the divinely conceived harmony of the universe" (*Canon Law and the Christian Community*, 127).

[67] See Yves Dossat, "Gui Foucois, enquêteur-réformateur, archevêque et pape," *Cahiers de Fanjeaux* 7 (1972): 23–57; Andreas Fischer, *Kardinale im Konklave: Die lange Sedisvakanz der Jahre 1268 bis 1271* (Tübingen: Niemeye, 2008), 133–35.

whether they worked for the king or for the pope, they understood themselves as involved in the same project.

Men who emerged from and worked within this *negotium*—such as Clement IV, Cardinal Henry of Susa (Hostiensis), St. Thomas Aquinas, and St. Louis IX—understood all law as ordered toward the right ordering of Christian society. This was neither solely the affair of the monarchy nor solely the affair of the papacy, but rather the affair of all authority, rooted ultimately in divine authority, and it was this authority upon which all law, secular and ecclesiastical, was constructed. This meant that the law (all law—civil, customary, and canonical) had always within it spiritual and temporal elements, and so spiritual and temporal authorities. Apostolic authority was therefore not some addition or exception to the government of the kingdom or the Church, something added in here and there, that had to be dealt with and reconciled with the real law of the land. Rather, apostolic authority was intrinsic to the practical law itself. We can easily see why Clement would be inclined to understand the office of the *de latere* legate, therefore, as that of a governor rather than as that of a delegated judge or ambassador, and indeed, as early as 1257, when Gui had not yet taken orders and was working as an *enquêteur* for the Crown, we find him stating that legates are proconsuls.[68] Within Clement's understanding, apostolic power was a necessary and ubiquitous constant of right order, which was as much ecclesiastical as secular. If apostolic power itself did not dissolve when a pope died, how did it make sense that the chief office wielding that power within a territory did?

We can see this also in a series of bulls he issued in 1265 concerning inquisitors into heresy, a matter concerning which Clement, of course, knew a great deal. He wrote to the various temporal powers of the Church instructing them to have the law of Frederick II against heresy written into their statutes. This was the standard secular complement to the papal com-

---

[68] *Consilium domini Guidonis Fulcodi*, 516.

mission of inquisitors, as we saw in an earlier chapter.[69] But more significantly, he promulgated a papal letter that asserted that the commissions of inquisitors did not expire with the death of the pope.[70] This is of major importance because, as we have seen in the case of legates, such a claim was essentially the assertion that inquisitors were ordinaries, that they were a fixed part of the hierarchy and not judge delegates. Along with papal privileges against all ecclesiastical censures from local ordinaries or from papal delegates, the inquisitors were elevated above all except the pope himself or his *de latere* legates.[71]

Within Clement's conception, emerging out of the *negotium pacis et fidei*, the need for a spiritual governor, an ecclesiastical proconsul, was obvious and natural. This was what he was asserting in his letter to Simon, and it was the basis for his construction of the legatine office over the course of his reign—the office that would come to be defined in the *Liber Sextus* as a *de latere* legation. While a full treatment of the role of apostolic power in France during Clement's reign will have to wait for a future work, a detailed examination of the legations of Simon de Brie and Radulph Grosparmi in the present will provide a window into its functioning and help explicate the understanding of the relationship between spiritual and secular power that was shared between Clement and Louis and that underwrote the construction of Louis's France.

---

[69] *Bullarium Franciscanum Romanorum Pontificum*, 3:52, 54; *Bullarium Ordinis FF. Prædicatorum*, 1:460.

[70] *Bullarium Franciscanum*, 3:42.

[71] *Bullarium Ordinis FF. Prædicatorum*, 1:469.

CHAPTER TWELVE

WITH THE COUNSEL AND ASSENT OF THE KING

> After the city comes the world community. This is the third stage in the hierarchy of human associations. First, we have the home; then the city; finally, the globe. And, of course, as with the perils of the ocean, the bigger the community, the fuller it is of misfortunes.

> —St. Augustine, *City of God* 19.7

WHEN GUI FOUCOIS CAME to the papal throne there were two large initiatives in France in which apostolic power figured centrally: the raising of funds and an army to send to the Holy Land, and the doing of the same to send against Manfred in Italy. In 1265 these initiatives were distinct: Giles, the Archbishop of Tyre, bore apostolic authority and worked to succor the Holy Land, and Simon of Brie, as a *de latere* legate, bore a commission to bring Charles of Anjou against Manfred. Both of these initiatives had been long-running, and in both of them the bearer of apostolic power partnered with the Crown.[1] Along with these two missions, the papal representatives in France assumed wide-ranging commissions concerning what we might call general Church government: reform of monasteries, reconciliation of feuding clerics, resolution of disputed elections, and things of that nature. In the nearly four years of Clement's reign, most of these manifestations of apostolic power were consolidated under a single *de latere* legate, and the office of *de latere* legate itself transitioned from being limited, in the sense that it was aimed at the completion of a narrow mission, to being wide-ranging and essentially permanent. The office described in the previous chapter was solidly built. The legate became the king's counterpart in the pursuit of the *negotium* of both Crown and Church—the establishment of peace, the protection of the faith, and the defeat of the infidel—a *negotium* that always involved both temporal and spiritual power and that, over the course of the career of Gui, as we have seen, was established as the social order of France.

Giles had come from the Holy Land during the papal vacancy between Alexander IV and Urban IV (1261) in order to raise support for the beleaguered Christians. Finding the curia without a head, he traveled to France and met with Louis IX in order to formulate a plan. With Urban's election, he quickly sought and received apostolic support for his mission in France.[2] From the beginning, then, Giles's mission was conducted along with the Crown: the succor of the Holy Land was, of course, extremely important to Louis, and it was an initiative that was by its very nature as much spiritual as temporal. At first Giles was commissioned to simply preach the Cross.[3] Urban had granted one hundredth of all ecclesiastical revenue for the succor of the Holy Land in 1262 but had commissioned its collection to local prelates, not Giles.

---

[1]   Contemporaries recognized these as the two primary initiatives in 1265; see *Ex Annalibus Clerici, ut videtur, Parisiensis* (MGH SS, 26:581).

[2]   LTC, 4:4849.

[3]   Ibid., 4:4788–91.

These prelates encountered strong resistance from much of the French clergy and were largely unsuccessful.[4]

In January of 1263 the pope, extremely anxious to help the Holy Land, consolidated all crusade-related operations under Giles.[5] He became the "executor of the business of the Cross" in all of its dimensions, from collecting the hundredth to raising recruits.[6] Everything that Giles did was to be done with the *consilium et assensum*, the counsel and the assent, of Louis.[7] "Because [he had] complete confidence in the king's laudable zeal for the succor of the Holy Land," Urban stated that the hundredth was to be used at the discretion of the king, who was given power to attach people to Giles's mission at his will.[8] Giles himself was given wide-ranging apostolic powers, elevating him above not only the local hierarchy but also all others bearing apostolic authority in the kingdom, above the whole complex tapestry of spiritual power that permeated society, at least in the pursuit of his commission, and the pope exhorted the French prelates and nobles to grant him *favorem, consilium,* and *auxilium*.[9] Those who failed to do so would be considered rebels and moved against accordingly.[10] Together, the king and Giles called a council in Paris at which they got the assembled prelates to agree "freely, not forced by apostolic letters or compelled by the secular arm," to pay the

---

[4]   *Eudes, Reg.*, 500, 501.

[5]   *Urban IV, Reg.*, 374, 395; LTC, 4:4804.

[6]   LTC, 4:4925.

[7]   *Urban IV, Reg.*,394; LTC, 4:4899, 4900. For example, when a certain noble petitioned the pope for a subsidy to be paid out of the hundredth for his imminent expedition to the Holy Land, Urban agreed under the condition that Louis consented (*Urban IV, Reg.*, 1813).

[8]   *Urban IV, Reg.*, 393; LTC, 4:4852.

[9]   LTC, 4:4808–09, 4811, 4813, 4823–35, 4839–40, 4842, 4849–51; MS Registra Vaticana, 26.127.246, 26.126.239, 26.127.245, 26.126.240, 26.126.241, 26.127.242, 26.126.238, 26.127.243, 26.127.244, 26.127.247, 26.127.248, 26.127.249, 26.128.250, 26.128.251, 26.128.253; *Urban IV, Reg.*, 373, 375–76, 390

[10] *Urban IV, Reg.*, 396.

hundredth.[11] The collection of revenue, its expenditure in aid of the Holy Land, and the preaching of the Cross were a single project, as much the king's as the papacy's, and Giles and Louis worked as a unit that bore the fullness of both apostolic and royal power. Desperate to help the Holy Land, Pope Urban IV exhorted Giles and Louis to plan and to execute a general passage for March of 1265.[12]

In the historiography, one frequently finds a certain narrative that the papacy of the 1260s had a single-minded obsession with Manfred and viewed Louis's obsession with the Holy Land as a hindrance to their Italian ambitions, but there is no evidence of this in the sources through 1264. Urban IV not only explicitly connected the resolution of the Italian business with the succor of the Holy Land[13] and granted wide-ranging powers to men such as Giles but also wrote letters exhorting kings and nobles throughout Europe to take the Cross.[14] The March 1265 date for a general expedition was set by the papacy, and apostolic power was fully deployed in the attempt to make it a reality. Urban not only was fully supportive of Louis's crusade plans but also was inclined to harangue the monarch to get on with it, to grant heaven the *auxilium* he owed it.[15] It was in the attempt to aid Louis in the raising of a crusade force that Urban consolidated so much apostolic power under Giles and attached him so directly to the royal initiative.[16] Giles had such power that some contemporary sources refer to him as a papal legate, even though neither the papacy nor the archbishop himself ever did so.[17] The point, though, is that by 1265 the whole business of succoring the Holy Land was organized under the king and a single cleric bearing wide-ranging apostolic power.

---

[11] *Gal. Christ.*, 2: Instrumenta, 293; Mansi, 23:1111.

[12] LTC, 4:4949; *Urban IV, Reg.*, 867–69.

[13] *Urban IV, Reg.*, 813.

[14] For example, see Ibid., 182, 183.

[15] For example, see Ibid., 344, 473; LTC, 4:4866.

[16] LTC, 4:4893, 4908; *Urban IV, Reg.*, 474.

[17] *Gal. Christ.*, 2:Instrumenta, 293.

Meanwhile, in the spring of 1263, with things going poorly in England, Albert, a papal notary, began serious negotiations with Charles of Anjou and Louis IX concerning the possibility of Charles taking the Sicilian throne and defeating Manfred,[18] and the talks continued through the rest of 1263.[19] By the spring of 1264 a tentative agreement had been reached, and in May Urban IV decided to send Simon of Brie as cardinal legate, at the request of Louis, in order to finalize the agreement and to help Charles and Louis put the plan into effect, a plan that included a tenth of all revenues from the French clergy for three years and the preaching of the Cross against Manfred.[20] Simon was commissioned with a full legation, that he might "rip up and plant," so that he might pursue whatever course was necessary for the success of the Sicilian business, and he was given a full dossier of papal letters attesting to his apostolic powers.[21]

The documents surrounding Simon's commission give a window into the real content to the *consilium et auxilium* concept that we discussed in Part II. They allow us to get behind legal rights, privileges, and dispensations, spiritual as much as temporal, that so many documents focus on and see how power was actually wielded. Of course, Urban wrote to the ecclesiastics of the kingdom requesting that they give the legate *consilium et auxilium*, and he likewise wrote to Charles and Louis.[22] This was perfectly normal, the ideal being universal cooperation.

We have, however, a few more papal letters to Louis of profound importance for understanding *consilium et auxilium*. The pope was understandably nervous about the French Church's reaction to a new tenth. The kingdom's prelates, after all, had only hesitantly and only after the king became involved agreed

---

18 LTC, 4:4853; *Urban IV, Reg.*, 269, 270,

19 TNA, 2:23–6; *Urban IV, Reg.*, 296, 300.

20 *Urban IV, Reg.*, 798–99, 802, 805, 807; LTC, 4:4934; TNA, 2:70.

21 Ibid., 802, 804–06, 813–14, 819–36; MS Reg. Vat., 28.110.104.

22 Ibid., 803, 807, 809, 812.

to pay the hundredth for the Holy Land. Urban wrote to Louis, "in whom only after God the Roman Church finds the foundation of her hope," stating that the success of the whole business rested on Louis and asking him to exert himself for its success. He should do so, the pope asserted, not only because of Louis's devotion to the Roman Church but also because of his personal devotion to Urban IV himself. In particular, the pope asked the king to attempt to get the prelates to show *favorem* to Charles and to pay the tenth. It was known, the pope asserted, that the Archbishop of Rouen and the bishops of Bayeux and Évreux were bound to the king *vinculo familiaritatis* and that these prelates were held in great *favorem* in the *consiliis* of the other prelates, who were accustomed to adhere to their "consilium." The pope asked, therefore, that the king show solicitude and attentiveness that the prelates might easily concede the tenth.[23]

The Archbishop of Rouen was the Franciscan Eudes, a particularly close friend to Louis and a regular part of his Parlement.[24] Eudes had worked closely with both Gui Foucois and Giles in Louis's negotiations with James of Aragon.[25] Both Bayeux and Évreux were sees with traditional ties to the Crown. Radulph Grosparmi, the keeper of the royal seal, had been the Bishop of Évreux before his elevation to the cardinalate along with Gui and Simon.[26] Bayeux was similar. The current occupant of the see had been the king's candidate in a disputed election in 1263 and had finally assumed control only after Urban IV settled the dispute in the king's favor.[27] The bishops of these sees were a part of the king's tightest network of *consilium et auxilium*, and they were themselves members of other networks and so had influence over bishops that both

---

[23] Ibid., 806.

[24] See, for example, *Eudes, Reg.*, 500–01, 527.

[25] LTC, 4:4775.

[26] For examples of Évreux's close connection to the Crown, see *Urban IV, Reg.*, 686, 2243; LTC, 4:4697.

[27] LTC, 4:4843, 5283; *Urban IV, Reg.*, 226.

the pope and the king lacked. The pope was sending Simon as legate, he asserted, because he was recognized to have a true devotion to Louis, from his "tender years," and so the pope asked that the king might support his legation with *consilio et auxilio*, with his *regio favore*, that he might be successful in the business commissioned to him.[28] The pope also asked Louis to induce Charles to follow the *consilium* of the legate.[29]

What the pope was spelling out here were the implications of the merger of the Crown and the papacy into a single, large network of *consilium et auxilium*. The king and the legates were members in a number of overlapping smaller networks that included the king, the nobles, the prelates, Charles, Alphonse, and the pope himself with his cardinals Gui, Simon, and Radulph. All these networks needed to be exploited and directed at the *negotium*. Urban was calling on Louis to deploy all his social power and to make the pope's initiatives his own, even as the pope made the king's initiatives his own (for example, in England and in the raising of funds and an army to succor the Holy Land). This was how large-scale initiatives could happen. Urban was asking that the whole, extended network be tightened up, with Louis and Simon the legate at the top, and directed toward a common goal, the defeat of Manfred. But this goal, the pope assured the king, was not distinct from his and Giles's work for the Holy Land: success in the Holy Land was dependent on success in Italy.[30] The chroniclers of St. Denis related that Louis supported Charles's campaign in Italy because he wanted to give *auxilium* to the Roman Church,[31] and it should not be forgotten that it was Louis who requested that Simon be sent as a legate into France.

And so we can see that the massive number of apostolic letters that were given to Simon—all his privileges and powers to manipulate, dispense with, and trump all other manifesta-

---

[28] *Urban IV, Reg.*, 806, 809.

[29] Ibid., 808; LTC, 4:4934.

[30] *Urban IV, Reg.*, 813.

[31] RHGF, 21:121.

tions of spiritual power in the kingdom—were only the legal support, the administrative and jurisdictional formalities, that constituted a *de latere* legation; his real "power" came from his integration into networks of *consilium et auxilium*. This is what Gui had lacked in his legation to England: he was a part of Louis's network, which was allied with the side in England that was then losing, and he was never able to even enter the kingdom. Simon, on the other hand, arrived in France as a member of the dominant network, a network that had been at work for most of the thirteenth century building a social order within which Simon, personally, as a cleric of the king and as a papal legate, was integral.

Simon arrived in Paris in August 1266, and together with the king called a council of the "majoires" of the kingdom, both prelates and nobles. The legate preached a stirring sermon against a certain type of blasphemy in which men were accustomed to swear on the saints or even Mary herself, and the king promulgated a statute against this bad custom. Then Simon and the king informed the gathered men that the pope had granted a tenth of ecclesiastical revenues for three years to aid Charles in his campaign against Manfred.[32]

This gathering is interesting for a couple reasons. First, its focus on blasphemy was a continuation of a theme for Louis. He had long associated success against the external enemies of Christ with success against the internal enemy of Christ in his own kingdom. Indeed, in 1260 in response to Pope Alexander IV's exhortations to action against the Muslims, Louis had held a similar council in Paris and had likewise legislated against blasphemy.[33] Simon, of course, was in agreement with Louis about this problem, and the legate and king acted together to remedy it—moral reform and crusade remained thoroughly bound up together, as it had been in the *negotium pacis et fidei*.

---

[32] *Eudes, Reg.*, 564; *Gal. Christ.*, 7:106; Mansi, 23:1121; Gaufrido de Belloloco, *Vita Sancti Ludovici* (RHGF, 20:19); *Beati Ludovici Vita* (RHGF, 23:174); *Ex Annalibus Normannicis* (MGH SS, 26:515).

[33] *Guillelmi de Nangiaco* (RHGF, 24:558); Mansi, 23:1029.

Second, there had been a similar council called in 1262 by the bishops who had been commissioned by the pope to collect the hundredth for the Holy Land. The assembled prelates on that occasion refused to accept the levy and appealed to the pope.[34] This council of 1266, however, presided over by both king and *de latere* legate, was of a different order, and while many prelates resented the tax, they could not outright refuse to cooperate with this network of *consilium et auxilium*.

Some prelates did resist, however, both the tenth for Sicily and the hundredth for the Holy Land. "Ducte spiritu voluntario rebellarent," as one partisan of Charles put it: they tried to hide revenue or to lie to Simon, Giles, or their deputies about the size of their prebends.[35] In these cases, it was only with the direct intervention of the secular power that money was collected,[36] and the collection of ecclesiastical revenues was most certainly as much a royal as a papal affair. It was, in fact, the affair of the whole network of *consilium et auxilium*, and as one would expect, prelates who were members of that network were far less inclined to resist payment.[37]

But Simon and Giles (and Gui as legate dealing with England through late 1264) were more than simply tax collectors. They were the chief representatives of apostolic power in the kingdom, and wherever the wielding of that power was necessary, they make an appearance in the sources. When relics were to be transferred, when a religious house needed correction, when an investigation into some crime had to happen, the pope often called upon his special representatives to perform the task.[38] Other special papal delegates, such as inquisitors into heresy, were likewise called upon to represent the pope in affairs that diverged widely from their

---

[34] *Eudes Reg.*, 500–01.

[35] *Andreae Ungari Descriptio Victoriae a Karolo Com. Reportatae* (MGH SS, 26:563–64; LTC, 4:5050; TNA, 2:244–46).

[36] *Majus chronicon lemovicense* (RHGF, 21:770).

[37] For example, see LTC, 4:5066, 5069.

[38] See, for example, *Urban IV, Reg.*, 650, 828, *Gal. Christ.*, 10:1280.

specific commissions.[39] Apostolic power was widely deployed throughout the kingdom, but throughout the reign of Urban it remained largely ad hoc.

Nevertheless, under Urban IV we can see the beginnings of the legate as proconsul, as spiritual governor. In 1264 Louis wanted to move a group of Dominicans to a new location and build them a house. This move was resisted by the local secular clerics, who did not want the friars in their jurisdictions. Louis asked the pope to intervene, but the pope responded that his intervention was unnecessary, as Louis had with him the legate, whose powers were more than sufficient to deal with the situation.[40] There had been some minor consolidation of power under Simon: only he, and no longer Giles, could take up provisions from the local prelates; only Simon could pass censure against the inquisitors into heresy.[41] But, overall, the papal representatives in France remained tied to specific initiatives, even if they were integrated into a stable network of power.

With the death of Urban IV in October of 1264, this whole apparatus ground to a halt. The restive prelates were inclined to take a strict view of the powers of papal legates during a vacancy, and Simon was left largely impotent.[42] When Gui was elected as Clement IV in February 1265, he was obliged to reissue the entire dossier of papal letters to Simon and to Giles and to exhort them to continue in their commissions.[43] This was very disruptive and it was the immediate context for the letter to Simon (discussed in the previous chapter) that asserted him to be a proconsul, a permanent part of the hierarchy, the holder of an office that certainly did not expire with the death of the pope. As we saw above, this claim had far-ranging

---

[39] *Bullarium Franciscanum Romanorum Pontificum*, 3:6.

[40] *Urban IV, Reg.*, 855–56.

[41] TNA, 2:81; *Bullarium Franciscanum*, 3:12.

[42] *Clément IV, Reg.*, 226, 812, 1426.

[43] Ibid., 1429–39, 1441–47; LTC, 4:4997–5011, 5013–23, 5026–32, 5042, 5045.

conceptual implications. It was only over the course of Clement's reign, however, that these implications became reality as he and the network of which he was a member sought to build the order they believed proper.

Like Urban before him, Clement IV was wholly committed to both a crusade to the Holy Land and the expedition against Manfred. There was no conceptual conflict between the two; they were understood as two manifestations of the same central problem.[44] Through 1265 preparations continued to be made for both expeditions, and Clement routinely exhorted men to take up the Cross and travel immediately to the Holy Land, exhorted Giles and Louis to quickly and effectively work for its succor, and assured the prelates of Palestine that help was on the way.[45] Louis's and Giles's operations actually increased during this year as they built a vast network of preachers and collectors of revenue. These men were largely Mendicants, who had been exhorted to the task by Clement himself.[46] Clement even extended the extent of Giles's apostolic power, definitively elevating him above all of its normal manifestations,[47] and he emphasized that everything Giles did was to be done with the consent and assent of Louis.[48] Giles continued to serve as a basically permanent representative of apostolic power, working with the king on issues that diverted widely from crusade.[49] This observation is made to point out that there is no support in the sources for the sometimes asserted narrative of these years that sees Louis as an idealist, even quaint, crusader, clinging to an outmoded and futile dream of

---

[44] *Clément IV, Reg.*, 216, 224, 903; TNA, 2:196; *Ludwigs des Heiligen Kreuzzug nach Tunis 1270*, 318.

[45] *Clément IV, Reg.*, 80, 113, 812, 825–26, 831, 898, 918; LTC, 4:5087.

[46] *Clément IV, Reg.*, 828; *Bullarium Ordinis FF. Prædicatorum*, 1:467; LTC, 4:5079, 5110, 5138; Léon L. Borrelli de Serres, "Compte d'une mission de prédication pour secours à la Terre Sainte (1265)," *Mémoires de la société de l'histoire de Paris et de l'Ile-de-France* 30 (1903): 243–80.

[47] LTC, 4:5058–64.

[48] LTC, 4:5012, 5076, 5087; *Clément IV, Reg.*, 812–14.

[49] *Gal. Christ.*, 10: Instrumenta, 235.

success in the Holy Land, even while the papacy had shifted its focus to the cynical and calculating issues of power politics in Italy.[50] Clement IV simply did not have different views concerning Christendom, crusade, kingship, or the Church than did Louis—positing such a disconnect between Gui Foucois and Clement IV is absurd: he was the same man and his life was internally coherent.

What did arise in the second half of 1265 were certain complexities of policy that compelled Clement to temporarily subordinate preparations for a crusade to the Holy Land in favor of success in the Sicilian expedition, and this did lead to some tensions between Louis and the pope. What happened is relatively simple. The papacy's arrangement with Charles of Anjou was ratified and he was solemnly invested with Sicily in July of 1265.[51] At the same time pressure from Manfred increased considerably and the government of the papal patrimony essentially collapsed.[52] Charles's campaign had to happen immediately. The problem was that not nearly enough of the tenth had been collected to finance the campaign, nor had a large enough army been raised.[53] Clement, therefore, sought to support Charles through borrowing against the tenth yet to be collected. The legate, Simon, was then to raise the money in France and pay the papacy's creditors.[54] Simon did so, but the money went too quickly. By late fall of 1265, as Charles crossed into Italy, the money was gone and Clement

---

[50] Not only did the papacy continue to support efforts to succor the Holy Land, but, as Housley has demonstrated, the campaign to Sicily had overwhelming royal support. Norman Housley, *The Italian Crusades: The Papal-Angevin Alliance and the Crusades against Christian Lay Powers, 1254–1343*, 152–53.

[51] *Clément IV, Reg.*, 1466.

[52] Daniel Philip Waley, *The Papal State in the Thirteenth Century* (New York: Macmillan, 1961), 172–75.

[53] *Clément IV, Reg.*, 970. Because of immediate need, the pope suspended the exemptions from the tenth of the Cistercians, the Templars, and the Hospitallers, a bold and resented move (*Clément IV, Reg.*, 1451; TNA, 2:153, 157).

[54] *Clément IV, Reg.*, 753–56, 1466, 1468–70, 1474–75.

was desperate.[55] He wrote to Simon, telling him to preach crusade, to commute crusader vows in favor of the Sicilian campaign, and to try to get a loan from Louis and Alphonse, secured by the tenth.[56] He wrote similar letters to Alphonse and Louis himself.[57] Clement wrote to friendly prelates and to the Mendicants of France, exhorting them to preach crusade and to raise more knights for the campaign.[58] The pope was trying to divert all the resources of the network of *consilium et auxilium* to the Sicilian campaign.[59] He seems to have had little luck, and by November his letters were increasingly frantic.[60] He begged Louis to give Charles *auxilium*.[61] Clement went so far as to extend the full crusade indulgence to those who simply paid the tenth that they owed.[62] Louis seems to have been hesitant to devote such resources to Charles's bid, and Giles complained bitterly that the needs of the Holy Land were being subordinated to those of Sicily and tried to exert pressure on the cardinals and others at the papal curia to change the situation.[63] Ultimately, though, the king did send money to Charles and on February 26 of 1266 his brother defeated and killed Manfred at the Battle of Benevento.[64]

---

[55] Ibid., 923, 968, 974.

[56] Ibid., 216, 968, 1142, 1472.

[57] *Epistole et dictamina Clementis pape quarti*, ed. Matthias Thumser (unpublished; last accessed Dec. 26, 2016, http://userpage.fu-berlin.de/~sekrethu/pdf/clemens.pdf), 108 (found also in *Clément IV, Reg.*, 977e), 43 (*Clément IV, Reg.*, 914), 68 (*Clément IV, Reg.*, 937); *Clément IV, Reg.*, 831; LTC, 4:5088.

[58] *Clément IV, Reg.*, 240.

[59] In the pope's letters to Alphonse and Louis, the theme of Manfred as anti-king is developed fully: he is outright evil, and he threatens the very fabric of Christendom. The resources of the network were to be devoted to Manfred's defeat because Manfred attempted to undermine its social architecture at the foundations (*Clément IV, Reg.*, 817; TNA, 2:196).

[60] TNA, 2:243–44.

[61] *Epistole et dictamina Clementis pape quarti*, 111 (*Clément IV, Reg.*, 980).

[62] TNA, 2:557.

[63] *Clément IV, Reg.*, 926, 1135; LTC, 4:5106–08, 5111–19.

[64] Ibid., 1485.

This brief tension between Louis and Clement is the only evidence that can be proffered for the supposed divergence between the Crown and the papacy over Italy and the Holy Land after it had been agreed that Charles would take the kingdom. What we are actually seeing is a disagreement among the leadership of a single network of *consilium et auxilium*, a disagreement that, because of the nature of such networks, could be settled only through exhortation, argument, and ultimately cooperation. This tension, however, concerned expediency, not principle. That this is the case becomes manifest in light of the fact that as soon as Manfred was defeated, Clement turned his whole attention toward the Holy Land, as he had promised throughout the Sicilian campaign.[65] As we have seen, at Clement's ascension to the papal throne the papacy had two primary initiatives with significant operations in France: the succor of the Holy Land and the defeat of Manfred. Clement initially pursued both, but then at the crucial moment, the turning point in the war against Manfred, he directed all his attention and resources to Sicily; with Manfred defeated, he turned back to the problem of the Holy Land.[66] Hopefully, we have established by now that Clement and Louis shared a worldview and worked toward the construction of the same social order. Such fundamental agreement in no way precludes particular disagreements or tensions. Nevertheless, it is the congruency between papacy and Crown that becomes manifest in the lead up to Louis's crusade of 1270, and it underwrote the seemingly perpetual legation of Simon and his successor and the construction of the proconsulate, the Jeremiahian legatine office.

In March of 1266, shortly after the defeat of Manfred, Clement wrote a letter to Louis in which he assured the king that their relationship of trust and friendship was most certainly sound. He promised the king that whatever he might

---

[65] LTC, 4:5118; *Clément IV, Reg.*, 918.
[66] *Clément IV, Reg.*, 1110.

ask of him, he would consider with full maturity and always with an eye toward Louis's well-being and salvation. Even if it might seem otherwise, the pope reassured him that he would always act in his favor as much as possible. If there was ever doubt or questions concerning the pope's actions, Louis should write to Clement and he would respond with a full explanation. The king should never question the pope's commitment to his welfare and there would be no secrets between them.[67] Based on their long-running friendship, we ought to take this letter at face value. The king and the pope's relationship was strained in the final phase of the Sicilian campaign, but it was over, and Clement wanted to make sure that he and the king remained united in *consilium et auxilium*, in friendship.

Immediately on the heels of Charles's victory, Clement started diverting resources to the succor of the Holy Land. He wrote to Simon in April that since Charles's whole expedition was a means towards the end of succoring the Holy Land, and since that mission was over, the legate was to stop preaching the Cross to Sicily and to begin preaching the Cross to the Holy Land. What is more, Clement instructed the legate to make his *auxilium et consilium* available wherever it might be useful, especially to the Archbishop of Tyre, Giles, and his collectors.[68] At the same time, Clement wrote to Louis exhorting him to lend *auxilium* to the Holy Land and to induce his magnates to the same, and he wrote to all the *crucesignati* of France telling them to leave the following March (1267).[69] Papal letters were written to the Archbishop of Tyre, to Alphonse, to the king of Navarre, and several to Simon, all for the purpose of making an expedition happen in the following spring.[70] Clement also wrote letters to the Christians of the

---

[67] *Epistole et dictamina Clementis pape quarti*, 157 (*Clément IV, Reg.*, 1026).

[68] *Thesaurus novus anecdotorum*, 2:312; LTC, 4:5199; *E Chronico Normanniae* (RHGF, 23:217).

[69] *Clément IV, Reg.*, 841, 843.

[70] Ibid., 844, 1491–93.

Holy Land promising them that his whole mind was bent on their troubles and that he was rousing the Christian princes to come to their *auxilium*.[71]

Clement's redirection of Simon to work for the succor of the Holy Land created an interesting situation in France. Giles, Archbishop of Tyre, in close collaboration with Louis, was still in charge of the preaching of the Cross and the collection of the tax. But, Simon was a *de latere* cardinal legate now charged with the same mission. Clement instructed Simon to show *favorem* to the archbishop, to grant him *consilium et auxilium*, and essentially to be of the same mind as the archbishop.[72]

Because the ideal was one of cooperation it was not strictly necessary for such an initiative to be ordered within a jurisdictional hierarchy. Nevertheless, with Giles's death in June of 1266, Simon simply assumed responsibility for the entire initiative.[73] Clement quickly issued Simon a full commission as a crusade preacher and collector of the crusade tax, putting Giles's large apparatus of delegated authority under his control and exhorting him to seek the "consilium" of Louis.[74] The dual-pole apparatus of delegated authority that had been built by the archbishop and Louis continued, now with Simon occupying the apostolic pole. For example, Master William de Sorbonne, a cleric of the king, had been deputized by Giles for the business of the Holy Land and bore letters from the king mandating that all the king's "friends" and *fideles* show him *auxilium et consilium*.[75] When Giles died, Simon immediately sent William himself to the Archbishop of Bordeaux asserting that nothing had changed and mandating that the bishop turn the hundredth over to William.[76]

---

[71] *Clément IV, Reg.*, 1117.

[72] LTC, 4:5199.

[73] Ibid., 4:5160.

[74] *Clément IV, Reg.*, 1117, 1499, 1504–07, 1513–14; LTC, 4:5175–77.

[75] LTC, 4:5161.

[76] Ibid., 4:5199.

This transfer and consolidation of apostolic power under a standing legate who had been sent to the kingdom on a different mission was most unusual, and it aroused opposition, with some arguing that with the Sicilian business finished, Simon's legation had come to an end. Clement reassured Simon that he had added the office of preaching the Cross to his legation and had not added a new legation to the office of preaching the Cross. It was for this reason that the pope had simply transferred to Simon the same letters that had been sent to Giles. His intention was that Simon would then delegate the preaching in the same way as had Giles. In short, his intention was that the preaching mission would be undisturbed. Indeed, Clement asserted that a new legation would have required a new agreement with the cardinals and that this was neither necessary nor desirable because the time was not right to make public the pope's plans.[77]

In his letter to Simon shortly after his ascent to the papal throne (considered in detail in the previous chapter), Clement had asserted that a legatine mission did not expire with the death of the pope who had sent it. With the transfer of the initiative to succor the Holy Land to Simon, Clement asserted that the completion of the initial mission of a legation did not necessarily end the legation itself. Rather, a legate's various commissions were distinct from the legation itself. This was a further move in the divorce of the legatine office from that of judge delegate or papal nuncio or executor of papal business, a move in the direction of the proconsul idea, the idea of a governor.

Clement clearly believed that this type of legatine office existed and that it was perfectly acceptable for Simon's legation to survive the completion of its initial mission, but nevertheless the immediate reason for this transfer and consolidation of commissions rather than the commissioning of a new legation was that Clement wanted to keep his crusade plans secret. He had planned on a general passage in March

---

[77] TNA, 2:416–17; *Clément IV, Reg.*, 1142.

of 1267, but by October of 1266 things had dramatically changed. Clement had received messengers from Louis, who informed the pope that the king intended to go beyond the pope's exhortations to give *auxilium* to the Holy Land: the king was going to take the Cross himself. Clement's response was decisive. He wrote to Louis, praising him and stating that in all things, "from end to end," the king's will and the pope's will agreed. He exhorted Louis to act "manfully" and assured him that the Lord and his vicar on earth would preserve his goods and honor.[78]

Clement wrote to Simon on the same day, telling the legate to attach himself directly to Louis. The legate should understand, Clement wrote, that he intended to grant Louis full *consilium et auxilium* in all things. Indeed, he wrote, "we would gladly help him personally even if the dignity of the apostolic see would suffer." The pope sent Simon letters addressed to the prelates of France containing mandates for the full marshaling of ecclesiastical resources in favor of Louis's crusade, and Simon was to keep them secret until the king publicly took the Cross. Then he was to act with his full office to compel the prelates to comply.[79] Clement also sent Simon a full dossier of letters definitively placing him at the head of the crusade effort, with almost limitless apostolic power, and instructing him to do everything with the *consilium* of Louis.[80] Immediately, Clement started transferring human resources from Charles in Sicily to Louis's expedition.[81]

---

[78] *Epistole et dictamina Clementis pape quarti*, 270 (*Clément IV, Reg.*, 1139). It is in the light of the narrative sketched above that we should understand Guillaume de Nangis's assertion, written a couple decades after the fact: "Nolens tamen subito aggredi tantum opus ex motu proprio cordis sui, per secretum nuntium et discretum humiliter et devote consuluit super hoc felicis recordationis dominum Clementem summum pontificum. Qui tanquam vir prudens in principio reformidans, diuque istud deliberans, tandem benigne consensit, ac pium ipsius propositum approbavit" (RHGF, 20, 438).

[79] *Clément IV, Reg.*, 1140.

[80] TNA, 2:419–20, 24; *Clément IV, Reg.*, 1516–19.

[81] *Epistole et dictamina Clementis pape quarti*, 280 (*Clément IV, Reg.*, 1149).

Clement was not here acting like someone who was annoyed by the king's simplistic obsession with the Holy Land, as has been suggested.[82] To the contrary, Clement believed that the success of his efforts hinged on the congruent efforts of the king. For example, Alphonse of Poitiers, Louis's brother, had taken the Cross years earlier and had not been able to satisfy the vow. He had periodically asked the pope for a subsidy to aid him, but in the middle of the Manfred affair, this subsidy did not come. In November of 1266, however, Clement wrote a most interesting letter to Alphonse. The pope had for a long time wanted very much to satisfy the count's most laudable devotion, especially because of the most urgent need of the Holy Land. But he had not been able to do so because the churches, already heavily burdened with taxes, resisted the addition of more. Even though these prelates could not take away the liberty of the pope, Clement wrote, still it was necessary that he wield his *plenitudinem potestatis* with moderation, as the Lord wants him to, so that he might be seen more as a father than as a lord. But things were about to change, the pope reassured Alphonse. The whole operation was dangling in suspense waiting for Louis to follow through, the pope wrote, and Alphonse's subsidy dangled with it. As soon as there was certainty, the pope could act. The count, therefore should wait and should know that the pope was not forgetful of the graces that the count had given him when he was constituted in minor offices and that he would always act to the count's advantage and honor.[83]

We can see that Clement recognized that a successful operation would have to be one of the whole network of *consilium et auxilium*. The pope's apostolic power was only one aspect of the fabric of this network, albeit an essential one. It had to be combined with royal power within the context of a total effort.

---

[82] James Powell, "Church and Crusade: Frederick II and Louis IX," *The Catholic Historical Review* 93, no. 2 (April 2007): 259–61; Jacques Le Goff, *Saint Louis*, 125.

[83] TNA, 2:427.

It was not that an alliance between the king and the pope was advantageous; it was rather that the very structure of society, of the order that pope and king had built, was such that the execution of a major initiative required apostolic and royal power to act in concert within the context of a vast network of *consilium et auxilium* that was made up as much of prelates as of laymen. It was through such networks that social power was wielded and the pope's fullness of power had to be deployed within this context. When Clement, Louis, Alphonse, and the others of the network worked together with one mind, then the resources of the kingdom, spiritual as much as material, could be marshaled against the enemies of the proper order, both within the kingdom and without.

Of course, crusades required both apostolic and secular power in their very nature, and in every account of Louis's taking of the Cross in March of 1267, Simon figures prominently. According to the major narratives, Louis was moved with his great piety to offer *consilium et auxilium* to the Holy Land.[84] He discussed the matter with the pope, who agreed with his plan.[85] Louis requested that a legate be sent, and Clement commissioned Simon to the task. Simon assembled a council in Paris and preached a stirring sermon, after which Louis, his sons, and a great number of barons and knights received the Cross from the legate's hand.[86] With Louis's vow, the full weight of the king's power was combined with that of the pope and a great mass of papal letters conceding material and spiritual privileges were released to the king and legate, including a tenth of all clerical revenues for three years.[87]

Despite the pope's plea that they extend their hands gener-

---

[84] *Vie de Saint Louis Par Guillaume de Nangis* (RHGF, 20:438).

[85] Ibid.; *Beati Ludovici Vita* (RHGF 23:174).

[86] *Vie de Saint Louis Par Guillaume de Nangis* (RHGF, 20:440); *Chronique Anonyme des Rois de France* (RHGF, 21:85); *Beati Ludovici Vita* (RHGF, 23:174); *E Chronico Normanniae* (RHGF, 23:217).

[87] *Clément IV, Reg.*, 464–46; LTC, 4:5274–78.

ously to the king, this grant of a tithe did not go over well with many of the French prelates.[88] As the archbishop and chapter of Auch complained to the pope, they had been giving a tenth to the king of England for five years to fight his barons and prepare for a crusade to England that never happened, and then to Charles of Anjou for three years to fight in Italy, and now another three to Louis.[89] On top of this there was the hundredth for the Holy Land. Such taxes had become basically permanent, as "crusades" of one form or another had become permanent. Indeed, as we saw above, crusading had become the way in which, ultimately, legitimate (moral and just) force was conceptualized within the dominant social order. The wars against Simon de Montfort, Manfred, Islam, and before that, heresy, were of a kind and all of them called for the congruent deployment of royal and papal power.

The permanence of these taxes was accompanied by the permanence of the legatine office. Simon himself had been a *de latere* legate in France already for over two years, and Giles, whose mission he assumed, had been operating in France since 1261. And after Louis's vow, Simon received a renewed and extended commission. Many of the bishops and abbots from the provinces of Rouen, Sens, and Rheims altogether refused to pay and indicated to the pope that they would rather remain in a state of excommunication than do so.[90] They claimed that they were "exhausted by intolerable extractions" and made "slaves rather than sons."[91] Clement replied that he was the Vicar of Christ and, invoking his *plenitudo potestatis*, threatened them with privation from their benefices and, if they contumaciously persisted, with the intervention of the secular arm, and he informed Simon to proceed with the collections.[92] Before, Louis's vow, before the full network of

---

[88] LTC 4:5279; *Clément IV, Reg.*, 479.

[89] *Clément IV, Reg.*, 508.

[90] Ibid., 595.

[91] *E Chronico Normanniae* (RHGF, 23:219).

[92] *Clément IV, Reg.*, (595, 1249).

consilium et auxilium was deployed, such an invocation of papal power would have been misplaced and incongruent, as Clement had explained to Alphonse, but within the context of the crusade it was more than just appropriate and more than just practical; it was the essential complement to the king's *plenitudo potestatis.*

Clement wrote to Simon (in a letter delivered by the marshal of the king) that it was Christ himself to whom they sought to give *auxilium* against the "despicable sons of darkness"; Louis, who was "relentless in his defense of the Christian religion," had "conformed his will" to that of the pope.[93] They were of one mind, and the pope, "not wanting to be in anyway remiss in this most important business of Christ," had committed the full material and spiritual resources of the Church. Simon was, therefore, commissioned with a full legation—"to rip up and to plant"—and was granted the power to do whatever was useful in the business, including the faculty to freely compel with excommunication "all contradictors and rebels."[94] To make sure that Simon and everyone else understood the extent of the legate's commission, Clement listed all the various ranks and orders of society, clerical as well as lay, against whom Simon could promulgate censures—no one lay outside Simon's power.[95] He was certainly elevated above the entire superstructure of ecclesiastical rights, uses, possessions, immunities, and powers—he had complete power, legally, to do whatever was necessary, and he was to use all his personal

---

[93] Ibid., 1203.

[94] AE, 22: 207.

[95] "discretioni tui exercendi libere censuram ecclesiasticam in omnes tam cathedralium quam aliarum ecclesiarum prelatos, exemptos et non exemptos, in universa quoque capitula et conventus, duces, marchiones, comites, necnon barones et quoslibet alios nobiles, in rectores etiam, balivos, potestates, consiliarios, universitates, populos et quascumque personas ecclesiasticas et seculars, etiam si Militie Templi, et Hospitalis sancti Johannis Jerosolimitani, vel sancte Marie Theutonicorum, seu Cisterciensis, Cluniacencis, Minorum aut Predicatorum ordinum fuerint, et in quaslibet alias publicas vel privatas tue legationis, cum videris expedire, non obstantibus . . . plenum et liberam concedimus auctoritate presentium potestatem" (*Clément IV, Reg.*, 492).

skills and all his apostolic power in support of the initiative and in total cooperation with the king.[96]

But the interplay between apostolic and royal power had manifestation beyond the raising of funds. The whole network became permeated with apostolic power, and Clement granted Louis a wide range of immunities and privileges. The pope put the kingdom under the protection of St. Peter and commissioned the Bishop of Bayeux, a cleric solidly in the king's network of *consilium et auxilium*, with the power to excommunicate anyone who contravened the apostolic act.[97] In addition, the pope granted Louis full immunity from all sentences of excommunication and interdict except those promulgated by him directly.[98] While this privilege was not itself novel, it was serious and was not some routine or empty formality. We can see how seriously Clement understood it in his denial of Louis's request that the privilege be extended to his three sons. Clement stated that the privilege elevated Louis above the power of the ordinary hierarchy of the Church, that it was granted because the apostolic see trusted him above all others, and that if it were extended, it would cause great unrest among both the barons and the episcopate. Louis's sons did not need the privilege anyway, Clement added, because Louis had with him a legate who had an ordinary jurisdiction second only to the pope himself.[99]

In France, the legate and the king were at the head of a vast network of *consilium et auxilium*, a network whose actions had complete royal and apostolic legal justification. But, the heads of this network were not themselves subject to these legal restraints. Again, it must be understood that unlike in modern legal positivism, the positive law here was not the ordering principle of society. It was a force that had to be introduced in order to counter force, it had to be justified according to

---

[96] *Clément IV, Reg.*, 463; LTC, 4:5280–81.

[97] LTC, 4:5283; *Clément IV, Reg.*, 467.

[98] *Epistole et dictamina Clementis pape quarti*, 481 (*Clément IV, Reg.*, 1350).

[99] Ibid.

some principle outside itself, and it was a consequence of a failure of the ideal, which was fraternal cooperation. And so, at the top of the network of social power, the positive law had to dissolve. The pope and the king were ultimately at the head of the network and their relationship was accordingly based on mutual *consilium et auxilium*, on friendship, and so was supralegal. Only the dissolution of the friendship, only the end of the *consilium et auxilium*, could justify the reintroduction of juridical elements in the relationship, and this was a dissolution that could be effected only by those at the top.

The king was therefore elevated above all ecclesiastical jurisdictions and judgments. In France, the king and the legate, who bore the full *vices* of the pope, and over whom only the pope could pass judgment,[100] operated together to direct their combined social power through their mutual network—the fullness of royal and of papal power merged together in their friendship, in their shared will and mutual trust. The apparatus that they built grew out of this unity at the top and reflected it. The king enforced apostolic mandates and the legate and pope enforced royal mandates because ultimately they were the same—they were the mandate of what was just and right.[101] Clement (sometimes represented by the legate) and Louis, at the very top gave each other advice, held strategic counsel, and deployed their power accordingly. Clement, for example, advised Louis against supporting Edward of England's plans to go to the Holy Land, and the pope worked in Italy to secure the diplomatic conditions that would facilitate Louis's expedition.[102]

Discord lower in the network was unacceptable, and both king and pope (and legate) evoked their power in order to compel subordinates to cooperate with the other pole.[103] When

---

[100] *Epistole et dictamina Clementis pape quarti*, 419 (*Clément IV, Reg.*, 1288).

[101] LTC, 4:5439; *Clément IV, Reg.*, 1411.

[102] *Epistole et dictamina Clementis pape quarti*, 419 (*Clément IV, Reg.*, 1288); *Clément IV, Reg.*, 1412; LTC, 4:5284.

[103] LTC, 4:5439; *Clément IV, Reg.*, 1411.

there was disharmony at the top, they attempted to deal with it amicably and not by evoking law. In May of 1268, the king had asked Clement, through Simon, for a fourth year to be added to the tenth. Clement responded that this request seemed to be at variance with Louis's customary goodness and that he could not possibly agree to mandate it.[104] He would, though, exhort the prelates to volunteer for a fourth year, which he was sure the king would recognize as just.[105] In another example, Clement had accidentally instructed the legate to provision clerics to certain prebends that he later learned fell to the right of the king. He asked Louis to forgive the mistake, confirm the clerics in their prebends, and to be assured that the papacy would in no way draw any legal conclusions from the affair.[106] The pope and the king were at the top of the social order that they had built, and in the ideal, at the top, the spiritual and the temporal powers would be perfectly united in charity, a thoroughly differentiated unity within which each became more truly what they were and both the fullness of papal and the fullness of royal power were fully realized in practice. This was an incarnational, Trinitarian worldview. In the kingdom itself, the legate bore the full apostolic *vices*, and it was he and the king who ruled, rarely leaving each other's company.[107]

The legate provided the authority necessary to marshal and direct all the resources of the kingdom that related to its ecclesiastical rather than its secular character. This included far more than just the collection of clerical taxes.[108] For example, the legate was active in commuting crusading vows made

---

[104] *Epistole et dictamina Clementis pape quarti*, 505 (*Clément IV, Reg.*, 1374).

[105] *Clément IV, Reg.*, 627, 1320; TNA, 2:557.

[106] *Epistole et dictamina Clementis pape quarti*, 290 (*Clément IV, Reg.*, 1159); LTC, 4:5312.

[107] Simon's surviving letters are all dated from Paris, and there are frequent remarks in the sources to the effect that Louis and Simon traveled together (see, for example, *Eudes, Reg.*, 564, 598, 668).

[108] Simon, though, was a zealous collector of revenue (*Clément IV, Reg.*, 789, 804; *Eudes, Reg.*, 678).

before Louis took the Cross to his expedition.[109] He and his delegates actively investigated who in the kingdom had taken the Cross, including when and under what circumstances, and then compelled them to join Louis. The spiritual power's control over wills and bequests was deployed to redirect funds and resources.[110]

And, of course, the apostolic authority made available the infinite resource of merit that it alone could distribute in the indulgence. Clement extended the full crusade indulgence to all those who paid their tenth,[111] and also, at the behest of Louis, to anyone who gave directly to the king a sum of money to be determined by a graduated scale tied to one's net worth.[112] All the activities of the legate were backed with apostolic censure followed by the intervention of the secular arm. But, the legate did more than promulgate ecclesiastical censures. He preached, offered Masses, and led processions. He oversaw the transfer of relics throughout the kingdom.[113] When the king's son, Philip, was knighted, Simon led a liturgical procession to Saint Denis in celebration, where he preached the crusade and a multitude of magnates took the Cross.[114] When Clement heard that the queen of France believed herself to have the head of St. Paul, the pontiff wrote to her, assured her that the head was in Rome and that the Greeks who told her otherwise were liars and instructed her to give the head to Simon lest such dangerous errors be sustained.[115]

Simon's activities went well beyond the application of ap-

---

[109] Clément IV, Reg., 496; Epistole et dictamina Clementis pape quarti, 343 (Clément IV, Reg., 1212).

[110] LTC, 4:5302; Clément IV, Reg., 538.

[111] TNA, 2:557.

[112] LTC, 4:5417; Ludwigs des Heiligen Kreuzzug nach Tunis 1270, und die Politik Karls I. von Sizilien, ed. Richard Sternfeld (Berlin: E. Ebering, 1896), 325.

[113] LTC, 4:5297–98, 5301; E Chronico Sanctae Catharinae de Monte Rotomagi (RHGF, 23:405).

[114] E Chronico Normanniae (RHGF, 23:218); Eudes, Reg., 669; Guillelmus de Nangiaco (RHGF, 20:561); Gal. Christ., 7:454.

[115] Epistole et dictamina Clementis pape quarti, 485 (Clément IV, Reg., 1354).

ostolic power to the needs of the crusade or to those narrowly of the king. The legate took on the role of governor of the Church. He held inquisitions into corrupt or destitute religious houses.[116] He dealt with disputed ecclesiastical elections and investigated and remedied irregularities surrounding them.[117] He sought to compel the bishop-elect of Lyon to assume the episcopal throne (he was hesitant to do so because he was worried about the security of his other properties).[118] When it was charged that the provost of Vienne not only was a pluralist but also had not even taken orders, Simon investigated,[119] and he looked into a personal matter for Clement having to do with a gift of a chalice and some vestments.[120]

These activities of ecclesiastical government were not sealed off from the monarchical government. As we have seen repeatedly in this book, they were intertwined. Alphonse wrote to his seneschals telling them to help the legate catch an apostate friar.[121] The pope ordered an abbot who was in a feudal dispute with the king to make peace, lest the legate act against him. Simon gave Eudes of Rouen the power to absolve one of the king's knights from the censure he had incurred by laying hands on a cleric, a crime reserved to the apostolic see.[122] Under Simon, the office of de latere legate became that of a proconsul, a standing governor wielding apostolic imperium, not tied to any single case or mission.

During the year and a half between Louis's taking the Cross and Clement's death, an extensive system of delegated apostolic authority was constructed aimed at maximizing the resources, both material and spiritual, available to the negotium. Most of this effort was transmitted through the legate to an

---

[116] Clément IV, Reg., 434, 440, 526, 583, 1521.
[117] Ibid., 512.
[118] Ibid., 587.
[119] TNA, 2:452.
[120] Clément IV, Reg., 1321.
[121] CAAP, 1:692.
[122] Eudes, Reg., 668.

army of delegates, very often Mendicant friars, who preached and collected revenue.[123] But sometimes laymen performed the same functions. We have an account of a knight preaching the Cross, and officers of the monarchy directly collected the clerical tax (with the full expectation of the apostolic indulgence for doing so).[124] This was a *negotium* of the entire network, and all of the resources of the network—juridical, sacramental, coercive, and personal—were marshaled. This was not an alliance; it was one operation.

For example, in February of 1268 Simon de Brie wrote to Simon of Paris, a cleric of the king[125] who was a lawyer and served in Parlement making inquisitions for Louis.[126] The legate wrote to him recounting that Clement had granted Louis the tenth so that he might complete his vow for the subsidy of the Holy Land, that this had been done with the *consilium* of the cardinals and Louis himself, and that it was in the service of this objective that Simon de Brie was commissioned.[127] The legate was here establishing his authority and the legitimacy of the whole *negotium*. It was legitimate because both poles of the network, the papal and the monarchal, were of one mind.[128] Simon de Brie told the other Simon how he had called together local councils throughout the kingdom, mentioning specifically the council of ecclesiastics from Sens, Tours, Rouen, and Reims—the very churches that Urban had asked Louis to pressure into supporting the legate. He then recounted how he had called a similar council for the South of

---

[123] LTC, 4:5339. The use of the Mendicants as preachers and collectors of revenue allows us to better understand exactly what type of activities the secular clerics who resisted them were opposed to and why the papacy was so solid in its support for the friars. See, for example, *Bullarium Franciscanum*, 3:162.

[124] *Majus chronicon lemovicense* (RHGF, 21:771); CAAP, 1:119.

[125] LTC, 4:5355.

[126] Olim, 1:283, 302.

[127] LTC, 4:5355.

[128] This formula was followed again and again in Simon's commissions of delegates (see, for example, LTC, 4:5373–74).

France but had fallen ill and could not attend (he actually fell off his horse[129]), and so Eudes, the Archbishop of Rouen, went in his place and read the apostolic letters.[130] Eudes was both a Franciscan and a close confidant and counselor to Louis, and there was no cleric in France more solidly in the king's *consilium et auxilium*.

Now that the apostolic letters had been read, the money had to be collected. The legate told Simon of Paris that he could not do it himself, and so he had to delegate. But the problem was that he did not have adequate knowledge of local circumstances in order to choose suitable delegates.[131] He did not know who could be trusted or who was in the network of *consilium et auxilium* at the local level, and so he granted Simon of Paris his *vices* and asked him to use his discretion to choose clerics from the local churches. This was to be done with the *consilium* of the local bishops, if they might be helpful, but otherwise Simon of Paris had the power to use censure and to call in the secular arm.[132]

What was in action here was a network of *consilium et auxilium*, a network that shared a certain vision for a social order and certain objectives, in this case the crusade. This network was not secular, and it was not ecclesiastical—it was necessarily both. For, its vision of reality and so of justice and legitimacy was sacramental and the spiritual and secular resources of society were wrapped up together in a single order of use, possession, custom, and law. The network had jurisdictional and juridical power—that is to say, it could produce legal justifications for its actions which had social power to the extent that others in society believed in their legitimacy. But its real power came from its mutual *consilium et auxilium*, the pooling of resources of all types and their use in both organizing the expedition and in accumulating the necessary resources from

---

[129] *Epistole et dictamina Clementis pape quarti*, 418.
[130] LTC, 4:5355.
[131] Ibid.
[132] Ibid.

society at large, even if this meant using force against "those whose hearts were made of iron."[133]

This was the network of *consilium et auxilium* that Clement and Louis had spent their whole lives building and extending, and during the run up to Louis's second crusade it was extended over even more of France. For example, the Archbishop of Sens, Guillaume de Brosse, had been a persistent problem for the king and the pope, resisting the ecclesiastical taxes and the power of the legate.[134] In 1267, the pope charged Simon to assign a co-adjudicator to Guillaume ("under whom the whole province sighed") to take control of the material and spiritual rights and properties of the bishop, and to make sure that in his so doing the tenth was paid to Louis.[135] Ultimately the archbishop was compelled to resign and the pope elevated Peter de Charny in his place. Peter had long been in the service of the papacy and Clement trusted him completely.[136] Clement wrote to Louis telling him that he had opened his mind to the new archbishop, assuring the king that Peter was zealous for Louis's cause, and telling him that any graces or honors that he gave Peter the pope would repute having been given to the pope himself.[137] He then instructed Peter to go personally to Louis and not to appoint new clerics without the king's approval, even though he had the legal right to do so,[138] and he asked Louis to act well in this business.[139] A similar sequence of events happened in Beauvais.[140] These clerics of Clement's and the king's network of *consilium et auxilium* worked in their own jurisdictions for the crusade effort.[141]

---

[133] *Clément IV, Reg.*, 627.

[134] TNA, 2:504.

[135] *Epistole et dictamina Clementis pape quarti*, 356; *Clément IV, Reg.*, 1521.

[136] Fernando Alberto Pico, "The Bishops of France in the Reign of Louis IX (1226–70)," 316.

[137] *Epistole et dictamina Clementis pape quarti*, 462 (*Clément IV, Reg.*, 1331).

[138] *Clément IV, Reg.*, 1332; TNA, 2:580.

[139] *Clément IV, Reg.*, 1379.

[140] LTC, 4:5296; *Epistole et dictamina Clementis pape quarti*, 361.

[141] See, for example, Mansi, 23:1165; *Eudes, Reg.*, 676.

During the reigns of Urban IV and Clement IV, apostolic and royal power grew closer together within a single social order. The whole order was predicated upon a sort of permanent and multi-tiered reform that applied the fullness of both royal and apostolic power to the order's construction and to the defeat of its enemies, internal as much as external. The preaching, the sacraments, and the indulgences of the spiritual power coupled with the order, organization, and labor of the temporal power positively built a society, while a sort of permanent crusade, the full deployment of both the spiritual and temporal swords, defended it.[142] This was the *negotium*, and within the *negotium* it is as unnecessary and inaccurate to posit the dominance of the monarchy over the papacy as it is to posit the submission of the monarchy to the papacy.[143] Clement, of course, had been a part of this project from the very beginning and he continued it during his papacy. Apostolic power was consolidated under a single standing legate and the legatine office transitioned into that of a spiritual proconsulate. This was Clement's understanding of right order from the very beginning of his reign, and so his actions during his pontificate were a continuation of his career—the construction and extension of a social order that brought secular and spiritual power together within the context of a single network of *consilium et auxilium*.

---

[142] Michael Lower is entirely correct when he sees Louis's crusade as an extension of his struggle for the reform and conversion of his own kingdom ("Conversion and St. Louis's Last Crusade," *Journal of Ecclesiastical History*, 58, no.2 [April 2007]: 230).

[143] Canon Nicolas's triumphalist reading that Louis was under Clément in the same way that a division is under an army is as wrong as the numerous histories that assert the relative decline of the papacy vis-à-vis the Crown (César Augustin Nicolas, *Un pape Saint Gillois: Clément IV dans le monde et dans l'Eglise, 1195–1268* [Nîmes, FR: Impr. Générale, 1910], 268).

CHAPTER THIRTEEN

SEDE VACANTE

For the will of God, who makes His angels spirits and His ministers a blazing fire, resides there [heaven] among spirits who are bound together in perfect peace and friendship, and melted together into one will by a kind of spiritual fire, as though on a high, holy, and mysterious seat, as though in His own home and in His own temple. From there He diffuses Himself through all things by certain most orderly movements of the creature, first the spiritual, then the material, and He uses all according to the unchangeable pleasure of His own counsel, whether incorporeal or corporeal things, whether rational or irrational spirits, whether the good by His grace or the wicked by their own will.

—St. Augustine, *On the Trinity* 3.4.9

ON NOVEMBER 29, 1268 Pope Clement IV died and the longest papal vacancy in history, thirty-four months, began. The legatine office in France, though, continued to function as an integral part of the kingdom's government apparatus and preparations for Louis's crusade continued. Indeed, the crusade itself happened, Louis being accompanied by a *de latere* legate with full apostolic power, while the papal throne sat unoccupied. This was possible because the legatine office was embedded in a network of *consilium et auxilium* and integrated into a web of law and procedure that not only allowed the office to operate without papal infusions of apostolic power but also required its existence. We saw in the last two chapters that Clement had a certain theoretical understanding of the legatine office, that of the Jeremiahian proconsul, and that he and Louis then built it in practice during the legation of Simon de Brie. In the present chapter we will see how this legatine office, through the papal vacancy and the expedition to Africa, required theoretical and legal definition and justification and that this was produced, as the office itself had been, by both Louis and the Roman Church, in this case the cardinals, especially the great canonist Hostiensis (Cardinal Henry of Susa).

In the summer of 1268 Clement IV fell ill and Simon de Brie was called back to the papal curia. However, as was appropriate to the office of proconsulate, Simon did not leave France until the arrival of his replacement, Cardinal Radulph Grosparmi. Radulph was one the cardinals elevated by Urban IV along with Simon de Brie and Gui Foucois himself. He had been a bearer of the royal seal, the Bishop of Évreux, a see solidly in the royal network of *consilium et auxilium*, and had been the legate in Italy with Charles of Anjou in his war against Manfred. Radulph's legation was an obvious continuation of the papal-monarchical initiative. With Radulph's arrival in Paris, Simon left France for the curia, and shortly thereafter Clement died.

The remarkable thing is that the apparatus constructed during Simon's legation continued to operate under Radulph—the crusade preparations and the governance of the Church pushed on. There were differences, but overall the legatine office continued to function. In order to see how this worked and how the legatine authority was integrated into the total governance of France, a specific example of delegated apostolic authority is useful. Sometime after the death of Clement IV, Louis's brother Alphonse of Poitiers wrote to the new legate, Radulph. He explained that the man who had been commissioned by the apostolic see to collect various funds had not begun fulfilling his mandate when the pope died. Because of this, the collector's mandate had expired. Alphonse, therefore, asked the legate to commission Peter Sorini to the task. Peter was a canon of Saintes and a "faithful master" of Alphonse who had served the count in various functions.[1] Radulph agreed and sent letters of commission to Alphonse, who forwarded them to Peter along with his own instructions.[2] Peter, somewhat unsure about the extent of his commission, asked Alphonse for clarification. Alphonse asked Stephan, the treasurer of Saint-Hilaire of Poitiers, to look into it, and Stephan did so by writing to Alphonse's procurator at the legate's curia, who talked to the legate and wrote back. Stephan then wrote directly to Peter clarifying the mandate.[3] (Stephan himself carried extensive apostolic powers, having been commissioned by the pope as the conservator of the immunities and privileges of Alphonse.)[4] At this point Peter went to work collecting the funds. A bit later, after having received complaints from Alphonse concerning certain ecclesiastics who were not respecting his crusader privileges, the legate wrote directly to Peter, mandating that he use apostolic authority to stop such molestations.[5]

Shortly thereafter, Alphonse wrote to Peter explaining that some of his rights were being violated, giving him a letter of Radulph's that granted him power to act against the perpetrators, and informing him that his men would be contacting

---

[1] CAAP, 1:641, 1102.
[2] Ibid., 1:1086.
[3] Ibid., 1:1103, 1101.
[4] *Urban IV, Reg.*, 2168, 2173, 2176; LTC, 4:4459, 4958.
[5] CAAP, 1:1000.

him soon. Alphonse instructed him to collect the names of ecclesiastics who were refusing to cooperate and to write to his own procurator at the legate's curia in order to receive letters against them. Also, if he was in need of any other letters from the legate, he should ask directly.[6] Radulph then wrote directly to Peter mandating that he collect the funds from redeemed crusader vows in his province and deposit them with the Friars Minor. Peter was concerned that this might prejudice the rights of Alphonse, so he wrote to him explaining the situation. Alphonse responded by stating that he did not believe the legate had any intention of prejudicing his rights. But, nevertheless, he instructed Peter to talk to the legate and clarify what his intentions were and what he believed his powers to be.[7] Sometime later, Alphonse told his seneschal in Poitiers that he had heard that some of his relatives were being dragged before an ecclesiastical court over feudal matters and instructed him to contact Peter, who held letters from the legate that might be helpful.[8] This type of thing goes on and on. Finally, throughout all his activities, Peter was consistently exhorted by both the legate and Alphonse to act always in a way that would best help the Holy Land. These communications of instructions and powers are demonstrated in the diagram on the facing page.

Such an order was not some sort of exception. Peter was simply one worker among hundreds, if not thousands, in the *negotium*. An example from the north of France is perhaps in order. Simon de Brie had commissioned the Bishop of Troyes to collect revenues in the counties of Champagne and Brie at the request of Louis and Theobald, the Count of Champagne and king of Navarre. The bishop, though, died. Radulph, therefore, again at the behest of the king, commissioned Thomas, the Abbot of Hautvillers, to the task.[9] Thomas was a cleric

---

[6] Ibid., 1:1001.

[7] Ibid., 1:1106.

[8] Ibid., 1:1025.

[9] LTC, 4:5515–56.

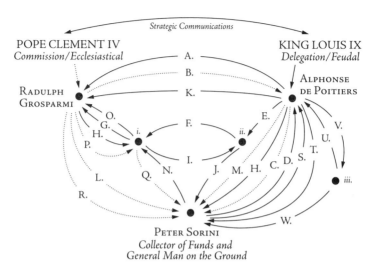

LEGEND

- i. *Alphonse's Procurator at the legate's court*
- ii. *Stephan, treasurer of St. Hilary of Poitiers*
- iii. *Seneschal of Poitiers*

Letters bearing Apostolic Authority

Instructions and other communications

(A selection of communications from April to August 1269 in chronological order)

A. Alphonse asks Radulph to commission Peter Sorini to collect certain funds.

B. Radulph agrees and sends letters of commission for Peter to Alphonse.

C. Alphonse forwards Radulph's letters of commission to Peter and gives him instructions on how to proceed.

D. Peter asks Alphonse for clarification concerning the extent of his authority.

E. Alphonse asks Stephan, the treasurer of St. Hilary, to look into Peter's question.

F. Stephan asks Alphonse's procurator at Radulph's court to ask the legate about Peter's question.

G. The procurator asks Radulph about Peter's question.

H. Radulph clarifies Peter's mandate to the procurator.

I. The procurator writes to Stephan with the legate's clarification.

J. Stephan writes to Peter with the legate's clarification.

K. Alphonse complains to Radulph that certain ecclesiastics are not respecting his privileges.

L. Radulph instructs Peter to use apostolic authority to stop the abuses.

M. Alphonse instructs Peter to act against certain violators of his rights and forwards letters from Radulph granting him further authority [Alphonse must have requested these from Radulph].

N. Peter asks Alphonse's procurator at Radulph's court to get further letters from the legate against the violators of Alphonse's rights.

O. The Procurator asks for the letters.

P. Radulph gives the procurator the letters.

Q. The procurator sends Radulph's letters to Peter.

R. Radulph mandates directly to Peter that he collect redeemed vow funds and deposit them with the Friars Minor.

S. Peter explains Radulph's mandate to Alphonse, worried that it might prejudice his rights.

T. Alphonse tells Peter that the legate is not prejudicing his rights and instructs him to talk to Peter directly, in letter or in person.

U. The seneschal of Poitiers complains to Alphonse that his relatives are being tried in an ecclesiastical court concerning feudal matters.

V. Alphonse tells the seneschal to contact Peter who holds letters from Radulph which might be helpful.

W. The seneschal of Poitiers writes to Peter asking for help.

of the king and used his new apostolic authority to maintain the network of preachers and that of deputies who collected revenue and deposited it directly with the king's men.[10] It was by the authority of the "lord legate" that he threatened and censured *contradictores et rebelles*, and it was with the power of the secular arm that force was ultimately applied.[11] Thomas was in frequent communication with both the legate and the king, working with their *consilium et auxilium*.

The men on the ground, the men collecting the taxes and preaching the Cross, the men doing the actual work of the network of *consilium et auxilium*, were at the bottom of a multi-polar power structure. Their tasks required that they bear both apostolic and royal power and that they work in constant consultation with both the monarchical and the apostolic poles, with their *consilium et auxilium*. The diagram above is actually simplified dramatically because Peter had multiple interactions with many other people—some men of the Crown, some of the legate—with whom he took *consilium*, carried messages, and cooperated on initiatives and projects.[12] There were an untold number of such delegates.

Such an organization does not sit well with modern theories of sovereignty that have dominated the study of medieval Church-State relations. But for every example from which one might argue that apostolic authority was being subsumed into the monarchy (in order to salvage such models as, for instance, Joseph Strayer's laicization thesis), another example could be offered that would seem to support the opposite dynamic. For instance, one of the rights claimed by *de latere* legates was the power to levy procurations on the local churches in support of their mission, and both Simon and Radulph had done so. However, there were clerics who refused to pay, and as a consequence, the legates excommunicated them. When they

---

[10] Ibid., 4:5542, 5545, 5586. He had the extensive cooperation of the Mendicant orders of the region (LTC, 4:5587).

[11] Ibid., 4:5585.

[12] CAAP, 1:1001.

continued to resist, the legates promulgated interdicts on their churches. After this, as Radulph wrote, "only one thing was left to use against such violent contumacy, the *auxilium* of the secular arm."[13] Radulph, therefore, appealed to the Crown for *auxilium*. Alphonse quickly ordered his seneschals and bailiffs to aid the legate by seizing the goods of the contumacious clerics, working under the direction of the legate. Alphonse had acquired letters from Radulph deputizing the count's men as collectors and granting them apostolic protection, and he forwarded these letters to his officers. He did the same throughout his domain.[14] Alphonse's officers and the apostolic delegates became largely the same men, men who "keep the business of the Holy Land in [their] heart."[15]

The order built in France over the course of the thirteenth century had, by 1270, developed to the point where the fullness of apostolic power was the necessary complement to the fullness of royal power, and this need was satisfied with the establishment of the *de latere* legation as a permanent aspect of the kingdom's governance. As had been the case with Simon, Radulph seldom left the side of the king and they are often presented in the sources as a unit.[16] Together, they occupied the top of the structure.

The importance of this apostolic power becomes clearer through an example again concerning Alphonse. The secular power was directly involved in the forceful collection of revenue from the local churches. By definition, this *negotium* allowed the "molestation" of the property of clergy and even force against their persons, but one aspect of the reforms that Louis and men such as Gui Foucois, along with their ecclesiastical counterparts, had implemented throughout the previous decades was the protection of the clergy from the exploitation of the local nobles. This took many forms, but

---

13 Ibid., 1:1004.
14 See Ibid., 1:984–86, 1004, 1157–59, 1176, 1196.
15 See, for example, Ibid., 1:683, 947, 1085
16 See, for example, LTC, 4:5608

one of the most common was the promulgation in local councils of very strongly worded canons against violence aimed at clergy or their property—the peace councils, and through them large councils, such as that held in Toulouse in 1229, serving as models.[17] Louis's own *Grande Ordonnance* of 1254 had included such language. Ironically, this legislation was being used against Alphonse's men, particularly in the province of Bordeaux, where, in 1262, a particularly strong statute had been promulgated.[18] Alphonse had complained in 1264 to Pope Urban IV that this statute often had the effect not only of harming the innocent but also of inhibiting the work of his officers, who sometimes licitly seized ecclesiastical goods, and of stirring up scandal between the secular officers and ecclesiastical persons, and he asked the pope to revoke or at least moderate it.[19] In response, the pope had given his lands a dispensation from the interdict stipulated in the statute, but he did not extend apostolic protection directly to the persons of Alphonse's officers, and the statute stayed in effect.[20] In 1269, however, this minimal protection was no longer sufficient. Alphonse's men needed direct protection, and so Radulph gave it to them. He provided the men, who were now working under both apostolic and secular authority, with privileges against this council, named directly in the *non obstante* section of his letters, thus trumping the ordinary

---

[17] See, for example, Mansi, 23:1117, 1263.

[18] Mansi, 23:1105: "We establish and this holy council defines with approbation, that places, towns, castles, cities, or parishes, in which the things of the church or of ecclesiastical persons or the same persons, are held captured, seized, invaded, or occupied, warning having been sent ahead, unless they be paid back, are *ipso facto* subject to interdict: also those who do the capturing, seizing, invading or occupying, detaining, are *ipso facto* subject to a sentence of excommunication. And if by chance the property is transferred to another place, when we learn of it, it too is subject to interdict and the first interdict preservers. And if it happens that they are transferred to many locations, we lead this to be observed in all of them."

[19] LTC, 4:4979; CAAP, 2:2049.

[20] *Urban IV, Reg.,* 2170, 2175.

hierarchy.[21] The *negotium* had working for it the fullness of both apostolic and royal power, and so there was no purchase for juridical opposition.

Unlike during the previous vacancy and Simon's legation, no one challenged Radulph's authority. No one argued that it had expired with the death of the pope. Clement's definition of 1265 seems to have been accepted. Nevertheless, in practice, legatine authority was limited. After Clement's death, direct papal interventions had ceased; there were no new infusions of apostolic power, and so we can see the limits of the ordinary authority of the legate. And what we see is that Radulph was frequently compelled to argue that he was but continuing the legation of Simon before him.[22] He did not innovate. Rather, he used his authority to maintain the apparatus and it was ultimately bound by existing papal concessions. This is significant because it reveals an important legal concept that would become crucial to the legal codification of the *de latere* legate in the *Liber Sextus*, with which we began Part III of this work. The concept was that of *res integra*.

In the 1240s the cardinal and canonist Goffredus of Trani had maintained that while the pope's death did end a legation, any processes the legate had begun were to be finished,[23] and Hostiensis agreed in his *Summa aurea*.[24] The decisive legal concept in Goffredus's and Hostiensis's reasoning was *res integra*, an unchanged legal situation. What it meant was that if a case had not yet been brought to court when the jurisdiction of a legate or his delegate was removed by the death of the delegator, then legally it was as if the legation had never existed at all; it was a *res integra* and therefore did not proceed. The status quo always took precedent. However, if the parties had appeared in court, the status quo had been upset—the

---

[21] CAAP, 1:986, 1004.

[22] See, for example, LTC, 4:5515, 5545, 5570.

[23] Goffredus of Trani, *Summa super titulis Decretalium* (Lyon, FR, 1519), 53r–54.

[24] Henry of Susa, *Summa aurea*, De officio legati, *et qualiter finiatur*.

process was a *res non integra* and must be finished, even after the delegator died.

Basically, nothing new could begin after jurisdiction was removed, but all pending cases were to be completed. When the canonists combined the traditional understanding of the effect of a pope's death (that a legation ended) with this concept, the result was a distinction between a general *de latere* legation that expired at the pope's death and one delegated to solve a specific case, which, if the case had begun, did not expire.[25] However, in 1265 Clement IV had flat-out denied this to be the case and had asserted that *de latere* legates were *instar proconsulum*—in the image of a proconsul—and that their offices survived the death of the pope. How were these positions to be reconciled? In his *Commentaria*, written in 1271, Hostiensis proposed an innovative solution. He argued that Radulph could continue to function because the entire apparatus of apostolic power was one large, perpetual *res non integra*.[26] Hostiensis was, of course, constructing a legal justification for what had occurred in practice during the previous three years, and in that practice we can see the concept he advanced: Radulph tried to present himself as simply continuing the legation of Simon and attempted to remain within the bounds of existing papal mandates, within the *res non integra*.

Under Clement IV several aspects of legation had received revision in the direction of the codification in the *Liber Sextus*: legations survived the death of the pope, and they survived the end of a particular mission, for missions were attached to legations and not vice-versa. Both of these revisions were put in practice by Simon and Radulph and seem to have been generally accepted. However, as the date for the general passage approached, a new problem arose. According to the traditional understanding, a legate's authority began when he entered his

---

[25] Robert C. Figueira, "The Canon Law of Medieval Papal Legations", 467.

[26] Henry of Susa (Hostiensis), *In primum [-sextum] decretalium librum commentaria* [hereafter, *Commentaria*] (Venice, 1581), ad 1.41.5.

province and expired when he left it. Canonically, legations were geographical. Radulph had received papal letters commissioning him with the kingdom of France and he had entered his province before the death of Clement, so his legation appeared a *res non integra* and according to Hostiensis's theory could continue. But by what authority could he travel with the crusading army?

Given the essential nature of the legate in St. Louis's government, we can understand why this question would trouble him, and in August of 1269 he wrote to the cardinals. He told them that he was very concerned about the authority of the legate, for while it was said that Pope Clement commissioned him with lands overseas, no letters existed, and furthermore he had not crossed into those territories before the pope's death. Louis was concerned that if the cardinals did not soon elect a pope, the Christian army, engaged in such arduous business, would have to go without the consolation and spiritual rewards that legates by custom provided them. He suggested that perhaps the legate's initial commission could be understood as two kingdoms in the place of one: one, France, being but preparation for the other, Jerusalem.[27]

In response, the cardinals wrote to Radulph borrowing directly much of Louis's language, posing the problem precisely as had the king, and then commissioning Radulph with a full legation to lands overseas. What is really interesting is the justification they provided for this action: they argued that from the commission of Simon and through to the commission of Radulph, the constant intention of Clement had been the prosecution of the *negotium* of the Holy Land and that Clement had formulated and implemented his plan after having taken solemn deliberations with the cardinals and having fully understood their *consilium*. Clement had intended for Radulph

---

[27] Louis to the Cardinals (August 5, 1269), in Wilhem Spatz, *Die Schlacht von Hastings* (Berlin, 1896; repr. Vaduz, LI: Kraus, 1965), 328; Fischer, *Kardinale im Konklave*, 376–83.

to go with Louis. The cardinals argued, therefore, in issuing a letter of commission to Radulph, they were adding nothing, but were rather ensuring that something was not taken away. They were essentially taking Louis up on his suggestion and were extending the *res non integra* idea to encompass the geographical limitations on legations.[28]

This action had serious ecclesiological and legal implications, and we are fortunate that Hostiensis justified it explicitly in his *Commentaria*. He stated that some of the cardinals had thought that the overseas segment of Radulph's legation had expired because with the death of Clement it was a clear *res integra*. This argument was tied to the geographical notion of legation. However, the majority of cardinals took Louis up on his suggestion and argued that Radulph's legation in France was preparatory to that overseas and that his having taken the Cross from the hands of Clement demonstrated as much. If the legation expired, great harm would befall the Christian people and the king of France would suffer, to whom, Hostiensis stated, the legate had been specially commissioned.[29] Radulph had been given a single mission, a mission that bound him to Louis, and this mission was *res non integra*.[30] In this exposition, Hostiensis borrowed language from the letter of the cardinals to Radulph, which had itself been borrowed from Louis. The net result of this argument was that *de latere* legations were not necessarily geographically limited, that the legate had ordinary jurisdiction wherever his mission might take him, and that in this case the mission was explicitly tied to a monarch.

But there is another dimension to Hostiensis's arguments that has perhaps greater significance. He argued that papal letters of commission were not necessary for Radulph because the pope had made his decisions with the *consilio* of the cardinals: they had been of one mind and the cardinals remembered

---

[28] *Annales Minorum*, 4:330–31.
[29] Henry of Susa, *Commentaria*, ad 1.41.5.
[30] Ibid.

his intentions.[31] It was this idea that justified the cardinals' commission to Radulph, and in that commission they emphasized their role in the pope's decision making process. We can see the same thing in another series of letters sent by the cardinals to St. Louis and Radulph while they were on crusade in 1270 outside the walls of Tunis. St. Louis informed the cardinals that he had been approached by representatives of the Greek emperor who asked him to arbitrate in the negotiations with Rome so that the emperor might rejoin the Catholic Church. Louis felt that such an action on his part would prejudice the prerogatives of the apostolic see, and so he asked the cardinals whether Radulph might be appointed to the task. The cardinals, stressing their involvement in both Urban IV's and Clement IV's efforts at reuniting the churches and their knowledge of the popes' intentions, commissioned Radulph to the task and commanded him to work closely with Louis on the initiative.[32]

Such a relationship between the pope and cardinals required explanation, and Hostiensis asserted that while the pope was the head of the universal Church and each of the faithful were generally his members, it was especially the case that the pope was the head of the cardinals and that the cardinals were members of his body in a special way. It was not fitting, he asserted, that the pope should extract oaths from his own members as if they were somehow foreign to himself. Indeed, the cardinals were the pope's entrails and fleshy parts, and hence they were sent as legates *de latere*, from his side. If the cardinals wanted to serve the pope with faith and obedience, Hostiensis argued, they ought to consider themselves bound by his own body and consider themselves to sin gravely if they betrayed his confidence, and the pope, if he wanted their faith and obedience, ought to bind the cardinals to himself as

---

[31] Ibid.

[32] *Acta Urbani IV, Clementis IV, Gregorii X (1261–1276) e registris vaticanis aliisque fontibus collegit*, ed. Aloysius L. Tàutu (Rome: Typis polyglottis Vaticanis, 1953), 29.

his own body. For this reason, it was not proper that the pope should act without the *consilium* of his brothers or that a cardinal should ever act contrary to his head, the pope—rather, he should always give him *auxilium*. Hostiensis added that, therefore, it is altogether fitting that the cardinals sent *de latere* wear the red and white vestments and gilded shoes of the pope.[33]

There is a difference between Hostiensis's discussion of the cardinals as the special body of the pope and the idea of the King's body or the corporate concept in Roman law. The first pope to use the corporeal image when discussing the relationship between himself and the cardinals was Innocent III, explicitly paraphrasing St. Paul,[34] and it became more common through the thirteenth century as the pope was increasingly identified with the Church itself (culminating in Hostiensis's "ubi papa, ibi Roma") and with Christ himself as *Vicarius Christi*.[35] When such images are combined with contemporary ecclesiological images of the Church as the body and spouse of Christ, we can get a sense of what Hostiensis now meant by *de latere*. His exposition is Pauline and matrimonial, and his discussion of *de latere* legates is better understood with images of the sacraments pouring *de latere Christi* or Eve emerging *de latere Adam* than with comparisons to the body politic.[36]

---

[33] Henry of Susa, *Commentaria*, ad 5.33.23. On the significance of clothing in the medieval, allegorical understanding of representation, see Ma Tapio Salminen, "In the Pope's Clothes: Legatine Representation and Apostolical Insignia in High Medieval Europe," in *Roma, Magistra Mundi*, ed. Jacqueline Hamesse (Louvain-La-Neuve, BE: Fédération Internationale des Instituts d'Études Médiévales, 1998), 339–54.

[34] *Die Register Innocenz III*, eds. Othmar Hageneder et al. (Vienna, AT: Verlag der Osterreichischen Akademie der Wissenschaften, 1964), 1:515, cited in Agostino Paravicini-Bagliani, *The Pope's Body*, trans. David S. Peterson (Chicago: University of Chicago Press, 1994), 64.

[35] Henry of Susa, *Commentaria*, ad 10.5.20. See also Paravicini-Bagliani, *The Pope's Body*, 70–71.

[36] See, for example, *Super Ioan* 19, lec. 1.5: "Et ideo haec duo specialiter pertinent ad duo sacramenta: aqua ad sacramentum Baptismi, ad Eucharistiam sanguis. Vel utrumque pertinet ad Eucharistiam, quia in sacramento Eucharistiae miscetur aqua cum vino; quamvis aqua non sit de substan-

There is therefore a deep continuity between this essentially theological understanding of *de latere* legation and that which Hostiensis had written in his *Summa aurea* some twenty years earlier (considered in chaper 11 above). The *de latere* legate continued to receive his mandate from a profoundly personal and physical relationship with the pope; it remained Christological and liturgical, an act rather than an institution. What had changed was the meaning of "the pope's body" to include the cardinals. The college of cardinals and the pope were a particularly tight network of *consilium et auxilium*, of differentiated friends of such intensity that they became one body. The force of law, therefore, in the ideal, stopped at the body of the college of cardinals. Legal instruments such as letters of commission were of little value in comparison with the memory of the cardinals. When the apostolic see was vacant, Hostiensis argued, the College held the plenitude of power with Christ himself as their head. Their exercise of it was limited not by law or by some sort of constitution (which would make no sense), but by their personal commitment of love and faithfulness to the deceased pope. They were his body and continued the functions, what might be called the *res non integra*, of that body, but they could not make innovations.[37]

---

tia sacramenti. Competit etiam hoc figurae: quia sicut de latere Christi dormientis in cruce fluxit sanguis et aqua, quibus consecratur Ecclesia; ita de latere Adae dormientis formata est mulier, quae ipsam Ecclesiam praefigurabat." Everytime a priest said or heard Mass, the words "Ex latere Christi sanguis et aqua exisse perhibetur et deo pariter commiscemur. Ut tu pius et misericors utremque sanctificare et benedicere digneris" would have been said as the water was mixed with the wine on the altar (Stephen J. P. van Dijk, OFM, *The Ordinal of the Papal Court from Innocent III to Boniface VIII and Related Documents* [Fribourg, CH: Fribourg University Press, 1975], 503). Guido de Baysio, in his *Rosarium Decretorum* (ca. 1300), would make explicit the identification between *legati de latere papae* and the *ecclesia de latere Christi* (Robert C. Figueira, "The Classification of Medieval Papal Legates in the *Liber Extra*," *Archivum historiae pontificiae* 21 [1983]: 221–22).

[37] For the formal development of this idea by Giles of Rome, see Paravicini-Bagliani, *The Pope's Body*, 163. During a vacancy, new cases were not heard at the Roman curia (Pascal Montaubin, "Le gouvernement de l'Église

This was not a "constitutional" or "democratic" arrangement, as some historians conclude,[38] but a moral, perhaps familial, one.

The question of what the cardinals could and could not do was therefore an ethical problem, not a legal one. It was for this reason that Hostiensis repeatedly stated that the cardinals could not take actions such as recalling a legate or issuing certain types of indulgences when the See was vacant *unless* the good of the Church demanded it.[39] Such exceptions have no place in modern jurisprudence, in which the law is the self-referential principle of order. In a world of primordial conflict, such exceptions would unleash chaos: Who decides when the exception is justified? Who is sovereign?[40] But these exceptions make perfect sense in a world in which the principle of order is not violence, but peace, one in which the law itself is the exception: it was an assumption of canon law that the papacy intended the good of the Church,[41] and if the cardinals did likewise, being of one mind, united in *consilium et auxilium*, there would be no conflict and law had no place.

The profoundly personal and theological relationship between the cardinals and the pope was expressed in the doc-

---

Romaine *sede vacante* aux XIIIe et XIVe siecles," in *Sede vacante: la vacance de pouvoir dans l'Église du moyen âge*, 139).

[38] Joseph Lecler, S.J., "Pars Corporis Papae . . . le Sacre College dans L'Ecclesiologie Medievale," in *L'Homme devant Dieu: Melanges offerts au Pere Henri de Lubac*, vol. 2 (Paris: Aubier, 1964), 190–91. See also Brian Tierney, *Foundations of the Conciliar Theory: The Contribution of the Medieval Canonists from Gratian to the Great Schism* (Cambridge: Cambridge University Press, 1955). Cary Nederman is certainly right that the terms "absolutism" and "constitutionalism" fail to capture adequately the way in which medieval thinkers conceived their political universe ("Conciliarism and Constitutionalism: Jean Gerson and Medieval Political Thought," *History of European Ideas* 12 [1990]: 189–209).

[39] Henry of Susa, *Commentaria*, ad 1.38.14.

[40] For Carl Schmitt, the person in society who decides upon the exception is by definition "sovereign" (*Political Theology: Four Chapters on the Concept of Sovereignty* [Chicago: University of Chicago Press, 2005]).

[41] Clarence Gallagher, *Canon Law and the Christian Community* (Rome: Università Gregoriana Editrice, 1978), 128; John A. Watt, *Theory of Papal Monarchy in the Thirteenth Century* (New York: Fordham University Press, 1965), 111.

uments and letters of the period. Beyond the routine papal exhortation for a cardinal to be well received "rather us in him,"[42] cardinals were often treated as extensions of the pope in both body and mind.[43] Writing to a layman who had been harassing a certain cardinal, Clement IV stated: "Therefore refrain from persecuting the said cardinal, who, as a special son of the Church, rather a noble member of her, you are not able to touch while leaving us and our other brothers untouched, since 'in the Lord we are one body and each is in each' (Rom 12:5; Eph 4:25)."[44] Cardinal Ottoboni, the legate to England after Gui, wrote of Gui's legation: "Since from the first hearing of such great error of her children the 'viscera' of mother church was run through with the sword of sadness, she sent her hand against the strong, taking from her womb (*de gremio suo*) she sent a holy and revered man [Gui]."[45]

Throughout the letters of Ottoboni the cardinal legates emerge from the womb, *de gremio*, of the Church rather than from the side of the pope. Indeed, the cardinals reside *in eius gremio*.[46] It is "mother Church" who accepts from the Lord the fullness of power over all her daughters, and the legates share in her solicitude.[47] Guido, the cardinal legate that Clement IV sent to Vienna in 1267, recalled to the council he had called the creation of man in God's image and man's fall in the garden. "From this," the legate stated, "domination of men and things was introduced. Because he did not know the rule of law, from human necessity man made law for himself." God, though, gave just laws through Moses, but these laws were but figures of Christ, through whose coming, in the fullness of time, the eternal law had been established. And this eternal law worked

---

[42] For example, see *Urban IV, Reg.*, 587.

[43] For example, see LTC, 4:4934.

[44] *Epistole et dictamina Clementis pape quarti*, 450.

[45] "Letters of Cardinal Ottoboni," ed. Rose Graham, *The English Historical Review* 15 (January 1900): 114.

[46] Ibid., 115, 117.

[47] Ibid., 108.

on earth through the papacy, "for the keys were given to Peter into perpetuity, from which the beauty of all ecclesiastical law flows." For the vindication of the nations and the reproofs of the people the apostolic see sent cardinal legates "just as if drawn off from a brook," that the malice and cupidity of men might be restrained under the "severity of the force of law," that they might learn to "live honestly, to not wound others, to assign to each his right."[48] The relationship between the pope and the cardinals was understood as one of complete unity, of the ideal relationship of *consilium et auxilium.*

There was no "sovereignty" here, but this is not because it was somehow egalitarian. The peace of such a society was rooted not in sameness, but in differentiation and so in fundamental inequality. And so, John Watt is mistaken to equate the papal *plenitudo potestatis* with Jean Bodin's "sovereignty," the power to give and cause the law, because the medieval conception of "law" was decidedly different from the absolutist, modern conception.[49] Friendship, not the violence of human law, was the fundamental principle of social order. And it is for this reason that the canonists of the period appear inconsistent concerning the extent of the prerogatives of the cardinals during a vacancy.[50] We are looking for legal structure where none existed, not because they had not yet cleared their heads, but because it would have been profoundly inappropriate. We can see in this understanding of the relationship between the cardinals and the pope a direct parallel to what Gui and Louis believed to be the essence of royal power in the context of the conflict in England. It was the introduction of law, of a constitution of sorts, between the king of England and his *consilium*, the reader will recall, that was utterly unacceptable, even abhorrent, to the king and the legate.

It was this idea that justified the cardinals' commission to

---

[48] Mansi, 23:1167.

[49] Watt, *The Theory of Papal Monarchy*, 84.

[50] Montaubin, "Le gouvernement de l'Église Romaine," 129.

Radulph of lands overseas,[51] and it allows us to see why the *res integra* concept had faded away by the time the gloss to the *Liber Sextus*, (with which Part III of this book opened) was written: it was a legal concept that had been absorbed into the supra-legal, essentially theological and ethical relationship between the pope and the cardinals. It is interesting that one of the more sustained arguments Hostiensis makes, in direct contradiction to his earlier writings, was that if the cardinals did not exercise papal power during a vacancy, then legations would necessarily expire when a pope dies, and that was "clearly not the case," for the legate bears the place of the apostolic see, which never dies.[52] This line of argument is, of course, circular—it had only been six years since Clement IV's letter to Simon declaring his legation to have survived the death of Pope Urban IV—and it makes sense only when we recognize that the law was being constructed as much to explain what actually existed as to dictate the Church's structure. Not only new decretals but also the meaning of old ones emerged out of this dynamic relationship between law and practice.

This section of Hostiensis's *Commentaria*, written in 1271 and predicated on the problem of Radulph and the crusade, offered an understanding of the law surrounding legations that while making no reference to Clement's 1265 letter treated above greatly impacted its gloss in the *Liber Sextus*. In fact, the gloss cites Hostiensis repeatedly. But it no longer needed to justify the notion that only cardinals are sent *de latere*, as had the earlier canonists. Rather, it states the opposite relationship, that some legates are called *de latere* precisely *because* they are cardinals. This is a logical reversal of the work of the canonists considered in Chapter 11, which preceded Clement's letter, a reversal that demonstrates that the canonical justifications came after the realm of practice had made cardinal *de latere* legations a reality. In the gloss the proconsul analogy is dominant and is extended from considerations of provincial rule

---

[51] For another example, see *Acta Urbani IV, Clementis IV, Gregorii X*, 29.

[52] Henry of Susa, *Commentaria*, ad 1.38.14.

into all aspects of legatine authority. In fact, the geographical aspect of legation is weakened: a legate need not have entered his province when the pope died, and the cardinals can transfer him. These concepts, as we have seen, grew up through the sequence of events surrounding Louis's second crusade and the long papal vacancy. And, of course, according to the gloss, a *de latere* legation survives the death of a pope because the legate now bears the place not of a man, who dies, but of the apostolic see, which never dies.[53]

With this gloss, written around 1304, an understanding of the legatine office that emerged over the course of decades in the interplay of various actors, ideas, and events became the definitive interpretation of the short and rather ambiguous letter of Clement IV written over fifty years earlier to the legate Simon. It is fascinating to consider, for example, how the petition of St. Louis in 1270 compelled the college of cardinals to controversial actions for which Hostiensis subsequently offered a justification that would then heavily influence the 1304 interpretation of a 1265 decretal, or how the frequent papal vacancies that provided the impetus for this whole shift in law were clearly the result of the increasing institutional coherence of the Church, the importance of monarchs in its governance, and the rise of the college of cardinals, all factors that played out in the discussion above.

The point is that all of the people involved in this history—Hostiensis, the popes and cardinals, St. Louis, and even Peter Sorini—approached the situation in which they found themselves, tried to make sense of it according to what they believed to be true and legal, and then acted. Most of this activity took place in the differentiated realm of *consilium et auxilium*, of use, possession, custom, and right, that had its order primarily in networks of friends. Law, including the law of the Church, spilled out of this multifaceted negotiation only where something went wrong. It is hard to imagine an office more directly a part of the institution of the medieval papacy than that of

---

[53] *Liber Sextus*, liber I, De officio legati, tit. XV, cap. II, in JC-1582.

cardinal *de latere* legate. And yet, as we have seen, not only were the *de latere* legates in France integral to royal rule, but the Crown was also instrumental to the office's very construction. There were two primary *ordines* of Christian society, the lay and the clerical, but they were not divorced from each other and were most certainly not self-sufficient or "parallel." Their unity can be seen most clearly when we step back from the abstractions of political theory and look at the actual people. Gui was "advocatus in utroque iure in curia regis Lodovoci sancti gratiam habuit in conspectu eius, unde et ipsum de suo secreto fecit consilio,"[54] and Louis was the "most Christian prince."[55]

---

[54] Tholomeus Lucensis, *Historia ecclesiastica nova* (MGH SS, 29:570).
[55] *Urban IV, Reg.,* 766.

St. Thomas Aquinas and the "Most Christian Kingdom"

Our City is as different from theirs as heaven from earth, as everlasting life from passing pleasure, as solid glory from empty praise, as the company of angels from the companionship of mortals, as the Light of Him who made the sun and moon is brighter than the light of sun and moon.

—St. Augustine, *City of God* 5.17

THE FRANCE THAT WAS BUILT over the course of the thirteenth century was, as the popes referred to it, a "most Christian kingdom."[1] This does not mean that it had a Christian ideology or that Christianity provided the language and imagery through which the "nation" or the "State" was built. It was not that the State was still working through a phase of ecclesiastical interference and rivalry or that the State was in the early phases of development. The State did not exist at all. The State exists only as a particular organizational scheme of thought and practice, as a particular social order at a particular time and place. It has no independent, transhistorical or transcultural existence, no universal applicability. It may be true that the State described by Max Weber, the sovereign, secular State that holds a delegable monopoly on the use of force within a certain territory that is wielded through an anonymous and rationally organized bureaucracy, had historical reality in the West during the modern period, but that was as transitory as was the social order of the thirteenth century: both were "complete acts" that were passing away as soon as they came into being. "The State" and its companion, "the secular," have a history, and there was a time before they existed. While Louis XIV may in some sense have been "the State," St. Louis IX certainly was not. In a similar way the modern "Church" did not exist in the thirteenth century—neither the voluntary spiritual communion characteristic of Protestantism nor the positive and enclosed jurisdictional structure of nineteenth-century Catholicism. The "religious" has a history, and the construction of the concept of the Church as the realm of the religious is a product of that history.

The narrative of the problem of Church and State in the Middle Ages, in which these modern categories are read back into history, is therefore flawed. It demands that we look for conflicts, alliances, submission, dominance, religious ideologies, and political motives where none may have existed because it is only through such concepts that the data of the sources can be

---

[1] See *Urban IV, Reg. [Les Registres d'Urbain IV]*, 804, 809.

sorted into categories that maintain the fundamental integrity of the "secular" and the "religious," the State and the Church. Modern historians sympathetic to Frederick II or Philip IV, as well as those sympathetic to the "papal monarchy," participate in the construction and maintenance of this narrative, which serves to legitimize the modern Western order by ultimately denying the possibility of other constructions. Within this vision, every society has a State and a Church, every society has the secular and the religious—some societies are simply more developed, more properly sorted, more enlightened, more civilized than others.

What I have attempted in the preceding chapters is to show the possibility of a different social architecture. I have attempted to show how the data of the sources can be assembled to build a different edifice and to tell a very different story. I have attempted to draw the ideas that underwrote this construction from its structural elements and from actual events in the lives of actual people. I am now positioned to offer an alternative to modern theoretical abstraction through my own theoretical description of this society. To do so, I will lean heavily on the work of St. Thomas Aquinas, who was most certainly a participant in this world. While I am aware that a thorough re-evaluation of Thomas would be a simply massive undertaking beyond the scope of the current work, I could not see a way of ending this book without at least a movement toward a reading of Thomas that is consistent with its general conclusions.

CHAPTER FOURTEEN

THE NEW LAW AND THE TWO SWORDS

Coming to the period of the kings, we find that Saul was ousted and that David became the first king to found a long dynasty in the earthly Jerusalem. Here, in the onward course of the City of God, was an event not to be passed over in silence, for it prefigured and heralded a tremendous change that was to come in respect to the two Testaments. I mean that the priesthood and kingship of the Old were transformed into the priesthood and everlasting kingship of Jesus Christ in the New. As a matter of fact, two occurrences—Samuel's supplanting of the rejected priest, Heli, to become both priest and judge, and David's establishment on the throne (after Saul had been cast aside)—foreshadowed this transformation.

—St. Augustine, *City of God* 17.4.1

THE TWENTIETH CENTURY SAW often spectacular fights among Catholic theologians and philosophers concerning the relationship between nature and grace, fights that focused largely on the thought of Aquinas. At our current distance it seems clear that straw men were erected and destroyed on both sides. It seems clear, for example, that the Neo-Thomism that drew so much fire was not nearly as "rigid" or as "two-storied" as its opponents sometimes made it seem. That being said, and setting the work of the most sophisticated thinkers aside, the manner in which this Neo-Thomism was simplified and used in other disciplines, such as history and political science, does indeed often resemble the caricature.

Within these disciplines, widespread among textbook articulations of Thomas's political thought is the implicit notion that he conceived of the divine law as an addition to the intact and universally accessible natural law in such a way that they existed side-by-side or in two clearly demarcated stories. We find often the notion that mankind not only has simple, rational access to the content of the natural law, but also has the ability to follow it, as if the divine law—and with it, grace—could be removed and the natural law would remain an unproblematic guide to human life which naturally virtuous humans could follow, as if, without divine law and grace, we would be left with "natural" government. In effect, social virtue (and so, "natural government") is treated as somehow immune from the effects of the Fall. While the theologians certainly acknowledge that Thomas thought that due to wounded human nature the individual cannot live according to the natural moral law without grace, somehow this acknowledgement is lost in many treatments of his political thought, within which Thomas is found suggesting that society could live by the moral law, that the "State" could be virtuous, that somehow the natural law, when considered socially, is clear and unproblematic and that un-graced mankind is capable of obeying it.

This is Thomas the Whig, even Thomas the liberal. This, it seems to me, is the Thomas who is often seen as responsible for demonstrating the "naturalness" (and so ultimately the "secularity") of the State against Augustine and his supposed belief that the State was a necessary evil under the reign of sin.[1] A thorough critique of this "Whiggish" Thomas falls well beyond the scope of the current study. Instead, I hope to paint a theoretical picture of the society within which Thomas lived and worked and to provide certain provisional intimations, certain suggestions, for how his thought can be seen to "fit," how he might be read as a part of the "complete act" of the thirteenth century. It should, of course, be remembered that Thomas taught and wrote as a member of that society focused on Paris and Rome, that of St. Louis and the Dominicans, and that he wrote to members of that society. The people who built the institutions of thirteenth-century France were Thomas's colleagues and friends. His thought must somehow fit. It is not that the people of the thirteenth century must be Thomists, but rather that he must be seen, somehow, to be one of them.

What follows, then, is a sketch, a provisional suggestion that is not properly nuanced or qualified and that does not account properly for professional Thomist scholarship. I have also attempted to avoid specialized theological or philosophical terminology, not only because I myself am not a master of such language but also because I want my suggestions to be intelligible to other non-specialists. My hope is that the following is useful and perhaps thought-provoking, rather than definitive. It represents my thoughts, as a historian, upon reading St. Thomas in light of my other research.

For Thomas, natural law is rational participation in the eternal law.[2] Natural law is the way God intends us, as human

---

1   See, for example, Brian Tierney, *The Crisis of Church and State, 1050–1300*, 165–67. For a thoroughgoing criticism of the "whiggish" interpretation, which has been a great help in the current study, see John Milbank, *Beyond Secular Order: The Representation of Being and the Representation of the People*, vol. 1 (Chichester, UK / Hoboken, NJ: Wiley-Blackwell, 2014), 240–47.

2   ST I-II, q. 91, a. 2. See also q. 93, a. 2: "So, then, no one except the blessed in heaven, who see God through his essence, can know the eternal law as it is in itself. However, every rational creature knows the eternal law with respect to more or less of what radiates from it. For any cognition of the truth is a sort of radiation from and participation in the eternal law, which is unchangeable

beings, to act concerning him, concerning ourselves, and concerning our fellow man. Indeed, Thomas states that the "first
general principles" of the natural law are that one ought to love
God and to love one's neighbor.[3] This is an expansive understanding of natural law: nothing that we *do* falls ultimately
beyond its reach.[4] Acts of all the virtues, Thomas says, fall
within its purview, and every act is governed by virtue.[5] This ex-
pansiveness of natural law should not be diminished, leaving us
with some cramped and abbreviated notion. Rather, to Thomas,
law itself is, as a matter of definition, a dictate of reason. The
eternal law as the source of all law is nothing else than divine
reason, and humans are human because they have a rational
nature that participates in this reason. Therefore, humanity's
right reasoning about what is to be done takes on, necessarily,
the nature of law.[6] This is to say that law is rational and that
practical rationality is legal; this is the crux of the natural law.

To Thomas, the expansive natural law is made particular
through human laws, which are the particular conclusions
that are drawn from the precepts of the natural law, "just as,
in the case of speculative reason, conclusions in the diverse
sciences, which are not naturally known to us but are instead
discovered by the activity of reason, are brought forth from

---

truth, as Augustine says in *De vera religione*. But everyone knows the truth in
some sense, at least with respect to the common principles of the natural law.
As for other matters, some participate to a greater degree and some to a lesser
degree in the cognition of the truth and, accordingly, they know more or less
of the eternal law." For all English translations from the "Treatise on Law" (ST
I-II, qq. 90–108), I use *Treatise on Law: the Complete Text*, trans. Alfred J.
Freddoso (South Bend, IN: St. Augustine's Press, 2009).

3   Ibid., q. 100, a. 3, ad 1: "Those two principles [love of God and love of
neighbor] are the first general principles of the natural law, and are self-ev-
ident to human reason, either through nature or through faith." See also q.
99, a.1, ad 2. See also Randall Smith, "What the Old Law Reveals about
the Natural Law According to Thomas Aquinas," *The Thomist* 75 (January,
2011): 114.

4   Ibid., q. 94, a. 2.

5   Ibid., q. 94, a. 3, resp.

6   Ibid., q. 93, a. 3.

naturally known indemonstrable principles."[7] In the same way, "in the case of practical reason, man naturally participates in the eternal law with respect to certain general principles, but not with respect to the particular determination of singular acts, even though the latter are contained within the eternal law. This is why it is necessary for human reason to proceed further to the particular sanctions contained in [human] laws."[8] Human law is nothing other than the practical determination of the natural law, its application.[9] It is the natural law lived socially—that is to say, applied for the common good in a certain time and place.[10] This application for the common good is also, for Thomas, a part of the definition of law itself.[11] This means that the natural law becomes law fully when it is applied and promulgated for a particular people through human law—it must be so "specified," or it remains empty. This makes sense when we again reflect on the definition of natural law as the rational participation of man in divine reason itself and note, as Thomas does, that humans are social and temporal in their very nature. For Thomas, then, mankind, even in paradise, would have had social organization; it would have lived under human law. While necessary to coordinate human action, the human law would have been perfectly congruent both with the natural law and with the reason of each individual, and so, it would not be an imposition, but a guide.[12]

To Thomas, even in paradise, natural law could not be

---

7   Ibid., q. 91, a. 3. See also Ibid., q. 94, a. 4, resp.

8   Ibid., q. 91, a. 3

9   Ibid., q. 95, a. 2, resp.; I-II, q. 93, a. 3, ad 2.

10   Ibid., q. 95, a. 4, resp.; I-II, q. 93, a. 3, resp.

11   Ibid., q. 90 a. 2, ad 3: "Just as nothing stands firm with regard to the speculative reason except that which is traced back to the first indemonstrable principles, so nothing stands firm with regard to the practical reason, unless it be directed to the last end which is the common good: and whatever stands to reason in this sense, has the nature of a law." See also q. 90, a. 4; q. 96, a. 3, resp.

12   A hierarchical division of labor, which included spiritual gifts, was natural to man: ST I, q. 96, a. 3–4; I-II, q. 111, a. 1, sc; a. 4–5; I-II, q. 112, a. 4, resp.; SCG III, ch. 81; *Super eth.* 1, lec.1.

fulfilled without divine help. This is so because man needs divine *auxilium* for every thought and every act, even the most natural. God enlightens man so that he might "see what pertains to natural knowledge."[13] This was God's promulgation of the natural law, promulgation being yet another part of the definition of law.[14] So aided by God, man was naturally capable of loving (*diligere*) God above all things, including himself, and his natural reason directed him to do so.[15] This divine, natural *auxilium*, however, was not the extent of divine involvement with man in paradise. Rather, Thomas tells us, man was the recipient of grace, which elevated his nature and allowed him to "do and wish supernatural good," which was, of course, his proper end. Without grace, mankind was capable of the good of "acquired virtue"—he could love (*diligere*) God and neighbor—but was not capable of the perfect virtue for which he was created, which was "infused virtue"; without grace, he could not perfectly love God and neighbor in Charity (*caritas*).[16] In paradise, however, he was never without this grace. In paradise, man's nature was perfected by grace.

We can see even here, in the garden, that the love of God and neighbor were united in human nature and in that nature's perfection in grace. Sin, however, shattered the foundation for both man's natural and his supernatural abilities.[17] Grace was removed, indeed, but man's natural abilities were also severely

---

[13] ST I-II, q. 109, a. 1–3.

[14] Ibid., q. 90, a. 4.

[15] Ibid., q.109, a.3.

[16] Ibid., q. 109, a. 3; q. 65, a. 2; q. 63, a. 4.

[17] Ibid., q. 109, a. 3, resp.: "Hence in the state of perfect nature man referred the love of himself and of all other things to the love of God as to its end; and thus he loved God more than himself and above all things. But in the state of corrupt nature man falls short of this in the appetite of his rational will, which, unless it is cured by God's grace, follows its private good, on account of the corruption of nature. And hence we must say that in the state of perfect nature man did not need the gift of grace added to his natural endowments, in order to love God above all things naturally, although he needed God's help to move him to it; but in the state of corrupt nature man needs, even for this, the help of grace to heal his nature." See also q. 109, a. 2.

damaged (though not destroyed[18]). Thomas writes:

> But in the state of integrity, as regards the sufficiency
> of the operative power, man by his natural endow-
> ments could wish and do the good proportionate to
> his nature, such as the good of acquired virtue; but not
> surpassing good, as the good of infused virtue. But in
> the state of corrupt nature, man falls short of what he
> could do by his nature, so that he is unable to fulfil it
> by his own natural powers. Yet because human nature
> is not altogether corrupted by sin, so as to be shorn
> of every natural good, even in the state of corrupted
> nature it can, by virtue of its natural endowments,
> work some particular good, as to build dwellings, plant
> vineyards, and the like.[19]

According to Thomas, then, man's ability to perceive, to
understand, and to act according to the natural law, was severely damaged through sin.[20] We here again need to keep in
mind Thomas's expansive understanding of natural law. Man's
natural capabilities to love both God and neighbor, the very
foundation of the natural law and the totality of the moral life,
were dramatically compromised. Indeed, Thomas asserts that
the consequence of original sin was an inborn, inordinate dispo-
sition "arising from the destruction of the harmony which was
essential to original justice." Fallen man consistently (though not
absolutely) replaced natural law in his practical reasoning with
what Aquinas calls the law of the stimulant [to sin], a "inclination toward sensuality." This law functioned as a type of a second
nature, a deeply flawed second nature, that was exaggerated
through actual sin and the construction of vices proper.[21]

---

18 Ibid., q. 85; q. 93, a. 6; q. 94, a. 6.

19 Ibid., q. 109, a. 2, resp.

20 Ibid., q. 93, a. 6, resp.

21 Ibid., q. 91, a. 6; , q. 82, a. 1, ad 4. See also, q. 85, a. 3: "Whatever is irregular
in a work of art, is unnatural to the art which produced that work. Now the
eternal law is compared to the order of human reason, as art to a work of art.

To Thomas, sin damaged severely man's ability to reason properly and act accordingly.[22] The rationality of man—his

---

Therefore it amounts to the same that vice and sin are against the order of human reason, and that they are contrary to the eternal law. Hence Augustine says (*De Lib. Arb.* iii.6) that *every nature, as such, is from God; and is a vicious nature, in so far as it fails from the Divine art whereby it was made.*" ST I-II, q. 71, a. 2: "I answer that, As a result of original justice, the reason had perfect hold over the lower parts of the soul, while reason itself was perfected by God and was subject to Him. Now this same original justice was forfeited through the sin of our first parent, as already stated; so that all the powers of the soul are left, as it were, destitute of their proper order, whereby they are naturally directed to virtue; which destitution is called a wounding of nature. Again, there are four of the soul's powers that can be the subject of virtue, as stated above, viz. the reason, where prudence resides, the will, where justice is, the irascible, the subject of fortitude, and the concupiscible, the subject of temperance. Therefore in so far as the reason is deprived of its order to the true, there is the wound of ignorance; in so far as the will is deprived of the order to the good, there is the wound of malice; in so far as the irascible is deprived of its order to the arduous, there is the wound of weakness; and in so far as the concupiscible is deprived of its order to the delectable, moderated by reason, there is the wound of concupiscence. Accordingly these are the four wounds inflicted on the whole of human nature as a result of our first parent's sin. But since the inclination to the good of virtue is diminished in each individual on account of actual sin, as was explained above, there four wounds are also the result of other sins, in so far as, through sin, the reason is obscured, especially in practical matters, the will hardened to evil, good actions become more difficult, and concupiscence more impetuous."

22 Ibid., q. 91, a. 6; q. 77, a. 2: "Thus, the law for man, which is given by divine ordination according to man's proper condition, is that he should act in accord with reason. This law was, to be sure, so strong in man's initial state that nothing either beyond reason or contrary to reason could take man unawares (*posset subrepere hominem*). But once man turned away from God, he fell into being carried away by the impetus of sensuality and this happens in a particular way to each man the more he recedes from reason, so that he becomes in a certain sense like the beasts, which are carried away by the impetus of sensuality." For a consideration of the distinction between speculative science and cognitive acts, which have always a moral dimension and so are subject to moral habit and directly affected by sin, and the social significance of this distinction, see Gregory M. Reichberg, "Contextualizing Theoretical Reason: Thomas Aquinas and Postmodernity," in *Postmodernism and Christian Philosophy*, ed. Roman T. Ciapalo (Mishawaka, IN: American Maritain Association, 1997), 183–203. See also Thomas Hibbs, "The Fearful Thoughts of Mortals: Aquinas on Conflict, Self-Knowledge, and

participation in the eternal law through the natural law, his natural love of God and neighbor, and his acquired virtue— had been the condition of the human nature that had been elevated through grace in the garden that man might achieve his supernatural end. Through sin, however, man turned away from what was natural to what was unnatural, an act contrary to the eternal law, and so a turning away from reason and a violation of the natural law. And so, both his natural and his supernatural ends lay beyond his reach.[23] Through original sin and the actual sin that follows on its heels, man's will and his intellect lay in tatters. He not only could not do what was right; he did not really know what was right: "the law of nature was destroyed by the law of concupiscence."[24] Thomas writes: "Even the intellect is one of the powers moved by the will. And so a deficiency of the intellect is also included materially in original sin, and this deficiency indeed consists of the lack of the natural knowledge that human beings would have possessed in their original state."[25]

In this condition "human law," such as it was, became law properly speaking only to the extent that the lawgiver acted virtuously despite his fallen nature. He had to both recognize the precepts of the natural law and determine their proper application in a particular situation,[26] and even to the extent that

---

the Virtues of Practical Reasoning," in *Intractable Disputes about the Natural Law: Alasdair MacIntyre and Critics*, ed. Lawrence S. Cunningham (Notre Dame, IN: Notre Dame University Press, 2009), 273–312.

[23] ST I-II, q. 86, a. 1.

[24] *In duo praecepta caritatis*, prol., quoted in Smith, "What the Old Law Reveals," 110.

[25] Thomas Aquinas, *De malo*, q. 4, a. 2, ad 2, in *On Evil*, trans. Richard Regan, ed. Brian Davies (Oxford/New York: Oxford University Press, 2003), 208. See also ST I-II, q. 71, a. 6. I thank my friend Jacob Wood for briefing me on the long-running debate among Thomists concerning whether St. Thomas changed his mind with regard to the relationship between the intellect and the will after the condemnations of 1270. I am taking his undisputed late position as representative of his thought generally and do not thereby intend to argue that he had never held a divergent opinion.

[26] ST I-II, q. 93, a. 1, resp.: "Just as a conception [*ratio*] of the things made

this might be the case, it was experienced as true law (and so in harmony with one's understanding of right) only to the extent that the people subject to it were themselves virtuous despite their fallen nature—a tall order.[27] Rather, man's fallen political and so legal situation was rather complicated. Thomas writes,

> For if the lawmaker's intention is directed toward the true good, i.e., the common good regulated in accord with divine justice, then it follows that through his law men become good absolutely speaking. On the other hand, if the lawmaker's intention is not directed toward the good absolutely speaking, but is instead directed toward a good which is advantageous or pleasant for himself or which is incompatible with divine justice, then his law makes men good not absolutely speaking, but only relatively speaking, viz., in relation to that sort of regime. This is the sense in which the good exists even in things that are per se evil, as when someone is said to be a good thief because he operates in a way that is appropriate for his end.[28]

Man cannot, Aquinas contends, be good in either an absolute or a relative sense without being related in the right way to the common good (again, either absolute or relative).[29] Man's practical reason involves necessarily propositions of law in either its proper or corrupted sense, and law (again, in either sense)

---

through his craft exists beforehand in a craftsman's mind, so too in anyone who governs there must exist beforehand a conception of the ordering of the things to be done by those who are subject to the governor's rule. And just as the conception of the things to be made through a craft is called an artistic conception [ars] or exemplar [exemplar] of the artifacts, so too the conception had by one who governs the acts of his subjects takes on the character of law, given the presence of all the other elements we described above as belonging to the nature of law." See also q. 90, a. 1, ad 3; q. 92, a. 1, ad 3.

[27] Ibid., q. 90, a. 3, ad 1.

[28] Ibid., q.92, a. 1.

[29] Ibid., q.92, a. 1, ad 3.

is intrinsically social. This means man's understanding of what is to be done is tied inextricably to his political community's understanding of what is to be done, of what is "good," and so to the relative legal regime under which he lives.[30]

Regardless of the merits of arguments surrounding the extent to which Aquinas believed proper practical rationality remains theoretically possible for fallen man, one thing that is clear is that in no sense could the natural law in anywhere close to the expansive manner understood by Thomas be fulfilled: the love of God and neighbor and congruency between the virtue of the ruler and that of the ruled were no longer practically possible to fallen man.[31] In this condition, "law" became coercive. Rulers used their power for their own advantage or, even if they used it for the common good, they found their subjects restive and so the objects of force. Human nature was not completely destroyed, however, and man retained a fundamental desire for happiness and an inclination toward reason and virtue, even if much diminished.[32] This incongruency was the root of anxiety and discontent in man concerning his internal condition, his relations with his fellow men, and his relations with God.[33] For Thomas, this was the so-called "nature" in which mankind found himself after the Fall—a thoroughly "unnatural" situation.

For Thomas, God instituted the Old Law, the first stage of the divine law, in order to begin to correct this condition. The Old Law corrected the defect in the knowledge of the natural law and the defect in the ability to apply it through human law. This was an external law focused on the intellect. Thomas writes:

---

[30] Ibid., q. 96, a. 5.

[31] Ibid., q. 109, a. 2–3; I-II, q. 94, a. 2, resp.

[32] Ibid., q. 85, a. 1; I-II, q. 93, a. 6, ad 2.

[33] Thomas Aquinas, *Super Ioan* 14, lec. 7, in *Commentary on the Gospel of John: Chapters 1–21*, trans. Fabian Larcher and James A. Weisheipl (Washington, DC: Catholic University of America Press, 2010).

Therefore, it was fitting for the Old Law to be given at a time appropriate for conquering men's pride. Man is proud with respect to two things, viz., knowledge and power. He is proud with respect to knowledge in the sense that thinking that natural reason can suffice for his salvation. So in order that man's pride on this score might be conquered, he was left to the guidance of his own reason without the support of a written law, and man was able to learn that he suffered from deficiencies of reason—and he learned this from experience, in virtue of the fact that by the time of Abraham men had fallen into idolatry and into the most shameful vices. And so it was necessary for the written Law to be given after that time as a remedy for human ignorance; for as Romans 3:20 says, "The knowledge of sin comes through the Law." But after man had been instructed through the Law, his pride was conquered in his weakness, when he was unable to fulfill the Law which he now knew. And so, as the Apostle concludes in Romans 8:3–4, "What the Law, weakened by the flesh, was powerless to do, this God has done by sending his own Son . . . so that the righteous decree of the law might be fulfilled in us."[34]

The Ten Commandments were the most basic dictates of the natural law. Through them, God re-promulgated a law that before sin had been immediately available to reason.[35] But

---

[34] ST I-II, q. 98, a. 6, resp.

[35] In response to the objection that the Decalogue is incomplete because it does not deal with sins against one's self, Thomas writes: "There are two possible replies to this objection. First, the precepts of the Decalogue are traced back to the precept of love. Now a precept had to be given to man concerning the love of God and neighbor, since in this regard the natural law had been obscured because of sin. By contrast, this was not the case with respect to the love of self, because (a) in this regard the natural law was still alive—or, alternatively, because (b) the love of self is also included in the love of God and neighbor, since it is in ordering himself to God that a man has genuine

the Old Law did not stop with these fundamentals. In fact, Thomas tells us, the totality of the natural law, the entire life in accordance with reason and so with virtue, was contained within the precepts of the Old Law.[36] Through the Old Law, God's promulgation of the natural law internally through the illumination of the human mind and through human reason's contemplation of creation, now compromised by sin, was re-accomplished externally through the revelation of the same law. The precepts of the Law "prohibited all the sins that are contrary to reason" and "made manifest the precepts of the law of nature and added certain precepts of its own."[37] It is revealing that Thomas has no problem extending these precepts of the Law conceptually back to the state of innocence by simply equating them with the precepts of the natural law under which prelapsarain man lived.[38] Indeed, the entire moral life was contained within them: the entire content of the natural law, which had before sin been clear internally, was now clear externally.

However, as mentioned above, the natural law became fully law only when it was specified and determined for a particular people at a particular time and place through human law. The problem after the Fall, of course, was that mankind had lost not only the ability to perceive accurately the content of the natural law but also the ability to understand the implications of that content or how it ought to be applied at a particular time and place.[39] For example, application of the law requires a line of reasoning such as this: fornication is unlawful; this particular

---

love for himself" (ST I-II, q. 100, a. 5, ad 1). See also ST I-II, q. 99, a. 2, ad 2; q. 100, a. 1, resp.; q. 100, a. 11, ad 1.

[36] Ibid., q. 98, a. 1, resp.; I-II, q. 100, a. 2, resp. See also Smith, "What the Old Law Reveals," 95–139.

[37] Ibid., q. 98, a. 1; a. 5.

[38] Ibid., q. 109, a. 4, resp." "And in this way man in the state of perfect nature could fulfill all the commandments of the Law; otherwise he would have been unable to sin in that state, since to sin is nothing else than to transgress the Divine commandments."

[39] Ibid., q. 94, a. 6.

act under consideration constitutes fornication; therefore, this particular act is unlawful.[40] The precepts of the natural law revealed through the Old Law made the first premise again reliably accessible to man. Through what Thomas, following the tradition, refers to as the "judicial precepts" of the Old Law, God revealed to Israel the middle premise, the "relative" specification of the natural law for them at that time, allowing the proper practical conclusion to follow. Thus, God revealed to Israel, through its human leadership, a great deal of what we would otherwise consider to be "human law": the specification of the precepts of the natural law for a particular people.

Indeed, the restoration of friendship between God and man was the primary function of the divine law. However, this friendship, Thomas tells us, could be restored only if man himself was first made good, which is the primary function of human law.[41] And so, *true* "human law" was necessarily contained within the divine law.[42] The community of men under

---

[40] Ibid., q. 77, a. 2.

[41] Ibid., q. 99, a. 2: "I respond: As is clear from Exodus 20:13 and 15 ('You shall not kill . . . You shall not steal'), the Old Law contained certain moral precepts. And this make sense. For just as the main intention of human law is to establish the friendship of men with one another, so too the intention of divine law is mainly to establish man's friendship with God. Nor since, according to Ecclesiasticus 13:19 ('Every beast loves its like'), likeness is a reason for love, it is impossible for there to be friendship between man and God, who is absolutely good, unless men are made good. Hence, Leviticus 19:2 says, 'You will be holy, for I am holy.' But the goodness of a man is virtue, which makes the one who has it good. And so precepts of the Old Law had by all means to be given concerning the acts of the virtues. And these are the moral precepts of the Law." See also q. 92, a. 1.

[42] A persistent problem in the interpretation of Thomas, it seems to me, is the inclination to place the various "laws" that Thomas discusses in parallel rather than in hierarchy. For example, in ST I-II, q.100, a. 2, resp., Thomas explains that "human law is ordered toward the civil community, which is a community of men with respect to each other . . . and so human law proposes precepts having to do only with acts of justice." He continues: "By contrast, the community directed by divine law is the community of men with God, whether in the present life or in the future life." The temptation to set these two laws and so the two communities that they govern side by side must be resisted, however, because Thomas goes on here to explain: "And so divine law sets forth precepts

God remained intrinsically a community of men, and so the law through which they were ordered to God also ordered them to each other.[43] The social life of man was one: "The end of human life and society is God."[44] We might say that the divine law occupied the "space" proper to human law; it fulfilled its function by elevating it beyond itself.[45]

The Old Law also revealed the "ceremonial precepts" which regulated the liturgical life of Israel. These, Thomas tells us, were the specification of that portion of the natural law that had to do with our love of God.[46] The ceremonial precepts were, therefore, the specification of the natural moral law for a particular people as much as were the judicial precepts. We might say that they were both a divinely revealed human law wherein, through God's aid, the leadership of Israel became the perfectly virtuous lawgivers who act always in accordance

---

having to do with all the things through which men are well-ordered toward their common life with God. Now man is joined to God by his reason, or mind, in which the image of God resides. And so divine law sets forth precepts having to do with all the things through which man's reason is well-ordered. But this ordering occurs through the acts of all the virtues; for the intellectual virtues render acts of reason well-ordered in themselves, whereas the moral virtues render the acts of reason well-ordered with respect to interior passions and exterior operations. And so it is clearly fitting for divine law to set forth precepts having to do with the acts of all the virtues." All of the "natural law" and all of the "human law" that governed justice are, to Thomas, integral to the divine law: they are in hierarchy, not in parallel.

[43] ST I-II, q. 100, a. 5, resp.: "As was explained above, just as the precepts of human law order man toward the human community, so the precepts of divine law order a man toward a sort of community or republic of men under God. Now in order for someone to live a good life in a community, two things are required. The first is that he behave well toward the one who presides over the community, and the second is that the man behave well toward the others who are his companions and co-participants in the community. Therefore, divine law must first lay down some precepts ordering a man toward God and, second, it must lay down other precepts ordering a man toward those others who are living together with him as neighbors under God."

[44] Ibid., q. 100, a. 6, resp.

[45] Ibid., q. 91, a. 5; q. 98, a. 1, 5; q. 99, a. 2, 4; q. 100, a. 2; q. 101, a. 2, 3; q. 103, a. 1.

[46] Ibid., q. 101, a. 1, resp.; q. 104, a. 1, resp.

with the natural law.[47] Within the divine law, then, a clear line
between the (just) laws of man and the laws of God is lacking:
God works through man to enact just human law.[48] Thomas
writes: "Law is ordered toward the common good as its end.
But there are two kinds of common good. The first is a sensible and earthly good, and it is to this sort of good that the Old
Law directly ordered [the people]."[49]

The Old Law restored to the people of Israel access to the
content of the natural law, both in principle and in specific
application. Through it, they knew how to live externally in
accordance with the eternal law and were habituated to do so.[50]
When Thomas offers us examples of "natural" government, it
is, therefore, often to Israel that he reaches, and it is in Thomas's treatment of the Old Law that he makes extensive use of
Aristotle's *Politics* and within which he situates his consideration of the best regime, pointing out Israel as an example.[51]
Without the grace that elevated human nature into the perfection of infused virtue, Israel under the Old Law was the closest
man ever came to living in a "natural" regime: he had access to

---

[47] Ibid., q. 99, a. 4, resp.: "I respond: As has been explained, it is the function
of divine law to order men to one another and to God. Both of these functions belong in a general way to the dictates of the law of nature, which the
moral precepts are concerned with, but both must be specified by divine law
or human law. For in speculative matters as well as in practical matters the
naturally known principles are general. Therefore, just as the specification of
the general precept regarding divine worship is accomplished through the
ceremonial precepts, so too the specification of the general precept of justice
that must be observed among men is specified through the judicial precepts.
Accordingly, one must posit three types of precepts in the Old Law, viz., (a)
the moral precepts, which have to do with the dictates of the law of nature,
(b) the ceremonial precepts, which are specifications of divine worship, and
(c) the judicial precepts, which are specifications of the justice that is to be
observed among men." See also q. 91, a. 5, ad 1 and ad 3; q. 98, a. 5, resp.; q.
99, a. 2, ad 2; q. 99, a. 3; q. 100, a. 3, resp.; q. 100, a. 8, resp., ad 3; q. 100, a.
11, resp.

[48] Ibid., q. 103, a. 1, resp.; q. 104, a. 1, resp.

[49] Ibid., q. 91, a. 5, resp.

[50] Ibid., q. 92, a. 1, ad 1–2.

[51] Ibid., q. 105, a. 1, resp.

the natural law and its specification, but without sanctifying grace. It was a "written" law of words and punishments, a law aimed at "a sensible and earthly good."[52] Thomas points out the very naturalness of the Old Law when he argues that there is no reason that a king outside Israel could not, in theory, adopt it for his people, even though it was unlikely to be a perfect fit, each people needing, of course, to have the natural law specified for their particularities.[53]

The Old Law, then, was primarily a "correction" of the deficiencies of fallen man. In it, Thomas tells us, there was real faith. Faith, to Thomas, was a preamble to perfection in Charity, and Faith itself transitioned from a "lifeless" to a "living" Faith to the extent that it was worked in Charity.[54] This was so in the life of the individual believer, in the life of the Church, and in the biblical narrative of salvation history. God first gave mankind knowledge, the "what" he is to believe and the "what" he is to do.[55] But, to Thomas, the Old Law was always pointing beyond itself to its fulfillment in Christ and the grace of the New Law.[56] Indeed, while the Old Law may have "restored" knowledge of the natural law, it did not restore the ability of mankind to fulfill that law: "A man cannot observe all the precepts of the Law unless he fulfills the precept of Charity, which cannot be done without grace. And so, what Pelagius claimed is impossible."[57] Even under the Old Law, some sort of "first

---

[52] Ibid., q. 91, a. 5.

[53] Ibid., q. 104, a. 3, resp.; ad 1–2; q. 105, a. 2, resp. Thomas compares the relationship between Israel and the Gentiles under the Old Law to that between clerics and the laity under the New Law. Israel had access to the natural law in a more perfect way than did the Gentiles in a way similar to that in which clergy and religious lived a more perfect form of the Christian life. The point, though, is that like the Gentiles, Israel under the Old Law remained subject to the natural law, though more perfectly known. Likewise, the clergy live a more perfect life under the New Law, but both they and the laity can achieve salvation through grace (see ST I-II, q. 98, a. 2, resp. and ad 3).

[54] ST II-II, q. 4, a. 4.

[55] Smith, "What the Old Law Reveals," 120.

[56] ST I-II, q. 98, a. 2, resp.; q. 101–02.

[57] Ibid., q. 100, a. 10, ad 3.

things" community remained impossible. This, to Thomas, required the New Law of grace.

As we have seen, the Old Law was an external law focused primarily on the intellect. The New Law, however, was an internal law focused on the will, a law that presupposes the restored, in faith, knowledge of the natural law. Thomas writes thus: "As the father of a family issues different commands to the children and to the adults, so also the one King, God, in His one kingdom, gave one law to men, while they were yet imperfect, and another more perfect law, when, by the preceding law, they had been led to a greater capacity for Divine things."[58] Within the New Law, then, human nature was redeemed, becoming once again itself and most fully "natural," even as grace elevated it past itself to its supernatural end.[59] "In this way the New Law is instilled into man, not only by indicating to him what he should do, but also by helping him to accomplish it."[60]

Indeed, the New Law was the fulfillment of law itself, but in being so it went beyond law. Thomas begins his treatise on law by distinguishing clearly between the two means by which God is the exterior principle of human action: his law, which instructs, and his grace, which assists.[61] After treating the various forms of law in depth, Aquinas ends the treatise with a treatment of the fulfillment of law in the New Law, which he defines ultimately as grace itself.[62] Law is fulfilled as it becomes something beyond its reach. (The treatise on law is followed immediately by the treatise on grace.) This is the logic of salvation, the logic of the Bible itself: the literal sense of Scripture anticipated its meaning in the allegorical, but both the literal and the allegorical were "intellectual" senses that were pointing toward their fulfillment in the interiorized tropological or moral sense, which concerned the will, leading

---

[58] Ibid., q. 91, a. 5, ad 1.

[59] Ibid., q. 91, a. 5.

[60] Ibid., q. 106, a. 1, ad 2.

[61] Ibid., q.90, prologue

[62] Ibid., q. 106, a. 1

it to the New Law of Charity, and so to the anagogical sense, which as perfect contemplation of God himself, was both the fulfillment of Scripture and its surpassing.[63]

For Thomas, then, the Old Law in and of itself was para-digmatic of law properly understood. It was rational: Thomas goes to great length to show the reasons for the precepts of the Law.[64] It was social, being directed definitively toward the common good and the right ordering of man to man and man to God.[65] It was given and promulgated by proper authori-ty.[66] It was coercive (an often overlooked aspect of Thomas's definitions of law).[67] It was external, dealing in and of itself with acts and things and written on stone tablets rather than the tablet of the heart.[68] And finally, it instructed rather than assisted.[69] Starting from this paradigmatic law, certain aspects of its definition can be seen in Thomas's work to become more difficult to apply in both the direction of the ideal natural law and in the direction of the graced New Law. The content of the natural law was, of course, clearly brought up into and sur-passed in the Old Law, and similarly the Old Law anticipated its own "surpassing" in the New Law through its thorough and essential figuration of the Incarnation.[70] Law, then, appears suspended; it appears in its nature to be transitory, reaching back to nature and forward to grace.[71]

In the garden, man's nature had been perfected in Charity through grace. His acquired virtue was a continuous prepa-ration for his constant reception of infused virtue, which was perfect virtue, disposing him to his true and final good. To

---

[63] ST I, q. 12; Supplementum. q. 92, a. 1; II-II q.175, a. 4; I-II, q. 106, a. 4, ad 1.

[64] ST I-II, q. 90, a. 1; q. 102; q. 105; q. 98, a. 1; q. 98, a. 2, ad 2.

[65] Ibid., q. 90, a. 2; q. 91, a. 5; q. 96, a. 1; q. 98, a. 1, 5; q. 99, a. 2, 4; q. 100, a. 2; q. 101, a. 2, 3; q. 103, a. 1; q. 101, a. 1, resp.; q. 104, a. 1, resp.

[66] Ibid., q. 95, a. 1; q. 90, a. 5, 6; q. 98 a. 2, 3.

[67] Ibid., q. 95, a. 1; q. 96, a. 5.

[68] Ibid., q. 91, a. 5; q. 101, a. 2; q. 106, a. 2, ad 3; q. 107, a. 1, ad 2, 3.

[69] Ibid., q. 103, a. 2, 3.

[70] Ibid., q. 98, a. 2; q. 99, a. 2, 3; q. 100; q. 102, a. 5; q. 104, a. 2; q. 107, a. 3.

[71] Ibid., q. 98, a. 6.

Thomas, the New Law fulfilled the Old Law in the same manner. The external promulgation of the natural law, along with God's ever-accelerating revelation of who he was and of his plans through the Son, prepared Israel for the reception of Christ and so for the full internalization of the Law in Charity. The New Law was, therefore, essentially, nothing else than the grace of the Holy Spirit that restored in "natural" men the Charity (which included ultimately true Faith and Hope) that supernatural friendship (and so, true peace) with God and neighbor required.[72] Perfect peace was, of course, salvation, the condition of the kingdom of God itself, which was the true and perfect society of the saints that, through the grace of the New Law, spilled over from heaven to earth. Peace was simple happiness, when all unrest was alleviated through the beatific vision, and through the New Law it was approached through Faith, Hope, and Charity. Faith united the intellects of men with each other and with God. Hope united all men in the pursuit of God, and Charity (which ultimately included both Faith and Hope) united all human will and action and directed them through the love of God. The peace of society, if it was to be a true and not simply an exterior peace, was a unity wrought through these virtues, horizontally and vertically; it was friendship between men and between men and God.[73] This means that true friendship in peace, both vertical and horizontal, was possible only through grace, especially that grace made available in the sacraments, because Faith, Hope, and Charity, along with all the minor virtues that worked in their service, were infused virtues.[74]

Charity was the perfection of the will in virtue, a perfection that carried with it the perfection of faith, transforming it from the lifeless faith proper to the Old into the living Faith

---

[72] Ibid., q. 106, a. 1, resp.

[73] ST II-II, q. 29; *Super Ioan* 14, lec. 7; SCG IV, ch. 50; ST I-II, q. 1, a. 5.

[74] ST I-II, q. 114, a. 2; II-II, q. 29, a. 3; *Super III sent.*, d. 23, q.1, a. 4 (Parma ed., 1858); ST I-II, q. 65, a. 3, resp.

of the New. It was perfect friendship with God.[75] In the New
Law, then, both the intellect and the will were perfected. There
was no aspect, no rightly ordered "department" of human life,
no sphere of the merely "natural," that somehow fell outside this
peace, that was not governed by the New Law. To Thomas, the
divine law was the natural law fulfilled and surpassed, moving
toward perfection, through revelation and grace, first externally in the people of Israel and then internally in the Church
of the New Law.[76] The Old Law was perfected in the New
Law, with the exteriorized precepts becoming perfected in the
interiorized Law of Charity in the same manner in which a boy
is perfected in becoming a man, with all that he was, without
remainder, "growing up" into manhood.[77] The total content of
the natural law was, therefore, perfected within the New Law.
It was made known through Faith and the right reason that it
supported, and it was interiorized and lived through Charity.
And so, Thomas follows the bulk of medieval legal tradition
in seeing the natural law ultimately as fully within the divine
law. As Gratian stated simply, "natural law is what is contained
in the Law and the Gospel."[78] The love of God and neighbor,
the fundamental content of the natural law, was, of course,

---

[75] ST I-II, q. 66, a. 5.

[76] Ibid., q. 107, a. 2, resp.

[77] See Gal 3:24–25; ST I-II, q. 91, a. 5; q. 98, a. 1, resp.; q. 99, a. 6, resp.; q. 106,
a. 3, resp.

[78] The first passage in the first distinction of Gratian's *Decretum* reads simply:
"The human race is ruled by two things, namely natural law and usages.
Natural law is what is contained in the Law and the Gospel. By it, each
person is commanded to do to others what he wants done to himself and
prohibited from inflicting on others what he does not want done to himself.
So Christ said in the Gospel: 'Whatever you want men to do to you, do so
to them. This indeed is the Law and the Prophets.'" Aquinas comments on
Gratian: "This passage should not be understood to mean that all the things
contained in the Law and the Gospel belong to the law of nature. For many
things set forth in the Law and the Gospel go beyond nature. Rather, the
passage means that what belongs to the law of nature is found more fully in
the Law and the Gospel" (ST I-II, q. 94, a. 4, ad 1). Similarly, as Aquinas
notes, "Augustine (*De Lib. Arb.* i.6) distinguishes two kinds of law, the one
eternal, the other temporal, which he calls human" (ST I-II, q. 91, a. 3, sc).

Christ's summation of the content of the divine law.[79] From within this line of thought, then, the grace that is required to both know and live the natural law is available only through the New Law: the only perfectly "natural" regime is a perfectly Christian regime—that is to say, the Church.[80] However, such a regime would, in fact, remain "legal" only to the extent that it was still coming into being. For, as we have seen, the New Law was properly grace itself, the fulfillment of law, and the perfect life under the New Law was a life of perfect Charity, the life of the Church triumphant, a life devoid of exterior law.

Under the reign of the New Law coming into being in time, however, the law would have to be specified for a particular time and place and for a particular people. As we have seen, under the Old Law this function was fulfilled by the judicial and ceremonial precepts. Under the New Law, because the grace of the Holy Spirit made true virtue once again possible, this function was at least partially returned to men, men now living in a state of grace, and so living the theological virtues.[81]

Those subject to those rulers, to the extent that they too achieved virtue, would perceive the human specification of the New Law not as an imposition, but as guidance and coordination in the construction of the society of peace, of the very

---

[79] Luke 10:26–28.

[80] ST II-II, q. 2, a. 5, ad 1: "If we understand those things alone to be in a man's power, which we can do without the help of grace, then we are bound to do many things which we cannot do without the aid of healing grace, such as to love God and our neighbor, and likewise to believe the articles of faith. But with the help of grace we can do this, for this help to 'whomsoever it is given from above it is mercifully given; and from whom it is withheld it is justly withheld, as a punishment of a previous, or at least of original sin,' as Augustine states." John Milbank writes of Thomas's thought: "The political, to be more fully its original paradisal self, must exceed itself through gradual entire inclusion within the ecclesial" (*Beyond Secular Order*, 246).

[81] Thomas's prince in his treatise *De regno* is a Christian of near perfect virtue. As regards the "ceremonial" precepts of the New Law, ST I-II, q. 107, a. 4 comments thus: "The teaching of Christ and the apostles added few precepts to those of the natural law; although afterwards some were added, through being instituted by the Holy Fathers." Human law within the New Law was, to Thomas, saintly law. See also ST I-II, q. 108, a. 1, 2.

kingdom of God, a construction that they understood to be the basis of their vocations and perfectly congruent with their understanding of the law.[82] As in paradise and under the Old Law, the love of God and the love of neighbor remained united in a single law, now the participation of the rational soul in the eternal law, perfected beyond itself through grace. Both the love of God and the love of neighbor were the object of this law, which was specified through both spiritual and temporal power to form a single "government." The alternative to the "government" of the interiorized New Law was, therefore, not the natural law simply, but first the government of the exteriorized law—this is the "government" of just human judgment possible through grace, government that no longer included the particular precepts of the Old Law, but did now include the particular precepts made by the virtuous spiritual and temporal lawgivers[83]—and failing that, the government possible to fallen nature without grace, that government possible through defective reason and the exteriorized rule of fear, a topic explored much more fully below.

Thirteenth-century France was, in the ideal, a society at peace, governed through the New Law. Throughout this book we have seen that peace was the goal of ecclesiastical and secular action, the goal toward which all earthly power rightly strove.[84] We can see how the networks of *consilium et auxilium*, of counsel and aid, that provided the real structure of government fit into this vision. They were, in the ideal, nothing short of groupings of friends who made each other's interests

---

[82] ST I-II, q. 107, a. 1.

[83] Ibid., q. 91, a. 4; q. 106, a. 1, resp.: "Still, the New Law contains certain elements that dispose us toward the grace of the Holy Spirit and certain elements that have to do with the use of that grace. These elements are, as it were, secondary aspects of the New Law, about which those who believe in Christ have to be instructed, through both the spoken word and the written word, regarding what they ought to believe and what they ought to do. And so one should reply that the New Law is in the first instance an instilled law, but that, secondarily it is a written law."

[84] *De regno* 1.2.

their own in Charity. What is more, they were animated with a sense of justice, an orthodoxy that united their members in Faith. Because they were groupings of fallen men in history, in truth, this charity and this faith remained relative—only approaching Charity and Faith proper to the extent that their members approached true virtue. Conflicts, therefore, occurred between these networks, and peace occurred not when they made a treaty or formed an alliance, but when the networks merged into each other. The network of the king, which grew to include the papacy under Urban IV and especially under Clement IV, sought to incorporate all of the kingdom into its circle of friends. This was how it made peace. This dynamic was clearly demonstrated in Gui's rise through the hierarchy, as well as in his and Louis's opposition to the "false peace" imposed upon the king of England, and we saw the principle perfected in the college of cardinals when they asserted themselves to be of one body and one will with the pope. The ideal kingdom, the kingdom of peace, was a kingdom of true friendship between man and man and between man and God.[85] This ideal kingdom, if it could be achieved, would be nothing short of the very kingdom of God, the Catholic Church, understood in the broadest sense possible.

The peace of the New Law included wholly both temporal organization and supernatural virtue through grace, and so, in the ideal, all humanity in all of its activities, spiritual and temporal, would find peace under the Law of Christ.[86] This

---

[85] *De regno* 1.10; ST I-II, q. 105, a. 2; q. 106, a. 4, ad 4.

[86] The acquired moral virtues, for example, were brought up into and fulfilled in the theological virtues as infused virtues: "All the moral virtues are infused together with charity. The reason for this is that God operates no less perfectly in works of grace than in works of nature" (ST I-II, q. 65, a. 3, resp.). These infused moral virtues were virtue simply and perfectly: "It is therefore clear from what has been said that only the infused virtues are perfect, and deserve to be called virtues simply: since they direct man well to the ultimate end. But the other virtues, those, namely, that are acquired, are virtue in a restricted sense, but not simply. . . . Hence a gloss of Augustine on the words, 'All that is not of faith is sin (Rom 14:23),' says: 'He that fails to acknowledge the truth, has not true virtue, even if his conduct be good'" (ST I-II, q. 65, a.

was a peace rooted in differentiation, both that of specialization and hierarchy and that of Charity through gift, and it was relational in its very foundation. We saw this understanding of peace manifested clearly on a sometimes microscale in our treatment of Parlement, which sought always to find the stable difference between parties, to find the peace rooted in differentiation that had been shattered and to reinstitute it. We also saw how this peace intrinsically included the spiritual and the temporal powers.

The equally spiritual and temporal nature of peace lets us see again the networks of *consilium et auxilium* and better understand why they cut across lines between clergy and laymen, why they were always conglomerations of spiritual and temporal powers. Peace required both powers, though in different ways. In true peace, the spiritual power would be active in the sense that it was the conduit through which grace flowed into society. The temporal power was active in the sense that it provided organization and direction to the grace-filled community as it satisfied the necessities of life. Of course, in true peace the New Law would be completely interiorized, and so even the threat of the sword would be out of place.[87] In the ideal of true peace, both the spiritual and temporal powers were essential, but neither the spiritual nor the temporal sword would function.[88] This is why the use of the sword was not the principle of order in this society, why it was a reaction to the loss of peace, something capable of restoring only exterior peace and so something transitory, preparatory for the Gospel, as the Old Law was preparatory for the New.

Under the reign of true peace, any sort of hard distinction

---

2). See also I-II, q. 63, a. 4.

[87] ST I-II, q.96, a. 3, ad 2.

[88] Ibid., q. 96, a. 5, resp.: "Someone is said to be subject to the law in the way that what is coerced is subject to what is doing the coercing. In this sense it is only bad men, and not virtuous and just men, who are subject to the law. For what is coerced and violent is contrary to one's will. And the will of good men is consonant with the law, whereas the will of bad men disagrees with the laws. Hence, in this respect only bad men, and not good men, are under the law."

between the spiritual and temporal powers tended to fade, collapsing entirely in the perfect peace of heaven. This is so because they "emerged" as distinct, social powers only within the context of the decidedly non-ideal reality of a fallen world in pursuit of its salvation. As was mentioned above, the New Law was first and foremost grace itself, which guided human action toward peace. However, it also had positive, "written" content.[89] The specification of this divine law by human law was a development within (or, in a hierarchical sense, below) the New Law and not alongside it, and it was with regard to such human law that the spiritual and temporal powers distinctly emerged.

But they did so as different legislators specifying in particular law the same body of general law, not as sources of distinct law codes.[90] The temporal power specified divine law,[91] and the spiritual power specified the same. Both the king and the bishop, each in their own way, were to the people of God what the "soul" was to the "body," or even what God was to all of creation (and a body has only one soul and the universe only one God).[92] We can see here how it was that the law created by St. Louis and the law created by the bishops and the papacy were not sealed off from each other. Instead, they emerged from the same sources and aimed at the same goals, different

---

[89] Ibid., q. 106, a. 1, resp.

[90] For example, Thomas writes in ST I-II, q. 95, a. 4, resp.: "Second, it is part of the definition of human law that human law is ordered toward the common good of the community. Accordingly, human law can be divided by the diversity of roles played by those who work specifically for the common good—e.g., priests, who pray to God on behalf of the people; rulers, who govern the people; and soldiers, who fight for the safety of the people. And so special laws are adapted to these men as such."

[91] *De regno* 1.15: "A king then, being instructed in the divine law, must occupy himself particularly with directing the community subject to him to the good life." The Dominican Vincent of Beauvais wrote to St. Louis: "Moreover, a prince's laws and statutes cannot be correctly made unless they are based on divine law, divinely written in sacred books" (*The Moral Instruction of a Prince*, 61).

[92] *De regno* 1.9; 1.12–13; ST I-II, q. 93, a. 5 resp.; I-II, q. 100, a. 8, ad 3.

manifestations of the single Law of God.[93] And it is simply impossible in actual fact for us to sort the contents of the civil/ feudal law simply into the category of specified natural law, just as it is impossible for us to sort the contents of the canon law into the category of specified divine juridical or ceremonial precepts. This was true, as we have seen, of the inquisitors and *enquêteurs*, of the functioning of the temporal and spiritual in Parlement, of Louis's treatment of the situation in England, and clearly in the making of canon law surrounding the status of legates during a vacant Holy See.

Thomas explains that the New Law directly prohibits or commands only "acts through which grace is introduced or acts which necessarily involve the correct use of grace."[94] The seven sacraments were instituted by Christ himself "because we are able to obtain grace only through Christ and not on our own," but the correct use of grace occurs through the works of Charity: "In so far as such works have a necessary connection with virtue, they pertain to the moral precepts, which were also handed down in the Old Law. Hence, on this score, it was not appropriate for the New Law to add anything to the Old Law with respect to exterior acts." However, specification of these precepts through both the ceremonial and the judicial precepts of the Old Law were "not themselves necessarily connected with interior grace." And so, under the New Law, they are "left up to human discretion. Some of these specifications are left up to the lower ranks and have to do with each individual taken one by one, whereas others are left up to temporal or spiritual authorities [ad praelatos temporales vel spirituales] and have to do with the common welfare."[95]

We can see here the legal "empty space" that was revealed in our treatment of Parlement. Christians "specified" the law of Charity amongst themselves through the mechanisms of "possession," "use," and "custom." This was how the "whole mul-

---

[93] ST I-II, q. 91.
[94] ST I-II, q. 108, a. 2, resp.
[95] Ibid.

titude," who to Thomas was the foundational human lawgiver, "legislated."[96] When they lived at peace they lived in the New Law and they lived in liberty under their own non-coercive "human law," such as it was. The spiritual and temporal powers, who "habet curam" for the multitude, intervened only when the particular peace of a time and place was upset.[97] What is more, we see that, to Thomas, spiritual and temporal legal authorities are both concerned with both judicial and ceremonial precepts, the specification of the natural law, within the New Law.[98]

For Aquinas, the law created by the spiritual and temporal powers in practice was not, however, simply the specifying law of a perfectly peaceful society under the New Law—a law that would be only instructional for an already virtuous people. Rather, it was constructed in a sinful world in need of conversion, a world that had to be brought to virtue and converted to true peace. It was not that people in the realm of sin did not want peace, which was nothing short of the fulfillment of all desire. Of course they did. It was that without virtue the only personal peace possible was that of fleeting pleasures and the only social peace possible was that provided by contracts for mutual gain or by force or the fear of force.[99] This was an exterior peace. Outside of the grace of the New Law, even the knowledge of what was right, of what God demanded of mankind, as was the case under the Old Law in of itself, was the source not of peace, but rather of anxiety and fear.[100] As

---

[96] Ibid., q. 90, a. 3.

[97] See Ibid.

[98] Ibid., q. 108, a. 2, ad 4: "Likewise, the judicial precepts, considered in themselves, have a necessary connection with virtue only with respect to the general nature of justice and not with respect to the particular specifications. And so our Lord left it up to those who were going to have spiritual or temporal care of others to specify the judicial precepts. However, as will be noted below, He did explain certain of the judicial precepts of the Old Law because of the Pharisees' defective interpretations of them." See also q. 108, a. 3, ad 3.

[99] ST II-II, q. 29, a. 2.

[100] See, for example, Hugh of St. Victor, *De Sacramentis*, II.2.2.

we have seen, the divine law had two stages—the Old and the
New, external and internal, Faith and Charity—two stages
that corresponded to the stages of mankind's return to God.
But, it was one divine law, and the New Law was its perfect
manifestation.[101] This means that the New Law fulfilled the
"exterior" functions of the Old Law in the ongoing dynamic
of salvation, though now in a manner capable of completion
internally in grace. Thomas writes that aside from the grace of
the Holy Spirit:

> The other element involves the Law of the Gospel
> in a secondary way, viz., the documents of the faith
> and the precepts that direct human affections and
> human actions. On this score, the New Law does not
> confer justification. Hence, in 2 Corinthians 3:6 the
> Apostle says, "The letter kills, but the spirit gives life."
> In *De Spiritu et Littera* Augustine explains that by
> "the letter" is meant any writing that exists exterior to
> men, even the writing of the moral precepts contained
> in the Gospel. Hence, even the letter of the Gospel
> kills unless the healing grace of faith is inwardly
> present.[102]

The precepts of the natural law, the moral precepts, all that
involved reason and virtue (which had been fully contained in
the specifications of the Old Law), remained contained in the
New Law, and their exterior enforcement remained the divine
mandate.[103] In a sense all the Old Law was preserved in the ex-

---

[101] ST I-II, q. 107, a. 1, resp.

[102] Ibid., q. 106, a. 2, resp.

[103] Ibid., q. 108, a. 1, ad 1: "The kingdom of God consists principally in interior
acts, but, as a result, all the things without which interior acts cannot exist
are likewise relevant to the kingdom of God. For instance, if the kingdom of
God is interior justice and peace and spiritual joy, then all the exterior acts
which are incompatible with justice or peace or spiritual joy must be incompatible with the kingdom of God. And so all such acts have to be forbidden
in the kingdom of God." See also q. 103, a. 3, ad 1; q. 107, a. 2, ad 1.

ternals of the New Law, in "deeds, moral and sacramental," and these externals retained the Old Law's character by pointing beyond themselves to their fulfillment in grace.[104] Within the Church, the peace that was possible outside sacramental grace, then, was at best the peace possible under the externalized law of the Gospel. Outside the Church, at its best, the peace that was possible was that through unhealed and unperfected nature's ability to understand the natural law, to specify it through human law, and to obey that law in virtue—the peace of the so-called "virtuous" Gentiles, which, as we have seen, was extremely limited, if not simply impossible. At its worse, in the realm of sin, peace was found only as the relative peace of tyranny. The problem faced by the spiritual and temporal powers in the Church was that the realm of perfected nature and the true, interior peace it proposed was everywhere and always (even in the heart of the individual Christian) intermingled with the realm of fallen nature and the exterior peace it proposed.

The spiritual and temporal powers' project was to bring people to interior peace, to life under the New Law. When they worked in the realm of sin, the powers became swords and inverted from their relationship in the realm of peace and virtue. Within the realm of sin, those who wielded the swords, because they were mere men, judged only the externals of human action and acted externally to affect such action.[105] In the realm of virtue, the spiritual power acted positively to convey grace and to make revelation present in sacred preaching. In the realm of sin, this grace was cut off both by the action of the sinner and by the positive action of the priesthood, most clearly through the sword of excommunication. In the realm of virtue, the temporal power provided guidance and the organization necessary to build a society of Charity, but there was no use for a sword. In the realm of sin, however, the positive action of the sword emerged as that which forged

---

[104] Ibid., q. 107, a. 1, ad 3.
[105] Ibid., q. 100, a. 9, resp.; q. 105, a .2, ad 7; q. 107, a. 1.

an exterior peace, the "peace" possible under the exteriorized Law, the peace which reigned under the Old Law in of itself. It was as they operated in the realm of sin that the most pronounced distinctions between the temporal and spiritual powers emerged: they became most clearly two powers when they were the two swords. What is more, we can see clearly how the patristic and monastic tradition of understanding the two swords as the Old and the New Testaments and the later tradition of understanding them as the temporal and spiritual powers where profoundly compatible interpretations that operated within the same fundamental schema.

Against the violence of sin, the temporal power was that authority that used force, and the spiritual power was that authority that invited the sinner back to the realm of true peace, that preached penance and offered mercy and so a return to grace through the sacraments. The dynamic was one in which the spiritual sword sought to scare the sinner back into the realm of grace before he really left it. Excommunication was first medicinal, and if there was any faith left in the sinner, being positively cut off from the grace of the sacraments would force him to seek absolution and so reunion with the society of peace. If this failed, if the mortal sinner or excommunicate accepted a life without grace, the temporal sword would be deployed to frighten or force him into accepting a worldly peace. This exterior peace not only protected the society of true peace from the violent but also created in the sinner habits that were conducive to acquired virtue and conversion, and it was the space within which the spiritual power sought conversions back to, first, a sort of faith and so subjection to the divine law (as had been the case under the Old Law), and then to Charity through grace and so freedom and true peace.[106]

Law (both civil and canon), in the judicial sense in which we are most used to understanding it, was what governed the transition between the conditions, the movement from simple fallen nature to the Law and through the Law to freedom.

---

[106] ST II-II, q. 29, a. 3, ad 3; I-II, q. 92, a. 2, ad 4; q. 95, a. 1.

Those in the state of sin were subject to the law through fear and force, and those with the beginnings of faith were subject to the law through their intellect, but it was a law properly administered by those in a state of grace, and their purpose was to bring the sinner out of both forms of subjection and into Charity.[107] This was a move that required the sacraments and so a law that dictated when and how they were to be administered. We can see how appropriate it was, then, that canon law grew up as an extension of penitential practice and why law books such as Gratian's *Decretum* spent so much time discussing the confessional. The regulation of the availability of the sacraments to a fallen world was the true content of positive canon law. This helps us understand Gui's treatment of the inquisitors as primarily confessors and their sentences as really penances.

The temporal power sought to build a society of virtue, a task that included education, good counsel, leadership, discipline (including the use of force), and protection from outside threats. The object of human society, Aquinas tells us, was precisely such a virtuous life, but the spiritual power was necessary for the achievement of this object because, as we have seen, true virtue was not possible without grace—if it were otherwise, kings would stand alone in their governance of society.[108] What is more, the end of human society was not simply the life of virtue, but rather, through it, to achieve the enjoyment of God, the beatific vision, which was perfect peace.[109] This required the grace of the sacraments and the knowledge of divine revelation, both given by the spiritual power. The royal and the priestly were therefore distinct but united in a single endeavor that was rooted in the united kingship and priesthood of Christ himself. The spiritual power was "higher" than the temporal

---

[107] ST I-II, q. 92, a. 1, ad 1–2; q. 93, a. 6; q. 99, a. 6, resp. and ad 1; q. 101, a. 3, resp.

[108] *De regno* 1.14

[109] ST I-II, q. 109, a. 2, resp.; a. 4, resp.; a. 6, resp.; a. 9, sc; a. 10, sc; II-II, q. 29, a. 4 sc.

power not because the rule of the temporal world of virtue was a delegation from the spiritual power, but because the temporal world was brought up and into true peace through the spiritual power: the temporal world achieved its end through the gifts of the spiritual power, and the spiritual in man, his soul, was higher in the microcosm of himself than was the temporal, his body.[110] Because man was both body and soul, the achievement of his end was both temporal and spiritual, but this did not make the division of spiritual and temporal concerns between different groups of men strictly speaking necessary. Such a division was rather a matter of divinely sanctioned fittingness, a fittingness that corresponded to the narrative of salvation history and the hierarchical structure of the universe and man's condition within it.[111]

It was fitting that the priests, who invited men to sacramental grace, should stand "above" the realm of sin, should

---

[110] *De regno* 1.14–15; ST II-II, q. 60, a. 6, ad 3; I-II, q. 147, a.3.

[111] *De regno* 1.15, 1.9: "So we read in the prophecy of Zacharias (ch. 12) that in the day of blessedness, when the Lord shall be the protector of those who dwell in Jerusalem—that is, in the vision of eternal peace—all houses shall be like to the house of David; for all will be kings, and will reign with Christ, as the members with the head. But the house of David will be like to the house of God because by wise government he faithfully carried out a divine task towards his people; and as a reward he will be nearer to God and joined to Him." In his most direct statement concerning the power of the papacy, Aquinas directly treats the pope as a man who is both king and priest, writing in *Super II sent.*, d. 44. Q. 3, a. 4: "Both the spiritual and the secular power derive from the divine power; consequently the secular power is subject to the spiritual only to the extent that this is so ordered by God; namely, in those matters which pertain to the salvation of the soul. And in these matters the spiritual power is to be obeyed before the temporal. In those matters, however, which concern the civil good, the secular power should be obeyed rather than the spiritual, according to what we are told in St. Matthew 'Render to Caesar the things that are Caesar's.' Unless, of course, the spiritual power and the secular power are conjoined, as in the pope, whose power is supreme in both, namely the spiritual and the secular, through the dispensation of Him Who is both priest and king; a Priest forever according to the order of Melchizedek, the King of kings and Lord of lords, Whose power shall not fail and whose dominion shall not pass away to all eternity. Amen."

stand within the true peace of the Gospel. The priest's sword of excommunication was wielded, it should be noted, not in the realm of sin, but at its very brink: it was wielded always against those who were still potentially within sacramental unity— excommunication was meaningless against the infidel. It was fitting that the priests, who had special access to revelation, should interact with the realm of sin primarily as preachers, trying to bring the sinner to some sort of faith and to the grace of the sacraments through which Charity was found. And it was fitting that the portion of the specified New Law that they administered, the canon law, was principally concerned with when and how grace could be poured out.

On the other hand, it was fitting that those Christians who wielded the temporal sword were also those who married and raised children, who toiled in the world. This was the realm of human cooperation, a realm ideally existing within perfect Charity. The people who lived in it and understood it were the ones who held the authority to organize it and who wielded the sword against those who would damage it. They maintained the borders against aggressors, internal or external, and they compelled such aggressors to accept at least the graceless peace of submission to force, an exterior peace from which they could transition, with the help of the preaching and the grace offered by the priests, to the true peace of Charity.[112]

This division of the spiritual and temporal powers into different groups of Christians was a fitting specification of the New Law operating in a fallen world, bringing it to conversion and peace. Its fittingness within the New Law helps us to understand why it is that in his treatment of law generally St. Thomas does not feel the need to treat temporal law and spiritual law as distinct "laws," even in the sense of branches of human law. Instead, they make an appearance only in passing and only to the effect that they are operating under the same

---

[112] *Super III sent.*, d. 30, a. 2, ad 8; ST II-II, q. 10, a. 8; I-II, q. 109, a. 8, ad 2.

aspect of law: the specification of the New Law.[113] We can see in what ways St. Louis and the papal legates depended on each other and operated together at the top of a vast "mechanism" of conversion, but without some sort of constitution. And we can see that it was entirely fitting that, unlike the monks and nuns, both the priests and the lords were called "secular." Both were directly engaged in the exterior manifestation of the law that subjected men to the extent that they did not live in virtue: the clergy facilitated the canon law and the laity the civil/feudal law, two laws that interacted with each other at every turn, two laws that were really only one. Both powers were, therefore, "political." They were two aspects of one dynamic, of the construction of a redeemed, intrinsically social humanity through the movement first to the exterior divine law and then through it to the interiorized divine law, which in salvation history was the movement from the Old to the New.[114]

We can see within this reading that the construction of legal institutions during the twelfth and thirteenth centuries was not a part of the process of "secularization," the process of building the foundations of the State at the expense of monastic and mystical faith, as it is often depicted in the mythology of modernity. Rather, it was the opposite: it was the effort to convert more and more of the world from violence to true peace, to produce in the law the bridge from fallen nature to redeemed nature. This was, of course, simply the dynamic of salvation itself: from fallen nature, to the Law, and through the Law to grace. It was the movement from the historical (nature) to the allegorical (Faith), on through the tropological (Charity) to the goal, the anagogical (which motivated the whole dynamic through Hope). In the spiritual life, it was the movement from sin to the purgative to the illuminative to the unitive ways; in the practice of the monks, from *lectio* to *meditatio* to *oratio* to *contemplatio*. We can understand clearly, then, why, in the *business of the peace and the faith*, heresy and violence went always

---

[113] ST I-II, q. 108, a. 2, resp., ad 4; q. 87, a. 1.
[114] Ibid., q. 72, a. 4; q. 99, a. 6, resp., ad 1.

together: they were the antitheses of Faith and Charity, which were the very building blocks of salvation.[115] Faith and Charity rose and fell always together, as did heresy and violence. This is why the *business of the peace and the faith* was necessarily as much about constructing a sacramental society of Faith and Charity as it was about waging war against a society of heresy and violence. The more successful this dynamic of salvation was, however, the more the juridical distinctions between the spiritual and the temporal powers would break down because more and more of the specifications of the New Law that were particular to each would be absorbed in the interiorization of the New Law itself. The specific law, both spiritual and temporal, that governed the interactions between people would be absorbed into the general law of Charity, the common understanding of Faith, and the practice of the sacraments.

We can see this dynamic most clearly in the monastic ideal, from which the entire reform movement of the High Middle Ages emerged. The monasteries were filled with both clerics (the ordained) and laypeople (the unordained), but their internal life was governed by one positive law, the Rule, specifying the New Law, and that life was aimed first and foremost at the interiorization of the New Law completely. Through this interiorization, the work of the monks in the fields or scriptorium and their work in the choir merged into a single liturgical reality that lived from sacramental grace.[116] We could, if we were so inclined, dissect the functioning of an ideal monastery and sort its life into "temporal" and "spiritual" categories, but why? It was a single life, fully temporal and fully spiritual—

---

[115] ST II-II, q. 4.

[116] See Jennifer A. Harris, "Building Heaven on Earth: Cluny as Locus Sanctissimus in the Eleventh Century," in *From Dead of Night to End of Day: The Medieval Customs of Cluny* [*Du coeur de la nuit à la fin du jour: les coutumes clunisiennes au Moyen Age*] (Turnhout, BE: Brepols, 2005) 131–51; Jean Leclercq, OSB, *The Love of Learning and the Desire for God: A Study of Monastic Culture* (New York: Fordham University Press, 1982); Mary Carruthers, *The Book of Memory: A Study of Memory in Medieval Culture* (Cambridge: Cambridge University Press, 1990).

this was the New Law, lived by the "religious," the model for all Christian society.

The reform movement poured out of the monasteries, and the law built by both the spiritual and the temporal powers of the High Middle Ages is more properly seen as emerging out of the Rules and Customaries of those religious houses and as attempting to turn all of Christendom into a single sacramental community of friends, into a single "monastic" society, rather than as emerging from the abstract study of the law of the Roman Empire by the secular "civilians" and the theocratic Gregorians and their nearly identical yet fundamentally incompatible drive to rationalize power and so build competing States. The dynamic was not one of dividing the social world into the "secular" and the "sacred," but rather of simultaneously sacralizing the secular and secularizing the sacred, of bringing them into each other, of closing the gap between the monastery and the world. The Cistercians, for example, attempted to build self-contained monastic societies with their own governance and their own economies that included all classes of people, redeemed worlds in miniature. This was a movement toward bringing society into the monastery. The Regular Canons and the Mendicant orders, on the other hand, under the same impulse reversed the movement and attempted to bring the monastery out into society, into the very hustle and bustle of urban life. The new orders of the twelfth and thirteenth centuries shared fundamentally a refusal to accept some sort of static codependence between a fallen world and saved religious.

By the turn of the thirteenth century, the married life itself, the seeming antithesis of the monastic life, was being referred to as the oldest religious order, and, of course, knighthood had become a clear "religious" undertaking.[117] Such active lives, St.

---

[117] See Giles Constable, *Three Studies on Medieval Religious and Social Thought* (Cambridge: Cambridge University Press, 1995), esp. 319–35. For the profoundly "religious" nature of "secular" life in the period, see Augustine Thompson, O.P., *Cities of God: The Religion of the Italian Communes, 1125–1325* (University Park, PA: Pennsylvania State University Press, 2005); see also the essays in André Vauchez, *The Laity in the Middle Ages: Religious*

Thomas tells us, are properly ordered to the contemplative life—all human action is in pursuit of contemplation, which is happiness.[118] It is not a coincidence that the same period that saw the massive expansion of the exterior law (what we might call the "Rule" of Christendom) saw also the so-called "discovery of the individual," the emphasis on interiorization.[119] The movement from the exterior to the interior is the very movement of Christian salvation, a movement that underwrote the entire monastic enterprise. Within this movement, the exterior law is not destroyed or somehow rendered moot by the coming of Christ. Rather, Christ makes the interior law achievable always through the exterior law, always as the fulfillment of the Law and not as its antithesis. Seen in this manner, the temporal and spiritual powers of the Church sought to subject more and more people to their law so that ultimately those people might be liberated in the New Law of Charity.[120]

What we are seeing is the construction of a sacramental social order. Like a monastery, the universal Church was as temporal as it was spiritual, as external as it was internal. It was made up of both laymen and clerics, kings and popes, but the temporal and the spiritual did not line up distinctly under one order or the other. They were distinct, but they were ev-

---

Beliefs and Devotional Practices, ed. Daniel E. Bornstein and trans. Margery J. Schneider (Notre Dame, IN: University of Notre Dame Press, 1993), and the now classic essays in M.D. Chenu, O.P., *Nature, Man, and Society in the Twelfth Century: Essays on New Theological Perspectives in the Latin West*, trans. Jerome Taylor and Lester K. Little (Chicago: University of Chicago Press, 1968).

[118] ST I-II, q. 3, a. 5.

[119] Colin Morris, *The Discovery of the Individual, 1050–1200* (Toronto: University of Toronto Press, 2012 [first published 1972]); Jennifer Harris, "Peter Damian and the Architecture of the Self," in *Das Eigene und das Ganze: Zum Individuellen im mittelalterlichen Religiosentum*, ed. Gert Melville and Markus Schürer (Münster: Lit, 2002), 131–58; Susan R. Kramer and Caroline W. Bynum, "Revisiting the Twelfth-Century Individual: The Inner Self and the Christian Community," in Melville and Schürer, in *Das Eigene und das Ganze*, 57–88.

[120] ST I-II, q. 108, a. 1, ad 2–3.

erywhere and always together, bound together in the very unity of Christ. This unity was most perfectly expressed at the Mass, where God was present in Body and Spirit, where the bread and the wine of temporal power, of lay human industry and organization, were turned into the Body and Blood of Christ through the spiritual power of the priesthood, and where the whole membership of the Church was united to each other and to God, both spiritually and corporally—this was a taste of salvation, a moment of the fulfillment of all law in the love of God and of neighbor, of the perfect regime that was the *ecclesia*.[121] Thomas writes: "And so it is appropriate that the grace flowing from the incarnate Word comes down to us through certain exterior and sensible things and that from this interior grace, through which the flesh is made subject to the spirit, certain sensible works are produced."[122] It is not a coincidence that the thirteenth century was a period of intense Eucharistic piety. The Feast of Corpus Christi grew up in France: it was made universal in 1264 by the French pope, Urban IV (who elevated Gui Foucois to the cardinalate), and its liturgy was composed by St. Thomas himself. The Eucharistic piety of the household of St. Louis is well known, as is that of the Mendicant orders. Pope Clement IV wrote a powerful defense of Eucharistic orthodoxy and as a young man demonstrated an intense devotion to the Virgin, a clear consequence of a profoundly incarnational understanding of reality.[123] The Mass was indeed the perfect sacrament, but all of the *ecclesia* was sacramental. Every aspect of the social life of the body of the baptized had intrinsic to it temporality and spirituality, including its "political" activities.

What this all means is that the perfected Church can be understood as a body that is indeed not "political." However, this can be so not because "politics" operates outside of it in a

---

[121] ST III, q. 73, a. 3, resp.; ST Supplementum, q. 71, a. 9, resp.

[122] ST I-II, q. 108, a. 1, resp.

[123] *Les Sept Joies de la Vierge par Guy Folqueis*, ed. C. Fabre (Le Puy, FR: Peyriller, Rouchon, and Gamon, 1920).

parallel, self-sufficient realm, but rather because to the extent that a people is converted "politics" is absorbed into the Church and fulfilled in the law of Charity, thereby ceasing to be "politics," in the modern sense, at all. The perfect Church is not political only because it is the fulfillment of politics, because politics is brought up into it and perfected beyond itself. Human coercive law, whether it be lay or clerical, operated at the boundary of the "political." As John Milbank has remarked, "for law to be law as just law, it must point beyond itself."[124] When the sword was used by the just against the unjust, it was wielded by one who stood within the interiorized law (the true peace), against one who stood outside this peace (one who was "subject" to the now exteriorized law).[125] At the point of the use of force, its object was necessarily in some sense both excommunicated and outlawed: he was outside the New Law (or perhaps it would be more accurate to say that the New Law was exterior to him), though subject to it. This is "politics." And so we see why excommunication, felony, and rebellion became

---

[124] "For Christianity the criterion of just law is that it must exceed the law's mere reactivity in the face of an always presumed evil, towards the recovered paradisal horizon of action as gratuitous and unnecessary positive offering, assuming no prior state of affairs to be remedied; this horizon can only be recovered through the ministries of mercy, forgiveness, reconciliation and reciprocal friendship. Thus now, for law to be law as just law, it must point beyond itself. Yet conversely, given the general state of human corruption, we are never, or at least rarely, in a relational condition where we can either act with pure paradisal spontaneity or proceed directly to reconciliation without an initial resort to corrective justice which will most frequently involve the coercive imposition of justice in some degree or other—given that, as the ancient Hebrews correctly thought, the defense of the weak and the abused cannot afford to wait upon the repentance of the wicked. Therefore it follows that the human existential situation, as understood by the gospel, is typically that of needing to bend a necessarily pre-reconciliatory and pre-(fully) restorationary justice towards the telos of genuine justice which is full reconciliation and an entire peaceful harmony of right apportioning. This situation and this bending are most acutely, crucially and publicly (but not exclusively) exemplified and manifest in the instance of public law" (John Milbank, *Beyond Secular Order*, 233).

[125] *De regno* 1.7–8.

different sides of the same offense, and we see again the fundamental coherence of the *business of the peace and the faith*.

Through this reading, we can come to understand that the distinction that really matters in understanding the thirteenth century is not that between spiritual and temporal authorities but that between the realms of the interiorized law and the exteriorized law, between the realms of virtue and vice, between the realms of true peace and worldly peace or violence, between servile fear and filial fear. These are the two "tiers" or "stories" of this society. In the realm of virtue, which is the realm of unity in Faith and Charity, both the temporal and the spiritual laws were descriptive and had a coordinating and pedagogical social function. They were also profoundly "religious." They were, as we have seen, the specifications of the New Law itself. In the realm of exteriorized law, they were profoundly "political." In this realm they remain authorities of the divine law, but it was not the perfectly fulfilled interiorized New Law. Rather, it began to cross back over to the exteriorized Law, we might say to the Old Law that remained contained within the New which itself included natural law.[126] But the Old Law was preparatory for the New; it was necessary for the New, which fulfilled it completely. What we see is a dynamic of salvation that was repetitive, even fractal. Salvation history itself, the functioning

---

[126] ST I-II, q. 107, a. 1, resp.: "All of the ascribed differences between the New Law and the Old Law are taken in a way corresponding to the perfect and the imperfect. For the precepts of any law are given concerning acts of virtue. But the imperfect, who do not yet have the habit of virtue, are inclined toward doing the acts of virtue in a way different from those who have been perfected through the habit of virtue. Those who do not yet have the habit of a virtue are inclined toward doing the works of the virtue by some extrinsic cause, e.g., the threat of punishment or the promise of some extrinsic reward such as honor or wealth or something of this sort. And so the Old Law, which was given to the imperfect, i.e., to those who had not yet attained spiritual grace, was called a 'law of fear' insofar as it induced one to the observance of its precepts by threatening certain punishments. . . . By contrast, those who have a virtue are inclined toward performing acts of that virtue out of love of virtue and not because of any extrinsic punishment or reward. And so the New Law, which consists principally in the spiritual grace poured into our hearts, is call a 'law of love.'"

of Christendom, the spiritual life of the individual believer, and even the structure of Aquinas's *Summa theologiae* itself all follow the same pattern: from fallen nature, to a type of faith through the Old, exteriorized law, to the New, interiorized law of Charity (and so true Faith) through grace.[127] This was the very "functioning" of Christianity, how God saved mankind.

Aquinas's understanding of this dynamic of salvation can be seen as ultimately rooted in man's *imago Dei* and the deep structure of creation through the analogical manifestation in time of the eternal processions of the Second Person (intellection) and the Third Person (volition).[128] Salvation history is, within this reading, the Trinity's interface with fallen, temporal, intellectual, and volitional (Trinitarian) man. Within this dynamic there is a constant circling back: the movements to Faith and Charity exist always with each other in dynamic relation, with an ever-present "procession" from Faith to Charity and back again to a more perfect Faith, and always with God, instructing through the law and assisting through grace, as the exterior principle of both virtues.[129] This movement is manifested in the movement from the Old into the New, and from the New back to the Old, a movement that happens historically and presently and at every level of scale: the "dead" faith of servile fear (itself a gift from God) through

---

[127] ST I-II, q. 98, a. 6, resp.; q. 103, a. 3, resp., ad 1; q. 107, a. 3, resp.

[128] ST I, q. 45, a. 7; ST I, q. 27, a. 2-3.

[129] ST I-II, q. 62, a. 4; q. 65, a. 4-5, 6; q. 113, a. 4; q. 17, a. 1; ST II-II, q. 4, a. 5, 7; q. 23 a. 7-8; ST, I-II q. 65 a. 4-5; ST, II-II q. 4 a. 3; ST I-II q. 90, prol.; ST I, q. 27, a. 3, ad 3: "Though will and intellect are not diverse in God, nevertheless the nature of will and intellect requires the processions belonging to each of them to exist in a certain order. For the procession of love occurs in due order as regards the procession of the Word; since nothing can be loved by the will unless it is conceived in the intellect. So as there exists a certain order of the Word to the principle whence He proceeds, although in God the substance of the intellect and its concept are the same; so, although in God the will and the intellect are the same, still, inasmuch as love requires by its very nature that it proceed only from the concept of the intellect, there is a distinction of order between the procession of love and the procession of the Word in God."

grace moves toward Charity, through which it is transformed into living Faith and so filial fear, which is inseparable from Charity, the fulfillment of the Law.[130] As the reader of Scripture, for example, moved deeper into Charity, not only did the tropological sense open to him, but his understanding of the allegorical sense grew ever deeper: as he conformed himself to Christ in the New Law of Charity, the Old Law emerged in Faith as ever more Christological.[131]

In this way, we can see that the dichotomy that is often posited between the supposed Augustinian belief that the State was the product of sin and so was not natural to man and the supposed Thomist belief that the State was indeed natural to man is, in fact, false. The "Augustinian" understanding and the "Thomistic" understanding are as integral to each other as the Old Law is to the New. Both temporal power and spiritual

---

[130] ST II-II, q. 7, a. 1-2; q. 19, a. 2, 4-7, 10.

[131] Henri de Lubac, *Medieval Exegesis: The Four Senses of Scripture*, vol. 2. St. Gregory the Great, for example, explained the two disciples on the Road to Emmaus's inability to recognize Christ not on account of Christ unilaterally hiding himself, but rather to their being unable, because of a lack of faith, to recognize him:

> "the Lord enacted outwardly, before their physical eyes, what was going on in them inwardly, before the eyes of their hearts. For inwardly they simultaneously loved him and doubted him; therefore the Lord was outwardly present to them, and at the same time did not reveal his identity . . . he simply showed himself to them physically exactly as he appeared to them in their minds: as a stranger, and therefore as one who would pass on."

The deficiency was within them. The deficiency began to be removed, however, as Christ expounded the allegorical content of Scripture. This was not adequate, however. Their vision was not healed until they moved to charity (the tropological) by pressing Christ to stay with them, an act of hospitality which culminated in the breaking of the bread and the full recognition of Christ (anagogical). "Consequently, they were not enlightened by hearing the precepts of God, but by doing them." Indeed, "Whoever," Gregory writes, "wishes to understand what he hears read out in church, should hasten to carry out in his actions those things which he understands already." Gregory the Great, *Reading the Gospels with Gregory the Great: Homilies on the Gospels, 21-26*, trans. Santha Bhattacharji (Fordham University Press: New York, 2002), 54–6.

power reached back into the Old and forward into the New. They operated in both the realm of sin and the realm of grace, and the "natural" was brought up into the "divine." This was how the Church saved humanity; this was the very dynamic of salvation played out through history and in the minutia of everyday life. Government was present across the human "field" from the garden, through the Fall, through the Old Law, and on to the redemption of nature in the New Law, but it manifested itself—it was specified—in different ways appropriate to the stage. Under the New Law still in time, this included the sword in the realm of sin. The king's use of the sword was, in a sense, a return to the Old Law and clearly a consequence of sin, a return that was always provisional, always temporary, always a "condescension" because of the "hardness of their hearts," and always ordered toward bringing the sinner back to virtue, to the interiorized New Law and the perfected "natural" government that existed therein.

Mankind's constant drift from the interiorized to the exteriorized law and back again was the setting for government, a very complicated setting. This drift occurred both at the individual level and at the level of communities.[132] The realms of virtue and vice were everywhere intermingled and confused. The same person, within the movement of a single act, could move between them without seam, as his intentions shifted.[133] This means that the line between the interior and the exterior was always blurred and under negotiation. What one authority believed to be clearly sin worthy of coercive remedial action another might believe to be within the realm of the pedagogical law, and yet another might believe to be no sin at all.

In this situation, the authorities themselves would be compelled to look at each other as possibly slipping into vice. Charity and Faith bound them and all Christians together in the realm of peace, but when in conflict few could admit that they were the ones who were no longer properly charitable and

---

[132] ST I-II, q. 106, a. 4, resp.
[133] ST I-II, q. 20, a. 6.

no longer properly faithful—ultimately excommunicated and outlawed. It is along these lines, then, that we find conflict— always between conglomerations of spiritual and temporal powers with conflicting relative readings of Faith and Charity and always threatening to become a type of "crusade." As we saw throughout this book, the drift of all sustained conflict, whether it be that in the South of France, in central Italy, or in England, was toward crusade. All "political" conflict had to be justified within a universal framework that aimed ultimately at the peace of all of humanity. All war had to be "religious," a fact that made war both less desirable, more difficult to wage, and more limited in scope. As is well known, during the reign of St. Louis, war between Christian princes was rare and relatively small-scale.

The final piece to this understanding of Christian society is the recognition that its realization as a society of perfect peace was ultimately impossible.[134] Perfection in Faith and Charity was something to be strived for and something to approach, but never something to be actually achieved in this life and before the consummation of the world.[135] This means that this world always had an eschatological dimension: what it pursued was ultimately beyond the reach of man in time. However, it was continually sought because, along with Charity and Faith, the realm of peace was the realm of the infused virtue of Hope.[136] Hope was what caused mankind to never settle for the realm of violence, for the realm of the peace of the world that was possible through exteriorized law. Hope was what always pulled man into the struggle to "reform" this realm into the fulfilled order of the interiorized New Law. Hope was what ultimately accounted for the real existence of the two realms because hope was what kept the realm of Charity and Faith always "under construction," and the realm of vice under perpetual reform.

---

[134] ST II-II, q. 29, a. 2, ad 4.
[135] ST I-II, q. 109, a. 10, ad 3; q. 5, a.3.
[136] *Super III sent.*, d. 23, q. 1, a. 5, resp. and ad 5.

What St. Thomas, St. Louis IX, and Clement IV would see, perhaps, in modern politics is the loss of this Hope: despair. To despair is to settle for the realm of exteriorized law, the realm of violence, and the compromise peace of this world. Charity and Faith might remain ideals, but the ideal is shifted exclusively to an otherworldly realm: to heaven, entrance to which is no longer something that mankind finds through struggle and with the aid of sacramental grace through actual transformation to virtue, but rather something that is or is not given to him regardless of a life lived entirely in the realm of sin, which, with the possibility of supernatural virtue removed, is all there is in this life. The "political" aspect of the dynamic of salvation, the aspect that "reached down" into sin or "back" to the Old Law, is thereby absolutized and the State emerges. From within this perspective it makes sense, I think, that "democracy," the least bad of the tyrannical regimes, has become the political ideal of modernity, the best we can imagine.[137]

Can we not perhaps see that the growth of the assumption of primordial violence in political theory is really a part of the same historical movement as that of the development of the doctrine of the total depravity of man, of *simul justus et peccator*, and of the denial of transformative grace? Is it not really the denial of the possibility of the "upper tier" of the New Law, the denial of the possibility of true peace in Charity, and the assertion that the best that can be hoped for is a type of concord, some sort of social contract?[138] This reading can offer an account, it seems to me, of Marsilius of Padua's elevation of the secular power over the spiritual in his quest for peace, of the nominalists' move toward an arbitrary law, of Machiavelli's

---

[137] *De regno* 1.3. Aquinas thought that monarchy was the best form of government because it was least likely to fall into tyranny, even if its tyranny was worse than that of a polity, a consideration that becomes moot if we assume truly virtuous government to be impossible (*De regno* 1.5).

[138] It is an assumption of liberal economic theory, for example, that peace in the sense that Aquinas understands it is impossible, that desire cannot be ultimately satisfied, that man always wants more, necessarily (see ST II-II, q. 29, a. 1).

contention that the prince must be amoral in order for "peace" to reign, of the congruency between Luther's doctrines of *sola fide* and the two kingdoms, as well as the rise of the absolutist monarchs, Catholic and otherwise. The transformational *sacramenta* of the Church, which, since the construction of the Carolingian Empire, had become the covenantal bond of unity in society, becomes the *sacramentum* of Hobbes, the oath through which man surrenders to the sovereign his power to inflict violence, the covenant that is simply a contract made in fear. Faith and Charity become faith and obedience.[139]

In a similar way, is not the modern Christian tendency to deny or ignore the spiritual senses of Scripture a denial that history can ever be more than the realm of nature, or perhaps of the Law, a denial that the Law is fulfilled (or, at least being fulfilled) in time? The spiritual senses operated within a dynamic of ascent from the literal (historical) to its fulfillment in the anagogical that was possible only through human ascent by means of cooperation with grace: the spiritual senses opened up to one as one grew in Faith and Charity, as one became ever more under the New Law.[140] As we saw in our treatment of the Capetian coronation rite, the David of the Old Testament was fulfilled in the David of the New Testament as the kingdom transitioned from the kingdom of men to the kingdom of God. Salvation was participatory, and so was the experience of society: the same David was at the same time a sword-wielding king to the sinner and the Prince of Peace to the righteous. In the move to the modern, such "spiritual" things are pushed outside the participatory, outside history or next to history or beyond history. Christ, the David of the New Testament, is now bodily at the right hand of the Father and not here among us.[141]

---

[139] For the sacraments as the basis of unity in Christendom, see Owen M. Phelan, *The Formation of Christian Europe: The Carolingians, Baptism, and the Imperium Christianum* (Oxford: Oxford University Press, 2014). See also Thomas Hobbes, *Leviathan* (1651), I.14, III.35, III.39, III.43.

[140] See de Lubac, *Medieval Exegesis*, especially vol. 2.

[141] Ulrich Zwingli stated, "He sits at the right hand of the Father, has left the world, is no longer among us" (quoted in Brad S. Gregory, *The Unintended*

What is more, once Christendom despaired of Charity and Faith (the anticipation of heaven on earth) and accepted the lower tier as its place of habitation, it seems a small step to dispense with heaven, the now socially irrelevant realm of virtue, altogether: it no longer exists on earth after all, even imperfectly. Heaven may or may not be real, but this becomes a matter for personal "religion" because its existence simply does not matter in the realm of absolutized politics, of simple history.

But, through this reading, we must see that the modern State remains "secular" only in the medieval sense. Or perhaps another way to put it is that the modern "secular" remains profoundly "religious." It is the bottom tier of exteriorized and highly specified law within the Christian dynamic divorced from the upper tier of interiorized and harmonized law. At its best, it is the realm of the truth of the Old Law (including the natural law), a realm of real faith, but without the grace of the sacraments necessary to satisfy it in Charity.[142] At its worst, it is the realm of vice, of despair, hatred, and infidelity—the "city of man." It is only because this lower tier is viewed as all there is on earth, only because the upper tier (Charity) has been pushed to the heavens, that the "secular" becomes the field on which all history is played. As in the thirteenth century, this lower tier remains where the "secular" side of both the spiritual and the temporal powers operate. Only now, because this lower tier has become all there is, the "secular" or "political" side of both powers is all that remains.

The spiritual power no longer wields a sword, which was always operative only in the upper tier of grace, and its positive, sacramental power, also operative in the upper tier, is simply ignored or denied any social consequence. Rather, the spiritual power is reduced to its function in the lower tier, to its preach-

---

Reformation: How a Religious Revolution Secularized Society [Cambridge, MA: Harvard University Press, 2012], 42).

[142] For the significance of the biblical account of the Hebrew polity in the formation of modern political thought, see Eric Nelson, *The Hebrew Republic: Jewish Sources and the Transformation of European Political Thought* (Cambridge, MA: Harvard University Press, 2010).

ing and its example of upright living, and canon law becomes little more than the bylaws of religious clubs. The temporal power is similarly reduced to its function in the lower tier: the maintenance of exterior peace through the wielding of the sword, the enforcement of contracts, and the waging of war. Each power therefore operates only within its most specified "share" of the law that once governed the transition between the tiers—the canonical and civil-feudal legal traditions at their most differentiated. As was stated above, it is in the lower tier that the division between the temporal and the spiritual powers become most pronounced. Absolutizing the lower tier, it seems to me, is therefore the origin of the modern division of Church and State. They remain bound up together and their division is rooted within the same social world, the lower tier of Christendom, now seen as all there is.

This reading helps us to understand, perhaps, the modern phenomenon of Christians who sincerely abhor violence, who, in fact, enforce what must be considered a taboo on "private" force, and yet who intuitively support the dynamic of more and more of social life being brought under the order provided by the institutionalized coercion of the State (in either the governmental/technocratic form common to the Left or the market/technocratic form common to the Right). In a world of ubiquitous violence, "peace" is to be found only through law and contract.[143] This, within the reading provided here, can be seen as closely related to the dualism discussed toward the beginning of this book, a dualism that combined pacifist asceticism with violent lordship. It is such dualism that Thomas points out as the error of Pilate: that kingship was nothing but

---

[143] For a discussion of how the foundations of the modern State ought to be found in the attempt to re-establish human unity and peace in a social world understood as made up of essentially individual actors in pursuit of their own interests at the expense of their fellow man and how this attempt was a perversion of the ecclesial attempt to affect true peace and unity, see William T. Cavanaugh, "The City: Beyond Secular Parodies," in *Radical Orthodoxy, a New Theology*, ed. John Milbank, Catherine Pickstock, and Graham Ward (London: Routledge, 1999), 182–200.

force and that truth was powerless in this world.[144]

This brings us back to the characteristic modern prejudice in favor of a primordial violence, the belief that social reality is ultimately a war of all against all, general conflict. Sovereignty is the only path to some semblance of peace because the actual violence will subside only when the wills of the many are condensed into the will of the one. But this is only an apparent peace because sovereignty is itself a perpetual act of violence, of suppression. Without Charity, as long as there is difference, there is war. The exterior law, then, becomes totalizing, the principle of order in a society that seeks to construct an undifferentiated space of rights, contracts, people and things because without the possibility of Charity, differentiation leads to conflict. It does not much matter whether sovereignty is legitimized with references to natural rights, divine right, or the right of the majority or whether it is denied all legitimacy and viewed simply as violence: whatever the case may be, the war must continue until difference is eliminated. And so, the dream of modern radicals was to find peace through the elimination of all difference, an elimination that fittingly could happen only through violent revolution and that would inaugurate the end of history. Modernity becomes the desperate attempt to establish the eternal, the abstract, within the flux of the temporal, the relative (in contradistinction to the medieval notion that the temporal was brought up and fulfilled without diminution in the eternal). To the postmodernists, of course, this dream of equality is repudiated in favor of an absolutized and all-encompassing "difference," but without Charity, violence remains the very structure of reality. I am convinced that it is the assumption that all difference is ultimately only bridged through conflict and subordination (which amounts

---

[144] *Super Ioan* 18, lec. 6. For an enlightening discussion of Aquinas's treatment of the discourse between Pilate and Christ and for its implications for our understanding of Aquinas political thought as fundamentally theological, see Frederick Christian Bauerschmidt, "Aquinas," in *The Blackwell Companion to Political Theology*, ed. Peter Scott and William T. Cavanaugh (Chichester, UK: Wiley-Blackwell, 2006), 48–61.

to the denial of Charity and Faith in favor of despair) that makes it impossible for moderns to conceptualize the relationship between the papacy and the monarchies of the Middle Ages as anything other than a fundamental contest.

The preceding chapters have presented a new reading of the relationship between the spiritual and temporal powers by following the lives of two men, Gui Foucois and Louis IX. I have constructed a narrative that rests ultimately on the coherence of the "complete acts" that are those individuals' lives and on the categories and concepts through which they viewed the world. I have not argued that the world of France in 1265 was a direct consequence of Gui's and Louis's lives, but rather, conversely, that they were at home in that world, as was St. Thomas Aquinas. By reconstructing the time, the places, events, and ideas of the span of their lives, we can construct a coherent thread of development, a description rather than a causal explanation.

And what this thread has revealed is the construction of a social order that was Christian. It was predicated not on war, but on the peace of differentiated relationships. And so, while law and jurisdiction were real and were essential, a description of the jurisdictional or legal apparatuses of this social order cannot capture its actual structure because, while the power wielded through these mechanisms was necessary, it was ultimately provisional within a society that understood benevolent relationships—relationships of *consilium et auxilium* wherein the differentiated power of one became the power of another— as the proper manner in which order was maintained. Peace was understood as the norm, and the status of the peace, what Thomas referred to as "custom," trumped all positive law: "It has the force of law, abolishes law, and is the interpreter of law."[145] Violence was unnatural and irrational—it happened, but it never belonged.[146] This was a Trinitarian understand-

---

[145] ST I-II, q. 97, a. 3, resp.
[146] Ibid., q. 6, a. 5, resp.

ing of difference.[147] Difference was not synonymous with war; rather, peace was possible precisely because difference made Charity—duty, gift, love—possible.[148] Inequality, difference, was the precondition of peace, and it was only where this difference broke down, where people approached each other as "the same," that conflict erupted. As is now hopefully clear, the best way to understand this order is not through recourse to the concepts of "State" or "Church," but through the concepts that the builders themselves deployed in discussing what it was that they were about: the *negotium pacis et fidei* or, more simply, the *negotium Christi.*

---

[147] See the structure of the argument of ST I, q. 27-45.

[148] Ibid., q. 96, a. 3, ad 2.

CHAPTER FIFTEEN

THE MOST CHRISTIAN KINGDOM

It is because God is ruling us that our soul is turned
into a spirit that no longer yields to itself for its own
ill but so orders us that our peace goes on increasing
in this life until, when perfect health and immortality
have been given us, we shall reign in utter sinlessness
and in eternal peace.

—St. Augustine, *City of God* 15.6

IN AUGUST OF 1268, just a few months before his death,
Clement IV wrote to St. Louis. The topic of the letter was
blasphemous oaths. Clement begins by stating that all thought,
all understanding, and all human power are the consequence
of a perpetual inflow of divine grace: if that grace were to
be removed, man and all of creation would retreat back into
the nothingness from which they had been called. Unaided,
mankind can perceive only the enigma of being. But the mag-
isterium of faith brings understanding and liberty, and this
comes to us through the Incarnation. God was made man and

conversed with man "that sharing in our humanity, previously wretched and abject, he might make us to participate in his divinity and to be co-heirs to his kingdom." The cost of this was his torture and death on the Cross. Therefore, the pope continues, it is remarkable that so many despise his humanity and in doing so offend his majesty. This is especially evident in those who, "with polluted and wicked lips," swear against their bodies, against their limbs, their heads, their eyes. They pile injury on the Son of God, swearing so against his body, who took up our body and "in man honored the great mass of humankind." Some try to defend themselves by arguing that such oaths are the custom of the land and that they swear so only with their lips and not with their hearts. Clement denied any validity to this claim, stating that these are "damnable customs." And so, Clement counsels the king ("warning as much as exhorting" and reflecting on the fact that his redeemer's injury is his own) to not put away the zeal that he has displayed against these blasphemers. Rather, with the "*consilio* of the prelates and barons," he should establish temporal punishments, "that those whom the fear of God does not recall from wickedness and monstrosity, might be called back by the 'censure of royal power.'" "Still," the pope concludes, "through this we do not want nor do we intend to absorb ecclesiastical censure," but rather, "by *mutuo auxilio* we believe each sword is to be aided, that the spiritual might direct [*dirigat*] the material and the material might support [*fulciat*] and sustain [*sustentet*] the spiritual."[1]

This letter illustrates many of the points that have been made throughout this book. It is the Incarnation of Christ that is the shared reference point between the king and the pope, the ultimate constant in their worldview. The world of men is a world where the material and the spiritual are united, and that unity makes everything possible. Those who assault the human Christ assault the foundations of the entire structure—they

---

[1] LTC, 4:5404.

are heretics.[2] This is an attack as much against the monarchy as against the Church, but the blasphemy is not simple. Clement reveals that it is imbedded in local customs of swearing and oaths, customs that are obviously of dramatic social importance to those who live under them. The pope exhorts the king to root them out. But, he reassures the king that this is not an act of violence on his part, for it is the blasphemers who have attacked God. Clement is exhorting the king to extend their shared orthodoxy and, of course, along with it their entire shared vision of social order. This is a counsel, however, and not a command, and the pope encourages the monarch to act with the *consilio* of the magnates of the realm. Their network of *consilium et auxilium* must act together against this shared threat. It must be extended to encompass more of the social space.

But it is in the final sentences of the letter that we can see most clearly the pope's understanding of the two powers: they are to give each other mutual *auxilium*. The spiritual directs (*dirigere*) the material and the material supports (*fulcire*) and sustains (*sustentare*) the spiritual. There is a temptation to read absolute subordination of the material to the spiritual in this statement because, in the modern understanding, it is the realization of one's will that is defined as power, and to modernity power is the object of the ubiquitous social conflict. But a look at the theological significance of these words in the writings of St. Thomas can help us see that this temptation is rooted in error. *Dirigere* was "to direct" something in the sense that an arrow is directed to its mark, or in the sense that habits direct thought.[3] To direct was not the same thing as to command, order, or rule, which would be *imperare, mandare,* or *regere.* Rather, *dirigere* was to point something in the right direction, to guide it, to show it its mark. To Clement this was the gift, the *auxilium*—in the form of sermons, the Eucharist, penance, and so on—that the spiritual gave to the temporal. The temporal

---

2 See ST I-II, q. 72, a. 4, obj. 3.
3 ST I, q. 103, a. 1, obj. 3; q. 79, a. 13, obj. 3.

returned the *auxilium* of support and sustenance. *Fulcire* was to support or to sustain, but it was used often figuratively. For example, one is "per consilium fulciatur."[4] It was the Eucharist "qui animae nostrae substantiam fulcit."[5] Indeed, the Church herself was upheld (*fulciatur*) by divine authority.[6] *Sustentare* was also to sustain or to hold up. But, it was normally more literal. One held oneself up or was sustained by food.[7]

The point is that the material power's sustenance of the spiritual power simply cannot be understood as subservience. It is more that the material "held in temporal being" the spiritual, constructed it, gave it shape, and kept it in place. The spiritual was operating in the world, after all, and needed protection, churches, food, clothes, oil, water, bread, men, and so on. But more than this, what made the spiritual power a power was that it operated in the material world of the temporal. In the same way, what made the temporal power a power, rather than the violence of the pagan kings, was that it operated within the spiritual, that it participated in divine law. The identity of each included that of the other. Fundamentally, the two powers were relational, and through this differentiated relationship, the Church as the City of God was built and maintained. In the Church the blind would be led by those who could see (the spiritual power) and the lame supported by those who were strong (the temporal power). In the ideal, like father and son or husband and wife, the spiritual and the temporal made their way together in peaceful differentiated unity toward the goal. Indeed, "to direct" and "to sustain" must be brought together within the Christian discourse on Charity. Aquinas himself did this in his discussion of the corporal works of mercy: to lead (*dirigere*) the blind and to support (*sustentare*) the lame were ultimately the same act of Charity.[8]

---

4 ST, I-II, q. 68, a. 5, obj. 3.

5 ST, III, q. 77, a. 6, obj. 1.

6 ST Supplementum, q. 55, a. 9, ad. 1.

7 ST III, q. 67, a. 7, obj. 3; I, q. 96, a. 3, corp.

8 ST II-II, q. 32, a. 2, ad 2: "Dicendum, quod omnes aliae necessitates ad

There was nothing in the pope's letter that Louis would have found objectionable. Indeed, in Louis's testament to his son written shortly before his death, the king offered a summation of the *negotium* of his rule that was thoroughly consistent with the pope's exhortation, though fittingly much more practical in tone. He exhorted his son to seek peace, to respect the customs and rights of the land, to protect the weak and the Church, to "strive to have wickedness expelled from your land," to "put down heresy as far as you can," and to suppress, with the counsel of good people, all those hostile to the faith. This was a vision of Christian kingship and Christian order that Gui and Louis shared. It did not change when the king's servant Gui became Pope Clement, and there is no reason to suppose any dissembling when Louis wrote to his son, "Dear son, I advise you always to be devoted to the Church of Rome, and to the sovereign pontiff, our father, and to bear him the reverence and honor which you owe to your spiritual father."[9] Similarly, there was no dissembling when Clement explained to Louis that he had loved the king's house from before the king was personally known to him, and that as he had advanced in the king's service and had come to obtain his friendship, this love had deepened. The pope continued that this had not changed after his election, but rather, while it was surely right that he should call Louis both "lord and friend, it was by the mercy of God alone that he had been called to the summit of the papacy and so he now calls him by the name of son, that his love might be shown."[10]

Clement and Louis were friends. They were also spiritual father and son. And it was together, with the fullness of royal power and the fullness of papal power united in their spiritual

---

has reducuntur: nam et caecitas, et claudicatio sunt infirmitates quaedam; unde dirigere caecum, et sustentare claudum reducuntur ad visitationem infirmorum."

9   David O'Connell, *The Teachings of Saint Louis: A Critical Text* (Chapel Hill: University of North Carolina Press, 1972).

10   *Epistole et dictamina Clementis pape quarti,* 12 (found also in *Clément IV, Reg.*, 883).

kinship, that (before Church and State) they built "the Most Christian Kingdom."

❧ BIBLIOGRAPHY

Manuscript Sources
MS Registra Vaticana, 26–28.

Primary Sources

Acta Conciliorum Epistolae Decretalies, ac Constitutione Summorum Pontificum. Edited by Jean Hardouin. Paris, 1714.

Acta Urbani IV, Clementis IV, Gregorii X (1261–1276) e registris vaticanis aliisque fontibus collegit. Edited by Aloysius L. Tàutu. Rome: Typis polyglottis Vaticanis, 1953.

Actes du parlement de Paris [*Actes*]. Edited by Edgard Boutaric. Paris: Henri Plon, 1863.

Ademari historiarum liber III. Edited by Georg Waitz. In MGH SS 4.

Alan of Lille. *Summa de arte praedicatori*. In PL, 210:109–98.

Andreae Ungari Descriptio Victoriae a Karolo Com. Reportatae. In MGH SS 26.

Annales Ecclesiastici [AE]. Edited by Odorico Rinaldi and Giacomo Laderchii. Paris: Barri-Ducis, 1870. *Annales Minorum seu trium ordinum a S. Francisco institutorum*. Edited by Luke Wadding. Florence, IT: Ad Claras Aquas (Quaracchi): 1931–1935.

Aquinas, Thomas. *Catena Aurea: Commentary on the Four Gospels, Collected Out of the Works of the Fathers*. Vol. 1, St. Matthew. Edited by John Henry Newman. Oxford: John Henry Parker, 1841.

———. *Commentary on the Gospel of John: Chapters 1–21*. Translated by Fabian Larcher and James A. Weisheipl. Washington, DC: Catholic University of America Press, 2010.

———. *Contra impugnantes Dei cultum et religionem*. In *Opera omnia iussu impensaque Leonis XIII P. M. edita* 41. Rome:

Ex Typographia Polyglotta S. C. de Propaganda Fide, 1970.

——. *De malo*. In *Opera omnia iussu impensaque Leonis XIII P. M. edita* 23. Rome: Ex Typographia Polyglotta S. C. de Propaganda Fide, 1982.

——. *De regno*. In *Opera omnia iussu impensaque Leonis XIII P. M. edita* 42. Rome: Ex Typographia Polyglotta S. C. de Propaganda Fide, 1979. *Beati Ludovici Vita*. In RHGF 23.

——.*Omnia opera*. Parma, 1856–1868.

——. *On Evil*. Translated by Richard Regan. Edited by Brian Davies. Oxford/New York: Oxford University Press, 2003.

——. *Opera omnia iussu impensaque Leonis XIII P. M. edita*. Rome: Ex Typographia Polyglotta S. C. de Propaganda Fide, 1884–2000.

——. *Scriptum super Sententiis* [*Super sent.*]. Parma, 1856–1858.

——. *Sententia libri Ethicorum* [*Super eth.*]. *Opera omnia iussu impensaque Leonis XIII P. M. edita* 47.1–2. Rome: Ex Typographia Polyglotta S. C. de Propaganda Fide, 1969.

——. *Summa contra gentiles* [SCG]. In *Opera omnia iussu impensaque Leonis XIII P. M. edita* 13–15. Rome: Ex Typographia Polyglotta S. C. de Propaganda Fide, 1918–1930.

——. *Summa theologiae* [ST]. In *Opera omnia iussu impensaque Leonis XIII P. M. edita* 4–12. Rome: Ex Typographia Polyglotta S. C. de Propaganda Fide, 1888–1906.

——. *Super Evangelium S. Ioannis lectura* [*Super Ioan*]. Turin, IT: Marietti, 1952.

——. *Super Jeremiam* [*Super Jer*]. Parma, 1863.

——. *Super Psalmos* [*Super Ps*]. Parma, 1863.

——. *Treatise on Law: The Complete Text*. Translated by Alfred J. Freddoso. South Bend, IN: St. Augustine's Press, 2009.

Assier, Alexander. *Vita Urbani papae quarti*. Troyes, FR: Bouquot, 1854.

Biblia cum glossa ordinaria. (Rusch, 1480/81)

Biblia Sacra cum Glossa Ordinaria et Postilla Nicolai Lyrani. Venice, IT: Magnam Societatem, 1603.

Bodin, Jean. *On Sovereignty: Six Books of the Commonwealth.* Translated by M. J. Tooley. Oxford: Basil Blackwell, 1955.

Borrelli de Serres, Léon L. "Compte d'une mission de prédication pour secours à la Terre Sainte (1265)." *Mémoires de la Société de l'Histoire de Paris et de l'Ile-de-France* 30 (1903): 243–80.

Bullarum diplomatum et privilegiorum sanctorum Romanorum Pontificum. Turin edition, 1857–1872.

Bullarium Franciscanum Romanorum Pontificum. Rome: Typis Sacæ Congregationis de Propaganda Fide, 1759–1804.

Bullarium Ordinis FF. Prædicatorum. Edited by Thomas Ripoll and Antonin Brémond. Rome: Ex Typographia Hieronymi Mainardi, 1729–1740.

Capitula Italica. In MGH *Leges Capit.* II, 1:217.

Capitulare Haristallense. In MGH *Leges Capit.* II, 1:51.

Capitulare Missorum. In MGH *Leges Capit.* II, 1:289–90.

Capitulare Missorum Generale. In MGH *Leges Capit.* I, 1:91–99.

Capitulare Missorum in Theodonis Villa Datum Secundum, Generale. In MGH *Leges Capit.* II, 1:122–26.

Capitulare Saxonicum. In MGH *Leges Capit.* II, 1:71–72.

Capitulatio de partibus Saxoniae. In MGH *Leges Capit.* II, 1:70.

Chartularium Universitatis Parisiensis. Edited by Heinrich Denifle. Paris: Ex typis fratrum Delalain, 1889–1897.

Chronica S. Petri Erfordensis moderna. Edited by Oswald Holder-Egger. In MGH SS 30.

Chronicon Girardi de Fracheto. In RHGF 21.

Chronicon Monasterii Sancti Taurini Ebroicensis. In RHGF 23.

Chronique Anonyme des Rois de France. In RHGF 21.

Collectio Capitularium Ansegisi. Edited by G. Schmitz. In MGH *Capit.* II, 1:637, 1996.

Concilia Galliae Narbonensis [CGN]. Edited by Stephanus Baluze. Paris: F. Muguet, 1668.

Consuetudines Feudorum. In *Corpus Juris Civilis*, edited by Giovanni Calza, 2:1149–94. Turin, IT: Edid. Heredes S. Bottae, 1829.

Corpus Documentorum Inquisitionis Haereticae Pravitatis Neerlandicae. Edited by Paul Fredericq. Ghent, BE: J. Vuylsteke, 1889.

Corpus Juris Canonici, emendatum et notis illustratum [JC-1582]. Rome, 1582.

Correspondance administrative d'Alfonse de Poitiers [CAAP]. Edited by Auguste Molinier. Paris: Imprimerie Nationale, 1895.

de Chartres, Guillaume. *De Vita et Actibus Inclytae Recordationis Regis Francorum Ludovici.* RHGF, 20: 27–41.

de Puylaurens, Guillaume. *Chronique, 1145–1275: Chronica Magistri Guillelmi de Podio Laurentii.* Edited by Jean Duvernoy. Paris: Le Pérégrinateur, 1996.

Decretales Gregorii Papae IX. Rome, 1582.

Decretum Gratiani. Edited by Emil Friedberg. In *Corpus Iuris Canonici* 1. Leipzig, DE: Bernhard Tauchnitz, 1881.

Decrees of the Ecumenical Councils [Tanner]. Edited and Translated by Norman P. Tanner, S.J. Washington, DC: Georgetown University Press, 1990.

Die Register Innocenz III. Edited by Othmar Hageneder et al. Vienna, AT: Osterreichischen Akademie der Wissenschaften, 1964–2010.

Documents of the Baronial Movement of Reform and Rebellion, 1258–1267. Selected by Reginald Francis Treharne and edited by Ivor John Sanders. Oxford: Clarendon Press, 1973.

Dondaine, Antoine. "Le manuel de l'inquisiteur (1230–1330)." *Archivum fratrum praedicatorum* 17 (1947): 85–194.

Douais, Celestin. *Documents pour servir a l'histoire de l'Inquisition dans le Languedoc.* Paris, 1890.

Duvernoy, Jean. "Cathares et Faidits en Albigeois vers 1265–1275." *Heresis: Revue d'hérésiologe médiévale* 3 (December 1984): 5–34.

E Chronico Normanniae. In RHGF 23.

Early Dominicans: Selected Writings. Edited by Simon Tugwell, O.P. New York: Paulist Press, 1982.

Enquêtes Administratives d'Alfonse de Poitiers: Arrêts de son parlement tenu à Toulouse, 1249–1271 [EAAP]. Edited by Pierre-Fr. Fournier and Pascal Guébin. Paris: Imprimerie nationale, 1959.

Epistole et dictamina Clementis pape quarti. Edited by Matthias Thumser. Unpublished. Accessed Dec. 26, 2016. http://userpage.fu-berlin.de/~sekrethu/pdf/clemens.pdf

The Établissements de Saint Louis: Thirteenth-Century Law Texts from Tours, Orléans, and Paris. Translated by F. R. P. Akehurst. Philadelphia: University of Pennsylvania Press, 1996.

Les Établissements de Saint Louis [Établissements]. Edited by Paul Viollet. Paris: Librairie Renouard, 1881.

Eudes Rigaud, *Registers.* In RHGF 21.

E Chronico Sanctae Catharinae de Monte Rotomagi. In RHGF 23.

E Floribus Chronicorum. In RHGF 21.

E Mari Historiarum, Auctore Johanne de Columna, O.P. In RHGF 23.

Ex Annalibus Clerici, ut videtur, Parisiensis. In MGH SS 26.

Ex Annalibus Normannicis. In MGH SS 26.

Foedera, Conventiones, Literae, et Cujuscunque Generis Acta Publica, inter Reges Angliae, et Alios quosvis Imperatores, Reges, Pontifices, Principes, vel Communitates [Foedera]. Edited by Thomas Rymer. London: J. Tonson, 1727.

Foucois, Gui. *Consilium.* In C. Carens, *Tractatus de Officio sanctissimae Inquisitionis et modo procedendi in causis fidei,* 322–47. Lyon, FR, 1649.

———. *Consilium domini Guidonis Fulcodi.* In César Augustin Nicolas, *Un pape Saint-Gillois, Clément IV dans le monde et dans l'Église, 1195-1268,* appendix. Nîmes, FR: Impr. Générale, 1910.

———. *Les sept joies de la Vièrge.* Edited by Cesaire Antoine Fabre. Le Puy, FR: Peyriller, Rouchon, and Gamon, 1920.

Gallia Christiana, in provincias ecclesiasticas distributa, in qua series et historia archiepiscoporum, episcoporum, et abbatum [Gal. Christ.]. Paris: V. Palmé, 1739–1880.

Gaufrido de Belloloco, *Vita Sancti Ludovici.* In RHGF, 20:1–27.

Gaydon: Chanson de geste du XIIIᵉ siècle. Edited and translated by Jean Subrenat. Louvain, BE: Peeters, 2007.

Geoffry of Beaulieu. *Vita Ludovici.* In RHGF, 20:3–27.

Glossae ordinariae. In PL 113 and 114.

Goffredus of Trani. *Summa super titulis Decretalium.* Lyon, FR, 1519.

Graham, Rose, ed. "Letters of Cardinal Ottoboni." *The English Historical Review* 15.57 (1900).

Gregory the Great, *Reading the Gospels with Gregory the Great: Homilies on the Gospels,* 21-26. Translated by Santha Bhattacharji. New York: Fordham University Press: 2002.

Guidonis, Bernardus. *De Foundatione et Prioribus Conventuum Provinciarum Tolosanae et Provinciae Ordinis Praedicatorum.* Edited by P. A. Amargier, O.P. Monumenta Ordinis Fratrum Praedicatorum Historica 25. Rome: Institutum Historicum Fratrum Praedicatorum, 1961.

———. *The Chronicle of William of Puylaurens.* Translated by W. A. Sibly and M. D. Sibly. Woolbridge, UK: Boydell Press, 2003.

Guillelmus de Nangiaco. In RHGF 20.

Henry of Susa (Hostiensis), *Summa aurea.* Venice, 1574.

———. *In primum [-sextum] decretalium librum commentaria.* Venice, 1581.

Histoire générale de Languedoc [HGL]. 3rd edition. Edited by J. Vaissete, C. Devic, and A. Molinier. 16 vols. Toulouse, FR: Edouard Privat, 1872–1904.

Historia Diplomatica Friderici Secundi [Hist. Frid.]. Edited by J. L. A. Huillard-Bréholles. Paris: Plon, 1860.

Historia universitatis parisiensis [HUP]. Edited by César Égasse du Boulay. Paris: Franciscum Noel, 1666.

Pope Innocent III. *Between God and Man: Six Sermons on the Priestly Office.* Translated by Corinne J. Vause and Frank C. Gardiner. Washington, DC: Catholic University of America Press, 2004.

Pope Innocent IV. *Apparatus in quinque libros Decretalium.* Frankfurt, 1570.

John of Joinville. *The Life of St. Louis.* Translated by René Hague from the text edited by Natalis de Wailly. New York: Sheed and Ward, 1955.

Karoli Magni Capitularia. Edited by A. Boretius. In MGH *Leges Capit*, II, 1890.

Layettes du Trésor des chartes [LTC]. Edited by Alexandre Teulet. Paris: H. Plon, 1863–1909.

Les olim ou registres des arrêts rendus par la cour du roi [Olim]. Edited by A. Beugnot. Paris: Imprimerie Nationale, 1899–1900.

Les Registres de Grégoire IX. Edited by Lucien Auvray. Paris: Albert Fontemoing, 1955.

Les Registres d'Alexandre IV. Edited by Charles de La Roncière et al. Paris: Albert Fontemoing, 1902.

Les Registres d'Urbain IV (1261–1264) [*Urban IV, Reg.*]. Edited by M. Jean Guiraud. Paris: Thorin et Fils, 1901.

Les Registres de Clément IV (1265–1268) [*Clément, IV, Reg.*]. Edited by Édouard Jordan. Paris: Thorin et Fils, 1845.

Li livres de jostice et de plet. Edited by François Adrien Polycarpe Chabaille. Paris: Firmin Didot Frères, 1850.

Liber extravagantium decretalium [X]. Edited by Emil Friedberg. In *Corpus Iuris Canonici* 2. Leipzig, DE: Bernhard Tauchnitz, 1881.

Lives of the Brethren of the Order of Preachers, 1206–1259. Translated by Placid Conway, O.P. Edited by Bede Jarrett, O.P. London: Burns, Oates, and Washbourne, 1924.

Ludwigs des Heiligen Kreuzzug nach Tunis 1270, und die Politik Karls I. von Sizilien. Edited by Richard Sternfeld. Berlin: E. Ebering, 1896.

Luther and Calvin on Secular Authority. Translated and edited by Harro Hopfl. Cambridge: Cambridge University Press, 2010.

Majus chronicon lemovicense. In RHGF 21.

Monumenta Germaniae Historica, Capitularia regum Francorum in MGH *Leges Capit*. I. Hanover, 1837.

Monumenta Germaniae Historica, Capitularia regum Francorum, Series II in MGH *Leges Capit*. II. Hanover, 1890.

Monumenta Germaniae Historica, Constitutiones et Acta Publica Imperatorum et Regum in MGH *Leges Const*. Hannover, 1893.

Monumenta Germaniae Historica, Scriptores in MGH SS. Hanover, 1841.

The Memoirs of the Lord of Joinville: A New English Version. Translated by Ethel Wedgwood. New York: E. P. Dutton, 1906.

O'Connell, David. *The Instructions of Saint Louis: A Critical Text.* Chapel Hill: University of North Carolina Press, 1979.

———. *The Teachings of Saint Louis: A Critical Text.* Chapel Hill: University of North Carolina Press, 1972.

Ordines Coronationis Franciae: Texts and Ordines for the Coronation of Frankish and French Kings and Queens in the Middle Ages. Edited by Richard A. Jackson. Philadelphia: University of Pennsylvania Press, 2000.

Ordonnances des Roys de France de la Troisième Race [Ordonnances]. 21 vols. Paris: Imprimerie Royale, 1723–1849.

Parisiensis, Matthaei. *Historia Anglorum.* Edited by Frederic Madden. London: Longmans, Green: 1869.

———. *Chronica Majora.* Edited by Henry Richards Luard. London: Longman: 1882.

———. *Matthew Paris's English History.* Translated by J. A. Giles. London: Enry G. Bohn, 1853.

Patrologiae cursus completus, Series latina [PL]. Edited by Jacques-Paul Migne. 217 vols. Paris, 1841–1864.

Pax Sigiwini Archiepiscopi Coloniensis. In MGH *Leges Const.*, edited by Ludewicus Weiland, 1:603–04. Hannover, 1893.

Pedro el Católico, Rey de Aragón y Conde de Barcelona (1196–1213): Documentos, Testimonios y Memoria Histórica. Edited by Martín Alvira Cabrer. Zaragoza, ES: Institución "Ferdando el Católico," 2010.

Pelhisson, Guillaume. *Chronique (1229–1244), suivie du récit des troubles d'Albi (1234).* Edited and translated by Jean Duvernoy. Paris: CNRS, 1994.

Peter of les Vaux-de-Cernay. *The History of the Albigensian Crusade: Peter of les Vaux-de-Cernay's Historia Albigensis.* Translated by W. A. Sibly and M. D. Sibly. Woodbridge, UK: The Boydell Press, 1998.

Processus legationis in Angliam Guidonis episcopi Sabinensis post-modum Clementis papae IV. In Joseph Heidemann, *Papst Clemens IV*, 194–248. Münster: Verlag von Heinrich Schöningh, 1903.

Recueil des historiens des Gaules et de la France [RHGF]. Edited by Martin Bouquet et al. Paris: Victor Palmé, et al., 1738–1904.

Recueil Général Anciennes Lois Francaises [RGALF]. Edited by A. J. L. Jourdan et al. Paris: Belin-Le-Prieur, 1822.

Regesta pontificum romanorum. Edited by August Potthast. Berlin: Rudolf de Decker, 1874.

The Register of Eudes of Rouen [*Eudes, Reg.*]. Translated by Sydney M. Brown and Edited by Jeremiah F. O'Sullivan. New York: Columbia University Press, 1964.

Royal and Other Historical Letters Illustrative of the Reign of Henry III. Edited by Walter Waddington. London: Longmans, Green, Reader, and Dyer, 1866.

Le sacre royal à l'époque de Saint Louis. Edited by Jacques Le Goff, Éric Palazzo, Jean-Claude Bonne, and Marie-Noël Colette. Paris: Gallimard, 2001.

Sacrorum conciliorum nova et amplissima collectio [Mansi]. 54 vols. Edited by Joannes Dominicus Mansi. Paris: Expensis Huberti Welter, 1903.

The Saxon Mirror. Translated by Maria Dobozy. Philadelphia: The University of Pennsylvania Press, 1999.

Summula Contra Hereticos: un traite contre les cathares du XIIIème siecle: Manuscrits Doat XXXVI de la B. N. de Paris, 379 de la B.M. de Toulouse. Edited by Jean Duvernoy, 1986. Accessed November 18, 2016. http://jean.duvernoy.free.fr/text/pdf/summula.pdf.

Thesaurus novus anecdotorum [TNA]. Edited by Edmond Martène and Ursin Durand. Paris: Sumptibus F. Delaulne, 1717.

Tholomeus Lucensis. *Historia Ecclesiastica Nova.* In MGH SS 29. Hannover, 2009.

Traver, Andrew G. *The Opuscula of William of Saint-Amour: The Minor Works of 1255–1256.* Münster, DE: Aschendorff Verlag, 2003.

"Une lettre addressée à Alfonse de Poitiers (24 mars 1251)." Edited by Ch.-V Langlois. *Bibliothèque de l'École des Chartes* 46 (Paris, 1885): 389–93.

Van Dijk, Stephen J. P., OFM. *The Ordinal of the Papal Court From Innocent III to Boniface VIII and Related Documents.* Fribourg, CH: Fribourg University Press, 1975.

Vincent of Beauvais, *The Moral Instruction of a Prince.* Translated by Priscilla Throop. Charlotte, VT: MedievalMS, 2012.

William of Nangis. *Gesta sanctae memoriae Ludovici regis Franciae.* In RHGF, 20:309–462.

———. *Chronicon.* In RHGF, 20:544–586.

William of Saint-Amour. *Tractatus brevis de periculis novissimorum temporum ex scripturis sumptus.* Edited and translated by G. Geltner. Louvain, BE / Paris: Peeters, 2007.

Secondary Works:

Affeldt, Robert. "The Problem of Private Property according to St. Thomas Aquinas." *Marquette Law Review* 34, no. 3 (Winter 1950–51): 151–82.

Asad, Talal. *Genealogies of Religion: Discipline and Reasons of Power in Christianity and Islam* (Baltimore, MD: Johns Hopkins University Press, 1993).

Edited by István P. Bejczy and Cary J. Nederman. *Princely Virtue in the Middle Ages 1200–1500.* Turnhout, BE: Brepols, 2008.

Baldwin, John. *Masters, Princes, and Merchants: The Social Views of Peter the Chanter and His Circle.* Princeton: Princeton University Press, 1970.

Barraclough, Geoffrey. *The Medieval Papacy.* New York: W. W. Norton, 1979.

Bauerschmidt, Frederick Christian. "Aquinas." In *The Blackwell Companion to Political Theology.* Edited by Peter Scott and William T. Cavanaugh, 48–61. Chichester, UK: Wiley-Blackwell, 2006.

Beebe, Bruce. "The English Baronage and the Crusade of 1270." *Bulletin of the Institute of Historical Research* 48 (1975): 127–48.

Bellah, Robert N. *Religion in Human Evolution: From the Paleolithic to the Axial Age* (Cambridge, MA.: Harvard University Press, 2011).

Berg, Beverly. "Manfred of Sicily and Urban IV: Negotiations of 1262." *Mediaeval Studies* 55 (1993): 111–36.

Berger, Adolf. *Encyclopedic Dictionary of Roman Law*. Philadelphia: The American Philosophical Society, 1953.

Berger, Peter. *The Sacred Canopy: Elements of a Sociological Theory of Religion*. New York: Anchor Books, 1967.

Bird, Jessalynn. "Paris Masters and the Justification of the Albigensian Crusade." *Crusades* 6 (2007): 117–55.

Bisson, Thomas N. "Consultative Functions in the King's Parlements (1250–1314)." *Speculum* 44 (1969): 353–73.

———. "The Military Origins of Medieval Representation." *The American Historical Review* 71.4 (1966): 1199–218.

———. *The Crisis of the Twelfth Century: Power, Lordship, and the Origins of European Government*. Princeton: Princeton University Press, 2009.

———. "The Organized Peace in Southern France and Catalonia, ca. 1140– ca. 1233." *The American Historical Review* 82 (1977): 290–311.

Bonne, Jean-Claude. "Images du sacre." In *Le sacre royal à l'époque de Saint Louis*, edited by Jacques Le Goff, Éric Palazzo, Jean-Claude Bonne, Marie-Noël Colette. Paris: Gallimard, 2001.

Bourdieu, Pierre. *Practical Reason: On the Theory of Action*. Stanford, CA: Stanford University Press, 1998.

Brown, Warren C. *Violence in Medieval Europe*. Harlow, UK: Longman, 2011.

Buisson, Ludwig. "Saint Louis: Justice et Amour de Dieu." *Francia* 6 (1978): 127–49.

Bull, Marcus. *Knightly Piety and the Lay Response to the First Crusade: The Limousin and Gascony, c. 970–1130*. Oxford: Clarendon Press, 1993.

Bünger, Ulrich. "Das Verhältnis Ludwig des Heiligen zu Papst Clemens IV (1265–1268)." PhD diss., Verheinigten Friedrichs-Universität, 1897.

Campbell, Gerard J., S.J. "The Attitude of the Monarchy toward the Use of Ecclesiastical Censures in the Reign of Saint Louis." *Speculum* 35, no. 4 (October 1960): 535–55.

———."Temporal and Spiritual Regalia During the Reigns of St. Louis and Philip III." *Traditio* 20 (1964): 351–83.

———. "Saint Louis's Ecclesiastical Policy in France." PhD diss., Princeton University, 1959.

———. "The Protest of Saint Louis." *Traditio* 15 (1959): 417–18.

Carolus-Barre, Louis. "La grande ordonnance de reformation de 1254." In *Septième centenaire de la mort de Saint Louis: Actes des colloques de Royaumont et de Paris (21–27 mai 1970)*, 85–96. Paris: Société D'Édition "Les Belles Lettres," 1976.

Carruthers, Mary. *The Book of Memory: A Study of Memory in Medieval Culture.* Cambridge: Cambridge University Press, 1990.

Cavanaugh, William T. "The City: Beyond Secular Parodies." In *Radical Orthodoxy, A New Theology,* edited by John Milbank, Catherine Pickstock, and Graham Ward. London: Routledge, 1999, 182-200.

———. *The Myth of Religious Violence: Secular Ideology and the Roots of Modern Conflict.* Oxford: Oxford University Press, 2009.

Charles, Rodger, S.J. *The Social Teaching of Vatican II.* San Francisco: Ignatius Press, 1982.

Chazan, Robert. "Archbishop Guy Fulcodi of Narbonne and his Jews." *Revue des études juives* 132 (1973): 587–94.

Cheney, Christopher Robert. "The Death of Popes and the Expiry of Legations in Twelfth-Century England." *Revue de droit canonique* 28 (1978): 84–96.

Chenu, M.-D., O.P. *Nature, Man, and Society in the Twelfth Century: Essays on New Theological Perspectives in the Latin West.* Translated by Jerome Taylor and Lester K. Little. Chicago: University of Chicago Press, 1968.

Chiffoleau, Jacques. "Saint Louis, Frédéric II et les constructions institutionelles du XIIIe siècle." *Médiévales: langue, textes, histoire* 17 (1998): 13–23.

Congar, Yves. "Ecce constitui te super gentes et regna (Jer. 1.10)." In *Theologie in Geschichte und Gegenwart*, edited by Johann Auer and Hermann Volk, 671–96. Munich, 1957.

———. "L'Église et l'état sous le regne de Saint Louis." In *Septieme Centenaire de la Mort de Saint Louis*, 257–71. Paris: Belles Lettres, 1976.

Constable, Giles. *Three Studies on Medieval Religious and Social Thought*. Cambridge: Cambridge University Press, 1995.

Crouch, David. *The Birth of Nobility: Constructing Aristocracy in England and France 900–1300*. Harlow, UK: Pearson, 2005.

de Lubac, S.J., Henri. *Corpus Mysticum: The Eucharist and the Church in the Middle Ages*. Translated by Gemma Simmonds, C.J. Notre Dame, IN: University of Notre Dame Press, 2007.

———. *Medieval Exegesis: The Four Senses of Scripture*, vol. 1. Translated by E. M. Macierowski. Grand Rapids, MI: William B. Eerdmans Publishing Company, 2000.

———. *Medieval Exegesis: The Four Senses of Scripture*, vol. 2. Translated by Mark Sebanc. Grand Rapids, MI: William B. Eerdmans Publishing Company, 1998.

Derrida, Jacques. "Difference." In *From Modernism to Postmodernism: An Anthology*, 2nd expanded edition. Edited by Lawrence Cahoon, 225–40. Malden, MA: Blackwell Publishing, 2003.

Dictionary of the Middle Ages: Supplement 1. New York: Charles Scribner's Sons, 2004.

Dondaine, Antoine, O.P. "Le Manuel de L'Inquisiteur (1230–1330)." *Archivum Fratrum Praedicatorum* 17 (1947): 85–194.

Dossat, Yves. "Gui Foucois, enquêteur-réformateur, archevêque et pape." *Cahiers de Fanjeaux* 7 (1972): 23–57.

———. *Les crises de l'Inquisition toulousaine au XIIIe siècle, 1233–1273*. Bordeaux, FR: Bière, 1959.

———. "Inquisiteurs ou Enqueteurs? À propos d'un texte d'Humbert de Romans." *Bulletin Philologique et historique* (1957): 105–13.

Douglas, Mary. *Natural Symbols: Explorations in Cosmology.* London: Routledge, 2003.

Douie, D. L. *The Conflict Between the Seculars and the Mendicants at the University of Paris in the Thirteenth Century.* London: Blackfriars, 1954.

Dufournet, Jean. "Rutebeuf et les moines mendiants." *Neuphilologische Mitteilungen* 85 (1984): 152–68.

Dudbabin, Jean. *Charles I of Anjou: Power, Kingship and State-Making in Thirteenth-Century Europe.* New York: Longman, 1998.

———. "The Political World of France, c.1200–1336." In *France in the Later Middle Ages, 1200–1500.* Edited by David Potter, 23–46. Oxford: Oxford University Press, 2002.

Dufeil, Michel-Marie. *Guillaume de Saint-Amour et la polémique universitaire parisienne, 1250–1259.* Paris: Picard, 1972.

Duggan, Charles. "Papal Judges Delegate and the Making of the 'New Law' in the Twelfth Century." In *Cultures of Power.* Edited by Thomas N. Bisson, 172–99. Philadelphia: University of Pennsylvania Press, 1995.

Dunbabin, Jean. *Charles I of Anjou: Power, Kingship and State-Making in Thirteenth-Century Europe.* New York: Longman, 1998.

———. *France in the Making, 843–1180.* Oxford: Oxford University Press, 1985.

Dykmans, M. "Les pouvoirs des cardinaux pendant la vacance du Saint Siège d'après un nouveau manuscrit de Jacques Stefaneschi." *Archivio della Societa Romana di storia patria* 104 (1981): 119–45.

Field, Sean L. *Isabelle of France: Capetian Sanctity and Franciscan Identity in the Thirteenth Century.* Notre Dame, IN: Notre Dame University Press, 2006.

Figueira, Robert C. "The Canon Law of Medieval Papal Legations." PhD diss., Cornell University, 1980.

———. "Legatus apostolice Sedis: The Pope's Alter Ego according to Thirteenth-Century Canon Law." *Studi Medievali* 3, no. 27 (1986): 527–74.

———. "The Classification of Medieval Papal Legates in the Liber Extra." *Archivum historiae pontificiae* 21 (1983): 211–28.

Firnhaber-Baker, Justine. "From God's Peace to the King's Order: Late Medieval Limitations on Non-Royal Warfare." *Essays in Medieval Studies* 23 (2006): 19–30.

Fischer, Andreas. *Kardinale im Konklave: Die lange Sedisvakanz der Jahre 1268 bis 1271.* Tübingen, DE: Niemeyer, 2008.

Francois, M. "Initiatives de Saint Louis en matiere administrative: les enquetes royales." In *Le Siecle de Saint Louis: 1226–1285,* 210–14. Paris: Tallandier, 1977.

Gallagher, Clarence. *Canon Law and the Christian Community.* Rome: Università Gregoriana Editrice, 1978.

Gautier, Léon. *Chivalry.* Translated by Henry Frith. London: George Routledge and Sons, 1891.

Gellner, Ernest. *Nations and Nationalism.* Ithaca, NY: Cornell University Press, 2006.

Georges, E. *Histoire du pape Urbain IV et de son temps (1186–1264).* Paris/Troyes: Frémont-Chaulin, 1866.

Gorski, Philip S. "Historicizing the Secularization Debate: Church, State, and Society in Late Medieval and Early Modern Europe, ca. 1300 to 1700." *American Sociological Review* 65.1 (200): 138–67.

Graham-Leigh, Elaine. *The Southern French Nobility and the Albigensian Crusade.* Woodbridge, UK: Boydell Press, 2005.

Grayzel, Solomon. "Jews and the Ecumenical Councils." *The Jewish Quarterly Review,* n.s., 57 (1967): 287–311.

Gregory, Brad. *The Unintended Reformation: How a Religious Revolution Secularized Society.* Cambridge, MA: Harvard University Press, 2012.

Griffiths, Quentin. "New Men among the Lay Counselors of Saint Louis' Parlement." *Mediaeval Studies* 32 (1970): 234–72.

Geuss, Raymond. *History and Illusion in Politics.* Cambridge: Cambridge University Press, 2001.

Hallam, Elizabeth M., and Judith Everard, *Capetian France, 987–1328*, 2nd ed. New York: Longman, 2001.

Ham, Edward Billings. *Rutebeuf and Louis IX.* Chapel Hill, NC: University of North Carolia Press, 1962.

Hampe, Karl, *Urban IV und Manfred (1261–1264).* In *Heidelberger Abhandlungen zur mittleren und neueren Geschichte* 11. Heidelberg: C. Winter, 1905.

Harris, Jennifer A. "Building Heaven on Earth: Cluny as Locus Sanctissimus in the Eleventh Century." In *From Dead of Night to End of Day: The Medieval Customs of Cluny* [*Du coeur de la nuit à la fin du jour: les coutumes clunisiennes au Moyen Age*], 131–51. Turnhout, BE: Brepols, 2005.

———. "Peter Damian and the Architecture of the Self." In *Das Eigene und das Ganze: Zum Individuellen im mittelalterlichen Religiosentum.* Edited by Gert Melville and Markus Schürer, 131–58. Münster, DE: Lit, 2002.

Hart, David Bentley. *The Beauty of the Infinite.* Grand Rapids, MI: William B. Eerdmans, 2003.

Hedeman, Anne, *The Royal Image: Illustrations of the Grandes Chroniques de France, 1274–1422.* Berkeley: University of California Press, 1991.

Heidemann, J. *Papst Clemens IV: Eine Monographie.* Vol. 1, *Das Vorleben des Papstes und sein Legationsregister.* Munster, DE: Schöningh, 1903.

Helmholz, Richard H. "Excommunication as a Legal Sanction." *Zeitschrift der Savigny-Stiftung für Rechtsgeschichte: Kanonistische Abteilung* 68, no. 99 (1982): 202–18.

Hibbs, Thomas. "The Fearful Thoughts of Mortals: Aquinas on Conflict, Self-Knowledge, and the Virtues of Practical Reasoning." In *Intractable Disputes about the Natural Law: Alasdair MacIntyre and Critics.* Edited by Lawrence S. Cunningham, 273–312. Notre Dame, IN: Notre Dame University Press, 2009.

Hobbes, Thomas. *Leviathan.* 1651.

Housley, Norman. *The Italian Crusades: The Papal-Angevin Alliance and the Crusades against Christian Lay Powers, 1254–1343.* Oxford: Clarendon Press, 1982.

Huizinga, Johann. *The Waning of the Middle Ages*. New York: Anchor Books, 1989.

Jones, Andrew W. "The Preacher of the Fourth Lateran Council." *Logos* 18.2 (Spring 2015).

———. "Quomodo vero praedicabunt nisi mittantur? The Authority to Preach in the Works of William of Saint-Amour and Thomas Aquinas: 1255–1256." Master's thesis, Western Washington University, 2007.

———. "The Two Swords and the Two Testaments: Pope Innocent III, the Senses of Scripture, and the Meaning of Kingship" Forthcoming.

Jordan, A. A. *Visualizing Kingship in the Windows of the Sainte-Chapelle*. Turnhout, BE: Brepols, 2001.

Jordan, William Chester. "The Capetians from the Death of Philip II to Philip IV." In *The New Cambridge Medieval History*. Edited by David Abulafia, 5:279–313. Cambridge: Cambridge University Press, 1999.

———. "The Case of Saint Louis." *Viator* 19 (1988): 209–17.

———. "Communal Administration in France, 1257–1270: Problems Discovered and Solutions Imposed." *Revue belge de philosophie et d'histoire* 59 (1981): 292–313.

———. "Isabelle of France and Religious Devotion at the Court of Louis IX." In *Capetian Women*. Edited by Kathleen Nolan, 209–23. New York: Palgrave, 2003.

———. *Louis IX and the Challenge of the Crusade: A Study in Rulership*. Princeton: Princeton University Press, 1979.

Kaeuper, Richard W. *Chivalry and Violence in Medieval Europe*. Oxford: Oxford University Press, 1999.

———. *Holy Warriors: The Religious Ideology of Chivalry*. Philadelphia: University of Pennsylvania Press, 2009.

Kantorowicz, Ernst. *The King's Two Bodies: a Study in Medieval Political Theology*. Princeton: Princeton University Press, 1957.

Kay, Richard. *The Council of Bourges, 1225: A Documentary History*. Aldershot, UK: Ashgate, 2002.

Kramer, Susan R., and Caroline W. Bynum. "Revisiting the Twelfth-Century Individual: The Inner Self and the

Christian Community." In *Das Eigene und das Ganze: Zum Individuellen im mittelalterlichen Religiosentum*. Edited by Gert Melville and Markus Schürer, 57–88. Münster, DE: Lit, 2002.

Krey, August. C. *The First Crusade: The Accounts of Eyewitnesses and Participants*. Princeton: Princeton University Press, 1921.

Krynen, Jacques. "Saint Louis législateur au miroir des mendiants." *Mélanges de l'Ecole française de Rome: Moyen Age* 113, no. 2 (2001): 945–49.

Kuttner, Stephan, and Antonio García y García. "A New Eyewitness Account of the Fourth Lateran Council." *Traditio* 20 (1964): 115–78.

Kyer, Clifford Ian. "Legatus and Nuntius as Used to Denote Papal Envoys: 1245–1378." *Mediaeval Studies* 40 (1978): 473–77.

La Due, William J., J.C.D, *The Chair of Saint Peter: A History of the Papacy*. New York: Orbis, 1999.

Le Goff, Jacques. *Saint Louis*. Paris: Gillimard, 1996.

———. "La structure et le contenu idéologique de la cérémonie du sacre." In *Le sacre royal à l'époque de Saint Louis*. Edited by Jacques Le Goff, Éric Palazzo, Jean-Claude Bonne, and Marie-Noël Colette. Paris: Gallimard, 2001.

———. *Saint Louis*. Translated by Gareth Evan Gollrad. Notre Dame, IN: University of Notre Dame Press, 2009.

———. "Aspect Religieux et Sacre de la Monarchie Française de X^e au XIIIe Siecle." In *Pouvoirs et Libertés au Temps des Premiers Capétiens*, 309–22. Maulévrier, FR: Hérault, 1992.

Lecler, Joseph, S.J. "Pars Corporis Papae . . . Le Sacre College dans L'Ecclesiologie Medievale." In *L'Homme devant Dieu: Melanges offerts au Pere Henri de Lubac*, vol 2: 183–94. Paris: Aubier, 1964.

Leclercq, Jean, OSB. *The Love of Learning and the Desire for God: A Study of Monastic Culture*. New York: Fordham University Press, 1982.

Lerner, Robert E. "The Uses of Heterodoxy, the French Monarchy and Unbelief in the XIIIth century." *French Historical Studies* 4 (1965): 189–202.

Little, Lester K. "Saint Louis' Involvement with the Friars." *Church History* 33.2. (June, 1964): 125–148.

Logan, F. Donald. *Excommunication and the Secular Arm in Medieval England: A Study in Legal Procedure from the Thirteenth to the Sixteenth Century.* Toronto: Pontifical Institute of Medieval Studies, 1968.

Lower, Michael. "Conversion and St. Louis's Last Crusade." *Journal of Ecclesiastical History* 58, no. 2 (April 2007): 211–31.

Lunt, W. E. *Papal Revenues in the Middle Ages.* 2 vols. New York: Octogon, 1934.

MacIntyre, Alasdair. *After Virtue.* Notre Dame, IN: University of Notre Dame Press, 2007.

Manent, Pierre. *Metamorphoses of the City: On the Western Dynamic.* Cambridge, MA: Harvard University Press, 2013.

Mann, Horace K. *The Lives of the Popes in the Middle Ages.* London: Kegan Paul, Trench, Trübner and Co., 1929.

Maritain, Jacques. *Man and the State.* Chicago: University of Chicago, 1951.

Ménard, Philippe. "Rotiers, soldadiers, mainadiers, faidits, arlots: Réflexions sur les diverses sortes de combattants dans la Chanson de la croisade albigeoise." *Perspectives Médiévales* 22 (1996): 157–62.

Milbank, John. *Theology and Social Theory: Beyond Secular Reason.* 2nd ed. Malden, MA: Blackwell Publishing, 2006.

———. *Beyond Secular Order: The Representation of Being and the Representation of the People,* vol. 1. Chichester, UK: Wiley-Blackwell, 2014.

Milbank, John, and Catherine Pickstock. *Truth in Aquinas.* London: Routledge, 2001.

Montaubin, Pascal. "Le gouvernement de l'Église Romaine *sede vacante* aux XIIIe et XIVe siecles." In *Sede vacante: La vacance de pouvoir dans l'Église du moyen age,* 116–49. Brussels, BE: Facultés universitaires Saint-Louis, 2001.

Moore, John C. "The Sermons of Pope Innocent III." *Römische Historische Mitteilungen* 36 (1994): 81–142.

Morris, Colin. *The Papal Monarchy: The Western Church from 1050 to 1250*. Oxford: Oxford University Press, 1991.

Mundy, John H. *Society and Government at Toulouse in the Age of the Cathars*. Toronto: Pontifical Institute of Mediaeval Studies, 1997.

Nederman, Cary. "Conciliarism and Constitutionalism: Jean Gerson and Medieval Political Thought." *History of European Ideas* 12 (1990): 189–209.

Nelson, Eric. *The Hebrew Republic: Jewish Sources and the Transformation of European Political Thought*. Cambridge, MA: Harvard University Press, 2010.

Nicolas, César Augustin. *Un pape saint-gillois, Clément IV dans le monde et dans l'Église (1195–1268)*. Nîmes, FR: Impr. Générale, 1910.

Nietzsche, Friedrich. *Beyond Good and Evil*. Translated by Walter Kaufmann. New York: Vintage Books, 1966.

Nongbri, Brent. *Before Religion: A History of a Modern Concept*. New Haven / London: Yale University Press, 2013.

Odegaard, Charles E. "Carolingian Oaths of Fidelity." *Speculum* 16.3 (1941): 284–96

Paravicini-Bagliani, Agostino. *The Pope's Body*. Translated by David S. Peterson. Chicago: The University of Chicago Press, 1994.

Pegg, Mark Gregory. *A Most Holy War: The Albigensian Crusade and the Battle for Christendom*. Oxford: Oxford University Press, 2008.

Pennington, Kenneth. *Pope and Bishops: The Papal Monarchy in the Twelfth and Thirteenth Centuries*. Philadelphia: University of Pennsylvania Press, 1984.

———. "The Formation of the Jurisprudence of the Feudal Oath of Fealty." *Rivista internazionale del diritto comun* 15 (2004): 57–76.

———. "Johannes Teutonicus and Papal Legates." *Archivum Historiae Pontificiae* 21 (1983): 183–94.

———. "Law, Feudal." In *Dictionary of the Middle Ages: Supplement 1*. New York: Charles Scribner's Sons, 2004.

Peters, Edward. *Inquisition*. Berkeley: University of California Press, 1989.

Petit-Dutaillis, Charles. *Étude sur la vie et le règne de Louis VIII, 1187–1226*. Paris: Librairie Emile Bouillon, 1894.

Phelan, Owen M. *The Formation of Christian Europe: The Carolingians, Baptism, and the Imperium Christianum*. Oxford: Oxford University Press, 2014.

Pico, Fernando Alberto. "The Bishops of France in the Reign of Louis IX (1226–70)." PhD diss., Johns Hopkins University, 1970.

Post, Gains. "Two Notes on Nationalism in the Middle Ages." *Traditio* 9 (1953): 281–320.

Powell, James. "Church and Crusade: Frederick II and Louis IX." *The Catholic Historical Review* 93.2 (April, 2007): 251–64.

Queller, Donald. "Thirteenth-Century Diplomatic Envoys: *Nuncii* and *Procuratores*." *Speculum* 35 (April, 1960): 196–213.

Reichberg, Gregory M. "Contextualizing Theoretical Reason: Thomas Aquinas and Postmodernity." In *Postmodernism and Christian Philosophy*. Edited by Roman T. Ciapalo, 183–203. Mishawaka, IN: American Maritain Association, 1997.

Renna, Thomas. *Church and State in Medieval Europe, 1050–1314*. Dubuque, IA: Kendal/Hunt, 1977.

Reynolds, Susan. *Fiefs and Vassals: The Medieval Evidence Reinterpreted*. Oxford: Oxford University Press, 1994.

Richard, Jean. *Saint Louis: Crusader King of France*. Edited by Simon Lloyd and translated by Jean Birrell. New York: Cambridge University Press, 1992.

———. *Saint Louis: roi d'une France féodale, soutien de la Terre sainte*. Paris: Fayard, 1983.

Robinson, I. S. *The Papacy, 1073–1198: Continuity and Innovation*. Cambridge: Cambridge University Press, 1990.

Salminen, Ma Tapio. "In the Pope's Clothes: Legatine Representation and Apostolical Insignia in High Medieval Europe." In *Roma, Magistra Mundi*. Edited by Jacqueline

Hamesse, 339–54. Louvain-La-Neuve, BE: Fédération Internationale des Instituts d'Études Médiévales, 1998.

Schmitt, Carl. *The Concept of the Political.* Chicago: University of Chicago Press, 2007.

———. *Political Theology: Four Chapters on the Concept of Sovereignty.* Chicago: University of Chicago Press, 2005.

Smith, Randall. "What the Old Law Reveals about the Natural Law according to Thomas Aquinas." *The Thomist* 75 (January 2011): 95–139.

Souplet, Maxime. *Jacques de Troyes le "pacificateur."* Verdun, FR, 1954.

Spatz, Wilhem. *Die Schlacht von Hastings.* Berlin, 1896. Reprint, Vaduz, LI: Kraus, 1965.

Spiegel, Gabrielle M. *Romancing the Past: The Rise of Vernacular Prose Historiography in Thirteenth-Century France.* Berkeley: University of California Press, 1993.

———. "The Cult of Saint Denis and Capetian kingship." *Journal of Medieval History* 1, no. 1 (1975): 43–69.

Strauss, Leo. *Natural Right and History.* Chicago: University of Chicago Press, 1953.

Strayer, Joseph. "La conscience du roi. Les enquêtes de 1258–1262 dans la sénéchaussée de Carcassonne-Béziers." In *Mélanges Roger Aubenas*, 725–36. Montpellier, FR: Faculté de droit et des sciences économiques de Montpellier, 1974.

———. "Crusades of Louis IX." In *Medieval Statecraft and the Perspectives of History*, 487–518. Princeton: Princeton University Press, 1971.

———. "The Laicization of French and English Society in the Thirteenth Century." In *Medieval Statecraft and the Perspectives of History.* Edited by John F. Benton and Thomas N. Bisson, 251–65. Princeton: Princeton University Press, 1971.

———. "The Political Crusades of the Thirteenth Century." In *Medieval Statecraft and the Perspectives of History.* Edited by John F. Benton and Thomas N. Bisson, 123–58. Princeton: Princeton University Press, 1971.

Szittya, Penn R. *The Antifraternal Tradition in Medieval Literature.* Princeton: Princeton University Press, 1986.

Tanner, Norman. "Pastoral Care: The Fourth Lateran Council of 1215." In *A History of Pastoral Care*. Edited by G. R. Evans, 19–31. London: Cassell, 1999.

Taylor, Charles. *A Secular Age*. Cambridge, MA: Harvard University Press, 2007.

Tellenbach, Gerd. *Church, State, and Society at the Time of the Investiture Contest*. Translated by R. F. Bennett. New York: Humanities Press, 1979.

———. *The Church in Western Europe from the Tenth to the Early Twelfth Century*. Translated by Timothy Reuter. New York: Cambridge University Press, 1993.

Thompson, Augustine, O.P. *Cities of God: The Religion of the Italian Communes, 1125–1325*. University Park: Pennsylvania State University Press, 2005.

Tierney, Brian. *The Crisis of Church and State, 1050–1300*. Toronto: University of Toronto Press, 1988.

———. *Foundations of Conciliar Theory: The Contribution of the Medieval Canonists from Gratian to the Great Schism*. Cambridge: Cambridge University Press, 1955.

Ullmann, Walter. *A Short History of the Papacy in the Middle Ages*. New York: Routledge, 2003.

———. *The Growth of Papal Government in the Middle Ages*. London: Methuen & Co., 1970.

Van Engen, John. "The Christian Middle Ages as a Historiographical Problem." *The American Historical Review* 19, no. 3 (June 1986): 519–52.

Vauchez, André. "Innocent III, Sicard de Crémone et la canonisation de Saint Homebon (†1197)." In *Innocenzo III: Urbs et Orbis*, 1:435–55. Rome: Roma Istituto Storico Italiano per il Medio Evo, 2003.

———. *The Laity in the Middle Ages: Religious Beliefs and Devotional Practices*. Edited by Daniel E. Bornstein and translated by Margery J. Schneider. Notre Dame, IN: University of Notre Dame Press, 1993.

Vicaire, Marie-Humbert, O.P. "'L'Affaire de paix et de foi' du Midi de la France (1203–1215)." In *Paix de Dieu et guerre sainte en Languedoc au XIIIe siécle*, 102–127. Toulouse, FR: Edouard Privat, 1969.

————. *Saint Dominic and His Times*. New York: McGraw-Hill, 1964.

Vodola, Elisabeth. *Excommunication in the Middle Ages*. Berkeley: University of California Press, 1986.

von Mises, Ludwig. *Human Action: A Treatise on Economics*. 4th rev. ed. San Francisco: Fox and Wilkes, 1996.

Wakefield, Walter L. *Heresy, Crusade and Inquisition in Southern France, 1100–1250*. Berkeley: University of California Press, 1974.

Waley, Daniel Philip. *The Papal State in the Thirteenth Century*. New York: Macmillan, 1961.

Watt, John A. "The Papacy." In *The New Cambridge Medieval History*. Edited by David Abulafia, 107–164. Cambridge: Cambridge University Press, 1999.

————. *The Theory of Papal Monarchy in the Thirteenth Century*. Fordham University Press: New York, 1965.

Whalen, Brett Edward. *Dominion of God: Christendom and Apocalypse in the Middle Ages*. Cambridge, MA: Harvard University Press, 2009.

Wood, Charles. "Mise of Amiens and Saint Louis' Theory of Kingship." *French Historical Studies* 6.3 6, no. 3 (Spring 1970): 300–10.

Wuthnow, Robert, James Davison Hunter, Albert Bergesen, and Edith Kurzweil. *Cultural Analysis*. Boston: Routledge, 1984.

Zerner, Monique. "Le negotium pacis et fidei ou l'affaire de paix et de foi, une désignation de la croisade Albigeoise á revoir." In *Prêcher la Paix et Discipliner la Société*, 63–102. Turnhout, BE: Brepols, 2005.

————. "Le déclenchement de la croisade Albigeoise retour sur l'affaire de paix et de foi." In *La Croisade Albigeoise, Actes du Colloque du Centre d'Études Cathares Carcassonne, 4, 5 et 6 octobre 2002*. Edited by Michel Roquebert, 127–42. Carcassonne, FR: Centre d'Études Cathares, 2004.